THE WELSH AND THE MEDIEVAL WORLD

The Welsh and the Medieval World
Travel, Migration and Exile

edited by

Patricia Skinner

UNIVERSITY OF WALES PRESS
CARDIFF
2018

© The Contributors, 2018

All rights reserved. No part of this book may be reproduced in any material form (including photocopying or storing it in any medium by electronic means and whether or not transiently or incidentally to some other use of this publication) without the written permission of the copyright owner except in accordance with the provisions of the Copyright, Designs and Patents Act 1988. Applications for the copyright owner's written permission to reproduce any part of this publication should be addressed to the University of Wales Press, 10 Columbus Walk, Brigantine Place, Cardiff, CF10 4UP.

www.uwp.co.uk

British Library Cataloguing-in-Publication Data
A catalogue record for this book is available from the British Library.

ISBN   978-1-78683-188-0 (hardback)
       978-1-78683-189-7 (paperback)
e-ISBN: 978-1-78683-1903

The rights of the Contributors to be identified as authors of this work have been asserted in accordance with sections 77 and 79 of the Copyright, Designs and Patents Act 1988.

The contributors gratefully acknowledge grants received from HEFCW and the University of Winchester to bring this volume to publication.

Typeset in Wales by Eira Fenn Gaunt, Pentyrch, Cardiff
Printed by CPI Antony Rowe, Melksham

CONTENTS

List of abbreviations   vii
List of figures, tables and appendices   ix
List of contributors   xi

Welsh diaspora history: reinstating the pre-modern
  Patricia Skinner   1

PART I: WALES AND THE NEIGHBOURS

1 Moving from Wales and the west in the fifth century: isotope evidence for eastward migration in Britain
  Janet Kay   17

2 Emma d'Audley and the clash of laws in thirteenth-century northern Powys
  Emma Cavell   49

3 Migration and integration: Welsh secular clergy in England in the fifteenth century
  Rhun Emlyn   75

4 'A vice common in Wales': abduction, prejudice and the search for justice in the regional and central courts of early Tudor society
  Deborah Youngs   131

Contents

PART II: WALES, EUROPE AND THE WORLD

5 Welsh pilgrims and crusaders in the Middle Ages
    Kathryn Hurlock   157

6 Welsh-French diplomacy in the Middle Ages
    Gideon Brough   175

7 Documents relevant to Wales before the Edwardian
    conquest in the Vatican archives
    Bryn Jones   215

8 Wales and the wider world: the soldiers' perspective
    Adam Chapman   241

9 The mixed jury in Wales: a preliminary inquiry into ethno-
    religious administration and conflict resolution in the
    medieval world, *c.*1100–1350 CE
    Michael Hill   267

Bibliography   293
Index   331

Abbreviations

AoC	R. R. Davies, *The Age of Conquest: Wales 1063–1415* (Oxford, 2000)
AWR	H. Pryce (ed.), with C. Insley, *The Acts of the Welsh Rulers 1120–1283* (Cardiff, 2005)
BBCS	*Bulletin of the Board of Celtic Studies*
Cal. IPM	*Calendar of Inquisitions post mortem*
CCR	*Calendar of Close Rolls*
CChR	*Calendar of Charter Rolls*
CLR	*Calendar of Liberate Rolls*
CPR	*Calendar of Patent Rolls*
CWR	*Calendar of Various Chancery Rolls, Supplementary Close Rolls, Welsh Rolls, and Scutage Rolls preserved in the Public Record Office, 1277–1326* (London: HMSO, 1912)
EAWD	J. C. Davies (ed.), *Episcopal Acts and Cognate Documents relating to Welsh Dioceses 1066–1272*, 2 vols (Cardiff, 1946–8)
EHR	*English Historical Review*
EME	*Early Medieval Europe*
GCO	Gerald of Wales (Giraldi Cambrensis), *Opera*, ed. J. S. Brewer, J. F. Dimock and G. F. Warner, 8 vols, Rolls Series 21 (London, 1861–91)
JEccH	*Journal of Ecclesiastical History*
JMH	*Journal of Medieval History*
MGH	*Monumenta Germaniae Historica*
WHR	*Welsh History Review*

Figures, Tables and Appendices

Figures

1.1a Geological map of Britain, with locations of $^{87}Sr/^{86}Sr$ values in relation to site locations. After Evans et al., 'Spatial Variations in Biosphere 87Sr/86Sr in Britain', *Journal of the Geological Society*, 167 (2010), fig. 1b

1.1b Map showing groundwater $\delta^{18}O_{dw}$ contours. After Darling et al., 'The O & H Stable Isotopic Composition of Fresh Waters in the British Isles. 2. Surface Waters and Groundwater', *Hydrology and Earth System Sciences*, 7.2 (2003), fig. 6

1.2 Map of all sites studied, laid over groundwater $\delta^{18}18O_{dw}$ contours. The line running from the Tyne to Cornwall divides the north/west and south/east halves of Britain. Acknowledgement: Permit Number **CP17/026** British Geological Survey © NERC 2017. All rights reserved

1.3 Strontium $^{87}Sr/^{86}Sr$ and oxygen $\delta^{18}O_{dw}$ values for all sampled individuals, according to period, displayed against twenty individuals that make up the north/western oxygen signature. Acknowledgement: Permit Number **CP17/026** British Geological Survey © NERC 2017. All rights reserved

1.4 Location of Sites and relative % that each regional population makes up of the entire sampled population from that cemetery. Acknowledgement: Permit Number **CP17/026** British Geological Survey © NERC 2017. All rights reserved

2.1 Simple genealogy of the D'Audley family

3.1 Welsh secular clergy ordained in London by decade

Tables

1.1 The quantity of burials with strontium (87Sr/86Sr) and oxygen ($\delta^{18}O_{dw}$) values from each cemetery or burial population

1.2 Regional origins according to site and chronological period, as indicated by isotope results

1.3 Regional origins according to site and chronological period, as indicated by isotope results, according to gender and age

2.1 Emma D'Audley's appearances in the Welsh assize court

3.1 Welsh secular clergy ordained in London by diocese

3.2 Welsh secular clergy ordained in Salisbury by diocese

8.1 Hywel Swrdal's military career

Appendices

3.1 Welsh secular clergy in London ordination lists

3.2 Welsh secular clergy in Salisbury ordination lists

6.1 Translated sources for Welsh-French diplomacy

List of Contributors

Gideon Brough gained his PhD from Cardiff University, where for over a decade he has taught on warfare, medieval France, medieval Wales and the Hundred Years War. He is the author of *The Rise and Fall of Owain Glyn Dŵr* (London: I. B. Tauris, 2017) and he made numerous contributions to *The Encyclopaedia of War* (Oxford: Wiley-Blackwell, 2012). He continues to work on medieval warfare and diplomatic relations..

Emma Cavell is a Research Officer on the AHRC-funded project 'Women Negotiating the Boundaries of Justice: Britain and Ireland *c.*1100–1750'. She was previously a Lecturer in medieval history at the University of Leeds. She has published numerous papers on the history of women in the Welsh Marches, and is currently completing a project exploring the interaction of gender, status and locality in shaping the lives of noblewomen of the Anglo-Welsh frontier between 1066 and 1282/3.

Adam Chapman is currently Editor and Training Coordinator with the Victoria County History based at the Institute of Historical Research. He received his PhD in 2010 from the University of Southampton, and worked there on the AHRC-funded project, 'The Soldier in Later Medieval England, 1369–1453'. His research interests include the cultural effects of war on medieval society, the development of the medieval landscape, and tracing the lives and careers of individuals through documentary records.

Contributors

Rhun Emlyn is an Associate Lecturer in history and Welsh history at Aberystwyth University, with special research interests in ecclesiastical and political history, as well as Welsh history. His current work concentrates on medieval Welsh students, their careers and their influence on European and Welsh society.

Michael Hill gained his PhD from Rutgers University in 2014, examining ethnicity and cultural change in medieval Wales. He has published on this subject in *Welsh History Review*, and is currently working for a private education company in Princeton as a specialist in European and world history.

Kathryn Hurlock is Senior Lecturer in medieval history at Manchester Metropolitan University. She is the author of *Wales and the Crusades, 1095–1291* (Cardiff: University of Wales Press, 2011), and co-edited *Crusading and Pilgrimage in the Norman World* (Woodbridge: Boydell, 2015) with Paul Oldfield, and *The Brill Companion to Medieval Wales* (Leiden: Brill, forthcoming) with Emma Cavell.

Bryn Jones is a PhD student at the University of St Andrews, where he holds the Saunders Lewis Memorial Scholarship. His project focuses on Wales and Rome before the Edwardian conquest.

Janet Kay completed her PhD at Boston College. She is now a Fellow of the Society of Fellows in the Liberal Arts at Princeton University. Her first book, *Norse in Newfoundland* (Oxford: British Archaeological Reports, 2012), explored the relationship between the Vinland Sagas and archaeological evidence for Norse exploration in the North Atlantic.

Patricia Skinner holds a Personal Chair in history at Swansea University. She has published extensively on medieval social and cultural history, and has a particular interest in minority histories. Her most recent book is *Living with Disfigurement in Early Medieval Europe* (New York: Palgrave, 2017).

Deborah Youngs is a Professor in medieval history at Swansea University, and director of the AHRC-funded project 'Women

Negotiating the Boundaries of Justice: Britain and Ireland *c*.1100–1750'. Apart from her publications on women and the life cycle, she is interested in early Tudor reading communities, and edited the Letter Book of Henry, Lord Stafford (1501–63) for the Staffordshire Record Society.

Introduction

Welsh diaspora history: reinstating the pre-modern

Patricia Skinner

How did the Welsh travel beyond their geographical borders in the Middle Ages? What did they do, what did they take with them in their baggage and what did they bring back? The contributors to this volume, working with archaeological, historical and literary evidence, seek to explore how the Welsh interacted with and made their mark on the medieval world through their expertise, creativity and enterprise. We deliberately omit the diffusion of the Arthurian legends from our consideration, since these have already formed the focus of a substantial body of scholarship. Moreover, the legendary character and broader appeal of the Arthur story make of it a transnational, rather than a peculiarly Welsh, phenomenon.[1] Instead we explore both the historical and the imaginary worlds: how 'Welshness' and Welsh culture has been shaped, re-interpreted outside Wales, how Welsh culture has been enriched by returning travellers, and how 'travel' might include exchanges of letters or other artefacts rather than the movement of people. Core to the book's purpose is the exploration of identity within and outside the Welsh territories, particularly since 'Welsh' may have became a fluid term to describe a stranger, often pejoratively. The contributors, who vary in their opinions as to whether there was anything specifically 'Welsh' about the experiences of medieval migrants and correspondents, also seek to explore the nature of 'Welsh history' as a discipline: how can Welsh historiography draw upon wider paradigms of nationhood, diaspora and colonisation; legal paradigms; gender relations; and the pursuit of educational, religious and cultural opportunities? And what can the medieval experience of Welsh people exploring the then known 'world' contribute to the longer-term history of emigration and exchange?

These questions have never formed the subject of a period-specific enquiry, although the modern era has seen extensive Welsh migration to all parts of the globe as well as immigration to Wales from Europe and beyond. The concept of *hiraeth* – a longing to be in Wales – was a rather more recent phenomenon, inspiring poetry and songs that reinforced some critics' image of Wales and the Welsh as inward-looking and reluctant to stray far from their land.[2] Nothing of course could be further from the truth – everyone knows, of course, the legend that it was the *Welsh* who discovered America in the twelfth century, with Owain Gwynedd's son Prince Madog immortalised in a fifteenth-century poem that came in handy for Elizabethan propaganda purposes when tussling with the Spanish for colonial rights in the New World.[3] Rather more securely documented, Welsh men and women were among the first to land on the east coast of America in the seventeenth century, and by the eighteenth century Pennsylvania had a substantial community of Welsh settlers and miners, attracted by the opportunity to bring existing skills to their new home.[4] Welshmen also played direct and indirect roles in the Atlantic slave trade from this period onwards.[5] Welsh poet Goronwy Owen settled and died in Virginia, and he was just one of many literary exports of the period.[6] By the early nineteenth century, Welsh miners and settlers were active across the United States, Chile and in Australia, with copper mining being a particular speciality.[7] The industrial age saw still more expansion, with manufacturing sites established by John Hughes in the Ukraine – the city known as Hugheovska eventually changed its name to Donetsk.[8] Welsh emigration to Patagonia, fuelled by a desire to settle in a land that did not require religious conformity or English to be spoken, set up a two-way traffic that continues to this day.[9]

Before addressing the missing, pre-modern part of the story of Welsh diasporas and exchange with the wider world, it is necessary to define 'Wales'. For the purposes of this book, 'Wales' is used to mark the modern boundaries of a territory that in the medieval period was politically fragmented and socially diverse, giving rise to a spectrum of different relationships with the outside world. The formation of the principality in the thirteenth century, followed swiftly by English conquest, gave a semblance of political unity, but only so long as it suited the new rulers to maintain this fiction. As Chris Wickham has pointed out in a short but important discussion, the increasing centralisation and accumulation of power evident in other post-Roman regions looks less inevitable when viewed through a Welsh lens: here, small, independent polities gave way far more slowly to the eventual and fragile process of unification under the rule of Gwynedd.[10] This history, as has long been recognised, was shaped by topography, the mountainous core of the peninsula forming a formidable barrier to effective overall control, but also limiting the opportunity for the accumulation of wealth that underpinned every medieval ruler's ability to rule.[11]

Yet the fragmented nature of power in Wales did not get in the way of a good story. The saga of the Jomsvikings, composed in Iceland in the thirteenth century and described by its editors as 'pure fantasy', includes an episode where the hero, Pálna-Tóki, marries the daughter of the ruler of 'Wales', Earl Stefnir. Not wishing to remain in Wales, however, he returns to Denmark with his wife Álof and leaves his affairs in the hands of one Bjorn the Welshman.[12] The story is set in the late tenth and early eleventh centuries, during which, in reality, 'between Rhodri Mawr and Gruffudd ap Llywelyn, c.850–1050 . . . a kingdom of Wales might have been in the making',[13] but there is absolutely nothing to suggest that 'Wales' here represents anything other than 'somewhere else', far removed from the main theatre of events in the Baltic Sea and Norwegian coast, but clearly accessible by sea. Yet the Icelandic author perhaps knew enough, based on the *thirteenth*-century reality, to recognise that he could propose a single ruler for Wales. And Wales's early connections with the Scandinavian world, as we shall see, were no fantasy.

It is no easier to define 'Welsh' in this period. Labels used for convenience by modern historiography to describe 'German' or 'French' or 'Spanish' or even 'Byzantine' cultures share with 'Welsh' the problem that such nomenclature would have been largely unintelligible to those living in the medieval regions to which such labels refer. Pálna-Tóki's mentor and companion, Bjorn 'the

Welshman' only needed to be identified as such because he was, for much of the saga, operating outside Wales. Toponymic surnames, as we shall see, form a partial element in tracking Welshmen beyond the borders of Wales. But Welsh texts are far more likely to use 'Briton' to identify those from within the country's borders (just as Byzantine authors were keen on maintaining they were 'Romans'). Finding a specifically 'Welsh' medieval identity, therefore, presents something of a challenge.

The present volume is structured around two themes of Welsh interaction with the medieval world. First, it examines Wales's relationship with its near neighbour, England, as geographical contiguity inevitably led to regular exchanges, and it is on this often fraught relationship that we have the most evidence.[14] The medieval history of Wales has of course fuelled modern debates around nationalism, Wales's relationship with the United Kingdom and the issue of assimilation, and many of these issues are visited here, particularly in chapters by Cavell and Youngs that explore mixed marriages and the fluid relationship between English and Welsh law. Whilst most of the written evidence dates to the central Middle Ages and later, Janet Kay demonstrates the exciting new inroads being made into the history of early Wales through archaeological analysis. Moreover, Welsh migration to places further afield might involve time spent in England. Rhun Emlyn's chapter traces Welsh clergy travelling to English sees: service in the Church offered the opportunity to engage in a truly transnational community.

The theme of mobility through religious devotion opens the second section of the book, which examines the Welsh on a broader European stage. Kathryn Hurlock follows Welsh pilgrims and crusaders to Spain, the Holy Land and Italy, where it becomes apparent that new appraisals of existing archival and poetic sources can bring new and exciting insights into Wales's position within Europe. Bryn Jones mines the Vatican Archive for evidence of Welsh-papal exchanges, whilst Gideon Brough surveys the evidence for Welsh-French diplomatic contacts across three key points in Welsh history. Adam Chapman suggests that it was as soldiers that most Welshmen travelled, and were encountered outside Wales. More work is surely required to actually *look* for Welshmen (and women) overseas, and it is hoped that the essays presented here provide a stimulus to such research. A final chapter in this section reflects upon how Wales's juridical cultures might productively be compared with others on an even wider scale, as Michael Hill brings the Welsh situation into dialogue with Islamic and Chinese practices.

A brief historical survey

Wales's links with the wider world, as is well known, pre-dated the medieval period. There is substantial evidence of Roman penetration into parts of the peninsula, attested by archaeological evidence and finds of coin hoards.[15] A Roman milestone from Port Talbot lay on the westward route from Caerleon, thought to end at Carmarthen.[16] In the sub-Roman period, conversion to Christianity led to regular connections both with Ireland and the near continent, as well as with Rome itself.[17] It also saw the often hostile interactions between Britons and Anglo-Saxons, immortalised in Gildas's *Ruin of Britain*, written a century after the events he relates.[18] At the heart of Gildas's polemic is a strongly held sense of British identity. Yet the Welsh situation cannot easily be fitted into models of ethnogenesis proposed by historians of other parts of early medieval Europe: resistance to the Anglo-Saxons meant that Wales did not experience the same 'barbarian' takeover that happened in Francia, Iberia, Italy and eastern Europe, each requiring retrospective histories to understand and justify the migration of these peoples to their new kingdoms.[19] As Janet Kay's paper in this volume demonstrates, it is possible to use archaeological evidence to show that there was clear evidence of movement and mixing between the Britons and Anglo-Saxons. Michael Garcia agrees: whilst the ambiguities in Gildas's text have permitted numerous interpretations of the 'division' between Britons and Saxons in this early period, spatial separation between the two groups is the least likely scenario.[20] The arrival of the latter did not represent a rupture in Welsh history: Gildas's pessimism derived as much from his disappointment in the petty kings of his own time as from the history he relates. As Nennius, too, echoed the condemnation of early British kings in submitting to the Saxons: 'let him that reads understand, that the Saxons were victorious, and ruled Britain, not from their superior prowess, but on account of the great sins of the Britons; God permitting it'.[21]

Increasingly, archaeological finds are providing a more nuanced picture of early interactions.[22] There has been a considerable amount of work to reconstruct early medieval Welsh history, and this reveals significant and sustained evidence of interactions with other regions of Europe.[23] These took the form of trade, religious pilgrimage and diplomatic exchanges. Trading links are the hardest to document, leaving only traces such as stray coin finds, such as an Anglo-Saxon penny of Cynethryth, struck in 787–92, a penny of Wulfred of Canterbury, struck around 810, ninth-century Carolingian deniers of Louis the Pious and Charles the Bald, and three lead weights of Viking type, all found by metal detectorists on Anglesey.[24]

The *Life* of St Samson of Dol attests to the mobility of ecclesiastics in this early period, as he served in Wales before eventually moving to Brittany.[25] Pilgrimage from Wales to holy sites in Rome and Jerusalem is rather better represented in early hagiography: St David's *Life* recounts several journeys.[26]

Wales's relationship with England, its closest neighbour, is rather less comprehensively explored for the early medieval period than later on. It is as if the building of the Mercian King Offa's dyke in the eighth century, and that king's ambitions to cement his relations with more powerful rulers on the Continent, effectively cut off cross-border relations and with them any Welsh interactions with Europe.[27] Yet as Thomas Charles-Edwards has recently argued, the idea that Wales became an isolated backwater is due more to historiographical bias than the realities on the ground. Regarding diplomacy, the rulers of Gwynedd in the ninth century are known to have had links with the court of the Frankish King Charles the Bald.[28] Both rulers suffered the effects of Viking raids, which began in earnest on Wales in 852. As Claire Holmes and Keith Lilley point out, however, the Viking history of Wales, including the Scandinavian etymology of the place-name Swansea and numerous other sites in the south-west, has been rather overlooked as scholars focused on relations with Ireland and other Celtic regions in this period.[29] Indeed, movement and interaction across and around the Irish Sea is well documented, giving rise to several recent studies,[30] and it was to Ireland that Rhodri Mawr was exiled in 877, after defeat at Viking hands.

Sedulius Scottus had been valued at the courts of Gwynedd and Francia for his talents as a poet and scholar. A similar case is the career of Asser (d. *c.*908): arriving at Alfred of Wessex's court having been tonsured at St David's, his promotion was due to his existing reputation.[31] As Charles-Edwards pithily comments, being from west Wales 'does not mean that [Asser] emerged from intellectual backwoods to be transformed in his outlook by a far more cosmopolitan group of scholars'.[32] Yet Wales still also formed a target for Anglo-Saxon slave-raiding activities, as David Wyatt has highlighted: the Old English *wealh* serving a double meaning of both 'foreign' and 'wealth' as well as 'Welsh'.[33] By the tenth century, the growing unity within England under the West Saxon dynasty provided a focus for more diplomatic exchanges. King Hywel Dda (d. 950) famously witnessed documents of the rulers of Wessex with the title *regulus*, his name ahead of other Welsh leaders, from 928 to 949. He was reluctant to join in periodic Welsh campaigns targeted against the English, but nor did he assist his English allies against his own countrymen, particularly in the major uprising of 937 against King Athelstan that culminated in the battle of *Brunanburh*.[34] The Welsh text known as *The Prophecy of Britain* or *Armes Prydein*, belongs to this period, written in south Wales around 930, and bears testimony to the hostility that some Welsh felt towards any closer relationship with the English.[35]

Hywel's name became associated with the first codification of Welsh law, although surviving books date much later. Legal autonomy and identity would form a strong thread in future relations with the outside world, particularly England, but it is notable how some Welsh laws on personal injury shared common motifs not only with other 'Celtic' traditions, but also have striking similarities to earlier continental laws whose transmission routes are now invisible to us.[36]

The eleventh century represented a watershed in Welsh relations with the wider world, as Norman aggression in England pulled Welshmen into military campaigns, willingly or not. Welsh resistance to Norman incursions was largely led by the kings of Gwynedd. Alongside written accounts of these campaigns, almost entirely produced by hostile Norman authors, archaeological investigation is beginning to reveal how the landscape influenced what was a protracted campaign.[37]

Norman penetration into Wales, and the creation of an Anglo-Norman realm that encompassed parts of France, meant that awareness of the region spread among foreign authors.[38] A by-product of this period was an increasing interest in what we would now term ethnographic literature, in which a Welshman, Gerald, archdeacon of Brecon, was an early participant.[39]

Robert Bartlett has written of a Norman diaspora across Europe in the eleventh and twelfth centuries, in particular focused on the spread of Norman culture and settlements through crusading expeditions.[40] Welshmen, whether under Norman lordship or not, participated in this expansion of Europe. Kathryn Hurlock has written extensively on the subject of the Welsh on crusade, and her paper in this volume further explores the theme, reflecting not only on the export of Welsh soldiers but also the importation of cultural themes into Welsh poetry and literature.[41] The crusade era also ushers in a period when Wales features more heavily in papal documents. As Bryn Jones outlines in his chapter, the relationship between the Welsh and the papacy, as evidenced in the Vatican archives, concerned everything from regularisation of queries regarding the election of abbots and bishops to the defence of church lands. From the pope's point of view, Wales (considered as part of Britain in most correspondence) contributed both funds and manpower to the crusade campaigns. Gerald's own report of his journey through Wales in 1188, alongside the archbishop of Canterbury, Baldwin, and personal involvement in preaching the crusade, reflects the latter phenomenon.

Another result of the imposition of Anglo-Norman and then Angevin rule was ongoing negotiation of the clear differences between Welsh and 'English' laws, particularly with regard to the rights of women.[42] Emma Cavell's chapter in this volume focuses on how even being associated indirectly with Welsh rebellion threatened to undermine one woman's claim to her property. The formation of the core of Welsh law is attributed to the time of King Hywel, but the differing traditions eventually crystallised in a series of thirteenth-century law books. These underline how uncertainty could dog any attempt to establish legal claims to property or other rights. Several chapters in this collection feature English commentators commenting negatively on their experience of the Welsh and their legal system, to the extent that by the fifteenth century such commentary had become almost a trope with which to damn the Welsh.

The Norman expansion also opened up and exploited Wales's pre-existing ties to Ireland, and numerous Norman families (including Gerald's own) benefited from land grants in both peninsula and island.[43] The thirteenth century marks another watershed, as Edward I planned and executed the definitive subjection of Wales to English rule. Although the settlement of this conflict is dated 1283, a true settlement in terms of harmonious relations was long in coming. Adam Chapman points out in his chapter, however, that it had not been unusual for Welshmen to fight in *English* armies, and this continued into the later campaigns of the Hundred Years War, with the prowess of Welsh bowmen celebrated in English texts.[44] Chapman suggests in fact that there was little particularly Welsh about their military participation in terms of pay and conditions. The aristocracy, too, participated in an international network of relationships that tied their Welsh and other interests together. The De Briouze/Braose family are a good example.[45]

Did English rule over Wales in fact contribute to the formation of a hybrid identity? Deborah Youngs points to continued difficulties in negotiating legal issues into the fifteenth century, and the revolt of Owain Glyndŵr certainly suggests that the relationship between Wales and its nearest neighbour was by no means settled. Gideon Brough considers the revolt in his longer survey of Welsh-French diplomatic relations.[46] The rebellion of Owain Glyndŵr was not the last episode of major tension between the Welsh and their neighbours, and the Acts of Union of 1536 and 1543, prescribing assimilation through the medium of the English language, represents the opening of a new era that takes us beyond the Middle Ages.[47]

Notes

[1] Not least the impressive series of volumes examining Arthur in different literary contexts: Gloria Allaire and Regina F. Psaki (eds), *The Arthur of the Italians: the Arthurian Legend in Medieval Italian Literature and Culture*

(Cardiff: University of Wales Press, 2014); Marianne E. Kalinke (ed.), *The Arthur of the North: The Arthurian Legend in the Northern and Rus' Realms* (Cardiff: University of Wales Press, 2011); Siân Echard (ed.), *The Arthur of Medieval Latin Literature* (Cardiff: University of Wales Press, 2011); Kristen Lee Over, *Kingship, Conquest and Patria: Literary and Cultural Identities in Medieval French and Welsh Arthurian Romance* (New York and Abingdon: Routledge, 2005). A more general survey demonstrating the reach of the legend is to be found in Helen Fulton (ed.), *A Companion to Arthurian Literature* (Oxford: Blackwell, 2009).

[2] Dora Polk, *A Book called Hiraeth* (Port Talbot: Alun Books, 1982).

[3] Gwyn Williams, *Madoc: the Making of a Myth* (London: Eyre Methuen, 1979).

[4] Charles H. Browning, *Welsh Settlement of Pennsylvania* (Philadelphia, 1912, repr. Ann Arbor, 1997).

[5] Chris Evans, *Slave Wales: the Welsh and Atlantic Slavery, 1660–1850* (Cardiff: University of Wales Press, 2010).

[6] John Gwilym Jones, *Goronwy Owen's Virginian Adventure: his Life, Poetry and Literary Opinions* (Williamsburg, VA: Botetourt Bibliographical Society, 1969).

[7] Eirug Davies, *The Welsh of Tennessee* (Talybont: Y Lolfa, 2012); W. D. Jones, 'Labour Migration and Cross-cultural Encounters: Welsh Copper Workers in Chile during the Nineteenth Century', *WHR*, 27.1 (2014), 132–154; W. D. Jones, 'Representations of Australia in Mid-Nineteenth-Century Welsh Emigrant Literature: Gwlad yr Aur and Awstralia a'r Cloddfeydd Aur', *WHR*, 23.2 (2007), 51–74.

[8] Susan Edwards, *Hughesovska: a Welsh Enterprise in Imperial Russia* (Cardiff: Glamorgan Record Office, 1992).

[9] Glyn Williams, *The Desert and the Dream: A Study of Welsh Colonization in Chubut, 1865–1915* (Cardiff: University of Wales Press, 1975). Geraldine Lublin, *Memoir and Identity in Welsh Patagonia: Voices from a Settler Community in Argentina* (Cardiff: University of Wales Press, 2017), brings the story up to date.

[10] Chris Wickham, 'Medieval Wales and European History', *WHR*, 25.2 (2010), 201–8.

[11] For a consideration of the topography and resources in comparative perspective, see Patricia Skinner, 'The mountainous problems of Wales and southern Italy', in Ross Balzaretti, Julia Barrow and Patricia Skinner (eds), *Italy and Early Medieval Europe: Papers for Chris Wickham* (Oxford: Oxford University Press, in press).

[12] N. F. Blake (trans.), *Jómsvíkinga Saga/The Saga of the Jomsvikings* (Edinburgh: Thomas Nelson, 1962), c.9 (p. 11). Pálna-Tóki's links

with Wales continue to be referred to throughout the saga: c.11 (p. 13), c.13 (p. 15) (Stefnir dies, Pálna-Tóki heir to Wales), cc. 14 and 15 (p. 16) (Pálna-Tóki and Bjorn at King Sveinn's feast, Pálna-Tóki puts Bjorn in charge of Wales), c.22 (p. 23) (Pálna-Tóki proposes to send young Vagn to Bjorn in Wales), c.24 (p. 25) Pálna-Tóki dies, Vagn inherits half of Wales), cc.30 and 34 (pp. 32 and 38) (Vagn and Bjorn the Welshman fight together at the battle of Hjorungavágr), c.37 (p. 43) (Bjorn, now 'an old man with white hair', and Vagn are spared death), c.38 (p. 43) (Bjorn goes home to Wales and rules there).

[13] Wickham, 'Medieval Wales', 204.

[14] See, e.g. for the Norman period, Brian Golding, 'Transborder Transactions: Patterns of Patronage in Anglo-Norman Wales', *The Haskins Society Journal*, 16 (2005), 27–46.

[15] Notably the Rogiet hoard, found near Caldicot: Edward Besly, 'The Rogiet Hoard and the Coinage of Allectus', *British Numismatic Journal*, 76 (2006), 45–146, online at *www.britnumsoc.org/publications/ Digital%20BNJ/pdfs/2006_BNJ_76_1_4.pdf* (accessed 19 November 2016).

[16] The road is tracked at *www.coflein.gov.uk/en/site/307253/details/roman-road-westwards-from-caerleon-rr60b-d#associated* (accessed 22 February 2017).

[17] Nancy Edwards and Alan Lane (eds), *The Early Church in Wales and the West* (Oxford: Oxbow, 1992).

[18] Gildas, *The Ruin of Britain and other Worlds*, trans. Michael Winterbottom (Chichester: Phillimore, 1978).

[19] The eastern emphasis of the ethnogenesis thesis is well represented in the essays in Florin Curta (ed.), *Borders, Barriers and Ethnogenesis: Frontiers in Late Antiquity and the Middle Ages* (Turnhout: Brepols, 2005).

[20] Michael Garcia, 'Gildas and the "grievous divorce from the barbarians"', *EME*, 21.3 (2013), 243–53.

[21] Nennius, *History of the Britons*, trans. J. A. Giles, III.45 (Cambridge, Ontario: In parentheses Publications, 2000), p. 20.

[22] E.g. Mark Redknap, 'Glitter in the dragon's lair: Irish and Anglo-Saxon metalwork from pre-Viking Wales', in James A. Graham-Campbell and Michael Ryan (eds), *Anglo-Saxon/Irish Relations before the Vikings*, Proceedings of the British Academy, 157 (Oxford: Oxford University Press, 2009), pp. 281–310.

[23] Wendy Davies, *Wales in the Early Middle Ages* (Leicester: Leicester University Press, 1982); Davies's major essays are collected in Wendy Davies, *Welsh History in the Early Middle Ages* (Aldershot: Variorum, 2009).

[24] The Charles coin is recorded on the Portable Antiquities scheme website with reference number PAS-BAA385: https://finds.org.uk/database/search/results/objecttype/COIN/broadperiod/EARLY+MEDIEVAL/countyID/25482 (accessed 22 February 2017).

[25] Fr. Fraine (ed.), *Vita Antiqua Sancti Samsonis Dolensis Episcopi* (*Analecta Bollandiana*, 6, 1887), pp. 77–150. See Karen Jankulak, 'The absent saint: St Samson in Wales', in J.-C. Cassard et al. (eds), *Mélanges offerts au professeur Bernard Merdrignac* (*Britannia Monastica* 17, Landevennec, 2013), pp. 197–212.

[26] Pilgrimage *to* St Davids seems to have been a slightly later phenomenon: J. Wyn Evans and Jonathan M. Wooding (eds), *St David of Wales: Cult, Church and Nation* (Woodbridge: Boydell, 2007).

[27] See D. J. Tyler's useful 'Offa's Dyke: a Historiographical Appraisal', *JMH*, 37 (2011), 145–61. The exception is Thomas Charles-Edwards's study 'Wales and Mercia, 613–918', in Michelle P. Brown and Carol Ann Farr (eds), *Mercia: an Anglo-Saxon Kingdom in Europe* (London: Continuum, 2001), pp. 88–105.

[28] Nora K. Chadwick, 'Early culture and learning in North Wales', in her *Studies in the Early British Church* (Cambridge: Cambridge University Press, 1958), pp. 29–120, at pp. 102–7, identifies the poet Sedulius Scottus as a link between the two courts.

[29] Claire Holmes and Keith Lilley, 'Viking Swansea', at www.medievalswansea.ac.uk/en/context/viking-swansea/ (accessed 19 November 2016).

[30] See the essays in Karen Jankulak, Thomas O'Loughlin and Jonathan M. Wooding (eds), *Ireland and Wales in the Middle Ages* (Dublin: Four Courts, 2007); Nancy Edwards, 'Early medieval sculpture in South-West Wales: the Irish Sea connection', in Rachael Moss (ed.), *Making and Meaning in Insular Art* (Dublin: Four Courts Press, 2007), pp. 184–97; Arlene Hogan, 'Wales and Ireland: monastic links', in Janet E. Burton and Karen Stöber (eds), *Monastic Wales: New Approaches* (Cardiff: University of Wales Press, 2013), pp. 163–76; Thomas Charles-Edwards, *Wales and the Britons 350–1064* (Oxford: Oxford University Press, 2013).

[31] See also Kaele L. Stokes, 'The Educated Barbarian? Asser's *Life of King Alfred* and Welsh Learning', *Quaestio Insularis*, 3 (2002), 45–58.

[32] Charles-Edwards, *Wales and the Britons*, p. 454; he also highlights other connections with Francia.

[33] David R. Wyatt, *Slaves and Warriors in Medieval Britain and Ireland, 800–1200* (Leiden: Brill, 2009), p. 127.

[34] R. C. Stacey, 'Hywel in the World', *Haskins Society Journal*, 20 (2009), 175–203; Kevin Halloran, 'Welsh Kings at the English Court, 928–956',

WHR, 25.3 (2011), 297–313; Charles-Edwards, *Wales and the Britons*, p. 526.

35 Rachel Bromwich and Ifor Williams (eds), *Armes Prydein: the Prophecy of Britain from the Book of Taliesin* (Dublin: Four Courts Press, 1982); on the text and its context see Helen Fulton, 'Tenth-century Wales and *Armes Prydein*', *Trans. Hon. Soc. Cymm.*, n.s. 7 (2001), 5–18; and more recently Gary German, 'L'"Armes Prydein Fawr" et "La Bataille de Brunanburgh": les relations géopolitiques entre Bretons, Anglo-Saxons et Scandinaves dans la Bretagne insulaire du Xe siècle', in Magali Coumert and Yvon Tranvouez (eds), *Landévennec, les Vikings et la Bretagne: en hommage à Jean-Christophe Cassard* (Brest: Editions du CRBC, 2015), pp. 171–209.

36 Discussed in Patricia Skinner, *Living with Disfigurement in Early Medieval Europe* (New York: Palgrave, 2017), pp. 67–101.

37 Jacqueline Veninger is currently researching the battle sites to recreate 'a cultural and societal native Welsh context that has been absent from our understanding of the Anglo-Norman incursion into Wales': see her presentation of her project in 'Landscapes of conflict: patterns of Welsh resistance to the Anglo-Norman conquest of North Wales, 1070–1250 – an overview of a new study', in Peter Ettel (ed.), *Château et frontière: actes du colloque international d'Aabenraa (Danemark, 24–31 août 2012)* (=*Chateau Gaillard*, 26, Caen: Université de Caen, 2014), pp. 353–6.

38 Sharon Kinoshita, 'Colonial possessions: Wales and the Anglo-Norman imaginary in the *Lais* of Marie de France', in Albrecht Classen (ed.), *Discourses on Love, Marriage and Transgression in Medieval and Early Modern Literature* (Tempe, AZ: Arizona University Press, 2004), pp. 147–62.

39 The literature on Gerald's works, particularly his *Description of Wales* and *Topography of Ireland*, is vast: for an introduction, see Robert Bartlett, *Gerald of Wales: a Voice of the Middle Ages* (Oxford: Clarendon Press, 1982), and Robert Bartlett, 'Gerald of Wales, c.1146–1220x3', *Oxford Dictionary of National Biography* (2004), online at http://dx.doi.org/10.1093/ref:odnb/10769 (accessed 22 February 2017).

40 Robert Bartlett, *The Making of Europe: Conquest, Colonization and Cultural Change, 950–1350* (London: Penguin, 1993), pp. 24–60.

41 Kathryn Hurlock, *Wales and the Crusades, c.1095–1291*, Studies in Welsh History 33 (Cardiff: University of Wales Press, 2011); Kathryn Hurlock, 'The Norman influence on crusading from England and Wales', in Kathryn Hurlock and Paul Oldfield (eds), *Crusading and Pilgrimage in the Norman World* (Woodbridge: Boydell, 2015), pp. 65–80.

[42] Dafydd Jenkins and Morfydd Owen (eds), *The Welsh Law of Women: studies presented to Daniel Binchy on his eightieth birthday* (Cardiff: University of Wales Press, 1980). The AHRC project 'Women negotiating the boundaries of justice', based at Swansea University, is further investigating this issue: *www.swansea.ac.uk/riah/research-projects/women-negotiating-the-boundaries-of-justice/*.

[43] See, e.g. Mark Hagger, *The Fortunes of a Norman Family: the de Verduns in England, Ireland and Wales, 1066–1316* (Dublin: Four Courts Press, 2001). The fortunes of the de Barry family in Ireland await a sustained study.

[44] Chapman has published what must now be the definitive study: *Welsh Soldiers in the Later Middle Ages, 1282–1422* (Woodbridge: Boydell, 2015); and Adam Chapman, 'Wales, Welshmen and the Hundred Years War', in L. J. Andrew Villalon and Donald J. Kagay (eds), *The Hundred Years War: Further Considerations* (Leiden: Brill, 2013), pp. 217–31. On the prowess of Welsh archers, already celebrated by Gerald of Wales, see Sean Davies, *War and Society in Medieval Wales, 633–1283: Welsh Military Institutions* (Cardiff: University of Wales Press, 2004), pp. 151–3, which nevertheless also dispels some common myths.

[45] See Daniel Power, 'The Briouze Family in the Thirteenth and Early Fourteenth Centuries: Inheritance Strategies, Lordship and Identity', *JMH*, 41.3 (2015), 341–61.

[46] And see also Richard Cavendish, 'Owen Glendower's French Treaty', *History Today*, 54.6 (June 2004), 54–5.

[47] Lloyd Bowen, 'Information, Language and Political Culture in Early Modern Wales', *Past and Present*, 228 (2015), 125–58, continues the story.

PART I:

WALES AND THE NEIGHBOURS

1

Moving from Wales and the west in the fifth century: isotope evidence for eastward migration in Britain

Janet Kay

It seems only fitting to start a book on the Welsh in the world by asking who, exactly, we are talking about, and where they lived – particularly at the very beginning of the medieval period. The focus of most research on Britain in the fifth century is on the collapse of the Roman administration and the concurrent *adventus Saxonum* – the arrival of immigrants from the Continent to what would later become Anglo-Saxon England. The fifth century, theoretically, had less of an impact on the people living in the part of the island we now know as Wales than it did on those in the eastern lowlands.[1] This is, however, the period that modern historians consider as the beginning of a concept of 'Wales', though the early medieval Welsh kingdoms would not exist until the middle of the sixth century at the earliest.[2] What, then, was 'Wales' in the fifth century, and who were the 'Welsh'? And how did these fifth-century people interact with the larger world around them?

The difficulty in studying the history of Britain in the fifth century, and of the western half of the island in particular, is the scarcity of the sources – textual or archaeological – that we have at our disposal.[3] We have no contemporary surviving texts, and the archaeological identification of sites from the period is almost impossible without radiocarbon dating.[4] There is no certain material culture tradition that can be attributed to the fifth-century British inhabitants of Wales; if anything, 'Britishness' in the fifth century and the early medieval period is very often defined as a lack of the material cultures found in eastern Britain.[5] And if a distinct 'Welsh' ethnicity coalesced later in the early medieval period, we have no evidence that it did in the fifth.[6]

This does not, however, mean that we cannot study what happened within modern Wales during the fifth century, even if these modern borders are meaningless for the very early medieval period. What we *do* know about the region in the fifth century is that it was at the centre of movements of people and objects across great distances; indeed, the best contemporary sources that we have are the result of international trade and migration. Pottery made in the Mediterranean and Gaul during the late fifth and sixth centuries was traded to high-status settlements in Wales, as well as Cornwall, Ireland and Scotland.[7] Inscriptions in both Latin and Ogham on stone monuments in Dyfed and Anglesey indicate a strong Irish immigrant presence during the fifth century, and possibly as early as the fourth.[8] And textual sources from a century or two later discuss the movement of people to Wales from Scotland, and from Wales to Brittany.[9]

The best way to study fifth-century Wales is therefore first by understanding that it was, in fact, part of the larger world around it (as the title of this book suggests), rather than the separate place in space-time it usually occupies in the history of post-Roman Britain. Here, and for the rest of this chapter, therefore, 'Wales' is imagined as the larger area of western Britain along the Irish Sea with which its people interacted – suggested through linguistic, material, textual and epigraphic evidence. Its geographical centre is the modern country, but its hypothetical boundaries reach as far south as Cornwall, eastward over the mountains, and north into western Scotland. The people who lived within this region, however, I will refer to as 'British'; their grandchildren and great-grandchildren may have been called 'the Welsh', but the people living in our reimagined 'Wales' during the fifth century were not.

In the last fifteen years archaeologists have increasingly turned to burial evidence, particularly of skeletons rather than grave goods, in order to learn more about how, when and possibly how far people moved in or into Britain during the late Roman and early medieval periods. One of the most recent (and very promising) bioarchaeological techniques is the study of stable isotopes.[10]

Oxygen and strontium isotopes are deposited in our teeth and bones when we eat and drink, and different relative quantities of these isotopes vary based upon where our food and water supplies come from. Studying these ratios can sometimes provide information about where people spent their early years by comparing the ratios present in their dental tissue to those found in drinking water, rainfall, bedrock and vegetation.[11] Stable isotope analysis therefore offers an objective and much needed method with which we can study migration in fifth-century Britain, by determining who had most likely grown up in the local area near the cemetery and who had moved there from somewhere else. By examining skeletons rather than material culture, we can see past the historiographical narratives of a specific cultural group and understand how communities and individuals moved across Britain at a time of considerable change in trade systems, political allegiances and subsistence strategies.

This chapter examines these fifth-century people from a biological perspective, through their stable isotopes, and considers how people moved to and from Wales and elsewhere in western Britain. I argue that recent results from these analyses from cemeteries used throughout Britain during the fifth century indicate that we need to reconsider our current narrative of a predominantly westward migration, in the model of the expulsion of the British from the eastern half of the island as the result of the movement of the 'Anglo-Saxons'. Rather, the isotopes suggest that there was also migration from our broadly conceived 'Wales' to the eastern half of the island. People from this region were on the move to other parts of Britain during a time period usually considered to be the reserve of the *adventus Saxonum*, and in a direction invisible in the epigraphic and textual evidence.

Stable isotopes and migration studies

Bioarchaeologists study the quantities of heavy isotopes strontium-87 and oxygen-18 within dental enamel, in relation to the normal-weight elements strontium-86 and oxygen-16; these two measurements are denoted as $\delta^{18}O$ and $^{87}Sr/^{86}Sr$.[12] Each tooth, which is formed at a different point in biological development, contains 'an enduring archive' of information on the geological and meteorological conditions at the time of its formation.[13] The strontium that ends up in skeletal material first leeches from the underlying geology into the water supply (and therefore is taken up by crops and animals) and becomes part of the human skeletal structure through consumption. Scientists can measure strontium ($^{87}Sr/^{86}Sr$) signatures in the bedrock of a specific region through water and soil testing, as well as from vegetation and animal bones taken either as archaeological samples or from the modern environment.[14] They then compare these values to human skeletal isotopes to determine whether or not a person predominantly drank water from and ate foods grown or raised on land above that bedrock. Certain types of hard geologies have consistent strontium values, which can be mapped across Britain.[15]

Oxygen isotopes are similarly taken into our skeleton from the water we drink, but vary according to climate and rainfall rather than hard geology. Oxygen is measured in two different quantities, $\delta^{18}O_p$ (phosphate in teeth) and $\delta^{18}O_{dw}$ (drinking water). The $\delta^{18}O_p$ levels from teeth are converted into a $\delta^{18}O_{dw}$ measurement, which can then be compared to rainfall and groundwater $\delta^{18}O_{dw}$ values to estimate where the person might have lived during their childhood, when tooth enamel forms.[16] Britain's weather system pushes its rain from west to east, and western Britain receives more of the heavier ^{18}O part of rain, while the lighter ^{16}O raindrops fall later as the rains reach the eastern coast (see Figures 1.1a and 1.1b). The farther west the site, therefore, the higher the $\delta^{18}O_{dw}$ expected within the local climate.[17] While climatic $\delta^{18}O$ can vary during different parts of the year, the average $\delta^{18}O_{dw}$ values have not changed significantly since the fifth-century.[18] Though recent studies show that the $\delta^{18}O_{dw}$ value of drinking water can also change through cooking or boiling, the relative effect that this has on skeletal isotopes is not yet known.[19]

Archaeologists studying skeletal isotopes in Britain generally group burials from each site into three isotopic categories, in order to avoid misconstruing the data by being too specific. The first – the 'immigrant' group – includes individuals whose oxygen isotopes are too high or low for Britain's climate. The second, 'local'

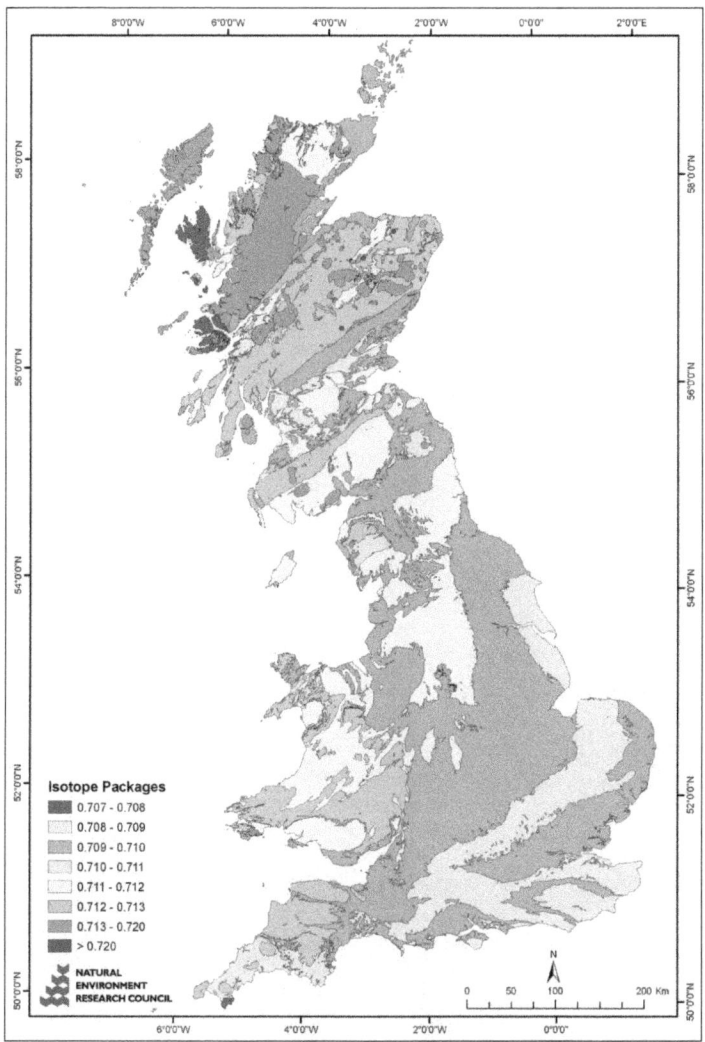

Figure 1.1a: Geological map of Britain, with locations of ^{87}Sr/^{86}Sr values in relation to site locations. After Evans et al., 'Spatial Variations in Biosphere 87Sr/86Sr in Britain', *Journal of the Geological Society*, 167 (2010).

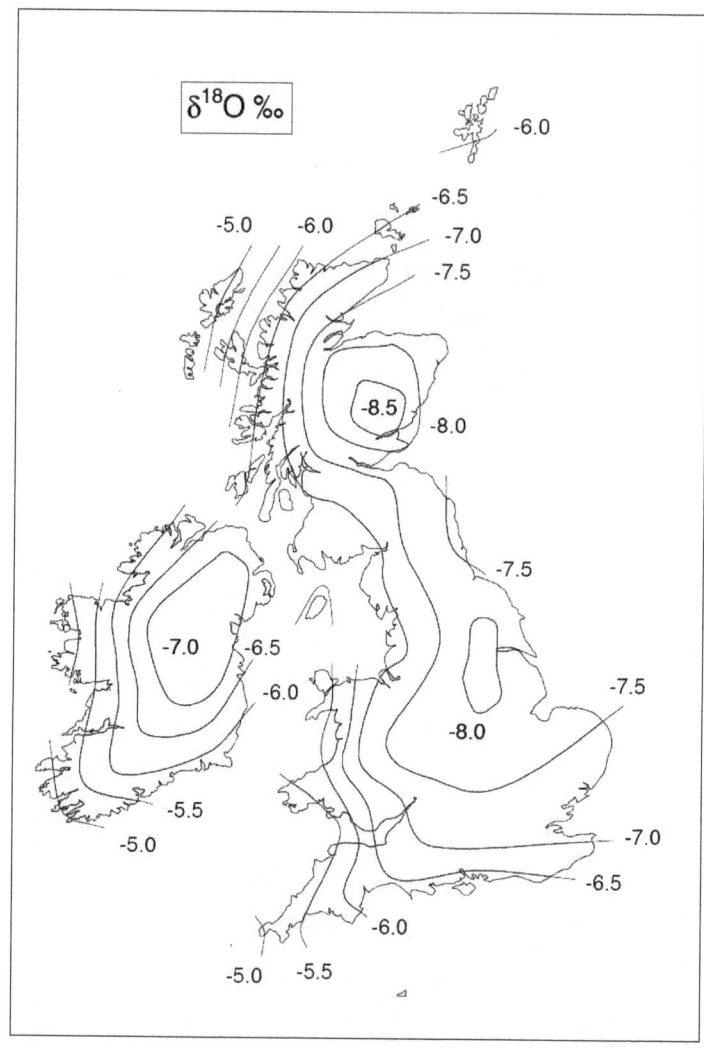

Figure 1.1b. Map showing groundwater $\delta^{18}O_{dw}$ contours. After Darling et al., 'The O & H Stable Isotopic Composition of Fresh Waters in the British Isles. 2. Surface Waters and Groundwater', *Hydrology and Earth System Sciences*, 7.2 (2003).

group includes people with $^{87}Sr/^{86}Sr$ levels that are possible on the underlying geology, and who also have oxygen in the expected British range ($\delta^{18}O_{dw}$ between -8.7‰ and -4.7‰).[20] Each investigative team determines their best estimate of how far within the landscape a community might have gone to bury its dead, and then takes samples from that environment to create a 'local' isotope signature.[21]

In the vast nebulous middle between 'locals' and definite 'immigrants' is an amorphous group of individuals who could have come from elsewhere in Britain, beyond the confines of the local area. Their oxygen isotopes fall within the British range, but their strontium isotopes are not possible on the local terrain. In many cases, archaeologists intentionally do not separate smaller regional categories within the wide 'non-local, yet still British' range of oxygen values, though many do identify people with very high $\delta^{18}O_{dw}$ ratios (<-4.5‰ to -5‰) as having likely come from the very western parts of Britain.[22] As skeletal and biosphere isotopic analysis and interpretation methods improve, it may be possible to one day determine more specifically where an individual was born and raised. The standard approach, which I use here, takes the simplest explanation as the best: that people whose isotopes are possible in Britain come from Britain, even if similar oxygen and strontium values can be found elsewhere in the Mediterranean or on the Continent.[23]

Isotopes and evidence for migration to and from Wales

The mobility of people out of western Britain in the fifth century has traditionally stopped at the theoretical border with England. The earliest historiographical narratives of post-Roman Britain argued that the proto-English, upon arrival, either evicted, married – or in extreme interpretations, exterminated – the British, to such an extent that their material culture and language disintegrated and disappeared in the east, and any surviving British – Romano- or otherwise – were pushed into Wales and the west.[24] This unidirectional narrative of migration within Britain from east to west in the fifth century, however, remains an overly simplistic conception of the possibilities of human movement during the interregnum between Roman Britain in the fourth century and the nascent Welsh and Anglo-Saxon kingdoms in the later sixth. It also is in stark contrast to our historical understanding of late Roman mobility, in which men, women and children moved throughout the empire, often across great distances.[25]

Two recent articles isotopic studies suggest that we need to change the way we understand the people living in Wales and western Britain during the fifth century. The first was an analysis by Katie Hemer et al. of the strontium and oxygen isotopes of thirty-three people from four early medieval cemeteries in Glamorgan and Pembrokeshire.[26] These isotopes showed that starting in the fifth century, and continuing for many centuries afterward, immigration was a fact of life in south Wales; while the majority of the sample population were local, several most likely came from other climates in Britain, while a few arrived from as far away as the Mediterranean.[27] The second study important for the mobility of people from fifth-century 'Wales' is, counter-intuitively, from a cemetery in Kent.[28] Rhea Brettell et al. compared skeletal isotopes from burials at the Anglo-Saxon cemetery at Ringlemere, Kent, to samples from burials at three contemporary cemeteries in France and Germany. All four sites had similar environmental conditions, and skeletons from all four sites were therefore expected to have relatively similar isotopic signatures.[29] At the continental sites, the majority of the sampled skeletons' isotopes were consistent with expected local values. Six of the seven people tested from Ringlemere, however, had oxygen values that fit better in Wales and western Britain than in Kent. The authors concluded that the unexpectedly higher oxygen values at Ringlemere were most likely the result of migration from western Britain.[30] These two articles, taken together, suggest that we need to reconsider how people from 'Wales' moved within their larger world during the fifth century.

In order to study migration within Britain in the fifth century, we need to understand the existing patterns of mobility in the fourth century, and track any changes through the fifth century and into the sixth. I first created a model of what oxygen and strontium values we might use to identify people who left Wales and were buried elsewhere in Britain using Hemer et al.'s data from early medieval

Pembrokeshire and Glamorgan. This is the best available isotopic study of roughly contemporary human skeletons buried within the boundaries of modern Wales;[31] and oxygen and strontium values similar to those in southern Wales can be found within the western and northern halves of Britain.[32] I then compared this population model to the published results from isotopic analyses of skeletons from cemeteries used for burial in the fifth century throughout Britain.

Testing oxygen and strontium isotopes of burials from four early medieval cemeteries in south Wales, Hemer et al. found that sixteen individuals of the total thirty-three sampled grew up near the places where they were buried, while four had moved from more extreme climate conditions on the outer coasts of western Britain.[33] I combined these twenty individuals into a sample population, which could be used as a comparative model against other isotopes tested from other skeletal remains elsewhere in Britain. First, the sample mean calculated from $\delta^{18}O_{dw}$ values for all twenty individuals produced an expected $\delta^{18}O_{dw}$ range for this model of -6.3‰ to -4.5‰.[34] The second criterion for this population model was strontium: an $^{87}Sr/^{86}Sr$ value of 0.7110 or higher. This is a common marker used to indicate a childhood on the older rocks found in the highlands of western and northern Britain, not only in Hemer et al.'s article, but also in all of the published isotope reports studied for this chapter.[35] Because the resultant $^{87}Sr/^{86}Sr$ and $\delta^{18}O_{dw}$ values for this model are found not only in modern Wales, but also along the Irish Sea – including Cornwall and western Scotland – I will refer to this model as 'north/western', for better comparison with isotopic signatures in the south and east. This north/western model predicts oxygen and strontium values that we might expect in people from our expanded conception of Wales in the fifth century. An individual must contain only one of these distinctive isotope markers to fall into this category, but many have both.

I re-organised the three standard 'local', 'immigrant' and 'non-local, yet still British' isotope categories discussed above to include the new model using the Welsh data. The 'local' group remains relatively unchanged from the standard approach, which originally includes those with both local strontium and oxygen values possible in the UK. However, because the north/western model claims all $\delta^{18}O_{dw}$ values between -4.5‰ and -6.3‰, the new 'local' group contains people whose isotope signatures fall into either one of two oxygen categories, both of which coincide with local strontium. The first of these is $\delta^{18}O_{dw}$ values between -6.3‰ and -8.7‰, the portion of UK values not included in the north/western model. The second, which only occurs at Lankhills, Winchester, is the presence in the skeleton of local $\delta^{18}O_{dw}$ values which would otherwise fall into the model constructed with the Welsh data. Unlike at the rest of the sites studied in this chapter, $\delta^{18}O_{dw}$ isotopes measured in the climate conditions and groundwater samples in Winchester overlap with the north/western model.[36] Therefore, the people buried at Lankhills whose strontium and oxygen isotopes are local to the Winchester area I considered part of the 'local' population, despite the same values being within the range calculated for the north/western model. It is important to note, in addition, that in the case of Porthclew, the 'local' values in Pembrokeshire were amongst the Welsh data set. The three individuals from Porthclew who fall into the north/western category therefore came from elsewhere in the north or west: one had oxygen values expected from the extreme western coast of Britain, while two had higher strontium levels than are possible around the cemetery area.[37]

I then split the 'immigrant' group into two categories based upon $\delta^{18}O_{dw}$ values. Those who most likely came from warmer climates fall under the category of 'Mediterranean', while those from the cooler parts of the Continent are 'Continental'. Finally, the last isotope category – the 'south/eastern' group – includes a few people whose otherwise British isotopes do not fit into either the local or north/western categories; this includes people with non-local strontium that is not high enough to otherwise fall into the north/western group, as well as people with considerably lower oxygen values than would be expected in the local area – both of these conditions are usually found in the southern and eastern parts of Britain.[38] Using this five-part isotopic model helps us look for changing international patterns of immigration, from either the heart of the Roman Empire or the Germanic homelands. More importantly, it allows us to identify in other parts of Britain some people who likely moved from our broadly conceived 'Wales'.

Out of the west

We can compare this north/western model to the data from the handful of isotope studies available for the fifth century. I examine in this chapter only those from cemeteries that were in use sometime during Britain's long fifth century, between c.350 and 550 CE. When the investigating archaeologists were able to differentiate between phases of burial within a cemetery, I excluded those isotope samples taken from people who most likely died much too early or too late to fit into this period.[39] And while some studies analyse either strontium or oxygen, this paper uses only those at which investigators tested both isotopes. This combination shows a more complete picture of human movement, as oxygen and strontium are independent measuring systems, and can provide information on movement in all cardinal directions. These combined criteria produced a study sample of 161 people within eleven cemeteries or burial populations throughout Britain (see Table 1.1 and Figure 1.2).

I arranged these eleven burial populations into three chronological groups, in order to study changes in human mobility from the late Roman period to the sixth century. Five populations date to the late fourth and early fifth centuries (henceforth known as Period I, c.350–425/450 CE). Only one of these five (the first phase of burial at Wasperton, Warwickshire) is rural:[40] those at the Scorton Hollow Banks Quarry and Catterick Bridge in North Yorkshire, the Wotton cemetery in Gloucester and Lankhills are all connected with towns or urban centres.[41] There are then three burial populations from the 'transitional' fifth century (Period II, from c.400 or earlier through c.500 CE or later). These include a second phase of burial at Wasperton, the Bainesse Farm cemetery outside Catterick and the rural cemetery at Berinsfield, Oxfordshire.[42] Finally, three cemeteries were in use from the late fifth century onward (c.450–550+ CE, Period III): the rural cemeteries at West Heslerton, North Yorkshire, Ringlemere, Kent and Porthclew, Pembrokeshire.[43] Though Hemer et al. tested skeletons from four early medieval cemeteries in modern Wales, I included in my comparative data set only those from Porthclew, for chronological reasons.[44]

Table 1.1: The quantity of burials with strontium ($^{87}Sr/^{86}Sr$) and oxygen ($\delta^{18}O_{dw}$) values from each cemetery or burial population

Site	Number of burials tested for strontium and oxygen isotopes	Date
Period I: sites ending during the first half of the fifth century (350–c.400/450 CE)		
Catterick Bridge	7	late 3rd–early 5th
Wotton Cemetery, Gloucester	9	3rd–4th
Lankhills, Winchester	55	mid-3rd–5th
Scorton, N. Yorks	8	4th
Wasperton, Warks. (Pd I)	14	3rd–mid-5th
Period I Total	**93**	
Period II: sites spanning the fifth century (including 400–500 CE)		
Berinsfield, Oxon	19	mid-4th–mid-7th
Catterick Bainesse SSD 10	8	3rd–mid-6th
Wasperton, Warks. (Pd II)	5	5th–mid-7th
Period II Total	**32**	
Period III: sites beginning during the fifth century (c.425/450 CE)		
Porthclew, Pembs	5	mid-5th–8th
Ringlemere, Kent	7	mid-late-5th
West Heslerton, N. Yorks	24	late 4th–7th
Period III Total	**36**	

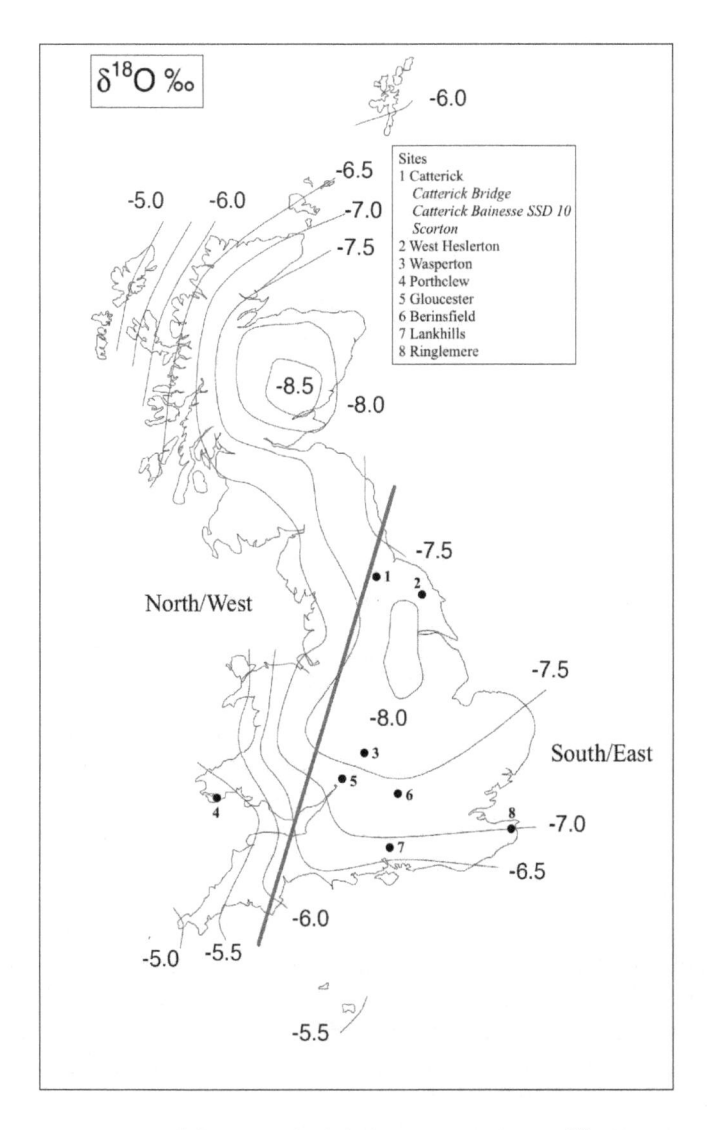

Figure 1.2. Map of all sites studied, laid over groundwater $\delta^{18}O_{dw}$ contours. The line running from the Tyne to Cornwall divides the north/west and south/east halves of Britain. Acknowledgement: Permit Number CP17/026 British Geological Survey © NERC 2017. All rights reserved.

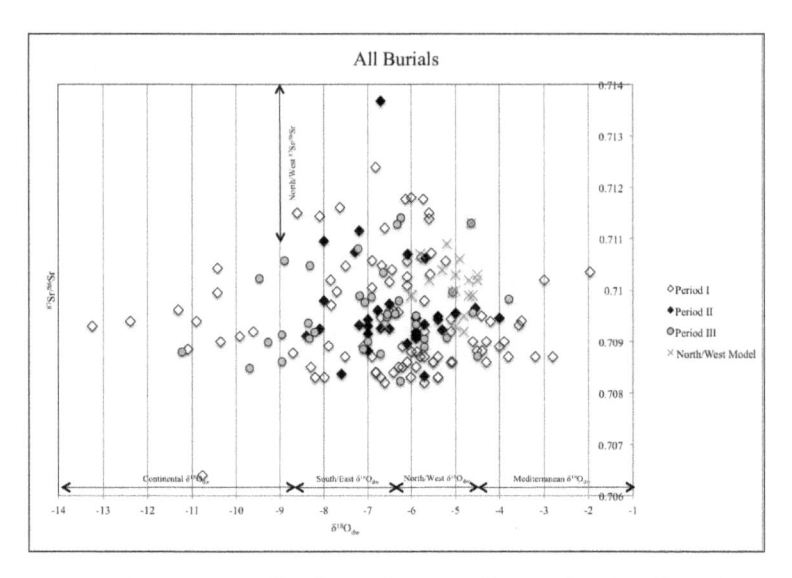

Figure 1.3. Strontium $^{87}Sr/^{86}Sr$ and oxygen $\delta^{18}O_{dw}$ values for all sampled individuals, according to period, displayed against twenty individuals that make up the north/western oxygen signature. Acknowledgement: Permit Number **CP17/026** British Geological Survey © NERC 2017. All rights reserved.

Over the course of the long fifth century, the results from these 161 sampled skeletons suggest that the height of human mobility in Britain occurred during the late Roman period, especially in communities burying in urban cemeteries. Figure 1.3 displays the $\delta^{18}O_{dw}$ and $^{87}Sr/^{86}Sr$ values for each of the individuals studied in this chapter from all three chronological periods (I, II and III), in comparison to the values from the twenty individuals from early medieval Wales who were included in the construction of the north/western model. The snapshot of mobility visualised in Figure 1.3 is described in Table 1.2, which displays the resulting breakdown of isotope signatures within each sample population, as part of its chronological period.

In Period I, just under one-third of the sample burials have 'local' isotopes. This means that a likely two-thirds of the ninety-three people in this chronological group moved from their childhood home before their deaths in the fourth and early fifth centuries. One-third immigrated from overseas, and a handful appears to have

Table 1.2: Regional origins according to site and chronological period, as indicated by isotope results

Site	Burial with isotopes	Locals	North/west Britain	South/east Britain	Mediterranean	Continental
Period I: sites ending in the fifth century (<450 CE)						
Catterick Bridge	7	6 (85.7%)	1 (14.3%)			
Gloucester	9	2 (22.2%)	4 (44.4%)	1 (11.1%)	2 (22.2%)	
Lankhills	55	16 (29.1%)	18 (32.7%)	4 (7.3%)	9 (16.4%)	8 (14.5%)
Wasperton (Pd I)	14	3 (21.4%)	8 (57.1%)		3 (21.4%)	
Scorton	8	1 (12.5%)	1 (12.5%)	1 (12.5%)	1 (12.5%)	4 (50.0%)
Period I Total	**93**	**28 (30.1%)**	**32 (34.4%)**	**6 (6.5%)**	**15 (16.1%)**	**12 (12.9%)**
Period II: sites spanning the fifth century						
Berinsfield	19	11 (57.9%)	8 (42.1%)			
Catterick Bainesse SSD 10	8	3 (37.5%)	4 (50.0%)		1 (12.5%)	
Wasperton (Pd II)	5	2 (40.0%)	3 (60.0%)			
Period II Total	**32**	**16 (50.0%)**	**15 (46.9%)**		**1 (3.1%)**	
Period III: sites beginning in the fifth century (c.425/450 CE)						
Porthclew	5	1 (20.0%)	3 (60.%)		1 (20.0%)	
Ringlemere	7	1 (14.3%)	6 (85.7%)			
West Heslerton	24	14 (58.3%)	3 (12.5%)			7 (29.2%)
Period III Total	**36**	**16 (44.4%)**	**12 (33.3%)**		**1 (2.8%)**	**7 (19.4%)**
TOTAL	**161**	**60 (37.3%)**	**59 (36.6%)**	**6 (3.7%)**	**17 (10.6%)**	**19 (11.8%)**

left the south-eastern lowlands of England. More importantly for our current study, our model suggests that one-third of the people in the Period I sample moved from Wales or elsewhere in the north or west to other parts of (eastern) Britain.

The group from Period II cemeteries looks considerably different. As the fifth century began, people and communities appear to have been more sedentary: isotopes suggest that all but one of the sampled burials from this chronological group was born in Britain. Half of the people from this period have locally available isotopes, and half have isotopes that fall into our north/western model. The percentage of the sampled population whose isotopic values suggest a childhood in Wales and the west therefore increased after the late Roman period. By the end of the fifth century and into the sixth (Period III), immigration to Britain picked up. As in Period II, however, roughly half of the sampled people have local isotopes: though immigrants formed a larger part of the population, they comprise only one-fifth of the total. Most of the immigrants in Period III, moreover, have isotopes available on the Continent. Unlike in Period I, where there were almost as many people from the Continent as there were from the Mediterranean, in Period III seven out of eight immigrants have the lower oxygen values associated with the Germanic homelands, Scandinavia and central Europe.

Given our current historical expectation of east-to-west migration within Britain during the fifth century, it is surprising to find that isotopic evidence suggests that people moved from Wales and north/western Britain to eastern Britain in almost the same percentages in both the late Roman Period I and Period III. In between, during the century which is usually characterised as the beginning of the *adventus Saxonum*, the proportion of the sampled population with isotopes falling within our north/western model is the highest. This is despite the fact that the sampling strategies at some of the Period II sites focused on people who were buried with Anglo-Saxon or continental material culture, and who therefore might have represented part of the immigrant population.[45]

Examining the movement within each chronological period in relation to age and gender further complicates our migration narrative. In the fourth century, our sample isotope evidence suggests that women were more likely to be local than men, and they were also

Moving from Wales and the west in the fifth century

Table 1.3: Regional origins according to site and chronological period, as indicated by isotope results, according to gender and age

Gender/ Age	Burial with isotopes	Locals	North/ west Britain	South/ east Britain	Medi- terranean	Continental
Period I: sites ending in the fifth century						
Male	32	9 (28.1%)	9 (28.1%)	2 (6.3%)	5 (15.6%)	7 (21.9%)
Female	29	10 (34.5%)	9 (31.0%)	3 (10.3%)	6 (20.7%)	1 (3.4%)
Juvenile	14	6 (42.9%)	7 (50.0%)		1 (7.1%)	
Unsexed	18	3 (16.7%)	7 (38.9%)	1 (5.6%)	3 (16.7%)	4 (22.2%)
Period I Total	**93**	**28 (30.1%)**	**32 (34.4%)**	**6 (6.5%)**	**15 (16.1%)**	**12 (12.9%)**
Period II: sites spanning the fifth century						
Male	11	6 (54.5%)	5 (45.5%)			
Female	10	3 (30.0%)	7 (70.0%)			
Juvenile	5	2 (40.0%)	2 (40.0%)		1 (20.0%)	
Unsexed	6	5 (83.3%)	1 (16.7%)			
Period II Total	**32**	**16 (50.0%)**	**15 (46.9%)**		**1 (3.1%)**	
Period III: sites beginning in the fifth century (c.425/450 CE)						
Male	9	4 (44.4%)	2 (22.2%)			3 (33.3%)
Female	17	7 (41.1%)	7 (41.1%)			3 (17.6%)
Juvenile	7	4 (57.1%)	1 (14.3%)		1 (14.3%)	1 (14.3%)
Unsexed	3	1 (33.3%)	2 (66.6%)			
Period III Total	**36**	**16 (44.4%)**	**12 (33.3%)**		**1 (2.8%)**	**7 (19.4%)**

slightly more likely than men to move within Britain (see Table 1.3). Immigration from the Continent was generally the preserve of the male population rather than women, while women were slightly more likely than men to have moved to Britain from the Mediterranean. In contrast, from the fifth century onward, men were more likely to remain in their local community, while women were more likely to move between childhood and death – in Period II, men were almost twice as likely to be local as were women. More than two-thirds of the sample female population in the early fifth century moved at some point during their lives, in comparison to half of the men. By the late fifth and early sixth centuries (Period III), men were still more likely to be local than women, though the relative proportion is less stark.

Our isotope evidence suggests that all of the people from the sampled population who moved within Britain after the early fifth century left their homes in Wales and the north/west and moved to south/eastern Britain. Figure 1.4 maps the proportion of where each site's sampled burial population came from. This visualisation of the data in Table 1.2 more clearly shows that migration within Britain during the fifth century is not the simple story of westward movement caused by the *adventus Saxonum*. This contradicts our current understanding of emigration from Wales as happening only westward along the Irish Sea or south to Brittany. It also challenges the expected narrative for contemporary eastern Britain.

While there are some immigrants from the Continent buried in the southern and eastern parts of Britain (at Lankhills, Scorton and West Heslerton), and people from the south and east of Britain moved to Gloucester, Scorton and Lankhills (all late Roman urban or fort cemeteries), a prominent picture of mobility from our sample is one in which people moved from our largely conceived 'Wales' to lowland eastern Britain, particularly from the early fifth century onward. In some cases, these cemeteries were quite close to the north/western zone, and the journey may have not been over great distances. People moving from the north/west to Gloucester, for example, may have only travelled a few miles, while a similar trip to Berinsfield or West Heslerton may have taken one or two days – and moving from the north/west to Ringlemere was very likely a one-way trip. And in disagreement with our current gendered

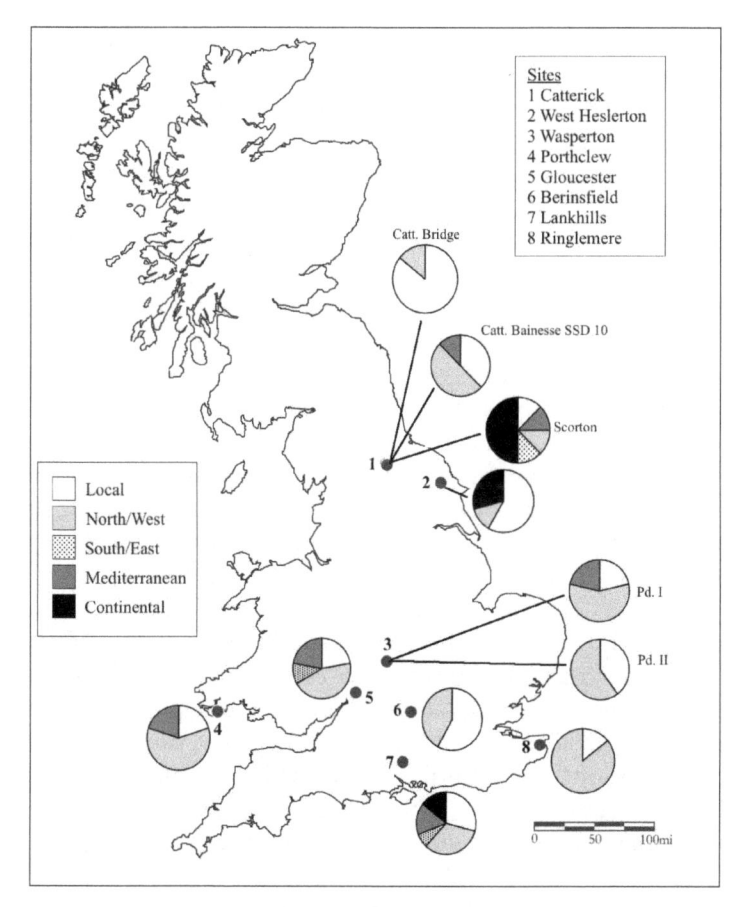

Figure 1.4. Location of Sites and relative % that each regional population makes up of the entire sampled population from that cemetery. Acknowledgement: Permit Number **CP17/026** British Geological Survey © NERC 2017. All rights reserved.

understanding of human mobility during and after the fifth century, within the sampled population, men were only slightly more likely to have moved from the Continent as they were from the north/west of Britain.

These isotope results suggest patterns of where people from certain places ended up. In the late Roman period, twelve of the fifteen people with Mediterranean-looking isotopes were buried in three of the four cemeteries associated with Roman towns – Lankhills, Gloucester and Scorton – but not at the Catterick Bridge cemetery. This may suggest that Catterick Bridge was the preserve of a small, local community. In the fifth century, however, only one sampled individual arrived in Britain from the Mediterranean: a young child, who was buried just outside Catterick. After the sixth century, similarly, the only likely immigrant from the Mediterranean was a child between seven and twelve years old. This child travelled to Porthclew, presumably with his or her family, following the trade routes that connected Wales to the Mediterranean, Cornwall and other places on the Irish Sea.[46] Migration to Wales from warmer climates after the fifth century was therefore not solely the preserve of adults. It might, however, have been limited within certain communities. People with Mediterranean-looking isotopes were not among the sampled population at the three sites where Anglo-Saxon material culture dominates – Ringlemere, Berinsfield and West Heslerton.

There are only three sites at which some sampled skeletons have isotopes almost certainly indicating a childhood on the Continent. The first two are the late Roman cemeteries at Lankhills and Scorton: these individuals likely illustrate the population movement from the Continent associated with the Roman military and administration.[47] The third is the Period III cemetery at West Heslerton, near the coast in North Yorkshire. None of the people buried on the other sites studied here, however, have isotopes that fit within our Continental model. In contrast, a substantial part of the population has isotopes that fall within our north/western model, suggesting a childhood in western Britain.

The relative percentages in Period III of people with local isotopes and those with isotopes from the Continent argue against the historiographical narrative of the solely westward migration of peoples or the eviction of the British by the Anglo-Saxons. What most of these studies find, in fact, is that there is no certain correlation between isotopic signatures and material 'ethnicity', at least not in funerary rites.[48] Grave goods at Period II of Wasperton and at Berinsfield, for example, are dominated by Anglo-Saxon material culture, and it is therefore surprising that isotope testing indicates that none of the twenty-four sampled skeletons from these sites were from continental Europe; rather, all of these people were most likely raised in the local community or in north or western Britain.

Where do we go from here?

Individually, each of these data sets from cemeteries in Britain used during the fifth century raises questions about how people arrived in their local communities. Taken as a collective group, however, the isotopic evidence suggests that we need to re-examine our historical narratives of how people from western Britain and the region we now know as Wales interacted with the larger world around them. Epigraphic, textual, linguistic and material culture evidence demonstrates that the people living in Wales were part of a much larger world, stretching beyond its shores to Scotland, the Irish Sea, Brittany and the Mediterranean; the isotopic evidence suggests that the grandparents and great-grandparents of the early medieval 'Welsh' were themselves active participants in such changes. They moved beyond the boundaries of the western half of the island to settle in the south and east in what is traditionally 'Anglo-Saxon' Britain.

We therefore need to also reconsider how we understand migration to and from Britain, particularly during a period whose historiography usually focuses on Germanic immigrants in the east. Stable isotope sampling provides one of the best methods to move our discussion of human mobility in the fifth century forward, and our research would benefit from a wider sampling strategy, with more samples per site. Though the cost of isotopic analysis means that a complete study of each cemetery is unlikely, the results from the burials studied in this paper indicate that we need to re-evaluate our current narrative of a predominantly westward migration during the fifth century. Similarly, we need to question not only our association of material culture with place of origin, but also the idea that most of the change in fifth-century Britain was the result of the arrival of a new cultural or ethnic group with the *adventus Saxonum*.[49] Instead, the stable isotopes from sites studied in this paper reveal that internal migration was likely more prevalent in fifth-century Britain than recent scholarship expects.

The proportion of sampled skeletons discussed here in fact suggests that for some parts of fifth-century Britain, the dominant migration narrative was one of movement from Wales and the west to the eastern lowlands, rather than the other way around. This, combined with the immigrants from other regions in the empire and from eastern or southern parts of Britain, tells a story of continual migration, in all directions. The story of the people living in what is now Wales during the fifth century, as well as in the rest of Britain, is therefore one in which people moved not only from east to west with the expansion of 'Anglo-Saxon' settlement and political power in the east, but also of movement from west to east, over the mountains and into lowland Britain. In future research on the fifth and sixth centuries, we may be able to learn more if we study how the Welsh – whatever people can be ascribed to that name in this period – impacted their neighbours to the east rather than the other way around.

Acknowledgements

I am extremely grateful to Patricia Skinner for her invitation to contribute to this volume, and for allowing me to change the direction of my research between the conference and this book. I also owe a great deal of thanks to Carolyn Twomey at Boston College, without whose timely assistance at Leeds this chapter would not have seen the light of day. The writing was assisted by a Mellon/ACLS Dissertation Completion Fellowship, and Duncan Schlee at Dyfed Archaeology kindly provided further information on the burials at Porthclew, Pembs. I would like to thank the entire medievalist cohort at Boston College, as well as Andrew Welton at the University of Florida, all of whom graciously read and endured long discussions on chemistry. I am also particularly thankful for the supervision of Robin Fleming and her comments throughout the many drafts. Any errors are, of course, my own. Permission to include the maps in this chapter has been provided by the British Geological Survey, Permit Number **CP17/026** British Geological Survey © NERC 2017. All rights reserved.

Notes

1. Christopher J. Arnold and Jeffrey L. Davies, *Roman and Early Medieval Wales* (Stroud: Sutton, 2000), pp. 142–3.
2. Wendy Davies, *Wales in the Early Middle Ages* (Leicester: Leicester University Press, 1982), pp. 102, 195; Chris Wickham, *Framing the Early Middle Ages: Europe and the Mediterranean 400–800* (Oxford: Oxford University Press, 2005), p. 48.
3. N. J. Cooper, 'Searching for the blank generation: consumer choice in Roman and post-Roman Britain', in J. Webster and N. J. Cooper (eds), *Roman Imperialism: Post-Colonial Perspectives* (Leicester: School of Archaeological Studies, 1996), pp. 85–98.
4. David Petts, 'Cemeteries and boundaries in western Britain', in S. Lucy and A. Reynolds (eds), *Burial in Early Medieval England and Wales*, Society for Medieval Archaeology Monograph Series 17 (London: Society for Medieval Archaeology, 2002), pp. 23–46, at p. 27.
5. David Petts, 'Burial in western Britain, AD 400-800: late antique or early medieval?', in R. Collins and J. Gerrard (eds), *Debating Late Antiquity in Britain*, BAR British Series 365 (Oxford: Archaeopress, 2004), pp. 77–88; Ken Dark, *Britain and the End of the Roman Empire* (Stroud: The History Press, 2010), pp. 77, 132–5.
6. John Hines, 'Welsh and English: Mutual Origins in Post-Roman Britain?', *Studia Celtica*, 34 (2000), 81–104, at 99–101; Chris Wickham, 'Medieval Wales and European History', *WHR*, 25.2 (2010), 201–8, at 202; W. Pohl, 'Introduction: strategies of distinction', in W. Pohl and H. Reimitz (eds), *Strategies of Distinction: The Construction of Ethnic Communities, 300–800* (Leiden: Brill, 1998), pp. 1–15.
7. Ewan Campbell, *Continental and Mediterranean Imports to Atlantic Britain and Ireland, AD 400–800*, CBA Research Report 157 (York: Council for British Archaeology, 2007), pp. 12–13, 25–6.
8. Davies, *Wales in the Early Middle Ages*, pp. 87–9; T. M. Charles-Edwards, *Wales and the Britons 350–1064* (Oxford: Oxford University Press, 2013), pp. 174–6; Bruce Copplestone-Crow, 'The Dual Nature of the Irish Colonization of Dyfed in the Dark Ages,' *Studia Celtica*, 16/17 (1981/2), 1–24.
9. Davies, *Wales in the Early Middle Ages*, pp. 89, 148; Hines, 'Welsh and English', 99–102.
10. Hella Eckardt (ed.), *Roman Diasporas: Archaeological Approaches to Mobility and Diversity in the Roman Empire*, Journal of Roman Archaeology Monograph, Supplementary Series 78 (Portsmouth, Rhode Island: Journal of Roman Archaeology, 2010); P. Budd, C. Chenery,

J. Montgomery, J. Evans and D. Powlesland, 'Anglo-Saxon residential mobility at West Heslerton, North Yorkshire, UK from combined O- and Sr-isotope analysis', in J. G. Holland and S. D. Tanner (eds), *Plasma Source Mass Spectrometry: Applications and Emerging Technologies* (Cambridge: Royal Society of Chemistry, 2003), pp. 195–208; John Moreland, 'Going Native, becoming German: Isotopes and Identities in Late Roman and Early Medieval England', *Postmedieval: A Journal of Medieval Cultural Studies*, 1.1/2 (2010), 142–9.

[11] Brian L. Beard and Clark M. Johnson, 'Strontium Isotope Composition of Skeletal Material can Determine the Birth Place and Geographic Mobility of Humans and Animals,' *Journal of Forensic Science*, 45.5 (2000), 1049–61; Merav Ben-David and Elizabeth A. Flaherty, 'Stable Isotopes in Mammalian Research: a Beginner's Guide,' *Journal of Mammalogy*, 93.2 (2012), 312–28; Janet Montgomery, 'Lead and Strontium Isotope Compositions of Human Dental Tissues as an Indicator of Ancient Exposure and Population Dynamics: The Application of Isotope Source-Tracing Methods to Identify Migrants Among I Archaeological Burials and a Consideration of Ante-Mortem Uptake, Tissue Stability and Post-Mortem Diagenesis' (unpublished PhD thesis, Department of Archaeological Sciences, University of Bradford, 2002).

[12] Jonathan Bethard, 'Isotopes', in E. A. DiGangi and M. K. Moore (eds), *Research Methods in Human Skeletal Biology* (Oxford: Academic Press, 2013), pp. 425–47; Montgomery, *Lead and Strontium Isotope Compositions*, p. 414. For the relative strengths and weaknesses of using longbone rather than dental samples, see P. Budd, J. Montgomery, B. Barreiro and R. G. Thomas, 'Differential Diagenesis of Strontium in Archaeological Human Dental Tissues', *Applied Geochemistry*, 15 (2000), 687-94; Janet Montgomery, 'Passports from the Past: Investigating Human Dispersals using Strontium Isotope Analysis of Tooth Enamel', *Annals of Human Biology*, 37.3 (2010), 325–46, at 326, 329–30; Susanne Hakenbeck, 'Potentials and Limitations of Isotope Analysis in Early Medieval Archaeology', *Post-Classical Archaeologies*, 3 (2013), 109–25, at 112.

[13] Montgomery, *Lead and Strontium Isotope Compositions*, p. 46.

[14] R. Alexander Bentley, 'Strontium Isotopes from the Earth to the Archaeological Skeleton: a Review', *Journal of Archaeological Method and Theory*, 13.3 (2006), 135-87; Montgomery, *Lead and Strontium Isotope Compositions*, pp. 265-6.

[15] J. A. Evans, J. Montgomery, G. Wildman and N. Boulton, 'Spatial Variations in Biosphere $^{87}Sr/^{86}Sr$ in Britain', *Journal of the Geological Society*, 167 (2010), 1–4; J. A. Evans, C. A. Chenery and J. Montgomery,

'A Summary of Strontium and Oxygen Isotope Variation in Archaeological Human Tooth Enamel Excavated from Britain', *Journal of Analytical Atomic Spectrometry*, 27 (2012), 754–64.

[16] Montgomery, *Lead and Strontium Isotope Compositions*, pp. 46–91. While there are a number of equations to convert $\delta^{18}O_p$ to $\delta^{18}O_{dw}$, the standard for use in the UK is a version (with correction for sample bias) of the one published in A. A. Levinson, B. Luz and Y. Kolodny, 'Variations in Oxygen Isotopic Compositions of Human Teeth and Urinary Stones', *Applied Geochemistry*, 2 (1987), 367–71. The corrected equation was formally published and explained in Carolyn Chenery, Gundula Müldner, Jane Evans, Hella Eckardt and Mary Lewis, 'Strontium and Stable Isotope Evidence for Diet and Mobility in Roman Gloucester, UK', *Journal of Archaeological Science*, 37 (2010), 150–63. The other two most commonly used are those in V. Daux, C. Lécuyer, M. Héran, R. Amoit, L. Simon, F. Martineau, N. Lynnerup, H. Reychler and G. Escarguel, 'Oxygen Isotope Fractionation between Human Phosphate and Water Revisited', *Journal of Human Evolution*, 55 (2008), 1138–47; and A. Longinelli and E. Selmo, 'Oxygen Isotopes in Mammal Bone Phosphate: a New Tool for Palaeohydrological and Palaeoclimatological Research', *Geochimica et Cosmochimica Acta*, 48 (1984), 385–90; see the Appendix to Chenery et al., 'Strontium and Stable Isotope Evidence for Diet and Mobility in Roman Gloucester', for a detailed discussion of the pros and cons of the different conversion formulas.

[17] W. G. Darling and J. C. Talbot, 'The O & H Stable Isotopic Composition of Fresh Waters in the British Isles. 1. Rainfall', *Hydrology and Earth System Sciences*, 7.2 (2003), 163–81, and W. G. Darling, A. H. Bath and J. C. Talbot, 'The O & H Stable Isotopic Composition of Fresh Waters in the British Isles. 2. Surface waters and groundwater', *Hydrology and Earth System Sciences*, 7.2 (2003), 183–95.

[18] If anything, ^{18}O would have been depleted (more negative) than it is today: Darling et al., 'Surface Waters and Groundwater', 194; Budd et al., 'Anglo-Saxon residential mobility at West Heslerton', p. 203; Evans et al. 'A Summary of Strontium and Oxygen Isotope Variation', 758.

[19] R. Brettell, J. Montgomery and J. Evans, 'Brewing and Stewing: the Effect of Culturally Mediated Behavior on the Oxygen Isotope Composition of Ingested Fluids and the Implications for Human Provenance Studies', *Journal of Analytic Atomic Spectroscopy*, 27 (2012), 778–85, at 781–2; also Rhea Brettell, Jane Evans, Sonja Marzinzik, Angela Lamb and Janet Montgomery, '"Impious Easterners": Can Oxygen and Strontium Isotopes Serve as Indicators of Provenance in Early Medieval European Cemetery Populations?', *European Journal of Archaeology*, 15.1

(2012), 117–45, at 125–6, 134–5. See also Lori E. Wright and Henry P. Schwarcz, 'Stable Carbon and Oxygen Isotopes in Human Tooth Enamel: Identifying Breastfeeding and Weaning in Prehistory', *American Journal of Physical Anthropology*, 106 (1998), 1–18; and Janet Kay, 'Old, New, Borrowed, and Buried: Burial Practices in Fifth-Century Britain' (unpublished PhD thesis, Boston College, 2017). Until this can be determined, the practice I have used here is to take measured $\delta^{18}O_p$ levels and their converted $\delta^{18}O_{dw}$ signatures at face value.

[20] Chenery et al. calculated expected oxygen values for archaeological individuals from Britain: 'Strontium and Stable Isotope Evidence for Diet and Mobility in Roman Gloucester'. Using a sample of fifty-seven people with local $^{87}Sr/^{86}Sr$ from nine sites in Britain, they calculated the population mean $\delta^{18}O_p$ value as -17.7 ± 0.9‰ (2σ, n=57). This produces a range of expected British $\delta^{18}O_p$ values from 16.8‰ to 18.6‰. Using the corrected Levinson equation to convert $\delta^{18}O_p$ into $\delta^{18}O_{dw}$, the total population mean from the results of nine sites converts to -6.7 ± 2.0 ‰ (2σ, n=57). This gives an expected British $\delta^{18}O_{dw}$ range of -4.7‰ to -8.7‰.

[21] J. H. Burton and T. Douglas Price, 'Seeking the local $^{87}Sr/^{86}Sr$ ratio to determine geographic origins of humans', in R. Armitage et al. (eds), *Archaeological Chemistry VIII*, ACS Symposium Series (Washington, DC: American Chemical Society, 2013), pp. 309–20; J. A. Evans and S. Tatham, 'Defining "Local Signature" in Terms of Sr Isotope Composition using a Tenth- to Twelfth-Century Anglo-Saxon Population Living on a Jurassic Clay-carbonate Terrain, Rutland, UK', *Geological Society, London, Special Publications*, 232 (2004), 237–48.

[22] Chenery et al., 'Strontium and Stable Isotope Evidence for Diet and Mobility in Roman Gloucester', 157.

[23] Evans et al., 'A summary of strontium and oxygen isotope variation', provide an excellent map of expected $\delta^{18}O_{dw}$ values within western Europe, and especially the Mediterranean (figure 12); see also Susanne Voerkelis, Gesine D. Lorenz, Susanne Rummel, Christophe R. Quétel, Gerhard Heiss, Malcolm Baxter, Christophe Brach-Papa, Peter Deters-Itzelsberger, Stefan Hoelzl, Jurian Hoogewerff, Emmanuel Ponzevera, Marleen Van Bocxstaele and Henriette Ueckermann, 'Strontium Isotopic Signatures of Natural Mineral Waters, the Reference to a Simple Geological Map and its Potential for Authentication of Food', *Food Chemistry*, 118 (2010), 933–40.

[24] Martin Carver, 'Wasperton in context', in M. Carver, C. Hills and J. Scheschkewitz (eds), *Wasperton: A Roman, British and Anglo-Saxon Community in Central England* (Woodbridge: Boydell, 2009),

pp. 127–40, at pp. 136–9; Nicholas Higham, *Rome, Britain and the Anglo-Saxons* (Seaby: London, 1992), pp. 1–16; Dark, *Britain and the End of the Roman Empire*, pp. 12–15; Michael E. Weale, Deborah A. Weiss, Rolf F. Jager, Neil Bradman and Mark G. Thomas, 'Y Chromosome Evidence for Anglo-Saxon Mass Migration', *Molecular Biology and Evolution*, 19.7 (2002), 1008–21; and Stephan Schiffels, Wolfgang Haak, Pirita Paajanen, Bastien Llamas, Elizabeth Popescu, Louise Loe, Rachel Clarke, Alice Lyons, Richard Mortimer, Duncan Sayer, Chris Tyler-Smith, Alan Cooper and Richard Durbin, 'Iron Age and Anglo-Saxon Genomes from East England Reveal British Migration History', *Nature Communications* (2015), 1–9. DOI: 10.1038/ncomms10408.

[25] Eckardt (ed.), *Roman Diasporas*.

[26] K. A. Hemer, J. A. Evans, C. A. Chenery and A. L. Lamb, 'Evidence of Early Medieval Trade and Migration between Wales and Mediterranean Sea Region', *Journal of Archaeological Science*, 40 (2013), 2352–9. The sites are Porthclew, Brownslade Barrow and West Angle Bay in Pembrokeshire and Llandough in Glamorgan.

[27] Hemer et al., 'Evidence of Early Medieval Trade', 2356–7.

[28] Brettell et al., '"Impious Easterners"'.

[29] Brettell et al., '"Impious Easterners"', 122–5, 128.

[30] Skeletal $\delta^{18}O_{dw}$ values for Ringlemere measured between -4.5‰ and -5.9‰, in an area of Britain for which the expected range is -6.5‰ to -7‰: Brettell et al., '"Impious Easterners"', 132–6). The authors also suggested that this seeming discrepancy might also be the result of different dietary habits, which can raise $\delta^{18}O_{dw}$ values.

[31] Though early medieval isotopes from the Isle of Man, which would also fall under the umbrella of a 'Wales' with indistinct geographical boundaries, have recently been published, those burials fell slightly outside the chronological purview of this paper: K. A. Hemer, J. A. Evans, C. A. Chenery and A. L. Lamb, 'No Man is an Island: Evidence of Pre-Viking Age Migration to the Isle of Man', *Journal of Archaeological Science*, 52 (2014), 242–9. The isotope results also determined that the population on the Isle of Man was more mobile than those from south Wales (Hemer et al., 'No Man is an Island', 245–7). Despite this important from the skeletons in Pembrokeshire and Glamorgan serve as a better proxy for isotopic signatures for our study of people raised in 'Wales' evidence for human mobility in the early medieval period, the results in the fifth century.

[32] Darling and Talbot, 'Rainfall'; Darling et al., 'Surface Waters and Groundwater'; Evans et al., 'Spatial Variations in Biosphere 87Sr/86Sr in Britain', figure 1b.

Janet Kay

33 Hemer et al., 'Evidence of Early Medieval Trade', 2354–6 and table 1. This isotope study originally assigns local/non-local oxygen values based on $\delta^{18}O_p$ rather than $\delta^{18}O_{dw}$, then converts the $\delta^{18}O_p$ into $\delta^{18}O_{dw}$. Four people had converted $\delta^{18}O_{dw}$ values (-4.6‰ to -4.5‰) that are possible on the extreme western coast of Britain. Though these four had $\delta^{18}O_p$ levels higher than possible in Britain (>18.6‰), their converted $\delta^{18}O_{dw}$ values (using the corrected Levinson equation) fell within the limits of values possible in the extreme west of Britain.

34 Sample mean -5.14 ± 1.16‰ (2σ), produces a population range of -6.30‰ to -3.97‰; this is adjusted to -6.30‰ to -4.5‰, accounting for the fact that $\delta^{18}O_{dw}$ values greater than -4.5‰ are not possible in Britain: Darling and Talbot, 'Rainfall'; Darling et al., 'Surface Waters and Groundwater'; see also Kay, 'Old, New, Borrowed, and Buried'. $\delta^{18}O_{dw}$ was used instead of $\delta^{18}O_p$ because the four individuals with warmer $\delta^{18}O_p$ values than are possible within Britain were included in this western population on the basis of their $\delta^{18}O_{dw}$ values. This model was constructed based upon the methods discussed in Chenery et al., 'Strontium and Stable Isotope Evidence for Diet and Mobility in Roman Gloucester', at 153.

35 Hemer et al. marked all burials with $^{87}Sr/^{86}Sr$ higher than 0.7110 as non-local to southern Wales, but expected that such values might be found in the mountains of eastern Wales or the Malvern Hills, near Worcester, or elsewhere in northern Britain: 'Evidence of Early Medieval Trade', 2356). See also C. Chenery, H. Eckardt and G. Müldner, 'Cosmopolitan Catterick? Isotopic Evidence for Population Mobility on Rome's Northern Frontier', *Journal of Archaeological Science*, 38 (2011), 1525–36, at 1531; Evans et al., 'Spatial Variations in Biosphere 87Sr/86Sr in Britain', figure 1b.

36 Expected local $\delta^{18}O_{dw}$ values are between -6.5 and -7.0‰ (Darling et al., 'Surface Waters and Groundwater', figure 6). Measured $\delta^{18}O_{dw}$ values for the Winchester area are -6.6 ± 0.7‰, 2σ (-5.9 to -7.3‰), and local $^{87}Sr/^{86}Sr$ values range from 0.7072 to 0.7092 (H. Eckardt, C. Chenery, P. Booth, J. A. Evans, A. Lamb and G. Müldner, 'Oxygen and Strontium Isotope Evidence for Mobility in Roman Winchester', *Journal of Archaeological Science*, 36 (2009), 2816–25, at 2820–1). There is therefore an overlap in $\delta^{18}O_{dw}$ values between those local to Winchester and the western model (from -6.32 to -5.9‰).

37 At Porthclew, skeleton 001 had extremely high $\delta^{18}O_{dw}$ (-4.6), while skeletons 004 and 005 had high $^{87}Sr/^{86}Sr$ levels (0.7114 and 0.7113, respectively): Hemer et al., 'Evidence of Early Medieval Trade', 2354).

[38] Evans et al., 'Spatial Variations in Biosphere 87Sr/86Sr in Britain', figure 1b; Darling and Talbot, 'Rainfall'; Darling et al., 'Surface Waters and Groundwater'.

[39] Because of this chronological restriction, isotopic studies at sites like Driffield and Trentholme Drive in Roman York, which date before *c*.350 CE, were too early to be included in this paper (S. Leach, M. Lewis, C. Chenery, G. Müldner and H. Eckardt, 'Migration and Diversity in Roman Britain: a Multidisciplinary Approach to the Identification of Immigrants in Roman York, England', *American Journal of Physical Anthropology*, 140 (2009), 546–61). Similarly, isotopic data from skeletons in studies on mid-late Anglo-Saxon studies were also excluded (e.g. the isotope data from Evans et al., 'A Summary of Strontium and Oxygen Isotope Variation'). For more on the chronological restrictions, and the exclusion of certain burials from the data set, see Kay, 'Old, New, Borrowed, and Buried'.

[40] Janet Montgomery, Jane Evans and Carolyn Chenery, 'Strontium and Oxygen Isotope Analysis of Burials from Wasperton, Warwickshire', in M. Carver (ed.), *Wasperton Anglo-Saxon Cemetery* [data set] (York: Archaeology Data Service, 2008) (DOI: 10.5284/1000052).

[41] H. Eckardt, G. Müldner and G. Speed, 'The Late Roman Field Army in Northern Britain? Mobility, Material Culture, and Multi-isotope Analysis at Scorton (N. Yorks.)', *Britannia*, 46 (2015), 1–33; Chenery et al., 'Cosmopolitan Catterick?'; Chenery et al., 'Strontium and Stable Isotope Evidence for Diet and Mobility in Roman Gloucester'; Eckardt et al., 'Oxygen and Strontium Isotope Evidence for Mobility in Roman Winchester'; and J. Evans, N. Stoodley and C. Chenery, 'A Strontium and Oxygen Isotope Assessment of a Possible Fourth Century Immigrant Population in a Hampshire Cemetery, Southern England', *Journal of Archaeological Science*, 33 (2006), 265–72.

[42] Montgomery et al., 'Strontium and Oxygen Isotope Analysis of Burials from Wasperton, Warwickshire'; Chenery et al., 'Cosmopolitan Catterick?'; S. S. Hughes, A. R. Millard, S. J. Lucy, C. A. Chenery, J. A. Evans, G. Nowell and D. G. Pearson, 'Anglo-Saxon Origins Investigated by Isotopic Analysis of Burials from Berinsfield, Oxfordshire, UK', *Journal of Archaeological Science*, 42 (2014), 81–92.

[43] Budd et al., 'Anglo-Saxon Residential Mobility at West Heslerton'; Brettell et al., '"Impious Easterners"'; Hemer et al., 'Evidence of Early Medieval Trade'; Duncan Schlee, pers comm. and *The Pembrokeshire Cemeteries Project: Excavations at Porthclew Chapel, Freshwater East, Pembrokeshire 2009, Second Interim Report*, Dyfed Archaeological Trust Report, 2010/20 (Llandeilo: Dyfed Archaeological Trust, 2010).

44 See Kay, 'Old, New, Borrowed, and Buried'. The earliest radiocarbon date from the sampled population at Brownslade Barrow was 610–770 CE, and at West Angle Bay *c*.890–1120: Hemer et al., 'Evidence of Early Medieval Trade', table 1). While some of the earliest radiocarbon dates from the entire cemetery at Brownslade Barrow date to the second half of the fifth century, these are bone fragments from uncertain deposits; all other radiocarbon samples range from the seventh through eleventh centuries, and therefore outside the purview of this chapter (Polly Groom, Duncan Schlee, Gwilym Hughes, Pete Crane, Neil Ludlow and Ken Murphy, 'Two Early Medieval Cemeteries in Pembrokeshire: Brownslade Barrow and West Angle Bay', *Archaeologica Cambrensis*, 160 (2011), 133–203, at 145–6). Similarly, radiocarbon dates indicate that burial at West Angle Bay did not begin until the second half of the sixth century, at the earliest (Groom et al., 'Two Early Medieval Cemeteries in Pembrokeshire', 177.) Llandough is a different conundrum. Of the more than one thousand burials within the cemetery, only about four dozen have any kind of dating evidence, and those dates range from the fifth century through the eleventh. There is considerable difficulty in trying to determine when amongst the cemetery's 700-year span any particular burial beyond those four dozen belongs. Of the fifteen skeletons from Llandough that were sampled for stable isotopes, only two have some kind of dating evidence, and only one falls within the long fifth-century restriction of this chapter: Burial 93 was interred sometime after 655 CE at the earliest, and Burial 2 between 370 and 640 CE (Neil Holbrook and Alan Thomas, 'An Early-Medieval Monastic Cemetery at Llandough, Glamorgan: Excavations in 1994', *Medieval Archaeology*, 49 (2005), 1–92, at 20 and 90–1). Without a secure way to determine which burials with isotope testing came from which chronological period (I, II, or III) used here, and because the cemetery was used frequently for a period of burial over seven centuries, I chose not to include any of the Llandough samples in this chapter.

45 Hughes et al., 'Anglo-Saxon Origins'; Evans et al., 'A Strontium and Oxygen Isotope Assessment of a Possible Fourth Century Immigrant Population in a Hampshire Cemetery'.

46 K. A. Hemer, 'Are we nearly there yet? Children and migration in early medieval Britain', in D. M. Hadley and K. A. Hemer (eds), *Medieval Childhood: Archaeological Approaches*, Childhood in the Past Monograph Series 3 (Oxford: Oxbow Books, 2014), pp. 131–44, at p. 133.

[47] Eckardt et al., 'Oxygen and Strontium Isotope Evidence for Mobility in Roman Winchester', 2822–4; Eckardt et al., 'The Late Roman Field Army in Northern Britain?', 25–8.

[48] In particular, see the results for late Roman Lankhills. In the first major excavation in the 1970s, Giles Clarke differentiated groups of 'exotic' foreigners from the local, 'native' population based upon their grave goods, and suggested that sixteen of the burials were of immigrants from Pannonia in modern Hungary: Giles Clarke, *Winchester Studies 3: Pre-Roman and Roman Winchester, Part II: The Roman Cemetery at Lankhills* (Oxford: BAR, 1979), pp. 377–89. In the last decade, however, two rounds of isotope testing on skeletons from both Clarke's excavations and a second phase of excavation at the site in the 2000s by Oxford Archaeology showed that funerary rites were not necessarily determined by where people were born: Evans et al., 'A Strontium and Oxygen Isotope Assessment of a Possible Fourth Century Immigrant Population in a Hampshire Cemetery'; and Eckardt et al., 'Oxygen and Strontium Isotope Evidence for Mobility in Roman Winchester', 2823–4.

[49] Carver, 'Wasperton in context', pp. 135–8; Guy Halsall, 'Ethnicity and Early Medieval Cemeteries', *Arqueologia y Territorio Medieval*, 18 (2011), 18–21; James Gerrard, *The Ruin of Roman Britain: An Archaeological Perspective* (Cambridge: Cambridge University Press, 2013), p. 14.

2

Emma d'Audley and the clash of laws in thirteenth-century northern Powys[1]

Emma Cavell

The widowhood of Emma d'Audley serves in many ways as a microcosm of a world in flux and a test case for tracking the aristocratic widow's experiences at law in the cultural melting pot of conquest-era Wales. The daughter of a prominent border lord and the wife of Gruffudd ap Madog, the ruler of northern Powys in the middle decades of the thirteenth century, Emma was part of a tried-and-tested pattern of intermarriage that increasingly linked Wales to England and opened it up to wider European influences. In her marriage she helped draw her husband into closer association with powerbrokers and elite social groups outside the borders of his dominion. After his death she witnessed forces from beyond those borders finally extinguish independent native rule in Wales. As a party to an Anglo-Welsh union, the matriarch of a mixed family, and the witness to all-out war between England and Wales, the widowed Emma perforce negotiated many of the conflicts, contradictions and mutual influences generated by the deeply ambivalent interaction between Welsh and English political societies in the thirteenth century. This chapter explores the surviving documentary evidence of Emma's widowhood in native Wales at the time of the Edwardian conquest and considers what the evidence reveals about the relationship between Wales and the wider world at this critical moment. It does this chiefly within the context of law, an issue – fundamental to Welsh identity and sense of self – at the very forefront of Anglo-Welsh relations in the final showdown between the two dominions. An investigation of Emma's direct engagement with law and legal process not only reveals the effects of (inter alia) conflicting legal systems and jurisdictions, divergent family expectations, and the politicisation and ideologisation of law on a widow's personal quest for justice, but also helps to illuminate the avenues by which English legal influences travelled into Wales, and the way in which Welsh law and legal practice was received in England, during the final years of Welsh independence.

Emma was a daughter of the influential Marcher baron Henry d'Audley (d.1246) and his wife Bertrada Mainwaring, and a sister to James d'Audley, *paterfamilias* from 1246 to 1272. Through their mother, Emma and her siblings could claim descent from the earls of Chester and, more distantly, Gloucester (see Figure 2.1). Their maternal grandmother was a daughter of Hugh de Kevelioc (d.1181), earl of Chester, while Hugh's own grandfather was none other than Robert earl of Gloucester, an illegitimate son of Henry I and the right-hand man of the Empress Matilda during the Anarchy (1135–54). By the early thirteenth century the Audley family, relative newcomers to border society, were entrenched in the north-eastern March and heavily involved, for good or ill, in border affairs.[2] Emma's marriage to the ruler of northern Powys, Gruffudd ap Madog, was presumably part and parcel of Audley ambitions in the region. The Welsh ruler was not her first husband, however. She had been married once before – to Henry Tuchet, lord of Lee Cumbray (modern-day Leegomery) in north-eastern Shropshire – but this marriage was childless. Tuchet was dead by 20 November 1242 and by 1 July 1244, with combined dower and *maritagium* in Shropshire, Staffordshire and Derbyshire, Emma had become the wife of a prominent Welsh powerbroker and a member of the increasingly diverse native elite.[3]

For Gruffudd ap Madog of northern Powys, the marriage was probably essential to his mastery of the rapidly shifting political landscape in Wales at the time. He was not alone among thirteenth-century Welsh rulers in choosing an English wife, but his was a lordship that was strategically significant in its location and unusually susceptible to the vagaries of Anglo-Welsh power play.[4] At the time of his marriage Gruffudd had recently done homage to Henry III,

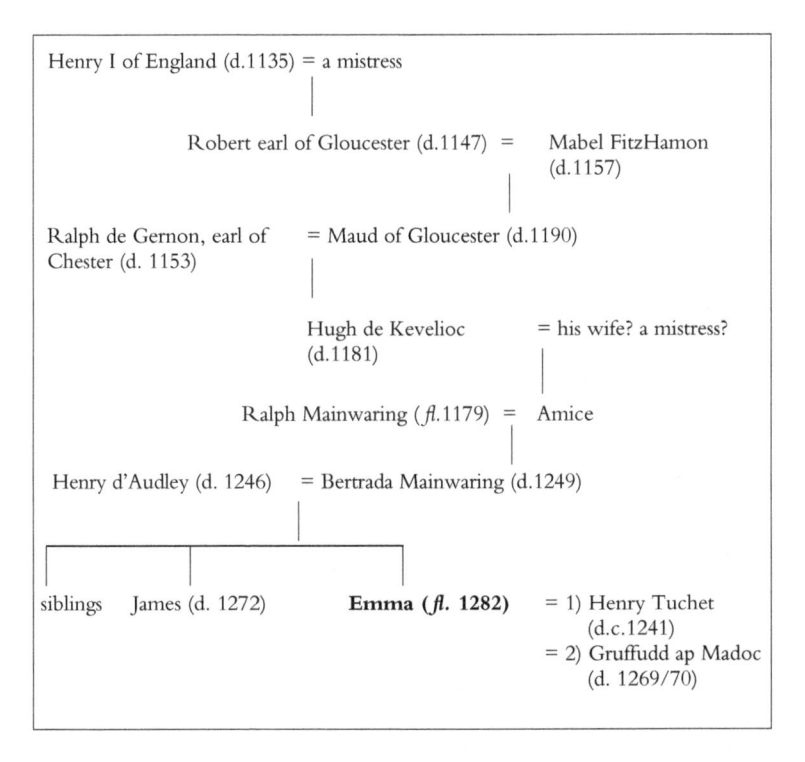

Clash of laws in thirteenth-century northern Powys

```
Henry I of England (d.1135) = a mistress
                        |
          Robert earl of Gloucester (d.1147) = Mabel FitzHamon
                                                (d.1157)
                                |
Ralph de Gernon, earl of    = Maud of Gloucester (d.1190)
Chester (d. 1153)
                        |
                Hugh de Kevelioc         = his wife? a mistress?
                (d.1181)                           |
            Ralph Mainwaring (fl.1179) = Amice
                                                |
Henry d'Audley (d. 1246)   = Bertrada Mainwaring (d.1249)
                        |
    ┌────────┬──────────────┐
siblings   James (d. 1272)  Emma (fl. 1282)  = 1) Henry Tuchet
                                                    (d.c.1241)
                                                = 2) Gruffudd ap Madoc
                                                    (d. 1269/70)
```

Figure 2.1: Simple Genealogy of the d'Audley family

cutting a path that preferred English royal suzerainty to the overlordship of the beleaguered prince of Gwynedd, Dafydd ap Llywelyn, bolstered his position against Venedotian encirclement, and reversed the long-standing policy of his father Madog ap Gruffudd (d.1238).[5] This was to set the pattern of his rule for the next decade and a half. Gruffudd's territorial reach, like that of his father, extended only to the northern half of the expansive old kingdom of Powys, but Matthew Paris counted him 'among the most powerful of the Welsh' (*quidam potentissimus Walensium*).[6] Although not yet at its greatest extent in the early 1240s, his dominion seems nevertheless to have comprised some form of lordship over all those lands possessed by his father when he died, namely the commotes of Maelor Gymraeg, Maelor Saesneg, Iâl, Cynllaith, Nanheudwy and Mochnant Is Rhaeadr.[7] This territory stretched from the rugged Berwyn highlands in the west, where the population was predominantly Welsh, to the fertile lowlands of the Cheshire and Shropshire borders. Its chief powerbase lay in the Maelor cantref, abutting the edge of Cheshire and northern Shropshire. Its rulers were often designated 'lord of Bromfield'; and by 1270 their chief residence was the impressive new hill-top fortress of Dinas Brân.[8] A well-enough rewarded but uneasy ally of Henry III of England when he married Emma, Gruffudd was ultimately to abandon his allegiance to the king. By October 1257, under pressure from Gwynedd, he had joined several of his brothers in the allegiance of Llywelyn ap Gruffudd and could be found harrying the borders of Herefordshire and Shropshire.[9] He was to remain with the prince of Gwynedd, seemingly as much a valued companion as a subordinate, for the rest of his life.[10]

Gruffudd died in the December of either 1269 or 1270 and was laid to rest, according to the Welsh annals, in his father's Cistercian foundation of Valle Crucis (Llynegwestl).[11] Widowed for a second time, Emma was now the mother of at least two daughters and five sons – Angharad, Margery, Madog, Llywelyn, Owain, Roger and Gruffudd Fychan.[12] She was also the mother-in-law to Margaret ferch Gruffudd, the wife of her eldest son Madog and sister to Llywelyn ap Gruffudd, prince of Wales. She was perhaps already a grandmother too.[13] Alongside her dower and *maritagium* in central and western England, Emma held significant life-interests in her late husband's dominion, most notably in the core district of Maelor. She seems to have regarded the latter territories as her priority, and was probably resident at Bromfield in that latter part of 1278 when the king directed a letter there addressed to 'the lady of Bromfield'.[14] Her late husband's hegemonic supremacy over Powys Fadog did not survive his death, however, and Emma witnessed the rapid partition of his territory among their sons under the direction of his erstwhile lord and companion, Llywelyn ap Gruffudd. Llywelyn had seized the constituent lands of northern Powys when Gruffudd died and, if we are to believe the complaint of Emma's sons Llywelyn Fychan and Owain, assigned to their elder brother Madog too large a share of the inheritance.[15] Certainly, Madog appears to have received the heart of the dominion centring on the cantref of Maelor and the castle of Dinas Brân, with all the symbolism of power and north-Powysian unity that impressive new fortress carried with it.[16]

It may have been intended that Madog would, like his father, assume seigneurial control over the whole of this strategic dominion; but in the April of 1277 English interventionism prevailed and Madog was compelled by the Crown to accept a new, more thoroughgoing partition. A month later the castle was burned by its garrison and abandoned.[17]

Such was the background against which Emma embarked upon her second period of widowhood. Having been almost completely silent on Emma's married life with Gruffudd ap Madog, the extant documentary evidence now provides the full measure of the competing pressures attendant upon her single life in conquest-era Wales. These pressures, generated by the peculiar circumstances of a mixed union within a precarious Anglo-Welsh political order, revolved in large measure around questions of women's property rights, family relations and a widow's personal quest for justice. Toward the end of the decade following Gruffudd's death, in the highly charged atmosphere that followed the first Welsh war (1276–7), Emma's name began to appear with some frequency in the English governmental records relating to those parts of Wales where the English king's authority now intruded (Table 2.1). She had become involved in three discrete lawsuits relating to her property rights.

Chiefly played out before the royal assizes mandated by the Treaty of Aberconwy in 1277, the lawsuits in which Emma was involved at times placed her at odds with members of her own family and tested the very means by which women in Emma's position, the wives of thirteenth-century Welsh rulers, were provided for in widowhood. In the surviving evidence we catch glimpses of intersecting, cooperating and conflicting interests, rights and loyalties, which showed little regard for the parameters of politics, culture or family. In the first of these suits, Emma appeared before the court at Oswestry on 28 November 1277 to demand the return of dower in Maelor, from which she claimed to have been evicted during the recent war between England and Wales; the following February at Oswestry she sued her second son Llywelyn over certain property rights in the commotes of Cynllaith and Nanheudwy;[18] and again at Oswestry in July that year, she and her sons Llywelyn and Owain defended their position in Cynllaith and Nanheudwy against their

Emma Cavell

Table 2.1: Emma d'Audley's appearances in the Welsh assize courts

Date	Location	Role	Justices	Adversaries	Cause
28 Nov 1277	Oswestry	plaintiff	Bishop of St Asaph Ralph de Fremingham	the king	Dower in Maelor Saesneg
			Walter de Hopton	Margaret widow of Madog ap Gruffudd (Emma's eldest son)	Dower in Eyton (Maelor Gymraeg)
9 Feb 1278	Oswestry	plaintiff	Ralph de Fremingham and fellows	Llywelyn ap Gruffudd Fychan of Bromfield (Emma's second son)	Land in the commotes of Cynllaith and Nanheudwy, of the gift of her late husband *Previously the subject of a hearing at Worcester*
9 Feb 1278	Oswestry	n/a	Ralph de Fremingham and fellows	the king	Dower in Maelor Saesneg: acknowledges king's right to take the land in exchange for interests in England
22 Jul 1278	Oswestry	co-defendant with sons Llywelyn and Owain	Walter de Hopton and fellows	Gruffudd ab Einion and five brothers, the sons of Einion ap Gruffudd of Iâl	Various properties and rights in the commotes of Cynllaith and Nanheudwy *Warranted by sons, plea moved coram rege*

kinsman Gruffudd ap Einion and his five brothers.[19] It is the first two of these lawsuits that reveal most about Emma's situation.

In fact, Emma had begun her quest for the restoration of her Maelor dower not at first by going to the Welsh assizes – they did not yet exist – but by a complaint addressed to the king in early

July 1277, as Edward was on his way to military confrontation with the prince of Wales. The royal writ instructing the justice of Chester, Guncelin de Baddlesmere, to investigate Emma's claims was issued from Worcester on 7 July, and by 18 July an all-Welsh jury had compiled its findings and sent them back to Chancery.[20] The materials survive today as a collection of separate documents in different scribal hands: the writ commissioning the inquiry, a detailed report returned by the investigating jurors, and three charters submitted in support of the jurors' findings.[21] No petition or written complaint from Emma has survived. It is nevertheless clear from those records that do still exist that Emma's husband had granted her some of his best land to support her in widowhood: first the whole of the commote of Maelor Saesneg (English Maelor), centring on the manor of Overton, and then the manor of Eyton in the neighbouring commote of Maelor Gymraeg (Welsh Maelor). Both grants were for her life only, and they had to revert to the patrimony fully intact when she died.[22] It was stipulated in the charter relating to Maelor Saesneg that this commote was not to be withdrawn from the authority of Llywelyn ap Gruffudd as *dominus Wallie* and – clearly – Gruffudd ap Madog's overlord at the time that he made the grant to his wife.[23] Emma seems to have entered these possessions while her husband was still alive and to have held them without trouble for some years. In the December of 1270, at Castell Dinas Brân, Emma's four adult sons, their father recently dead, had confirmed her endowment. Llywelyn ap Gruffudd, prince of Wales, ratified their deed.[24] During the course of the war, however, Emma had been ejected from these properties, and by 6 July 1277 her quest in respect of her dower had begun.

Taken together, the materials lodged with Chancery in July 1277 and the records of the litigation initiated before the Welsh assize justices later that year hint at the complexity and volatility of the socio-legal world in which Emma was operating. This was as true when it came to the creation of Emma's dower by her living husband as it was her defence of those interests after his death. The political climate in northern Powys following the first Anglo-Welsh war of 1276–7 and the dramatic curtailment of the power and prestige of the prince of Wales, made things still more knotty. An examination of all the surviving documentation relating to Emma's Maelor rights makes it immediately clear that the identification of these rights as dower occurs only in the record of Emma's litigation before the royal justices on the Welsh circuit and one or two of the associated administrative documents.[25] By contrast, the small bundle of materials returned to Chancery in mid-July merely depicts land-grants from a living husband to his wife, life tenures that could not be alienated in any way and were to revert to the patrimony on Emma's death, and Emma's seisin during her husband's lifetime. True, the conditions of inalienability and compulsory reversion so carefully articulated in Gruffudd's charters, and the unequivocal statement in the jurors' own report that Gruffudd had made these grants 'when he married Emma' (*quando Emmam . . . duxit in uxorem*), make Emma's endowment *look* very much like traditional English church-door dower (*dos nominata*); but the jurors' report also explicitly denied that this is what the grants were. Ordered by the king's writ to determine the means by which the grants were made to Emma, the jurors found that it was by enfeoffment (*per feoffamentum*) and not in the name of dower (*nomine dotis*).[26]

Indeed, look more closely at the evidence and it becomes clear that, even if Emma had originally been endowed with Maelor Saesneg at the time of her marriage in the early 1240s, perhaps as a spoken promise at the church door, the charter itself is of later provenance. It designates Llywelyn ap Gruffudd supreme lord of the territory being granted, a fact of life for the married couple only from the autumn of 1257, when Gruffudd ap Madog abandoned his allegiance to the king in favour of the prince of Wales. The deeds were also witnessed by the couple's four grown, or nearly grown, sons. Nor can Emma have received the manor of Eyton in any meaningful fashion at the time of marriage. That manor was held by her husband's younger brother Hywel until his death at some point after September 1267.[27] Moreover – and this is hard to ignore – not only was dower quite foreign to the precepts of native law packaged up in the textbooks of Welsh lawyers at that time (widows' property rights under 'the law of Hywel' were almost entirely associated with chattels), but the form of dower used was also, by English standards, rather old fashioned by the middle of the thirteenth century. In contemporary England the automatic third, calculated on the landholder's property when he died, was generally preferred. Dower was not typically conveyed by charter in England either, but by spoken word before witnesses on the day of the marriage or by administrative process after the husband's death. There is much that is curious, therefore, about Emma's endowment.

The situation was highly unusual, but it was not unique. Emma's may be the best documented case, and the only one we know to have been submitted to close investigation. Yet it is nevertheless clear that similar provisions were made for certain of her contemporaries, other married women, both native and foreign, from thirteenth-century Welsh ruling society.[28] No arrangement was stranger than the grant of the commote of Anhuniog which Owain ap Maredudd, ruler of Ceredigion, made in 1273 to his wife Angharad, the daughter of the native ruler of Cydewain. Although this was a husband-to-wife gift intended for Angharad's maintenance in her widowhood, as in Emma's case, the grant preserved in Owain's charter was couched in terms of a *maritagium*. The common law *maritagium*, a gift of land originating with the bride's family and not the groom or his family, was something altogether different from dower.[29] The hybridisation of forms of distinctly English-flavoured land conveyance is nowhere clearer than here. As in the case of Emma's endowment we have access to both the charter in which the grant was recorded and to the record of litigation at the Welsh assizes; and once again it is not until Angharad pleaded disseisin before the justices on the Welsh circuit that her endowment was called dower.[30]

We are undoubtedly fortunate therefore that, in the case of her Maelor properties, we can more or less follow Emma d'Audley on the road to remedy and catch glimpses of the open channels of communication between England and Wales in the context of Emma's legal rights. We have seen that Emma's quest for justice began as an extra-curial affair when, on or shortly before 6 July 1277, she apprised the king of her complaint and procured a royal writ ordering an investigation into her claims. She presumably wrote directly to Edward himself on his way to Wales, or to the chancellor Robert Burnell, as the man in the royal entourage fielding all such complaints and requests.[31] A vernacular (French) petition of *c.*1282–3, by which Emma appealed for Edward's assistance in another property-related matter, coupled with evidence of use of mounted *nuntii* in her communications with the king in 1278, may indicate the manner in which she proceeded in July 1277.[32] If so, we may assume that the written word carried the particulars of Emma's Welsh tenure and disseisin from native Wales to the English king's circle, couched in terms that reflected both Emma's own understanding (or representation) of the situation and the Anglo-centric socio-legal framework in which these rights and processes were viewed by both widow and sovereign. An appeal to the English king's authority was a natural choice for Emma given not only her own political allegiance, but also the altered balance of power in northern Wales and the judicial vacuum that power-shift had brought with it. The judicial processes attached to Edward's inter-war settlement had yet to be established, and the central courts of England had no authority beyond England's borders.

The findings returned by the inquisition in July 1277 differed from Emma's complaint in two ways. The first was on the matter of who was responsible for ejecting her from her properties. Although Emma seems initially to have believed that it was the king's bailiffs – that vigorous agent of royal power in the region, Roger Lestrange, being the most likely candidate[33] – the inquisition found that it was actually Llywelyn ap Gruffudd who was responsible for her eviction. He had taken the land, according to the investigating jurors, because it was 'the custom of Wales [*consuetudo Wallie*] that if any one, for fear of war or for other reasons, relinquishes his lands and leaves Wales for other parts the lord is permitted to seize the land as his escheat and do whatever he likes with it'.[34] Perhaps Emma had left the land during the war only to find Lestrange and company in charge when she returned to the region. The second difference is the jurors' reference to another 'custom of Wales' relating to Emma's Maelor tenures: 'that every Welshman could, if he wished, give his wife lands and tenements either before marriage or afterwards'.[35] It is this device that almost certainly holds the key to the dower-like rights in their husbands' patrimonial lands which Emma, Angharad and others held, in clear contradiction of a body of law which, strictly speaking, allowed no such thing.

In fact, the law books of the age, in which the classical rules relating to women were fossilised, also made room for the operation of legitimate, alternative practices – or customs – that could, provided they were just, circumvent law *sensu stricto*.[36] The law texts much thumbed by native men of law thus kept pace with practical realities and social change, despite the ancient and venerable nature of the law contained within the texts themselves. These realities – the creeping shadow of English political dominance over Wales, the function of land in the Anglo-French aristocratic framework to which Welsh elite society increasingly belonged, and the place of women within this same socio-political framework – paved the way for landholding by women in a way that mirrored English practice and remained acceptable and perfectly defensible within the native Welsh legal system. Land was too powerful a currency, and women too central to its circulation within elite societies of this milieu, for the wives and widows of the Welsh ruling classes to be denied property rights akin those enjoyed by aristocratic woman outside Wales, however those rights were actually formulated. For the women of English or Marcher origin, whose attitudes presumably took shape in circles governed by the common law of England, the expectation that the Welsh ruler would provide a substantial landholding for his prospective widow may have been still greater.

We hear nothing more about Emma's interests in Maelor Saesneg and Maelor Gymraeg in the extant evidence until, nearly five months later, in the circumstances of the post-war settlement, the cogs of the new royal judicial machinery in Wales slowly began turning. Before Walter de Hopton and his fellows sitting at Oswestry on 28 November 1277, Emma entered two separate pleas against two different defendants: one for Overton against the king, who now held Maelor Saesneg; the other for Eyton in Maelor Gymraeg against her daughter-in-law Margaret ferch Gruffudd. Both interests are termed 'dower' in the record of the litigation. Emma had clearly taken some sort of advice on her case. By then she knew who had ejected her from her lands, or at least whom to sue. By February 1278 it had been determined that Overton should be restored to Emma, subject only to the king's will, but the matter of Eyton was more complicated. In seizing the lands from Emma, loyal to the Crown during the upheavals, Llywelyn had bestowed them on a favourite of his own: Emma's eldest son Madog. Madog was now dead. Emma's argument was that Gruffudd had dowered her with

Eyton in Maelor Gymraeg during his life and placed her in seisin immediately, and that she had retained possession of the manner from that point until it was occupied by Llywelyn in time of war. Llywelyn had bestowed it on Madog, who in turn had granted it to Margaret 'in the name of dower'.[37] Margaret's defence was that Emma had given the manor to her son willingly and in peacetime.[38] In the event, the two women came to an agreement before the case was taken any further: Emma was to have the lordship of Eyton and Margaret to hold it of her at farm for an annual rent of 10 marks. Emma could reoccupy the property in the event that Margaret defaulted on her payment or died during her mother-in-law's lifetime.[39]

Such was the importance of Maelor Saesneg to Edward I's politico-military agenda in north Wales, on the other hand, that the restoration of this land to Emma was always likely to be precarious. As a loyal adherent of the king in a contested region, she must have been fully aware of this fact. Although the commote and constituent interests were returned to Emma by the royal justices at Oswestry on 9 February 1278, she was compelled to acknowledge before the same men that she claimed only a lifetime interest in these lands and would relinquish them to the king should he offer her an alternative in England.[40] Whether Edward had by then already notified Emma of his intention to make an exchange is unclear, but by the beginning of October moves were already afoot for his permanent acquisition of Maelor Saesneg.[41] On or shortly before 3 October 1278, with Edward lodged in Macclesfield, king and subject came to an agreement: in return for Emma's surrender of Maelor Saesneg, Edward promised to give her interests in England to the same value – a value that was to be determined by an extent (survey) of Maelor Saesneg. Letters from the king at Macclesfield were conveyed to 'the lady of Bromfield' around this same time, almost certainly indicating that Edward and Emma were corresponding about the issue.[42] A little over a month later the two parties to the exchange and their associates converged on Westminster, the heart of English government, to complete the business. On 10 November, in the presence of a strikingly Welsh-free cohort of witnesses that included bishop of Hereford and the Marcher barons Roger Mortimer and Roger de Clifford, Emma quitclaimed to the king and his heirs all her rights in Maelor Saesneg. She received in return a lifetime grant of 100s. (£5) per annum from the farm of the town of Derby and the manors of Claverley (Shrops) and Tattenhall (Staffs).[43] Emma's compliance was clearly well rewarded, and there are hints that she preferred a stable income from English properties, in counties with which she was already familiar, over the challenges of a vulnerable estate in her late husband's turbulent lands. Yet her acquiescence in the king's demands ran directly counter to the interests of her sons and grandsons. It is difficult to imagine that she was oblivious to the impact on her own family of the king's agenda in Wales following the war of 1276–7.

Yet the Westminster exchange was still more than a year away when Emma's rights to land in her late husband's lordship first came up against those of her surviving sons in the king's courts of law. Madog's death in the summer of 1277, combined with the determined encroachment of royal power onto native soil at that time, had propelled the family into a series of appearances before the English king's justices in Wales, as they negotiated inheritance shares, widows' property interests and wardship rights.[44] Now too some of the effects of the increasingly ideological and emblematic status of Welsh law in the face of external threat become evident. While the dower-disagreement between Emma and her daughter-in-law Margaret had been articulated before the court and settled out of it without much ado, this was not the case with the suit that Emma brought against her second son, Llywelyn Fychan. In the presence of Ralph de Fremingham and his fellows at Oswestry on 9 February 1278, the very same session at which she had briefly recovered Maelor Saesneg, Emma sued Llywelyn for the restoration of rights which she had previously held within the commotes of Cynllaith and Nanheudwy, in the east of her late husband's lordship, abutting Oswestry itself. The extant plea-roll entry is typically brief and bald, and furnishes only limited information about the disputed properties: Emma claimed from her son the vill, or township, of Llanarmon and the cattle enclosure at Llwythder in Cynllaith, and half of the township of Trefor in Nanheudwy, to be held as she had previously held them.[45] Additional evidence demonstrates that these properties came with the right to *amobr* (a native virginity payment, with similarities to English *merchet* and *leyrwite*, rendered to a woman's lord on the occasion of her marriage)[46] and to a 30s. rent in the township of Trefor, and that she had received charters of grant and her sons' confirmation for all or some of these rights.[47] Despite their similarities to Emma's Maelor rights, these interests are not called dower in any of the extant records. At the Oswestry session that February, Llywelyn appeared before the justices, perhaps encountering his mother there in person, and restored the disputed properties to her.

This was not, however, the first that Llywelyn had heard of Emma's demands: at the same session he was also penalised for failing to comply with an earlier order regarding his mother's rights. A previous judicial bench at Worcester had already instructed Llywelyn to restore the property to his mother. He had not done so.[48] There is not much to go on in the case of Emma's initial action against her son – no commission of *oyer* and *terminer* like those preceding her Maelor pleas, no inquisition, and seemingly no surviving record of litigation – and it is not clear whether the Worcester court was linked to the king's personal presence in the city. Nevertheless, the determination of Emma's rights in Cynllaith and Nanheudwy by the justices of the Welsh assizes belonged squarely to the context of royal intervention in Wales and princely disempowerment, of which the king's appearances in Worcester at this juncture were also part; and we may presume that Emma appealed to the king's authority on this occasion in much the same way as she had when first seeking reinstatement in her Maelor properties. She may even have used the same communiqué, which reached the king's entourage in or near Worcester in the opening days of July 1277. While in Worcester, with war still underway, the king and his council determined that the lands captured from Llywelyn ap Gruffudd would be returned to claimants only after due inquisition or legal process.[49] Emma's claims to Maelor Saesneg and Eyton were certainly subject to very close scrutiny. Although Cynllaith and Nanheudwy had not, in the manner of Emma's Maelor properties, been seized directly from the prince of Wales, it was certainly the case that Llywelyn Fychan, whose share of Powys Fadog included rights in Cynllaith and Nanheudwy, had form as an agent of princely power in the region.[50] Perhaps he had used the cover of war and the excuse of his political allegiance to move in on those of his mother's territories that fell within his lordship. She certainly employed the advancing tide of royal power, and the judicial framework carried with it, to reclaim those lands.

It is conceivable, moreover, that heirs to native 'princely' dominions born to mixed marriages resented (or effected to resent in the circumstances of the moment) their English mother's expectation of land rights in their regnal patrimony. Those heir-widow land disputes so common in England had the potential to assume political and ideological trappings in peri-conquest Wales, particularly in the context of a mixed marriage. After all, Llywelyn Fychan and his brothers, Emma's own sons, were among the most strident champions of *Cyfraith Hywel* at this time, no matter how much it otherwise suited them to exploit the brave new political order and its socio-legal consequences. The ambivalence is understandable. Northern Powys had long been brutally exposed, like a rock face in driving wind, to the influences sweeping in from England and the Continent. In her marriage and in her active negotiation of her own legal rights in widowhood, Emma was effectively a conduit of such influences and an agent of change. Influence and change were scarcely further reaching than in the arena of law.

On the other hand, as far as it is reflected in the legal proceedings of the Welsh assizes and analogous records, Emma's relationship with Llywelyn Fychan, by all accounts the most fractious of her sons, was not wholly antagonistic.[51] Notwithstanding the curial conflict outlined above, she subsequently came to an agreement with Llywelyn that he could hold the township of Llanarmon, 30s. rent from Trefor, and the *amobr* due on all her properties in Cynllaith and Nanheudwy until the end of her life – provided, that is, that he paid her £7 a year for the privilege and that the interest came back to her if he died first. The agreement was set down in writing (*un escrit*), but that document is now lost.[52] In addition, Emma joined forces with Llywelyn and another son Owain in fending off the claims of their kinsman Gruffudd ab Einion and his five brothers to a collection of vills in Cynllaith. The plea of the six sons of Einion was originally directed against Llywelyn and Owain alone, before Ralph de Fremingham and his fellows at Oswestry on 9 February 1278.[53] When their case appeared again at Oswestry on 22 July, Emma had been drawn into the litigation. On this occasion the six-brother team claimed eight individual vills – Nancennin, Tregeriog, Nantyr, Llangollen Fechan, Ysgwennant, Dolwen, Hafodwen and Llwythder – as their inheritance from their father, and they claimed these vills against mother and sons together: Owain, they said, held Nancennin; Llywelyn held Tregeriog, Nantyr, Llangollen Fechan and Ysgwennant; and Emma held the remaining three (Llwythder, of course, having just been returned to her by Llywelyn Fychan).[54]

It would appear that Owain and his mother travelled from Wales to the Oswestry court in person (or, less likely, through unrecorded proxies), Emma to answer for herself and Owain to answer for himself and Llywelyn. Owain pleaded Welsh law and invoked the Treaty of Aberconwy as justification of his request to have the case settled according to *Cyfraith Hywel*[55] – though it would naturally be tried within the framework, and presumably under the procedural norms, of royal justice. For her part, Emma offered that she held her three vills as the result of a life-grant from her husband, and that upon his death the grant had been confirmed by her two co-defendants, her sons Llywelyn and Owain, with a charter. Since Llywelyn and Owain thus effectively took the place of their father as the original grantor, Emma called them to warranty. That was Owain's task, and again he spoke for himself and his brother in repeating his position 'with the same answer as above'.[56] The extant record provides a summary of proceedings in court over a number of separate sessions – a summary that smacks of forethought and planning on the part of the defendants. Owain's appeal to Welsh law and the specific counter-arguments he set against the plaintiffs' claims, Emma's call for her sons to warrant her, and Owain's prompt fulfilment of that role, all seemingly took place at one sitting. One suspects that the defendants' conduct had been worked out in advance, through discussion, cooperation and, almost certainly, lawyerly advice. There are no surprises, no defaults, no technical hitches and no adjournments. A date was set for judgment, but it was Owain's appeal to Welsh law that introduced a delay. Like several other causes initiated that day that invoked native law, this suit was transferred out of the assize courts to the immediate purview of the eagle-eyed English king. The royal justices acknowledged that the interpretation of the Treaty of Aberconwy was beyond their remit (and probably their ken), and the suit was referred *coram rege* to await the king's will on the matter.[57] Nothing more is heard of it. In any case, Emma, warranted by her sons, had dropped out of proceedings and was not required in court for this matter again. In January 1279 the suspicion was raised that Justice Ralph de Fremingham had improperly accepted gifts of horses from Emma and Owain.[58] Perhaps such concerns were connected to the above litigation, which had been initiated before Fremingham nearly a year earlier. Whether or not Emma was ever tempted to use bribery as a form of legal self-help, the allegations were soon found to be untrue.

While we see no more of Emma in the law courts after the summer of 1278, her challenges were far from over. Having lost her eldest son Madog, but recently reconciled to the king, in the summer of 1277, Emma was to lose still more when war broke out again in 1282. Though she herself appears outwardly never to have faltered in her loyalty to the Crown, her sons were deeply ambivalent. The turbulent Llywelyn Fychan had been among the first of the prince's followers to capitulate in 1276, but when day broke on Palm Sunday 1282 he was at the head of a destructive Welsh raiding party that descended on Oswestry.[59] With him was his brother Gruffudd, Emma's youngest son.[60] The pair returned with their armies to devastate the border town for a second time in the September of that year.[61] The prince of Wales himself claimed ignorance of the original conspiracy, which was apparently spearheaded by his own younger brother Dafydd, but he had soon assumed leadership of a full-scale revolt. If Emma was similarly unaware of her sons' choices, or simply choosing to turn a blind eye to activities that ran counter to her own public stance, it soon became an immediate issue for her. When the second war ended, in bloody fashion, on a wintry field in the vicinity of Cilmeri on 11 December 1282, it was not just the prince of Wales who was dead. Two of Emma's sons, Llywelyn and Owain, had also perished during or soon after the war. Llywelyn Fychan had been killed with his lord that very day, while Owain, apparently in the king's faith on 15 June 1282, and perhaps still in January 1283, had died 'the king's enemy and rebel' some time after the latter date.[62] Little is known of Roger. Of her five sons, only Gruffudd Fychan seems to have survived. He returned to the king's allegiance under very restrictive terms.[63]

In fact, the events of 1282 resulted in the near complete dispossession of the remaining members of Emma's marital family. Although Gruffudd Fychan was reinstated in Glyndyfrdwy in the west of Powys Fadog, a tenant-in-chief at the will of the king, and his own son Madog received part of Cynllaith, a different fate awaited the rest of Gruffudd ap Madog's old dominion.[64] This was reconstituted as a series of Marcher lordships in the hands of the likes of the earl of Surrey (Bromfield and Yale), Roger Mortimer the younger (Chirk), and others.[65] Of Emma's young grandsons, the offspring of her eldest son Madog, nothing more is known after outbreak of war in 1282.[66] In the care of their own mother Margaret until the end of 1277, they had then been entrusted to the wardship of guardians John de Warenne and Roger Mortimer junior and simply disappeared from the records – drowned in the River Dee on royal orders, according to early modern rumour.[67] Only in the legendary Owain Glyndŵr, a descendant of Gruffudd Fychan, did any trace of her husband's direct line survive the conquest of Wales.[68] We may speculate about her feelings. It is likely, too, that Emma no longer lived in Wales. It is difficult to ignore her absences from her Maelor properties or those exchanges which she effected with the king, her son Llywelyn and her daughter-in-law Margaret and which replaced direct management of her Welsh lands with monetary incomes and access to resources in England.[69] Nevertheless financial necessity, personal choice, social expectation, or a combination of factors, compelled Emma to continue the defence of her rights to property in Wales that had been given to her so long ago by her husband. Having allowed Llywelyn Fychan to rent certain of her interests in Cynllaith and Nanheudwy for life, she had lost their reversion when Roger Mortimer the younger seized all of her late son's lands at the end of the war. Soon after Llywelyn Fychan's death in December 1282, therefore, Emma turned once again to the king for help, 'as he is chief lord and can do justice to all' (*issicome il est chef seignor e puyt fere dreytur a touz*).[70] English royal power now had no rival in Wales.

The French petition to the king represents Emma's last appearance in the records that remain. By then she can have been no less than about sixty years old. The world into which she had married was gone. Little remained of her husband's dominion and only one son had survived the English onslaught. In 1241 Emma's marriage as a young widow to the ruler of Powys Fadog had been one of those unions that served to bring Wales into ever closer inter-connection with England and Europe beyond. At the forefront of the relationship between Wales and the world beyond lay the problem of law, and Emma's widowhood in Wales on the eve of the Edwardian conquest, in so far as it is reflected in the extant documentation, revolved in large measure around the negotiation of justice on a complex and shifting legal landscape. In her husband's land *Cyfraith Hywel* was as stridently championed as it was subject to the influences of the common law of England and the constraints of English royal justice. Emma's experiences reflected this and her actions were tailored accordingly. Through creative, legally viable mechanisms that paid heed to the rapidly changing socio-political realities of thirteenth-century Wales, Emma and others, like Angharad wife of Owain ap Maredudd of Ceredigion, were provided with forms of landholding that were broadly fashioned on women's landholding outside Wales and cut across the age-old tenets of *Cyfraith Hywel*. When her rights were challenged Emma had recourse to a unique judicial platform: the laws and customs of Wales interpreted, mediated and applied within a framework, and by the agents, of English royal justice (among which agents we must count the king himself). The king's will and the long arm of his law is ever apparent. Thus the examination of the case of one woman in thirteenth-century Wales, a woman who was not herself Welsh and probably had little connection with *pura Wallia* before she married the ruler of northern Powys, throws into relief the relationship of a soon-to-be-conquered realm with its would-be conquerors. Her marriage and her actions helped to further connections with England, both to channel information to the king and his agents on the ground and to embed further change in the native society where she lived.

Notes

[1] This article is based in part upon research currently being undertaken as part of the AHRC-funded collaborative project: 'Women Negotiating the Boundaries of Justice: Britain and Ireland, c.1100–c.1750' (PI: Deborah Youngs, Swansea University). I owe a debt of thanks to Trish Skinner, David Stephenson and Sparky Booker for their careful appraisal of earlier drafts of this chapter. It is far stronger for their input. All remaining errors are, of course, my own.

[2] See, for example, David Stephenson, *Medieval Powys. Kingdom, Principality and Lordship, 1132–1293* (Woodbridge: Boydell, 2016), pp. 120, 130, 138–40, 286; David Stephenson, '*Potens et Prudens*: Gruffudd ap Madog, Lord of Bromfield 1236–69', *WHR*, 22 (2005), 409–31, at 419; Janet Meisel, *Barons of the Welsh Frontier: the Corbet, Pantulf and FitzWarin Families, 1066–1272* (Lincoln, NB and London: University of Nebraska Press, 1980), pp. 15–16, 26, 44, 53, 83, 119, 120–2.

[3] The National Archives, C60/40, Fine Rolls of Henry III, the roll for 27 Henry III (28 October 1242–27 October 1243), no. 57; Charles Roberts (ed.), *Excerpta e Rotulis Finium in Turri Londinensi Asservatis. Henrico Tertio Rege A.D. 1216–1272*, 2 vols (London: Record Commission, 1835, 1836), i, pp. 271, 390 (henceforth *Rot. Fin.*); *Cal. IPM*, i, no. 156; *CPR, 1247–58*, p. 627; *CCR, 1256–9*, pp. 201–2; R. W. Eyton, *The Antiquities of Shropshire*, 12 vols (London, 1854–60), vii, pp. 343–5. A cursory outline of Emma's career may be found in Gwenyth Richards, *Welsh Noblewomen in the Thirteenth Century: An Historical Study of Medieval Welsh Law and Gender Roles* (Lewiston NY, Queenstown ON and Lampeter: Edwin Mellen Press, 2009), pp. 148–50.

[4] Stephenson, *Medieval Powys*, pp. 115–16; Stephenson, '*Potens et Prudens*', 410.

[5] *CLR, 1226–40*, p. 477; *CChR, 1226–57*, p. 263; Stephenson, '*Potens et Prudens*', 415–18; Stephenson, *Medieval Powys*, chapter 6.

[6] Matthew Paris, *Chronica Majora*, ed. Henry R. Luard, 7 vols (London, 1872–1883), iv, pp. 159–50; v, pp. 597, 613, 646. See *AoC*, pp. 227–36, for a brief but eloquent description of Powys and its principal divisions.

[7] See especially the map 'Powys and its Neighbouring Districts in the Thirteenth Century' in *AoC*, p. 232 and the three maps showing Powys's internal divisions and geographical contexts on pp. xiv–xvi of Stephenson, *Medieval Powys*.

[8] *AoC*, p. 230; Stephenson, *Medieval Powys*, pp. 116, 127–8.

[9] *CPR*, 1247–58, pp. 560, 627; *CCR*, 1256–9, p. 99; *Annales Cestrienses; or, Chronicle of the Abbey of S. Werberg, at Chester*, ed. Richard Copley Christie (London, 1887), p. 74–5; Stephenson, 'Potens et Prudens', 418, 423–6; Stephenson, *Medieval Powys*, p. 122.

[10] Stephenson, 'Potens et Prudens', 426.

[11] *Brut y Tywysogyon: Peniarth MS. 20 Version*, trans. Thomas Jones (Cardiff: University of Wales Press, 1952) for the year 1269. December 1269, for Gruffudd's death, is the date to which historians have typically adhered. However, the issue on 22 December 1270 of that charter by which Gruffudd's sons confirmed their father's grants to their mother (*AWR*, no. 526), likely expedited in the immediate aftermath of the ruler's death, caused J. E. Lloyd to suggest that Gruffudd in fact died twelve months later than traditionally believed: J. E. Lloyd, *Owen Glendower* (Oxford: Oxford University Press, 1931), p. 9 and n. 1. The history of the Abbey of Valle Crucis is best outlined in Janet Burton and Karen Stöber, *Abbeys and Priories of Medieval Wales* (Cardiff: University of Wales Press, 2015), pp. 213–17.

[12] Stephenson, *Medieval Powys*, p. xxi, names another possible son of Gruffudd and Emma – Einion.

[13] Madog had probably married the prince of Gwynedd's sister Margaret more than a decade before his father's death. On his own death eight years later Madog left two underage sons: *CWR*, pp. 161, 162, 170, 181.

[14] TNA, C47/4/1, fol. 40v. The likelihood is that this was Emma d'Audley. Although her daughter-in-law Margaret was also associated with Bromfield, in 1278 it was Emma who held both the whole of Maelor Saesneg and the lordship of Eyton in Maelor Gymraeg, and it was Emma with whom the king needed to negotiate to effect an exchange.

[15] *The Welsh Assize Roll, 1272–1284*, ed. James Conway Davies (Cardiff: University of Wales Press, 1940), p. 247.

[16] Stephenson, *Medieval Powys*, pp. 127–31. For a brief run-down of the prince of Wales's division of northern Powys among the brothers, see Stephenson, *Medieval Powys*, p. 159.

[17] *Welsh Assize Roll*, p. 247; *AWR*, no. 527; *Littere Wallie*, ed. J. G. Edwards (Cardiff: University of Wales Press, 1940), pp. 53–4; *Calendar of Ancient Correspondence Concerning Wales*, ed. J. Goronwy Edwards (Cardiff: University of Wales Press, 1935), p. 83; J. B. Smith, 'Dynastic succession in medieval Wales', *BBCS*, 33 (1986), 199–232, at 229; J. B. Smith, *Llywelyn ap Gruffudd: Prince of Wales* (new edn, Cardiff: University of Wales Press, 2014), pp. 423–4.

[18] *Welsh Assize Roll*, p. 238.
[19] *Welsh Assize Roll*, pp. 256–8.
[20] Edward reached Worcester from Gloucester on 3 July, and pressed on to Stourton (Worcs) on 6 July: Henry Gough, *Itinerary of King Edward I throughout his reign A.D. 1272–1307, exhibiting his movements from time to time so far as they are recorded*, 2 vols (Paisley: Alexander Gardner, 1900), i, p. 73.
[21] TNA, C145/35 (39). The set is printed in full, but not without errors, in Frederic Seebohm, *The Tribal System in Wales: being part of an inquiry into the structure and methods of tribal society* (2nd edn, London and New York: Longmans Green, 1905), Appendix D, pp. 101–5 and calendared in *Cal. IPM*, i, no. 1095. The two charters of Gruffudd himself and the confirmation deed of his sons are printed in *AWR*, nos 515–16 and 526 and catalogued in K. L. Maund (ed.), *Handlist of the Acts of Native Welsh Rulers, 1132–1283* (Cardiff: University of Wales Press, 1996), nos 235–6 and 238.
[22] TNA, C145/35(39); *AWR*, nos 515–16; Seebohm, *Tribal System*, pp. 102, 103–4. The charter relating to Eyton is incorrectly endorsed 'Emma daughter of Gruffudd ap Madog' (*Emma filia Griff' ap Madogi*).
[23] TNA, C145/35(39); *AWR*, no. 515; Seebohm, *Tribal System*, p. 102.
[24] TNA, C145/35(39); *AWR*, no. 526; Seebohm, *Tribal System*, p. 105.
[25] E.g. *CWR*, pp. 170–1.
[26] At the same time, other interests in his patrimonial territories which Gruffudd granted to Emma during his lifetime are never associated with dower at any point: *Welsh Assize Roll*, p. 238; *AWR*, no. 520; *Calendar of Ancient Petitions relating to Wales*, ed. William Rees (Cardiff: University of Wales Press, 1975), p. 441.
[27] Hywel was still alive at the time of the Treaty of Montgomery in late September 1269: *AWR*, no. 363. For information on Hywel's career and political allegiances, which did not always match Gruffudd's, see e.g. Smith, *Llywelyn ap Gruffudd*, pp. 112, 132, 138, 169, 179, 181; *AWR*, nos 284, 513, 522–3; Stephenson, *Medieval Powys*, pp. 124, 128, 203, 259, 283.
[28] These include arrangements for Elen wife of Maredudd ab Owain of Ceredigion (*AWR*, no. 69; *CPR*, 1232–47, p. 487), Hawise Lestrange, wife of Gruffudd ap Gwenwynwyn of southern Powys (*AWR*, nos 606, 607; *CWR*, pp. 171–3, 179; *CPR*, 1340–3, pp. 96–7), Juliana de Lacy, wife of Maredudd ap Rhobert of Cydewain (*CCR*, 1251–3, p. 185; *AWR*, no. 15; *Welsh Assize Roll*, p. 255), Margaret Lestrange, wife of Rhys ap Gruffudd ab Ednyfed Fychan (*CWR*, p. 285) and the case of Angharad ferch Owain discussed below. Other examples may also be found.

[29] TNA, C146/9502; *AWR*, no. 71; and printed as an appendix to J. B. Smith, 'Dower in Thirteenth-Century Wales: a Grant of the Commote of Anhuniog, 1273', *BBCS*, 30 (1983), 348–55, 354–5. For information on the common law *maritagium*, see e.g. Joseph Biancalana, *The Fee Tail and the Common Recovery in Medieval England, 1176–1502* (Cambridge: Cambridge University Press, 2001), pp. 10, 39–69; J. M. Kaye, *Medieval English Conveyances* (Cambridge: Cambridge University Press, 2009), pp. 139–40.

[30] *Welsh Assize Roll*, p. 242; *CWR*, p. 171.

[31] The timeframe – nine days between the commission of inquiry to Guncelin de Badlesmere and the execution of the commission at Farndon on the Wales-Cheshire border – is likely too short for the mediation of Chancery itself.

[32] *AWR*, no. 520 (the petition of December 1282 x 1283). An extant account book of the Wardrobe for 1278 reveals that letters from the king were conveyed by a *nuncio* to 'the lady of Bromfield' in October, while in September royal letters were conveyed to unidentified recipients in Bromfield: TNA, C47/4/1, fols 39, 39v, 40v. See above, n. 14.

[33] *CWR*, p. 162.

[34] Seebohm, *Tribal System*, p. 103: *consuetudo Wallie talem quod quocienscumque aliquis pro timore guerre vel alia occasione reliquerit terram suam et recesserit de Wallie ad alias partes bene licebit domino terram illam seysire tamquam escaetam suam et facere inde voluntatem suam.*

[35] Seebohm, *Tribal System*, p. 102: *unusquisque Walicus ad voluntatem suam dare potest uxori sue terras et tenementa sua ante sponsalia vel post prout sibi cederit voluntati.*

[36] This issue is discussed at length in Emma Cavell, 'Widows, Welsh Law and the Long Shadow of England in the Thirteenth Century', unpublished article, under review.

[37] *Nomine dotis*: TNA, JUST1/1147, m. 7. *Welsh Assize Roll*, p. 245 translates it as 'by way of dower'.

[38] The original plea-roll entry for the dispute between Emma and Margaret variously describes the endowments thus: *ut dotem, in dotem, ut dotem suam*, as well as *nomine dotis*, as cited above, n. 30: TNA, JUST1/1147, m. 7.

[39] *Welsh Assize Roll*, pp. 245–6 and *AWR*, no. 517. For an explanation of the common law grant in fee farm, see Kaye, *Medieval English Conveyances*, pp. 104–5, 207.

[40] *Welsh Assize Roll*, p. 239.

[41] Evidence that he was already considering substitution in early January 1278 can be found in *CWR*, pp. 170–1.

42 TNA, C47/4/1, fols 39, 39v, 40v and above nn 13, 31. The king was probably in Macclesfield on that occasion from 26 September to 3 x 5 of October.

43 *AWR*, no. 519; *CCR*, 1272–9, p. 513; *CPR*, 1272–81, pp. 282–3. The king was certainly at Westminster from the latter part of October to mid-November (Gough, *Itinerary*, pp. 88–9) and it looks very likely that Emma, like the witnesses, travelled there for the exchange too.

44 As illustrated especially by *Welsh Assize Roll*.

45 *Welsh Assize Roll*, p. 238.

46 Technically *amobr* was due for any sexual liaison, but had by this time effectively become a marriage payment. It was still levied by Marcher lords after the conquest and was not, as in England, restricted to villein tenants: R. R. Davies, 'The status of women and the practice of marriage in late medieval Wales', in Dafydd Jenkins and Morfydd Owen (eds), *The Welsh Law of Women: studies presented to Daniel Binchy on his eightieth birthday* (Cardiff: University of Wales Press, 1980), pp. 93–114, at pp. 96–7, 103–6, 110–12; Dafydd Jenkins, 'Property interests in the classical Welsh law of women', in *The Welsh Law of Women*, pp. 69–92, at p. 73; D. B. Walters, 'The European context of the Welsh law of matrimonial property', in *The Welsh Law of Women*, pp. 115–31, at p. 124.

47 *AWR*, nos. 518, 520; *Cal. Ancient Petitions*, p. 441; *Welsh Assize Roll*, p. 257.

48 *Welsh Assize Roll*, p. 238. Presiding in Worcester on that occasion were Roger de Seyton, Ralph de Hengham and Hywel ap Meurig. Llywelyn was similarly disobedient to other royal judicial pronouncements: *Welsh Assize Roll*, p. 305 and see Stephenson, *Medieval Powys*, p. 162.

49 *Welsh Assize Roll*, pp. 2, 35 makes reference to a parliament at Worcester, but there is no record of a formal parliament at this time or in Worcester. A meeting of the king and council is more likely.

50 See *Littere Wallie*, p. 54; *AWR*, nos 533–8.

51 For some of Llywelyn's antagonisms and frustrations, see Stephenson, *Medieval Powys*, pp. 162–3.

52 *AWR*, no. 520; *Cal. Ancient Petitions*, p. 441.

53 *Welsh Assize Roll*, p. 238.

54 *Welsh Assize Roll*, p. 256.

55 *Welsh Assize Roll*, p. 258: *per legem Walensicam qui vocatur Keueryth eis et omnibus Walensicis per dominum Regem concessam*.

56 *Welsh Assize Roll*, p. 258.

57 *Welsh Assize Roll*, p. 258: *videtur Iusticiariis domini regis per ipsos non esse facturi ad interpretandum predictam composicionem pacis per ipsum dominum Regem conditam* [i.e. the Treaty of Aberconwy].

58 *Welsh Assize Roll*, p. 264; *Calendar of Inquisitions Miscellaneous (Chancery), preserved in the Public Record Office*, 8 vols (London: HMSO, 1916–69), ii, no. 285. Fremingham appears to have been removed from the king's affairs in Wales between the commencement of this suit in February 1278 and its resumption, this time before Walter de Hopton and others, in July 1278. He was sent on royal business in Rome in the summer of 1278: *Welsh Assize Roll*, introduction, p. 99.

59 *Welsh Assize Roll*, pp. 352–3; *AoC*, p. 348. See also *Brut y Tywysogyon: Peniarth MS. 20*,p. 120, *Brut y Tywysogyon: Red Book of Hergest Version*, ed. and trans. T. Jones (Cardiff: University of Wales Press, 1955), pp. 269–71. For Llywelyn Fychan's capitulation in December 1276, see *CPR, 1272–81*, p. 186.

60 *Welsh Assize Roll*, p. 352.

61 *Welsh Assize Roll*, p. 352.

62 Smith, *Llywelyn ap Gruffudd*, p. 565; *CWR*, pp. 226, 262, 271, 272; Stephenson, *Medieval Powys*, pp. 164–5.

63 *CWR*, pp. 265, 266; *CCR, 1279–88*, p. 231; *AWR*, no. 532.

64 For Gruffudd Fychan, see above, n. 60; for his son Madog: Lloyd, *Owen Glendower*, pp. 11–12.

65 *CWR*, p. 240. See *AoC*, p. 363, for the fate of several native *regna* after 1282.

66 *CWR*, p. 240.

67 *CWR*, pp. 161, 240. See Smith, *Llywelyn*, p. 520 and n. 40.

68 Stephenson, '*Potens et Prudens*', 431; A. D. Carr, 'An Aristocracy in Decline', *WHR*, 5 (1970), 103–29, at 110, 112; Stephenson, *Medieval Powys*, pp. 159–65.

69 Even her engagement with the Welsh assize courts was all at Oswestry in the Shropshire borderlands, rather than at any of the sessions in Wales itself.

70 *AWR*, no. 520; *Cal. Ancient Petitions*, p. 441.

3

Migration and integration: Welsh secular clergy in England in the fifteenth century[1]

Rhun Emlyn

In June 1441, two Welshmen left the same border area of northeast Wales for very different reasons. Guto'r Glyn, who later became the most prominent poet of his age, went to fight in Normandy in the army of the duke of York; David Blodwell became canon of Hereford cathedral and studied canon and civil law at Cambridge.[2] Both of these men illustrate the opportunities that had opened up for Welshmen in the later Middle Ages to work and travel outside Wales as the Edwardian conquest brought peace as well as increased political, economic and social connections between the Welsh and their English neighbours.[3] Guto'r Glyn soon returned to Wales; David Blodwell, however, spent the rest of his life mainly in England, becoming commissary-general of Canterbury by the end of his life. We know much about Guto and his fellow Welsh soldiers; there were surely many like David Blodwell who left Wales to seek preferment in the Church in England, and yet we know little about these men. Who were they? How common was it to seek a career in England? How widespread was mobility among the Welsh clergy? To what extent did large numbers of them settle in England? These questions have rarely been explored in depth, research having been focused on notable individuals, specific groups such as the students of Oxford, or the personnel of the Church in Wales.[4]

Recently, as shown in the content of this volume, increasing attention has been paid to the travel of Welsh men and women in England and further afield and the importance of these connections for medieval Wales. In his work, Adam Chapman has highlighted the involvement of Welsh soldiers in later medieval English armies and Kathryn Hurlock has discussed the relationship between Wales and the crusades.[5] Other recent explorations include Deborah Youngs's study of the travel of female apprentices to England and Katharine Olson's discussions of pilgrimage to Rome.[6] My previous work has focused on the extent of travel among the higher clergy, a group for whom mobility was common as shown by David Lepine.[7] The higher clergy, however, were the elite of Welsh clergy and would have been only a small proportion of the men who travelled from Wales in search of ecclesiastical positions. What about the majority who might not have been as successful, but who also migrated to England for shorter or longer periods of time? Some historians, in particular Virginia Davis, have started addressing the nature of clerical mobility in general and have shown the diverse nature of these men's experiences and motivations.[8] The aim of this chapter is to discuss some of these ideas in a Welsh context by considering the migration of Welsh secular clergy to England in the fifteenth century and defining the nature of this movement, exploring their integration into the Church in England.[9] This will enrich our knowledge of the relationship between Wales and England in the later medieval period, demonstrating how widespread mobility was among Welshmen in the fifteenth century, and help us to understand the type of Welsh society they left behind.

Before continuing we must first define who the 'Welsh clergy' were. How can we recognise a Welsh cleric outside Wales? How meaningful is the term 'Welsh clergy'? We are sometimes reliant on names, such as patronymics and toponyms, in order to identify Welsh men and women in England in this period. The advantage in studying clergy is that the Church often recorded details about the origins of its personnel, which enables us to be more certain when looking for patterns in the migration of Welsh individuals to England. Some Church records note the clerics' diocese of origin, allowing us to identify those who were from the Welsh dioceses.

The diocese was the geographical unit used by the Church when recording the details of clergy; therefore, for the purposes of this chapter, a Welsh cleric is one who is identified as coming from one of the four medieval Welsh dioceses of Bangor, St Asaph, St David's and Llandaff.[10] In describing an individual as being one of the Welsh clergy no presumption is made about how they would have defined themselves; it is likely that there are some included in this study who would never have considered themselves to be Welsh, being of Anglo-Norman descent or living in the border areas, but none the less had their geographical origins in the country.

In order to discover the presence of Welsh clergy in England one type of source is essential: bishops' registers. In the fifteenth century Wales was divided into four dioceses, while there were seventeen in England, each with its own bishop. The official business of the bishop in governing his diocese would be recorded in the register and as a result a vast range of information is usually included: institutions to benefices; wills proved before the bishop; ordination lists; licenses and dispensations (such as for clerics to be absent from their parishes); legal acts; letters and documents relating to the execution of royal writs. As a result, these registers display a profusion of names and biographical details of clergy, from the un-beneficed to the episcopate, and allow us to track their careers and movements. Some English registers survive from the thirteenth century and the survival rate is fairly high for the fifteenth century, although there are still a number of significant gaps.[11] A number of these registers have been edited and published, most notably by the Canterbury and York Society, but many remain unpublished. Because of the limited survival of Welsh bishops' registers those in England are extremely useful sources for the study of Welsh clergy and the Welsh Church, and as they are so rich in detail they provide a better picture of mobility than found in most medieval records, contributing towards our ideas about the movement of Welshmen in general. It is therefore not surprising that we must turn to these records if we are to gain a deeper understanding of the migration and integration of Welsh clergy in England.

Migration

Bishops' records throw light upon the extent to which Welsh clergy travelled to and within England in pursuit of a career. Names of Welsh clerics appear in various parts of the bishops' registers but the ordination lists in particular are extremely useful in identifying Welsh clergy who were present in England at key junctures of their careers. Joining the ranks of the clergy required ordination and clerics were ordained to a number of different orders in turn. There were four minor orders of doorkeeper, lector, exorcist and acolyte; and three major orders of subdeacon, deacon and priest, although not every cleric would have attained the priesthood. Ordination lists, usually recording the ordination of men as acolytes and then to the three major orders, appear in most surviving bishops' registers. Candidates would usually present themselves to their own bishop for ordination but they could also receive letters dimissory from their bishop, permitting them to be ordained in another diocese. In these cases the diocese of origin was noted, allowing us to identify clerics from the four Welsh dioceses being ordained in England. An individual's presence in the ordination lists of a diocese other than his own reveals his location at the time of his ordination and provides us with a snapshot of where that individual was seeking work or where he was travelling at that moment in time. As clerics would be ordained to a number of various orders we can also track where they were at different times, allowing us to discern whether they just happened to pass through a diocese, if they were highly mobile or if they were more permanently resident in one place. Ordination ceremonies usually occurred four times a year and by the later medieval period an individual would often be ordained to successive orders at successive ceremonies, although some would be ordained acolyte and subdeacon at the same ceremony.[12] According to canon law there should have been an interval of a year between ordination as acolyte and subdeacon, three months before becoming a deacon and a further three months before ordination as a priest.[13] These intervals were not observed in the case of many Welsh clergy, but this lack of observance was not a particularly Welsh phenomenon.[14] Ordination lists record other biographical details which may add to our information about their careers and travels. These details include degrees attained and their title (their benefice or a source of financial support until they had their own benefice), implying a connection to a geographical area.

In order to gain a full picture of the Welshmen being ordained in England we can look at the ordination lists of dioceses that experienced different levels of migration of Welsh clergy. The two border dioceses of Hereford and Coventry and Lichfield included communities that would have been considered as Welsh at that time and some parts that now fall to the west of the current Wales-England border. Ordination ceremonies in these two dioceses would have been conveniently located for some clerics from the Welsh dioceses. Hereford in particular was closer to many from the eastern half of the sprawling diocese of St David's than the ceremonies held within their own diocese. In the fifteenth century the ceremonies in St David's diocese were mainly held at the bishop's palace at Lamphey, but some were held at Haverfordwest, Pembroke, Llawhaden and the cathedral in St David's, all within the modern county of Pembrokeshire in the west of the diocese.[15] There are a few examples of ceremonies being held further east – at Carmarthen, Abergwili and Swansea – but even these were distant for large swathes of the diocese, and only one ceremony being held in the east of the diocese, in Brecon. Welshmen listed in the ordination lists of these two English dioceses, therefore, were not necessarily travelling for any length of time in England. There are other dioceses in England where fairly large groups of Welsh clergy resided and as a result we would expect the number of Welshmen ordained in these to be greater than in most English dioceses. These would include London, which had a large body of immigrant clergy, and the dioceses of Lincoln and to a lesser extent Ely, where the universities of Oxford and Cambridge were located. At the other end of the scale, the more remote dioceses of Carlisle and Durham are less likely than most to see a large body of Welsh clergy in their ordination lists as they are further from Wales and the main centres that would have attracted Welsh clergy. A number of dioceses in southern England are more likely to have experienced some migration of Welshmen, especially Worcester, Salisbury, Winchester and Bath and Wells. These were on or near the main routes from London or Oxford to south Wales, or Bristol, which had strong connections with the country.[16] The following discussion will focus on two particular dioceses, London and Salisbury, which are likely to give different perspectives on the migration of Welsh clergy.

We will turn our attention first of all to a diocese that would have been among the most attractive to Welsh clergy in pursuit of employment. London in the fifteenth century attracted men and women from all walks of life in search of work, large numbers of clergy among them. The city was much larger than any other in medieval England. The population had declined as a result of the Black Death, from a high point of possibly 80,000, but it is estimated that the population was around 40,000 in 1400 and around 50,000 in 1500; nowhere else in England came close in terms of population.[17] The city's clerical population would have numbered in the thousands; around 300 would have been attached to St Paul's cathedral alone, and the city had 107 parish churches with between three and twenty-five serving each of them in the late fourteenth century.[18] There was a constant demand for chantry and mass priests and work was to be found in royal service, in the households of bishops and members of the aristocracy, so that the city was reliant on the migration of clergy from outside to serve its needs.[19] The appeal of London is evident in the fact that the vast majority (80 per cent) of clergy ordained in London in the fifteenth century were from outside the diocese.[20] It is unfortunate that we have no surviving ordination lists of Thomas Kempe, bishop of London between 1450 and 1489, leaving a significant gap in the record of ordinations in the diocese. As a result we can only learn the identities of Welshmen ordained in London in the first fifty and last ten years of the fifteenth century.[21]

A total of 196 Welshmen appear in the London ordination lists.[22] These individuals would have migrated to London for at least a short period, probably in search of preferment. Although part of a larger body of Welsh clergy present in the city comprising both those newly ordained in London as well as those ordained elsewhere, they provide us with an idea of the number of Welsh clergy present in London during the century. In order to make these numbers more meaningful we can break them down according to diocese of origin (see Table 3.1).

Welsh clergy in London came from all corners of the country, but there is a clear difference between St David's and the smaller

Table 3.1: Welsh secular clergy ordained in London by diocese
(with earlier figures for comparison)

Diocese	1361–99 (exc. 1375–82)	1400–49	1489–1500	Fifteenth-century total
Bangor	2	19	7	26
Llandaff	7	20	3	23
St Asaph	8	19	25	44
St David's	37	92	11	103
Total	54	150	46	196

dioceses. A number of clergy from Llandaff, Bangor and St Asaph were ordained during the periods of the fifteenth century for which ordination lists survive (twenty-three, twenty-six and forty-four respectively), with clergy from the latter clearly more successful in finding their way to London. A different picture emerges when we look at St David's, the largest of the Welsh dioceses. In total, 103 men from this diocese are known to have been ordained in London during the century. It is possible that some of these variations can be explained in terms of different migration patterns from the north and south of the country; after all the south had more direct connections to London and other major towns in England. One clear difference between north and south is that a higher proportion of clergy from the northern dioceses were ordained as priests; they had often progressed further in their clerical careers by the time of their arrival in London and were more likely to stay for longer periods.[23] As I will discuss shortly, the migration patterns of north and south also developed differently over time. The main reason for these differences however is the character of St David's diocese. It was the largest Welsh diocese by far, and included Carmarthen, Brecon and Haverfordwest, the three largest Welsh towns.[24] The diocese also had good connections with several English ports and important links with the royal court.

We can provide more context for these numbers by comparing them to clergy from English dioceses. Virginia Davis has calculated the number of clergy who were ordained priests, rather than the whole cohort, from the sixteen English dioceses (excluding London itself) for periods of forty years, allowing a comparison with Welsh dioceses.[25] Between 1400 and 1439 the number of priests from the three smaller dioceses was relatively modest: six each from Bangor and Llandaff and seven from St Asaph. This is what one would expect for fairly small and remote dioceses; indeed, these numbers are close to those of Hereford, Rochester and Carlisle (eight, seven and seven respectively). During the same period twenty-five men from St David's diocese were ordained priests. Considering the size of the diocese, this figure is smaller than we might expect, being in the same range as dioceses such as Worcester, Durham and Winchester which were geographically smaller. And yet we should probably not be too surprised, as Wales was less heavily populated than England and the total population of the country is unlikely to have been above a quarter of a million during the fifteenth century.[26] This suggests that Welsh clergy were slightly less likely than their English counterparts to travel to London for ordination, certainly early in the century, but also that migration to London functioned in a similar way for Welsh and English dioceses. While not being exact guides to the number of clerics present, a diocese's size and, in some cases, proximity to London had a clear relationship with levels of migration to the city. London seems to have been almost as attractive and as accessible to Welsh clergy as to English clergy.

These general figures conceal more significant details. Using the figures for these four decades is not in reality a fair comparison between Welsh and English dioceses as very few Welsh clergy were ordained in London in the first decade of the fifteenth century. Apart from William Chirk from St Asaph diocese, ordained deacon and priest in 1401, no Welshman was ordained in London until 1408 and only a few were ordained at the end of the decade. This decade saw a general decrease in ordinations in London, explained by Virginia Davis in terms of demographic patterns following the Black Death and disillusionment with the Church as a result of the Papal Schism,[27] but the near complete absence of Welsh clergy in London ordination lists before 1408 can only be

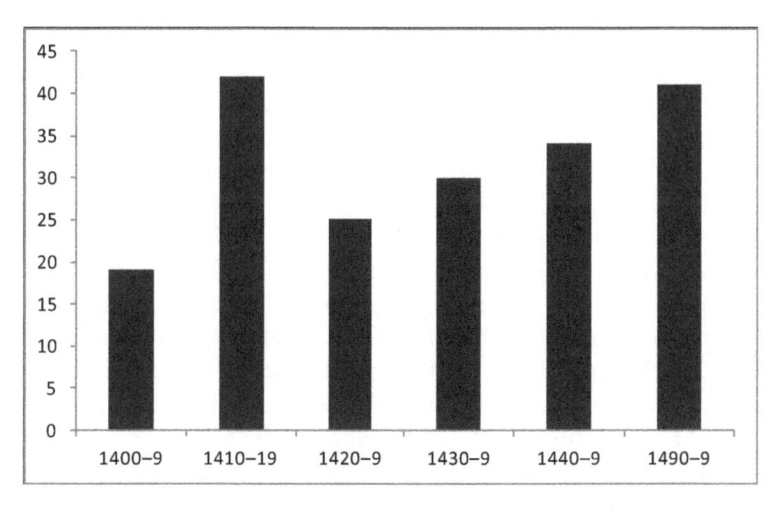

Figure 3.1: Welsh secular clergy ordained in London by decade

explained by the turmoil caused by the Glyndŵr rebellion, with Welshmen only travelling to London and receiving ordination there once the rebellion was coming to an end.[28] It seems that very few Welshmen were starting their pursuit of a career in London while the rebellion was ongoing, although there is plentiful evidence that those already progressing in their careers were still successful in England.[29] The fact that the numbers from Welsh dioceses are not very far behind English dioceses of similar size and distance from London is significant as we are comparing Welsh dioceses over three decades with English dioceses over four decades.

Following the failure of the rebellion there seems to have been a growing momentum of Welsh clergy leaving the country to seek opportunities elsewhere, as shown in Figure 3.1. The second decade of the century saw the highest number of Welshmen recorded in the ordination lists of any decade in the century; this rise was particularly dramatic in St David's diocese, with thirty-two clergy leaving the country and appearing in the London ordination lists. After this sudden upsurge, numbers decreased in the 1420s but from then on the century saw a gradual increase of Welsh clergy appearing in London decade by decade, with the number for the 1490s coming close to the high point of the 1410s. The rebellion evidently did not adversely affect the travel of Welsh clergy to London in the long term, although it may have lessened the attraction of staying at home. Indeed the rebellion, and the political and social context which followed it, seems to have given impetus to the exodus of clergy from Wales. The number of Welsh clergy in London in the first decades of the fifteenth century was significantly higher than the last decades of the fourteenth century, which saw very few Welshmen being ordained in the city (see Table 3.1). The fact that this growth in the fifteenth century was a Welsh phenomenon is made clear by the striking contrast with the general pattern: in general the number of ordinations in London was higher in the fourteenth century than the fifteenth century.[30] There was clearly a trend of increasing migration of Welshmen to London throughout the fifteenth century as the failure of the Glyndŵr rebellion made leaving their homeland more appealing while opportunities were opening up elsewhere.

At the end of the century there is another intriguing set of figures. A sharp increase of Welsh clergy moving to London would be expected following the accession of Henry VII and it has been suggested that there was an increase in Welshmen being ordained in Winchester.[31] Glanmor Williams writes that: 'there were, after 1485, fresh, enhanced, and more numerous opportunities for Welshmen. They now went to England in larger numbers than ever before and made a much more palpable impact on the life of that country.'[32] Following a gap of forty years, ordination lists have survived in London from 1489 onwards. Compared to the century's earlier decades there was a modest increase in the number of Welsh ordinations in the final decade; this seems to be a continuation of the pattern of gradual increase seen earlier in the century rather than demonstrating a significant change following Henry Tudor's success. There was a dramatic rise however in the number of clergy from St Asaph diocese. Twenty-five individuals from that diocese were ordained in London between 1489 and 1499, including individuals who would later rise to prominence such as Robert ap Rhys, personal chaplain and crossbearer to Cardinal Wolsey as well as chancellor and vicar-general of his home diocese, and Richard Whitford, friend of Erasmus and author of devotional literature.[33] This is more than the other three dioceses combined and also more than the number that came from St Asaph during the first fifty years of the century.[34] Clearly, if the accession of Henry VII had any immediate influence on the presence of Welsh clergy in London, it was only felt in the north-east of the country. The increase in numbers from St Asaph in particular is not easy to explain, although there was a corresponding dramatic rise in students from the diocese in the University of Cambridge in the second half of the century.[35] There was also a less significant rise in number from Bangor diocese during this decade which suggests that this may have been a northern phenomenon. It is also interesting to note that the same period saw a similar increase in London of clergy from dioceses in the north of England, including Coventry and Lichfield which shared a border with St Asaph.[36]

While the visits of some of these Welsh clergy to London might have been brief, it is clear that for many their residency in London was more permanent. A number were ordained to three or four consecutive orders in the city, showing their presence at different times over months or years. David Mathew from St Asaph diocese was ordained acolyte in London in March 1408 and to the three major orders in February, March and May 1410. We can trace others in London over longer periods of time: Roger Elisse, also from St Asaph diocese, was ordained subdeacon in February 1496 and deacon in April of the same year before his ordination as priest four years later in April 1500. Not all the clergy would have stayed in London for the whole period between ceremonies, as is seen in examples where clergy were ordained to non-consecutive orders. One such example is Richard Wogan from St David's diocese who was ordained acolyte and subdeacon in the same ceremony in December 1413 and priest in March 1416, suggesting that he had been ordained deacon elsewhere and was not staying permanently in London. In addition to differences between Welsh clergy in their length of residence in the city they also seem to be appearing in the city by different routes. Very often Welsh ordinands in London were ordained to the title of a religious house in their home diocese, implying that their strongest connections were still with home, but there were three other locations that appeared fairly often as the location of their title. A significant number had as their title religious foundations either in the English cities closest to Wales, such as the Hospital of St Oswald in Worcester for David ap Hywel ap

Gwilym of Llandaff diocese, or in the university cities of Oxford and Cambridge, for example Rewley Abbey at Oxford which served as the title of Richard Says of Bangor diocese. A third group were ordained to the title of churches and institutions in London, such as St Bartholomew's Hospital in Smithfield which is noted as the title of seven Welsh ordinands.

It would seem that the clergy discussed above were a very mixed group, containing some who were recent arrivals from Wales, some who had been resident in the city for at least a short period, some who had developed connections with the English border counties on their way to London and others who had come from the English universities.[37] This serves to emphasise the importance of connections between south Wales and certain English towns and cities, especially Bristol, and the key role of university education in drawing Welsh clergy to England. As some of the London clergy were only ordained as deacons or priests in the city, a study of other bishops' registers, especially in dioceses with universities or those located close to Wales, might reveal details of previous ordinations thereby showing the routes that these indviduals took to London.

It is clear that London attracted significant numbers of Welsh clergy, and that the Welsh were part of the great migration of clergy to the city in the fifteenth century. However, looking at other English dioceses shows that there was constant migration of clergy from Wales to other parts of England. Salisbury is a good general indicator of migration into England, being neither one of the main centres that attracted the most clergy nor remote, and close to the main roads used by Welshmen in England. In order to study the presence of Welsh clergy in the diocese we can look at the ordination lists of two episcopates at both ends of the century: Robert Hallum (1407–17) and Thomas Langton (1485–93).[38]

Fifteen secular Welsh clergy were ordained in Salisbury during Hallum's episcopate and seventeen during the shorter episcopate of Langton.[39] At some ceremonies a number of Welshmen were ordained together, such as the ceremony held in Ramsbury in February 1491 when John ap David ap Gwyn of St Asaph was ordained acolyte, William Howell of St David's ordained subdeacon and, from St Asaph, Thomas ap John, Geoffrey de Meyndek ap

Table 3.2: Welsh secular clergy ordained in Salisbury by diocese

Diocese	1407–17	1485–93
Bangor	0 or 1	3
Llandaff	1	2
St Asaph	0	6
St David's	13 or 14	6
Total	15	17

Pell and Richard Howell were ordained as priests.[40] Although Welsh clergy travelled to Salisbury diocese throughout the century there were notable differences between the beginning and the end of the century, some of these reflecting the patterns seen in London.

Earlier in the century Salisbury diocese was a less important destination for Welshmen wishing to be ordained. Far fewer Welshmen travelled to Salisbury for ordination than to London during Hallum's episcopate: fifteen in Salisbury compared to fifty-two in London.[41] As shown in Table 3.2, nearly all of these in Salisbury came from St David's diocese, alongside one from Llandaff and one from either Bangor or St David's; it may be that no cleric from the two northern dioceses was ordained in Salisbury during this period.[42]

In addition nearly half of the Welsh clerics were ordained at ceremonies held within about ten miles of Oxford, and so could have been Oxford students who crossed the border into Salisbury diocese for the sole purpose of being ordained, an issue discussed below. It seems that, reflecting a pattern seen in London, clergy from St David's diocese were much more likely than those of other dioceses to appear in ordination lists in England and a number were travelling from that diocese from 1408 onwards at the time of the gradual decline of the Glyndŵr rebellion. However, migration numbers from the three other Welsh dioceses to English dioceses (apart from London) were very low. To put this in some perspective, we can compare with those from Hereford, an English diocese which occurs around as often in the London ordination lists and which also does not share a border with Salisbury. Hereford was among the English dioceses that sent the smallest number of priests to London during this period, with only eight priests from the diocese appearing in the London ordination lists throughout the first forty years of the century.[43] The number of clergy from Hereford that appeared in Salisbury was also small, only three individuals, but this was more than the one or zero from Bangor, St Asaph and Llandaff. It seems that while Welsh clergy were represented fairly well in the ordination lists of London they were less likely than English clergy to travel to other parts of England.

By the end of the century a very different pattern had emerged. More Welsh clergy were ordained in Salisbury during Langton's episcopate than during the longer episcopate of his predecessor, suggesting an increasing number of Welsh clergy migrating to England by the end of the century. Numbers had increased to the extent that they were similar to those seen in London. In fact, in the few years where we can directly compare Salisbury and London (between April 1489 and June 1493) more Welshmen were ordained in Salisbury than in the capital.[44] We should be wary of depending too heavily on evidence from a four-year period, but it seems that migration to other English dioceses was much more in line with London by the end of the fifteenth century. There does not seem to be a sudden increase in Welshmen being ordained in London following the accession of Henry VII, but his accession may have had an effect on Welsh migration to other parts of England, as noticed in Winchester by Virginia Davis.[45] The main contributor to the increase in Salisbury was the appearance of clergy from the northern dioceses, in particular a growth in the numbers from St Asaph as was also the case in London; there were no clerics from St Asaph in the earlier period but six were ordained under Langton, including the four ordained in the Ramsbury ceremony mentioned earlier. There was also a slight increase in clergy from certain English dioceses, but not as sharp a rise as seen in those from the dioceses of north Wales.[46] It is likely that this rise reflects an increased connection with Salisbury, rather than an increase in Oxford students visiting the diocese for their ordination, as during the later period Salisbury ordination ceremonies were infrequently held in close proximity to Oxford. The Welsh by the end of the fifteenth century were more widely travelled when compared to their focus on London earlier in the century.

In order to gain a clearer understanding of the nature of this migration it is worth exploring further the relationship between ordinands and the diocese of Salisbury. The connection of some of these men to the diocese of Salisbury must have been minimal. During Hallum's episcopate seven of the ordinands were ordained close to Oxford, in either Abingdon or Sutton Courtenay, and for six of the seven their ordination is their only known link to the diocese. As Oxford was on the edge of the large diocese of Lincoln, ceremonies held in Abingdon and Sutton Courtenay might have been more convenient for Oxford students than ceremonies held in their own diocese of residence. Of these six men with no other known connection to the diocese, Philip David is known to have been a student at Oxford and Walter ap David had received a licence of non-residence from the bishop of St David's to allow him to study at a university.[47] In the later period only one Welsh cleric, Thomas Dagnall, was ordained in close proximity to Oxford and he is known to have studied at the university.[48] Most Welsh clergy, however, were ordained in the heart of the diocese, in places such as Ramsbury, Potterne, Sherborne and in and around Salisbury itself, and it is clear that many were based more permanently in or near the diocese. Some appear more than once in the ordination lists, such as David Willyam from St David's diocese who was ordained subdeacon at Potterne in September 1408 and deacon at Sherborne in December of the same year.[49] In his case we have further evidence of his links with the diocese. He was ordained to the title of Cerne Abbey, in the south of the diocese, and appears elsewhere in the bishop's register as a proctor.[50] Others are also known to have held positions in the diocese: David ap Rhys was rector of Brightwalton, and had been ordained earlier in the diocese by Hallum's predecessor, while David Maynell was vicar choral of Salisbury cathedral.[51] There were others with connections to places near the diocese, such as Thomas Hore who was ordained to the title of Bruton Priory just over the border in Bath and Wells diocese.[52] These examples highlight how the experience of migration could differ among Welsh clergy ordained in England and how some would travel across different parts of England in search of a career.

Integration?

Ordination lists show that there was significant migration of Welsh clergy to England during the fifteenth century. It is a different question entirely whether they were successful in gaining preferment. To what extent did Welsh clergy gain appointments, establish careers for themselves and integrate into the Church in England? In order to answer these questions, and to provide a more complete picture of the integration of Welsh clergy within a particular area, we will again consider the diocese of Salisbury.

A survey of this diocese suggests that fifteenth-century Welsh clergy were successful in finding benefices in England. As well as listing the names of those who were ordained, bishops' registers provide details of institutions to benefices within the diocese; the register of Thomas Langton can serve as a case study of Welshmen ordained in English dioceses. An examination of the register shows that, during the eight years between June 1485 and June 1493, at least thirty-five Welshmen were appointed to or left their benefices in this diocese alone.[53] These are mainly records of appointments to, or vacations of, parish churches, such as the appointment of Robert ap David as rector of Long Crichel in February 1490 and the resignation of John Ryse as rector of Long Bredy in March 1487.[54] In some instances a Welshman resigned to be succeeded by one of his compatriots, such as the appointment in April 1493 of David Jonys as keeper of the Hospital of St John the Baptist in Cricklade following the resignation of Thomas Gogh.[55] One would expect to find high numbers of Welsh clergy in dioceses such as Hereford, Lincoln and London, but their strong presence in Salisbury is illuminating and suggests that a study of other dioceses in southern England would be worthwhile. It is also clear that the ordination lists examined earlier in this chapter reveal only a sample of Welsh clergy present in the diocese; at thirty-five, the number of those appointed or leaving their benefices is double the number ordained in the diocese during the same period, and this number does not include all the clergy who may have held a benefice in the diocese throughout the period. Interestingly no names are repeated as being both ordained and installed in Langton's register: they are two separate groups of individuals.[56] Combining both groups, we have a complex picture of a body of over fifty Welsh clerics appearing in Salisbury diocese during these eight years. Some were seeking employment, some were successful in obtaining a benefice, some were leaving to pursue further opportunities while yet others were merely passing through.

We cannot be certain that all those appointed to benefices were resident or active in the diocese, but some are recorded in the register as engaging with the work of the Church there. As well as being rector of Godmanstone, James Vaughan was present at a heresy trial at Salisbury.[57] Another Welshman, John Howell, was present at heresy trials in the diocese, but not recorded elsewhere in the register.[58] Some were involved in the administration of the diocese in various ways, none more so than William Jonys, who was appointed at various times as commissary-general and sequestrator in the archdeaconries of Berkshire and Wiltshire, commissioner to punish offenders following the bishop's visitation, collector of a charitable subsidy and commissioner for patronage inquisition.[59] David Husband was another who was engaged in the work of the diocese, serving as proctor for the dean and chapter of Salisbury cathedral, and is an example of how clerics from Wales could be successful in being appointed to a number of rectories in different parts of England.[60] Before his appointment in Salisbury diocese in 1472 as rector of Wroughton, Wiltshire, he had held the rectories of Biddenden in Kent, Alresford in Hampshire as well as Brighstone on the Isle of Wight.[61] The successful appointment of Welsh clergy to English benefices was evidently not restricted to the diocese of Salisbury.

Up to now we have considered the Welshmen who gained appointments at parish level in the diocese of Salisbury, but what about the higher clergy, such as members of cathedral chapters? These were desirable positions, providing their holders with status and wealth; acquiring a canonry was a sign of a highly successful career.[62] During the fifteenth century at least ten Welshmen became members of the cathedral chapter at Salisbury. Not all canons were required to be permanently resident, although one of the Welsh canons, Maurice ap David, was declared contumacious for not attending the election of the dean.[63] Two of the Welsh canons went on to become bishops in other dioceses, Henry Ware at Chichester and Richard Martyn at his home diocese of St David's.[64] Some of the Welsh canons were also appointed to other prominent positions in the diocese: Richard Caunton, for example, became archdeacon of Salisbury.[65] Another of these canons, however, merits further consideration. Geoffrey Crukadan was a highly qualified cleric who became the highest official of the diocese during the second decade of the fifteenth century. Already a bachelor of canon law and licentiate of civil law, probably of Oxford, he matriculated at the University of Cologne in 1401.[66] By 1406 he had become rector of Tadmarton in Oxfordshire as well as canon of Salisbury and prebendary of Bitton.[67] As a Welshman in England, Crukadan had to pay for a licence in 1413 to allow him to stay in the country following the turmoil of the Glyndŵr rebellion but his career continued to flourish.[68] He was evidently trusted and respected by the bishop of Salisbury, Robert Hallum, who appointed Crukadan as his vicar-general to administer the diocese during his absence at the Council of Pisa in 1409 and again at the Council of Constance between 1414 and 1417.[69] Crukadan also served as official of the diocese from 1409, presiding over the bishop's consistory court.[70] These were highly responsible and prominent positions at the heart of the administration of the diocese, but it was not uncommon for Welshmen to fill such roles in England. David ap Rhys, ordained in Salisbury, served the diocese of London over three decades in various capacities as vicar-general, keeper of the spiritualities, commissary-general and official, and was one of many Welshmen who were appointed to high administrative positions in London during the fifteenth century.[71] Geoffrey Crukadan, David ap Rhys and others show how some Welsh clerics had become thoroughly integrated into the Church in England during the fifteenth century.

Conclusions

Until now we have seen that there was substantial migration of clerics from Wales to England in the fifteenth century and that a number of them were successful in gaining preferment. But can we glean more than this from the sources? What further can be understood of the nature of clerical mobility? What are the emerging patterns that can develop our understanding of Welsh migration to England in general in this period? The pre-eminence of London as the destination of Welsh clergy is beyond doubt. Welshmen travelled for ordination to different parts of Salisbury diocese but London had a clear and lasting appeal. This is especially seen in the decades following the Glyndŵr rebellion when there seems to have been an exodus of clergy from Wales to London. London attracted clergy from the Welsh dioceses in a similar way to how it drew clergy from dioceses in England, which does not seem to be the case in Salisbury in the early fifteenth century. The importance of London is also suggested by the fact that Welsh clergy were more likely to stay there for longer periods and be ordained to multiple orders (compared to Salisbury). A similar pattern has been noticed by Virginia Davis with regard to Irish clergy. A 'substantial proportion' of Irish clergy in English ordination lists were ordained in London, with very few appearing in other dioceses.[72] This focus on London was a pattern common to non-English clergy.

The pre-eminence of London was less marked among the Welsh by the end of the century as migration from Wales to other parts of England increased. While Irish clergy seemed to have continued to direct their focus on London and saw only a modest increase in their numbers there, the fifteenth century was a period of growth in migration from Wales with increasing numbers appearing in other parts of England.[73] Even when their numbers were at their lowest point in the first decade of the century the Welsh were by far the most populous non-English group in the London ordination lists; by the end of the century this numerical advantage had increased.[74] This had not been the case in the second half of the fourteenth century when there were nearly as many Irish clergy (forty-nine) as Welsh clergy (fifty-four) ordained in London. It would seem that during the century following the Glyndŵr rebellion Wales became further integrated with England as individual Welshmen decided that their future lay in England. That the greatest change was seen in north Wales, which previously had fewer ties with England, only serves to confirm this impression.

Welsh clergy in England were highly mobile, moving back and forth across the country. Students crossed the borders of dioceses in order to receive ordination; rectors received benefices in different parts of the country; ordinands were ordained to titles in locations far from their ordination ceremony. The clearest indication of this migration is when the same individuals were ordained to various orders in different dioceses. No fewer than eleven of those ordained in Salisbury also occur in the London ordination lists, allowing us to plot their movements from one diocese to the other, and in some cases back again.[75] David Pontan from St David's diocese was ordained acolyte at St Paul's cathedral on 22 September 1414 and subdeacon at Fulham parish church in London diocese on 22 December of that year; he then travelled to the Dominican friary at Fisherton near Salisbury for his ordination as deacon on 23 February 1415 and was back in Fulham manor chapel for his ordination as priest on 16 March.[76] For some, travel in England indicated their commitment to stay in the country in the long term to further their careers, but in other cases a period in England was followed by a return to Wales. One such example is Maurice Gwyn from St David's diocese who was ordained deacon in London in April 1495 but was soon back in his home diocese where he was appointed to numerous benefices, culminating in becoming canon of the cathedral and prebendary of Clydey.[77] Their travel was clearly not only in one direction. Due to the poor survival of Welsh bishops' registers it is difficult to assess how many of the clergy ordained in England returned home. Some are known to have later received prominent positions back in Wales, such as the three clerics from Bangor – David Nant, Hugh Alcock and Hugh Tregarn – who became members of the cathedral chapters of Bangor or St Asaph.[78] In some cases, such as John Morgan who became bishop of St David's, advancement in the Church in England was key to their appointment to prominent positions back home in Wales.[79] Those who returned would have brought back with them important connections forged while in England (such as Robert ap Rhys who was the agent of Cardinal Wolsey), the benefit of their education if they had been to university as well as a different outlook.[80]

The relatively high number of Welsh clergy within the Church in England would have made them a significant body and led to the development of networks and, in some cases, communities of Welsh clergy in England. It is not usually easy to see tangible links between individuals within the Church structure but we have an interesting glimpse in the will of Philip Morgan, bishop of Ely and one of the most successful of the Welsh clergy in England. He died, in October 1435, on one of his estates in south-east England, yet his executor and many of the witnesses were Welsh: John Blodwell (who was almost certainly related to David Blodwell mentioned at the beginning of this chapter), Maurice Wynter, Morgan Wynter, Thomas Howell, Maurice Cradock and Geoffrey Davy.[81] John Blodwell, Maurice and Morgan Wynter had also been appointed rectors in the diocese.[82] These were men who had benefitted from the patronage of Philip Morgan and were at his side when he died. It is unfortunate that his register as bishop of Ely has not survived to allow us to see who he ordained and installed in the diocese, but it is apparent that he had created and maintained a circle of Welshmen under his auspices in the diocese. Further research will be required in order to establish if similar groups existed in other parts of England.

When considering patronage it is tempting to look at individuals such as Philip Morgan and emphasise the role of Welshmen as patrons of their compatriots in England. In Langton's register, examined earlier, there are certainly examples which suggest that Welsh connections played a part in a cleric's advancement: John Davyd, alias Kidwely, became rector of Hamstead Marshall on an exchange of benefices with John Tudir, and Jasper Tudor was the patron who presented John ap Lothyum to the rectory of Milston.[83] Welsh patronage was vital for some individuals, but in reality most Welshmen who stayed in England were supported by English individuals and institutions. This, more than anything, highlights the integration of Welsh clergy into the English Church and illustrates the development of the relationship between Wales and England by the end of the fifteenth century.

Rhun Emlyn

APPENDICES

Below are the details of clergy from the four Welsh dioceses who were ordained in London and Salisbury dioceses in the periods studied in this chapter. Appendix 3.1 includes all those ordained in London except for the years between 1450 and 1489 when there is a gap in the records. Appendix 3.2 includes those ordained in Salisbury during the episcopates of Robert Hallum (1407–17) and Thomas Langton (1485–93). Individuals are listed chronologically in order of their first ordination. The details include their names with variations in the spelling of surnames and, in brackets, degrees noted in the registers;[1] orders with dates and locations of the ceremonies;[2] and their title (i.e. their benefice, patrimony or patron, usually a religious foundation or an individual).[3] Unless stated otherwise, the parishes that serve as their title are within their diocese of origin and hospitals that appear as their title are in London. The following are the abbreviations used in the appendices.

---

[1] Forenames, including patronymics, are given in their modern standard spelling when this is identifiable. Where there exists Welsh and English modern versions of the name (e.g. Gwilym and William) the English version has been used unless the name is of Welsh origin or the Welsh version is clearly meant. Variants of the surname appear in their chronological order. Unless stated otherwise, their degrees are noted in the record of their first ordination.

[2] In some instances no location is given for the ceremony and there are examples where a different location appears in entries in the database for ceremonies held on the same date. Ceremonies were held in the parish church of the stated location unless stated otherwise. A number of ceremonies were held in religious houses that had multiple names or used terms such as priory and hospital interchangeably; in these cases the names have been standardised, following Caroline M. Barron and Matthew Davies (eds), *The Religious Houses of London and Middlesex* (London: Institute of Historical Research, 2007). The modern name Much Hadham is used instead of Great Hadham, the name that appears in the original records.

[3] Further details are given where parishes and religious houses may otherwise be confused, although some are unidentified.

Abbreviations used for degrees:
B.Cn.L.   Bachelor of Canon Law
B.C.L.   Bachelor of Civil Law
B.Cn.+C.L.   Bachelor of Canon and Civil Law
D.C.L.   Doctor of Civil Law
M.A.   Master of Arts

Abbreviations used for orders:
ac.   acolyte
sdn.   subdeacon
dn.   deacon
pr.   priest

Abbreviations used for ordination locations:
A.   Abbey
C.   College
F.   Friary
H.   Hospital
Holy Trinity   Holy Trinity Priory, Aldgate
M.   Manor
P.   Priory
Pal.   Palace
St.   Street
St Bart's   St Bartholomew's Hospital
St Mary B.   St Mary without Bishopsgate Hospital (also known as St Mary Spital)
St Mary C.   St Mary within Cripplegate Hospital (also known as Elsingspital)
St Thomas   St Thomas of Acon Hospital

Abbreviations used for title:
d.   diocese
H.   Hospital
preb.   prebendary of

Rhun Emlyn

APPENDIX 3.1:

Welsh secular clergy in London ordination lists

The individuals are listed below according to diocese of origin.

Bangor diocese

Gregory ap Joy
ac. and sdn. 22/09/1408 (St Paul's)   Llandyfrydog
dn. 22/12/1408 (Fulham)   as above
pr. 2/03/1409 (St Paul's)   as above

Matthew Ledwygan/Lodwygon
sdn. 18/03/1413 (St Paul's)   Priestholme Cell
dn. 8/04/1413 (St Paul's)   as above

John de Boste/Bosto
ac. and sdn. 23/12/1413 (Much Hadham M.)
                                        Llanrhaeadr-yng-Nghinmeirch
dn. 3/03/1414 (Much Hadham M.)   as above
pr. 24/03/1414 (St Paul's)   as above

David Nant (Magister when ac., B.Cn.+C.L. when dn.)
ac. 14/03/1416 (St Paul's)   Aberdaron
dn. 23/09/1419 (Fulham)   Aberdaron (portioner)
pr. 23/12/1419 (Fulham M.)   as above

Robert Hilton
sdn. 21/12/1420 (St Paul's)   Royston Priory

George ab Ieuan ab Ithel
dn. 20/12/1427 (Much Hadham M.)   Bangor cathedral
pr. 28/02/1428 (St Paul's)   as above

Migration and integration

Andrew Hules (*Magister*)
dn. 28/02/1428 (St Paul's)　　　he is archdeacon of Anglesey

Hugh Alcock
ac. 18/12/1428 (Lambeth Pal.)　Clynnog (co-portioner)
sdn. 19/02/1429 (St Bartholomew's P.) as above
pr. 28/03/1433 (Bishop's Pal.)　as above

Geoffrey ap Llywelyn ap Hywel
dn. 26/03/1429 (Wykham M.)　Penmon Priory

Geoffrey Kymmere (B.C.L.)
dn. 26/03/1429 (Wykham M.)　Kyme Priory

John Spycer/Spicer
dn. 15/03/1432 (Holy Trinity)　Bangor cathedral
pr. 14/06/1432 (St Thomas)　as above

Hugh Tregarn
dn. 7/03/1433 (Bishop's Pal.)　Llanddwyn

Richard Says
ac. and sdn. 21/03/1439 (St Mary B.) Rewley Abbey

Ieuan ab Edmund
sdn. 21/03/1439 (St Mary B.)　Aberconwy Abbey
dn. 30/05/1439 (Much Hadham)　as above

John Benet
sdn. 20/02/1440 (Much Hadham)　Rewley Abbey

Lewis Anglesey
ac. 26/05/1442 (St Mary B.)　　-

Lewis ap Hywel
sdn. 16/03/1443 (St Paul's)　Barnwell Priory

John ap Maredudd ab Ieuan
pr. 11/04/1444 (St Paul's)　　　　Beddgelert Priory

William Edward
ac. 17/12/1446 (St Mary C.)　　　 -
sdn. 4/03/1447 (St Thomas)　　　 Oriel College, Oxford

Lewis Gwynny
sdn. 6/03/1490 (Holy Trinity)　　 Beddgelert Priory
dn. 27/03/1490 (St Bartholomew's P.) as above

John Byrd/Byrde
dn. 21/04/1492 (St Paul's)　　　　Osney Abbey
pr. 1/06/1493 (St Mary B.)　　　　as above

John Elys
ac. 2/03/1493 (St Thomas)　　　　 Penmon Priory
sdn. 23/03/1493 (Holy Trinity)　　as above
dn. 6/04/1493 (St Paul's)　　　　 as above

John Gwynne (B.C.L.)
dn. 19/09/1495 (St Paul's)　　　　'St Lonani de Kilwelon',
　　　　　　　　　　　　　　　　　St David's d.
pr. 26/02/1496 (St Bartholomew's P.) as above

Lewis John
pr. 19/09/1495 (St Paul's)　　　　Penmon Priory

John ap Lloyd ap Med.
ac. 10/03/1498 (St Bartholomew's P.) -
sdn. 31/03/1498 (St Thomas)　　　 Penmon Priory
dn. 14/04/1498 (St Paul's)　　　　as above
pr. 21/09/1498 (St Bartholomew's P.) as above

William ap Metto
pr. 21/09/1498 (St Bartholomew's P.) Penmon Priory

Llandaff diocese

Richard Parker
sdn. 2/03/1409 (St Paul's)   Tintern Abbey

Lawrence David
ac. 21/12/1409 (Much Hadham)   -

David ab Ieuan
ac. and sdn. 20/09/1410 (Fulham)   Bristol Augustinian Abbey
dn. 20/12/1410 (Fulham)   as above

Clement Oginor/Ogmor
ac. and sdn. 27/02/1412 (Much Hadham M.)
                                   Neath Abbey
dn. 2/04/1412 (St Paul's)   as above
pr. 28/05/1412 (Fulham)   as above

Robert Webbe
pr. 24/09/1412 (St Paul's)   H. of St John the Baptist,
                                   Bridgwater

John Fouler/Foulere
ac. 18/03/1413 (St Paul's)   preb. Llangwm in Llandaff
sdn. 8/04/1413 (St Paul's)   as above
pr. 23/12/1413 (Much Hadham M.) as above

William Smyth
ac. 21/12/1415 (St Paul's)   -

Richard Caerlyon (*Magister*)
dn. 11/03/1419 (St Bride, Fleet St.)   Tintern Abbey

Thomas Spycer (possibly the same as John Spicer, below)
sdn. 21/09/1420 (St Paul's)   St Mary de Pré Priory

John Spicer (possibly the same as Thomas Spycer, above)
dn. 21/12/1420 (St Paul's) St Mary de Pré Priory
pr. 8/03/1421 (Fulham M.) as above

Walter Hardyng
sdn. 19/02/1429 (St Bartholomew's P.) Keynsham Abbey

John Melan
sdn. 19/02/1429 (St Bartholomew's P.) Bristol Augustinian Abbey

David ap Hywel ap Gwilym
dn. 19/02/1429 (St Bartholomew's P.) H. of St Oswald, Worcester

Hugh Thomas
sdn. 20/12/1432 (Fulham M.) Osney Abbey
dn. 7/03/1433 (Bishop's Pal.) as above
pr. 28/03/1433 (Bishop's Pal.) as above

Thomas London
ac. and sdn. 25/05/1437 (Maldon F.) bishop and cathedral of Llandaff
dn. 21/09/1437 (St Paul's) Llandaff cathedral, dean and chapter
pr. 21/12/1437 (Much Hadham) as above

Lewis Neth
ac. 12/03/1440 (Ludgate F.) -

Hugh Bryton
ac. 11/03/1441 (Holy Trinity) -

Alexander Whyte
ac. 11/03/1441 (Holy Trinity) -

Morgan Philipp
dn. 22/05/1445 (St Edmund, Lombard St.)
 St Mark's Bonhommes, Bristol

Philip Uske (D.C.L.)
ac. 4/03/1447 (St Thomas)   Battle Abbey
pr. 3/06/1447 (Holy Trinity)   as above

Philip ap Rhys
dn. 19/12/1489 (St Bartholomew's P.) Neath Abbey

William Glover
dn. 2/04/1496 (St Paul's)   Grace Dieu Abbey

Adam ap Thomas
sdn. 13/06/1500 (St Thomas)   Holy Trinity Priory, Aldgate
dn. 19/09/1500 (St Bartholomew's P.) as above
pr. 10/04/1501 (St Paul's)   as above

St Asaph diocese

William Chirk
dn. 19/02/1401 (Holy Trinity)   Llandegfan, Bangor d.
pr. 19/03/1401 (Holy Trinity)   as above

David Mathewe/Mathew
ac. 31/03/1408 (no location given)   –
sdn. 15/02/1410 (no location given)   H. of St John the Baptist, Bristol
dn. 23/03/1410 (Lambeth Pal.)   as above
pr. 17/05/1410 (Barking A.)   as above

Adam Hore
sdn. 2/03/1409 (St Paul's)   Valle Crucis Abbey

David Elys
dn. 2/03/1409 (St Paul's)   St Bartholomew's H.

Edward Littyle/Lytyl alias Bagh
ac. 1/06/1409 (Fulham M.) -
sdn. 21/06/1409 (Much Hadham) Walter Grendon, Prior of
 the Hospitallers
dn. 21/12/1409 (Much Hadham) as above
pr. 23/03/1410 (Lambeth Pal.) as above

John Clochy/Clochyd/Clothby/Clothyd
ac. 19/09/1411 (St Paul's) -
sdn. 27/02/1412 (Much Hadham M.) Ivychurch Priory
dn. 19/03/1412 (Much Hadham M.) as above
pr. 2/04/1412 (St Paul's) as above

Hugh ap Llywelyn
pr. 1/06/1420 (Fulham M.) Rewley Abbey

Thomas Eslake
pr. 22/12/1436 (St Bartholomew's P.) Whitford

John Morton/Merton
sdn. 28/02/1437 (St Bride, Fleet St.) Llanrhaeadr-yng-Nghinmeirch,
 Bangor d.
dn. 11/04/1444 (St Paul's) as above
pr. 6/06/1444 (St Thomas) as above

Gruffudd ap [illegible] ap Llywelyn
dn. 7/06/1438 (St Bartholomew's P.) Strata Marcella Abbey

David Kissmer/Kismer
ac. and sdn. 28/02/1439 (St Paul's) Whitland Abbey

John ap Hywel ab Adda
pr. 28/02/1439 (St Paul's) Strata Marcella Abbey

William Oswestre
sdn. 21/03/1439 (St Mary B.) Halston Knights Hospitallers

Migration and integration

Geoffrey ab Edmund
pr. 10/06/1441 (St Mary B.)   'Sancti Spirito in Armus' Priory

Geoffrey Allynton/Alenton
sdn. 17/03/1442 (St Bartholomew's P.) St Mary Graces Abbey, London
dn. 31/03/1442 (St Laurence Pountney C.)
                               as above

David ap Ken. [Cynwrig?] ap Robert
dn. 26/05/1442 (St Mary B.)   Aberconwy Abbey
pr. 16/03/1443 (St Paul's)   as above

Geoffrey Owgan
ac. 6/06/1444 (St Thomas)   –

John Penne
ac. 19/12/1444 (St Mary B.)   –
sdn. 23/12/1447 (St Bartholomew's P.) St Frideswide Priory, Oxford

David Chirke (M.A.)
dn. 8/04/1447 (Bishop's Pal.)   Aberconwy Abbey
pr. 3/06/1447 (Holy Trinity)   as above

Richard Whitford alias Rich ap Gruffudd ap Bell
sdn. 18/04/1489 (St Paul's)   Basingwerk Abbey

Thomas ab Ithel
pr. 19/09/1489 (St Paul's)   St Frideswide Priory, Oxford

Maurice Westbury
pr. 5/06/1490 (St Thomas)   Osney Abbey

Cadwaladr ap John
ac. 17/12/1491 (Holy Trinity)   –
sdn. 17/03/1492 (St Bartholomew's P.)
                               Strata Marcella Abbey
dn. 7/04/1492   as above
pr. 21/04/1492 (St Paul's)   as above

Robert ap Rhys (no location given)
ac. 22/02/1494 (St Paul's) –

Lewis ap William
sdn. 22/02/1494 (St Paul's) Leighs Priory
dn. 10/03/1494 (Holy Trinity) as above
pr. 24/05/1494 (St Thomas) as above

John ap Richard
pr. 22/02/1494 (St Paul's) Valle Crucis Abbey

John ap Maredudd
sdn. 10/03/1494 (Holy Trinity) Valle Crucis Abbey

Robert Apkete
sdn. 10/03/1494 (Holy Trinity) Aberconwy Abbey

Edward David
sdn. 10/03/1494 (Holy Trinity) Holy Trinity Priory, Aldgate

Thomas Johones
pr. 10/03/1494 (Holy Trinity) Valle Crucis Abbey

Geoffrey ap Rhys
pr. 24/05/1494 (St Thomas) Valle Crucis Abbey

Owain Lewes
ac. 14/03/1495 (St Bart's) –

Richard Llond (*Magister*)
dn. 4/04/1495 (St Mary C.) Aberconwy Abbey

John Williams
pr. 4/04/1495 (St Mary C.) Basingwerk Abbey

Migration and integration

Eliseus Mathew/Mathon
ac. 13/06/1495 (St Paul's)   –
sdn. 19/09/1495 (St Paul's)   Hurley Priory
dn. 19/12/1495 (St Thomas)   as above
pr. 29/05/1496 (St Paul's)   as above

Thomas ap William alias Groundre/Gronen
ac. 19/09/1495 (St Paul's)   –
sdn. 26/02/1496 (St Bartholomew's P.) Valle Crucis Abbey

Roger Elesa/Elisse/Elissa
sdn. 26/02/1496 (St Bartholomew's P.) Valle Crucis Abbey
dn. 2/04/1496 (St Paul's)   as above
pr. 18/04/1500 (St Paul's)   as above

Geoffrey ap Richard
sdn. 2/04/1496 (St Paul's)   Valle Crucis Abbey
dn. 29/05/1496 (St Paul's)   as above
pr. 24/09/1496 (St Bartholomew's P.) as above

David Conwey
pr. 23/09/1497 (St Mary B.)   Aberconwy Abbey

Thomas ap Gwyn
pr. 23/02/1499 (St Mary B.)   Valle Crucis Abbey

Geoffrey Lloyd
ac. 24/05/1499 (St Mary C.)   –
sdn. 4/04/1500 (St Bartholomew's P.) H. of St John the Evangelist,
                                     Cambridge
dn. 18/04/1500 (St Paul's)   as above
pr. 20/12/1500 (St Mary C.)   as above

John ap Richard
pr. 24/05/1499 (St Mary C.)   Valle Crucis Abbey

Edward Almere
pr. 21/09/1499 (Holy Trinity)   Chester Abbey

Geoffrey ap Hywel
pr. 21/12/1499 (St Bartholomew's P.) Cymer Abbey

St David's diocese

Walter ap David
dn. 31/03/1408 (Fulham)   Llanychâr

Hywel ab Ieuan
dn. 31/03/1408 (Fulham)   H. of St Nicholas, Salisbury

Philip Payn
dn. 31/03/1408 (Fulham M.)   Alcester Abbey

Thomas Kayn
sdn. 22/09/1408 (St Paul's)   his patrimony

David John
dn. 22/09/1408 (St Paul's)   Llangynllo, Cardiganshire

John Mathewe/Mathew
ac. 2/03/1409 (St Paul's)   –
dn. 1/06/1409 (Fulham M.)   St Frideswide Priory, Oxford

Hugh Mannsell/Maunsell
sdn. 2/03/1409 (St Paul's)   Holy Trinity Priory, Aldgate
dn. 23/03/1409 (St John's A., Colchester)
                                      as above
pr. 6/04/1409 (St Paul's)   as above

John Bole
pr. 21/06/1409 (Much Hadham)   Carmarthen Priory

Richard Gryndam
ac. 21/12/1409 (Much Hadham)   –

Lewis ap Rhys
sdn. 21/12/1409 (Much Hadham)   St Bartholomew's H.

Philip David
pr. 21/12/1409 (Much Hadham)   Llansadyrnin

David Mortymer
pr. 15/02/1410 (no location given)   he is vicar choral of St David's cathedral

Adam Philipp
pr. 20/09/1410 (Fulham)   he is vicar choral of St David's cathedral

David (ap) Henry
ac. and sdn. 7/03/1411 (St Paul's)   Penderyn

David ap Gruffudd
dn. 7/03/1411 (St Paul's)   H. of St David, Swansea
pr. 28/03/1411 (St Paul's)   as above

George Coke
dn. 19/09/1411 (St Paul's)   John Hanard junior, of Brecon
pr. 19/12/1411 (St Paul's)   as above

Peter Russell
ac. 19/12/1411 (St Paul's)   –
sdn. 27/02/1412 (Much Hadham M.)   his patrimony

David Pedwern/Pedwerne
sdn. 27/02/1412 (Much Hadham M.)   St Frideswide Priory, Oxford
dn. 19/03/1412 (Much Hadham M.)   as above
pr. 2/04/1412 (St Paul's)   as above

Rhun Emlyn

Hugh Herle (*Magister*)
ac. and sdn. 19/03/1412 (Much Hadham M.)
                                        Llangadog, Carmarthenshire
dn. 2/04/1412 (St Paul's)   as above

John ap Hywel
pr. 28/05/1412 (Fulham)   Talley Abbey

Richard Waryn
pr. 24/09/1412 (St Paul's)   St Dogmaels Abbey

Philip Poytyn
sdn. 18/03/1413 (St Paul's)   Poughley Priory
dn. 8/04/1413 (St Paul's)   as above
pr. 22/04/1413 (St Paul's)   as above

John Widelock (possibly the same as Richard Widelok, below)
ac. 23/12/1413 (Much Hadham M.)   -

Richard Wogan
ac. and sdn. 23/12/1413 (Much Hadham M.)
                                        Manorbier
pr. 14/03/1416 (St Paul's)   Narberth

Richard Widelok (possibly the same as John Widelock, above)
sdn. 23/12/1413 (Much Hadham M.) Osney Abbey

David Ponten/Pontan/Poutan
ac. 22/09/1414 (St Paul's)   -
sdn. 22/12/1414 (Fulham)   Talley Abbey
pr. 16/03/1415 (Fulham M.)   as above

Philip Husband
dn. 22/12/1414 (Fulham)   Rewley Abbey
pr. 23/02/1415 (Fulham M.)   as above

Thomas Hore
ac. 23/02/1415 (Fulham M.)   -

Henry Rikard/Richard/Ricard
ac. 21/12/1415 (St Paul's)   –
sdn. 14/03/1416 (St Paul's)   David Hawell, knight of Wales
dn. 4/04/1416 (St Paul's)   as above

John Willy/Wylly
ac. 21/12/1415 (St Paul's)   –
dn. 27/03/1417 (St Bartholomew's P.) St Mary without Bishopsgate H.
pr. 10/04/1417 (St Bartholomew's P.) as above

Nicholas Bukton
ac. 14/03/1416 (St Paul's)   –

Henry Hopkyn
ac. 14/03/1416 (St Paul's)   –
sdn. 4/04/1416 (St Paul's)   John Wogan the younger, knight, Begelly

Roger Somer
sdn. 14/03/1416 (St Paul's)   Bruern Abbey
dn. 4/04/1416 (St Paul's)   as above

William Ady
sdn. 14/03/1416 (St Paul's)   Haverfordwest Priory
dn. 4/04/1416 (St Paul's)   as above

David Baron
pr. 10/04/1417 (St Bartholomew's P.) St Bartholomew's H.

John Laundrey
pr. 10/04/1417 (St Bartholomew's P.) St Bartholomew's H.

Hugh ap Gruffudd
ac. and sdn. 19/02/1418 (St Mary B.) St Dogmaels Abbey
dn. 12/03/1418 (St Mary C.)   as above
pr. 21/05/1418 (St Paul's)   as above

John Ricardby
ac. and sdn. 19/02/1418 (St Mary B.) Lampeter
dn. 8/03/1421 (Fulham M.) as above

John Thorlec
sdn. 21/05/1418 (St Paul's) Llanfeugan

William Legburn
pr. 21/05/1418 (St Paul's) preb. Llannerch Aeron in
 Llanddewibrefi

William Chaumberleyn
dn. 17/12/1418 (Stratford atte Bowe chapel)
 Cilgerran

Maurice ap Meurig
ac. 11/03/1419 (St Bride, Fleet St.) -

Lewis ap David
dn. 11/03/1419 (St Bride, Fleet St.) St Frideswide Priory, Oxford

Thomas Stevenes
sdn. 2/03/1420 (Fulham M.) Humphrey Stovyle, knight of
 Somerset

David Tappa
pr. 1/06/1420 (Fulham M.) Osney Abbey

John Dyovall
sdn. 8/03/1421 (Fulham M.) St Bartholomew's H.
dn. 22/03/1421 (St Paul's) as above

John Lewis
sdn. 8/03/1421 (Fulham M.) Carmarthen Priory

Philip Coffyn
dn. 22/03/1421 (St Paul's) Haverfordwest Priory

Richard Lloid
pr. 22/03/1421 (St Paul's)   Strata Florida Abbey

John Palmer
ac. 19/12/1422 (St Paul's)   –
sdn. 27/02/1423 (St Paul's)   Sheen Priory
dn. 20/03/1423 (Newgate F.)   as above
pr. 3/04/1423 (St Paul's)   as above

Thomas Herry
ac. 18/12/1424 (St Paul's)   St Bartholomew's H.

Roger Smyth
sdn. 19/04/1427 (Much Hadham M.) St Bartholomew's H.
dn. 14/06/1427 (Much Hadham M.) as above

Lewis Rede
ac. 20/09/1427 (St Mary C.)   –

John Watkyn
sdn. 28/02/1428 (St Paul's)   patrimony of Thomas Lote and
                              St Paul's
dn. 20/03/1428 (Holy Trinity) St Mary Graces Abbey, London
pr. 3/04/1428 (St Laurence Pountney C.)
                              as above

Richard Hore
sdn. 28/02/1428 (St Paul's)   'Langham'[1]
dn. 24/02/1431 (St Paul's)   as above

Philip Ewyas
ac. 19/02/1429 (St Bartholomew's P.) –
pr. 24/09/1429 (Bishop's Pal.) Rewley Abbey

Thomas Lassery
ac. 11/03/1430 (St John's A., Colchester)
                              Haverfordwest Priory

[1]   Possibly Llangwm or Llan-gan.

Richard Caunton (*Magister* when ac., B.Cn.+C.L. when pr.)
ac. 11/03/1430 (St John's A., Colchester)
                                                Llanfairorllwyn
pr. 10/06/1430 (St Paul's)   as above

John Bernard
sdn. 11/03/1430 (St John's A., Colchester)
                                                 H. of St Bartholomew, Gloucester

William Prey
dn. 11/03/1430 (Bishop of St David's house)
                                               he is archdeacon of Carmarthen

Philip Lute
sdn. 24/02/1431 (St Paul's)   London Charterhouse Priory

John ap David
ac. 22/12/1431 (St Bartholomew's P.) –

Geoffrey ap Rhys
ac. 14/06/1432 (St Thomas)   –

Philip ap Rhys
sdn. 20/12/1432 (Fulham M.)   Maenordeifi

John Wyd
sdn. 12/03/1435 (St Thomas.)   Haverfordwest Priory

Thomas More (M.A. when sdn.)
ac. 22/12/1436 (St Bartholomew's P.) –
sdn. 28/02/1437 (St Bride, Fleet St.) Osney Abbey
dn. 16/03/1437 (St Mary B.)   as above

Philip Walter
ac. 28/02/1437 (St Bride, Fleet St.) –

John Lewys
sdn. 28/02/1437 (St Bride, Fleet St.) Carmarthen Priory

Migration and integration

William Howell
ac. 16/03/1437 (St Mary B.) –

Thomas Fadir/Fadyir/Fadre/Fades
ac. 7/06/1438 (St Bartholomew's P.) –
sdn. 17/12/1446 (St Mary C.)   Llangoedmor
dn. 8/04/1447 (Bishop's Pal.) as above
pr. 3/06/1447 (Holy Trinity)   as above

Philip Lord/Llord
ac. and sdn. 28/02/1439 (St Paul's)   Angle

John Fyssh
sdn. 28/02/1439 (St Paul's)   St Mary within Cripplegate H.
dn. 21/03/1439 (St Mary B.)   St Mary without Bishopsgate H.

Gruffudd ap David Dow
dn. 28/02/1439 (St Paul's)   Cilrhedyn

Robert Fysthe
ac. 20/12/1439 (Much Hadham)   –

Thomas Thy
ac. 20/02/1440 (Much Hadham)   –

William Conway
pr. 21/05/1440 (St Osyth's A.)   Llanglydwen[2]

Richard Towker/Touker (B.C.L.)
ac. and sdn. 24/09/1440 (Much Hadham)
                              Osney Abbey

Thomas Llewellyn
sdn. 24/09/1440 (Much Hadham)   Haverfordwest Priory

---

[2] 'Llanglodwyn', identified by Virginia Davis as Llangolman, is more likely to by Llanglydwen.

Robert Howell
sdn. 1/04/1441 (St Mary C.)   H. of St John the Baptist, Oxford
dn. 15/04/1441 (St Paul's)   as above

William Lessham
pr. 26/05/1442 (St Mary B.)   Port Einon

John Gruffuth
dn. 22/12/1442 (Holy Trinity) Haverfordwest Priory

William Somur/Somor
ac. 16/03/1443 (St Paul's)   -
sdn. 6/04/1443 (Ludgate F.)   Haverfordwest Priory

Richard Orchard
ac. and sdn. 21/09/1443 (St Bart's) Angle

Richard Canuton
ac. 21/12/1443 (St Bartholomew's P.) -

Philip Devenold
ac. 21/12/1443 (St Bartholomew's P.) -

David Harvy
ac. 7/03/1444 (St Paul's)   -

Richard Keteley
ac. 7/03/1444 (St Paul's)   -
ac. (again) 28/03/1444 (St Mary C.) H. of St John the Baptist, Oxford
sdn. 11/04/1444 (St Paul's)   as above
pr. 6/06/1444 (St Thomas)   as above

David ap Thomas (ap David Vachan)
ac. 13/03/1445 (Bishop's Pal.) -
sdn. 27/03/1445 (Bishop's Pal.) St Mary within Cripplegate H.

John Gareyn
ac. 12/03/1446 (Stepney)   -

John Gardyner
sdn. 2/04/1446 (St Bartholomew's P.)   Strata Marcella Abbey
dn. 11/06/1446 (Stepney)   as above
pr. 24/09/1446 (St Bart's)   as above

Richard Machon
ac. 11/06/1446 (Stepney)   –

John More (B.C.L.)
ac. 24/09/1446 (St Bart's)   –

William Bowen
pr. 18/04/1489 (St Paul's)   Osney Abbey

Lewis ap Morgan
dn. 7/04/1492 (no location given)   Talley Abbey
pr. 21/04/1492 (St Paul's)   as above

William Morgan
sdn. 21/04/1492 (St Paul's)   St Helen's Priory, London

Reginald Phillip/Philips (*Magister* when sdn., B.C.L. when pr.)
sdn. 21/04/1492 (St Paul's)   All Souls College, Oxford
pr. 22/09/1492 (St Bart's)   as above

John Richarson
ac. 22/09/1492 (St Bart's)   –

Thomas Williams
sdn. 10/03/1494 (Holy Trinity)   Clifford Priory

Maurice ab Ieuan ap Rhys
dn. 4/04/1495 (St Mary C.)   Carmarthen Priory

Maurice Gwyn (*Magister*)
dn. 4/04/1495 (St Mary C.)   St Dogmaels Abbey

Rhun Emlyn

Stephen Williams
pr. 13/06/1495 (St Paul's)　　　Carmarthen Priory

Reginald ap Rhys
ac. 18/02/1497 (St Thomas)　　–
sdn. 11/03/1497 (St Mary C.)　　Talley Abbey
dn. 25/03/1497 (St Paul's)　　as above

Gruffudd Pacdon (B.C.L.)
pr. 24/05/1499 (St Mary C.)　　Vale Royal Abbey

APPENDIX 3.2:

Welsh secular clergy in Salisbury ordination lists

The individuals are listed below according to episcopate rather than diocese of origin, with their diocese included in brackets after their names. References have been provided to the published registers.

Register of Robert Hallum (1407–17)

Thomas Coyne (St David's)[1]
ac. 13/04/1408 (St Nicholas, Abingdon) –

David John (St David's)[2]
sdn. 13/04/1408 (St Nicholas, Abingdon)
                           Llangynllo, Cardiganshire

Philip David (St David's)[3]
dn. 13/04/1408 (St Nicholas, Abingdon)
                           Llansadyrnin

Philip Payne (St David's)[4]
pr. 13/04/1408 (St Nicholas, Abingdon)
                           Alcester Abbey

William Hoper (St David's)[5]
ac. 9/06/1408 (Sutton Courtenay)   Aberedw

Walter ap David (St David's)[6]
pr. 9/06/1408 (Sutton Courtenay)   Llanychâr

[1] *The Register of Robert Hallum*, p. 158.
[2] *The Register of Robert Hallum*, p. 158.
[3] *The Register of Robert Hallum*, p. 159.
[4] *The Register of Robert Hallum*, p. 159.
[5] *The Register of Robert Hallum*, p. 160.
[6] *The Register of Robert Hallum*, p. 160.

Rhun Emlyn

David ap Rhys (St David's)[7]
pr. 9/06/1408 (Sutton Courtenay)   Brightwalton, Salisbury d.

David Wyllyam/Willyam (St David's)[8]
sdn. 22/09/1408 (Potterne M.)   Cerne Abbey
dn. 22/12/1408 (Sherborne A.)   as above

Peter Russell (St David's)[9]
dn. 2/04/1412 (Salisbury cathedral)   his patrimony

Richard Waryn (St David's)[10]
dn. 28/05/1412 (Sonning)   St Dogmaels Abbey

John Rampney (Llandaff)[11]
pr. 22/04/1413 (Sonning M.)   Ieuan ap Lewys ap Morgan

David Pontan (St David's)[12]
dn. 23/02/1415 (Salisbury Dominican F.)
    Talley Abbey

David Maynell (St David's/Bangor)[13]
sdn. 19/09/1416 (Salisbury Dominican F.)
    he is vicar choral of Salisbury cathedral
pr. 5/06/1417 (Salisbury Dominican F.) as above

---

[7] *The Register of Robert Hallum,* p. 161. His diocese of origin is not included in the record of his ordination, but he is known from other sources to be from St David's diocese. See Emden, *A Biographical Register of the University of Oxford,* i, pp. 549–50.
[8] *The Register of Robert Hallum*, pp. 161, 163.
[9] *The Register of Robert Hallum*, p. 174.
[10] *The Register of Robert Hallum*, p. 175.
[11] *The Register of Robert Hallum*, p. 179.
[12] *The Register of Robert Hallum*, p. 185.
[13] *The Register of Robert Hallum*, pp. 189, 195.

Migration and integration

Thomas Hore/Hoore (St David's)[14]
dn. 27/03/1417 (Sherborne A.)   Bruton Priory
pr. 5/06/1417 (Salisbury Dominican F.) as above

John ap John (St David's)[15]
ac. 5/06/1417 (Salisbury Dominican F.) -

Register of Thomas Langton (1485–93)

Thomas Dagnall (St David's)[16]
ac. 20/05/1486 (Cumnor M.)   -

Thomas Hewys (St Asaph)[17]
sdn. 13/06/1489 (Ramsbury)   Dorchester Abbey, Lincoln d.

Thomas Williams (Llandaff)[18]
pr. 13/06/1489 (Ramsbury)   Margam Abbey

Richard ap John (St Asaph)[19]
pr. 18/09/1490 (Ramsbury)   Strata Marcella Abbey

John ap David ap Gwyn (St Asaph)[20]
ac. 26/02/1491 (Ramsbury M.)   -

William Howell (St David's)[21]
sdn. 26/02/1491 (Ramsbury M.)   Osney Abbey

---

[14] *The Register of Robert Hallum*, pp. 192, 195.
[15] *The Register of Robert Hallum*, p. 193.
[16] *The Register of Thomas Langton*, p. 99.
[17] *The Register of Thomas Langton*, p. 101.
[18] *The Register of Thomas Langton*, p. 101.
[19] *The Register of Thomas Langton*, p. 106.
[20] *The Register of Thomas Langton*, p. 108.
[21] *The Register of Thomas Langton*, p. 108.

Thomas ap John (St Asaph)[22]
pr. 26/02/1491 (Ramsbury M.)   Valle Crucis Abbey

Geoffrey de Meyndek ap Pell (St Asaph)[23]
pr. 26/02/1491 (Ramsbury M.)   Basingwerk Abbey

Richard Howell (St Asaph)[24]
pr. 26/02/1491 (Ramsbury M.)   Basingwerk Abbey

David Lloyd (St David's)[25]
ac. 19/03/1491 (Sherborne A.)   -

Walter Vaugham (Llandaff)[26]
sdn. 2/04/1491 (Ramsbury M.)   Llantarnam Abbey

Lewis Richard (Bangor)[27]
ac. 17/03/1492 (Ramsbury)   -

David Cadigan (St David's)[28]
dn. 17/03/1492 (Ramsbury)   Osney Abbey
pr. 7/04/1492 (Ramsbury)   as above

Morgan Williams (St David's)[29]
ac. 7/04/1492 (Ramsbury)   -

Reginald Philip (St David's)[30]
ac. 7/04/1492 (Ramsbury)   -

---

[22] *The Register of Thomas Langton*, p. 108.
[23] *The Register of Thomas Langton*, p. 108.
[24] *The Register of Thomas Langton*, p. 108.
[25] *The Register of Thomas Langton*, p. 108.
[26] *The Register of Thomas Langton*, p. 109.
[27] *The Register of Thomas Langton*, p. 112.
[28] *The Register of Thomas Langton*, pp. 112, 114.
[29] *The Register of Thomas Langton*, p. 113.
[30] *The Register of Thomas Langton*, p. 113.

John Birde (Bangor)[31]
sdn. 7/04/1492 (Ramsbury)　　　　Osney Abbey

Henry Davy (Bangor)[32]
ac. 23/03/1493 (Ramsbury)　　　　–

[31] *The Register of Thomas Langton*, p. 113.
[32] *The Register of Thomas Langton*, p. 117.

Notes

[1] I am grateful to audiences in Aberystwyth and Leeds for their comments and suggestions on versions of this chapter, and wish to thank Professor Virginia Davis for being willing to discuss some aspects of this study and providing access to some of her unpublished work.

[2] For a biography of Guto'r Glyn's see E. A. Rees, *A Life of Guto'r Glyn* (Talybont: Y Lolfa, 2008), and see also Adam Chapman's chapter in this volume, below. The details of David Blodwell's career can be found in A. B. Emden, *A Biographical Register of the University of Cambridge to A.D. 1500* (Cambridge: Cambridge University Press, 1963), p. 66.

[3] *AoC*, chapters 15 and 16.

[4] Glanmor Williams in particular has discussed Welsh clergy in the later medieval period. For examples, see Glanmor Williams, *The Welsh Church from Conquest to Reformation* (rev. edn, Cardiff: University of Wales Press, 1976); Glanmor Williams, 'Two neglected London-Welsh clerics: Richard Whitford and Richard Gwent', in Glanmor Williams, *Welsh Reformation Essays* (Cardiff: University of Wales Press, 1967), pp. 67–89. For Welsh students at Oxford, see Gwilym Usher, 'Welsh Students at Oxford in the Middle Ages', *BBCS*, 16 (1954–5), 193–8; Rhŷs W. Hays, 'Welsh Students at Oxford and Cambridge Universities in the Middle Ages', *WHR*, 4.4 (1969), 325–61; Rhun Emlyn, 'Myfyrwyr canoloesol Cymreig a'u gyrfaoedd' (unpublished PhD thesis, University of Wales, Aberystwyth, 2012); Alexandre Delin, 'Les étudiants Gallois à l'université d'Oxford, 1282–1485' (unpublished PhD thesis, Université Paris 1 Panthéon-Sorbonne, 2013).

[5] In particular, see Adam Chapman, *Welsh Soldiers in the Later Middle Ages, 1282–1422* (Woodbridge: Boydell, 2015); Kathryn Hurlock, *Wales and the Crusades, c.1095–1291*, Studies in Welsh History 33 (Cardiff: University of Wales Press, 2011); and see their further comments in their chapters in this volume, below.

[6] Deborah Youngs, '"For the Preferement of their Marriage and Bringing Upp in their Youth": The Education and Training of Young Welshwomen, *c.*1450–*c.*1550', *WHR*, 25.4 (2011), 463–85; Katharine K. Olson, '"Ar Ffordd Pedr a Phawl": Welsh Pilgrimage and Travel to Rome *c.*1200–*c.*1530', *WHR*, 24.2 (2008), 1–40.

[7] Rhun Emlyn, 'Serving Church and state: the careers of medieval Welsh students', in Linda Clark (ed.), *The Fifteenth Century XI: Concerns and Preoccupations* (Woodbridge: Boydell, 2012), pp. 25–40; David Lepine, *A Brotherhood of Canons Serving God: English Secular Cathedrals in the Later Middle Ages* (Woodbridge: Boydell, 1995), pp. 41–8; David

Lepine, '"Loose canons": the mobility of higher clergy in the later Middle Ages', in Peregrine Horden (ed.), *Freedom of Movement in the Middle Ages: Proceedings of the 2003 Harlaxton Composium* (Donington: Shaun Tyas, 2007), pp. 86–103.

[8] Virginia Davis, 'Episcopal ordination lists as a source for clerical mobility in England in the fourteenth century', in N. Rogers (ed.), *England in the Fourteenth Century* (Stamford: Paul Watkins, 1993), pp. 152–70; Virginia Davis, *Clergy in London in the Late Middle Ages: A Register of Clergy Ordained in the Diocese of London Based on Episcopal Ordination Lists 1361–1539* (London: Centre for Metropolitan History, 2002).

[9] All references to clergy in this chapter will refer to secular clergy only; very few Welsh regular clergy appear in the English sources examined below.

[10] It is possible that the diocese noted in Church records sometimes refers to the location of a cleric's benefice rather than their diocese of origin. This seems to be the case with Andrew Hules who was noted as coming from Bangor diocese in the London ordination lists; see A. B. Emden, *A Biographical Register of the University of Oxford to A.D. 1500*, 3 vols (Oxford: Oxford University Press, 1957–9), ii, pp. 949–50. Andrew Hules has been included in the study as it is likely that the same would have happened in the case of some Welshmen who had benefices in England.

[11] See David M. Smith, *Guide to Bishops' Registers of England and Wales: A Survey from the Middle Ages to the Abolition of Episcopacy in 1646* (London: Royal Historical Society, 1981); David M. Smith, *Supplement to the 'Guide to Bishops' Registers of England and Wales: A Survey from the Middle Ages to the Abolition of Episcopacy in 1646'* (York: Canterbury and York Society, 2004).

[12] Peter Heath, *The English Parish Clergy on the Eve of the Reformation* (London: Routledge & Kegan Paul, 1969), p. 13; R. N. Swanson, *Church and Society in Late Medieval England* (Oxford: Blackwell, 1989), pp. 42–3. Ceremonies were held on 'the Saturdays in the third week of Advent, the first week of Lent, the vigil of Trinity, and in September following the octave of the Virgin's Nativity': Heath, *The English Parish Clergy*, p. 13.

[13] Davis, *Clergy in London*, p. 12. Clergy could take longer between ordination ceremonies, especially if they started young as there were minimum age requirements for the various orders: Heath, *The English Parish Clergy*, p. 15; Swanson, *Church and Society*, p. 40.

[14] See Deborah Youngs's chapter below for English views of Welsh lawlessness.

[15] The surviving bishops' registers of St David's have been published as R. F. Isaacson (ed.), *The Episcopal Registers of the Diocese of St David's 1397–1518*, 3 vols, with discussion by R. Arthur Roberts (London: Cymmrodorion, 1917–20). No ordination list appears in the surviving section of the register of Stephen Patryngton, published as H. D. Emanuel, 'A Fragment of the Register of Stephen Patryngton, Bishop of St David's', *Journal of the Historical Society of the Church in Wales*, 2 (1950), 31–45. Some of the diocese's ordination ceremonies were held in England.

[16] For the main routes in this period, see F. M. Stenton, 'The Road System of Medieval England,' *The Economic History Review*, 7.1 (November 1936), 1–21; B. P. Hindle, 'The Road Network of Medieval England and Wales', *Journal of Historical Geography*, 2.3 (1976), 207–21; J. F. Edwards and B. P. Hindle, 'The Transportation System of Medieval England and Wales', *Journal of Historical Geography*, 17.2 (1991), 123–34. For the connections between Wales and Bristol, see Ralph A. Griffiths, 'Medieval Severnside: the Welsh connection', in Ralph A. Griffiths, *Conquerors and Conquered in Medieval Wales* (Stroud: Alan Sutton, 1994), pp. 1–18, and in particular pp. 12–14.

[17] Caroline M. Barron, *London in the Later Middle Ages: Government and People 1200–1500* (Oxford: Oxford University Press, 2004), pp. 238–42. It is difficult to estimate the population of England's towns and cities in the later Middle Ages, but an idea of their comparative sizes is provided by the recorded number of taxpayers of the 1377 poll tax. London had 23,314 taxpayers in 1377 and the city with the second highest number of taxpayers was York which had 7,248. See Alan Dyer, 'Appendix: ranking lists of English medieval towns', in D. M. Palliser (ed.), *The Cambridge Urban History of Britain Volume I: 600–1540* (Cambridge: Cambridge University Press, 2000), pp. 747–70, and in particular pp. 758–60.

[18] Barron, *London in the Later Middle Ages*, p. 4. See also Marie-Hélène Rousseau, *Saving the Souls of Medieval London: Perpetual Chantries at St Paul's Cathedral, c.1200–1548* (Farnham: Ashgate, 2011).

[19] Davis, 'Episcopal ordination lists', p. 165; Davis, *Clergy in London*, p. 22.

[20] Davis, *Clergy in London*, pp. 28–9.

[21] The ordination lists can be accessed through the database contained in a CD-ROM in Davis, *Clergy in London*. All following references to these ordination lists can be found in this database.

[22] For details of these individuals, see below, Appendix 3.1.

[23] During the first forty years of the century around half of the clergy from Bangor and St Asaph were ordained priests while from St David's and Llandaff only a third were ordained to that order.

[24] For a recent discussion of the character of St David's diocese, see Ralph A. Griffiths, 'The Significance of St Davids and its Bishops during the Fifteenth Century', *WHR*, 27.4 (2015), 672–706. The students of the diocese seem also to have been more numerous at Oxford than students from the other Welsh dioceses, although the survival of the diocese's bishops' registers contributes towards this impression: Emlyn, 'Myfyrwyr canoloesol Cymreig', 25–6.

[25] Davis, *Clergy in London*, pp. 27–8 and in particular table 5.

[26] R. R. Davies, *The Revolt of Owain Glyn Dŵr* (Oxford: Oxford University Press, 1995), p. 35. It has already been noted how a smaller proportion of clergy from St David's were ordained priests, which might affect this analysis.

[27] Davis, *Clergy in London*, p. 23.

[28] The main study of the rebellion is Davies, *Revolt of Owain Glyn Dŵr*. For the effect and aftermath of the rebellion see also Glanmor Williams, *Renewal and Reformation: Wales c. 1415–1642* (Oxford: Oxford University Press, 1993), chapter 1; Ralph A. Griffiths, 'After Glyn Dŵr: An Age of Reconciliation?', *Proceedings of the British Academy*, 117 (2002), 139–64.

[29] Emlyn, 'Serving Church and state', pp. 39–40.

[30] Davis, *Clergy in London*, pp. 21–4.

[31] Davis, *Clergy in London*, p. 28.

[32] Glanmor Williams, 'The Welsh in Tudor England', in Glanmor Williams, *Religion, Language and Nationality in Wales: Historical Essays* (Cardiff: University of Wales Press, 1979), pp. 171–99 (quotation from p. 173).

[33] For Robert ap Rhys, see Williams, *The Welsh Church from Conquest to Reformation*, pp. 322–6. For Richard Whitford, see Williams, 'Two neglected London-Welsh clerics', pp. 67–75.

[34] The sudden rise in clergy from St Asaph can also be shown by comparing with English dioceses. More priests from St Asaph were ordained in London between 1489 and 1500 than from Rochester and Hereford for a forty-year period between 1490 and 1529. For the figures from English dioceses, see Davis, *Clergy in London*, p. 28 and table 5.

[35] Emlyn, 'Myfyrwyr canoloesol Cymreig', 28–9.

[36] Davis, *Clergy in London*, p. 27.

[37] A. B. Emden felt confident enough to include in his register of Oxford students clergy who were ordained to the title of religious houses in Oxford. See Emden, *A Biographical Register of the University of Oxford*, i, p. xxxvii.

[38] Joyce M. Horn (ed.), *The Register of Robert Hallum, Bishop of Salisbury 1407–17* (York: Canterbury and York Society, 1982), pp. 158–95;

D. P. Wright (ed.), *The Register of Thomas Langton, Bishop of Salisbury 1485–93* (York: Canterbury and York Society, 1985), pp. 96–119.

[39] For details of these individuals, see Appendix 3.2. There were also one or two others who might be Welsh but whose dioceses of origin are not clear.

[40] *Register of Thomas Langton*, p. 108.

[41] Hallum made his profession of obedience and received the spiritualities of the see on 28 March 1408 and therefore the numbers ordained in both dioceses are from the period between that date and June 1417: Joyce M. Horn (ed.), *Fasti Ecclesiae Anglicanae 1300–1541: Volume 3, Salisbury Diocese* (London: Athlone Press, 1962), p. 2.

[42] When David Maynell was ordained subdeacon his diocese of origin is noted as St David's but when he became a priest it is said that he came from Bangor: *The Register of Robert Hallum*, pp. 189, 195.

[43] Davis, *Clergy in London*, p. 28. There were between six and seven priests each from Bangor, St Asaph and Llandaff during the same period.

[44] In this period thirteen Welshmen were ordained in London while sixteen were ordained in Salisbury.

[45] Davis, *Clergy in London*, p. 28.

[46] There were five clergy from Hereford, compared to three in the earlier period, and numbers from York, the diocese with the greatest number of priests in London at the end of the century, had gone from twenty-three to twenty-five even though Langton's episcopate was shorter than that of Hallum.

[47] Emden, *A Biographical Register of the University of Oxford*, i, p. 548; *The Episcopal Registers of the Diocese of St David's*, i, p. 391.

[48] Emden, *A Biographical Register of the University of Oxford*, i, p. 554. Although ordained further into the diocese, in Ramsbury, three others are likely to have been closely connected to Oxford at the time of their ordination as they were ordained to the title of Osney Abbey in the city. One of these, David Cadigan, is described as a scholar when he was granted his letters dimissory: *The Episcopal Registers of the Diocese of St David's*, ii, p. 604.

[49] *The Register of Robert Hallum*, pp. 161, 163.

[50] *The Register of Robert Hallum*, pp. 60, 161.

[51] *The Register of Robert Hallum*, pp. 161, 189. For David ap Rhys's career, see Emden, *A Biographical Register of the University of Oxford*, i, p. 549.

[52] *The Register of Robert Hallum*, pp. 192, 195.

[53] Dioceses of origin were not included when recording institutions and therefore these numbers are less precise than the numbers of those ordained. In many cases we know from other records of the Welsh origin of these individuals but in some cases we can say that they are

probably from Wales due to details such as the use of the 'ap' patronymic in their names. There are probably others not included within the thirty-five that were in fact Welsh.

54 *The Register of Thomas Langton*, pp. 12, 29.
55 *The Register of Thomas Langton*, p. 46.
56 This does not mean that those ordained and installed were always two separate groups. Those ordained by Langton might have been installed in the diocese by his predecessor or successor.
57 *The Register of Thomas Langton*, pp. 12, 64.
58 *The Register of Thomas Langton*, pp. 77–8.
59 *The Register of Thomas Langton*, pp. 14, 52, 61.
60 *The Register of Thomas Langton*, p. 84.
61 Emden, *A Biographical Register of the University of Oxford*, ii, p. 989. He had also been canon at Hereford and Chichester cathedrals and prebendary in St Mary's Abbey, Winchester: Joyce M. Horn (ed.), *Fasti Ecclesiae Anglicanae 1300–1541: Volume 2, Hereford Diocese*, revised by David Lepine (London: Institute of Historical Research, 2009), p. 62; Joyce M. Horn (ed.), *Fasti Ecclesiae Anglicanae 1300–1541: Volume 7, Chichester Diocese* (London: Athlone Press, 1964), pp. 20, 29.
62 Lepine, *A Brotherhood of Canons Serving God*, p. 18.
63 *The Register of Thomas Langton*, p. 54.
64 *Fasti Ecclesiae Anglicanae 1300–1541: Volume 3, Salisbury Diocese*, pp. 10, 52, 81, 96; *Fasti Ecclesiae Anglicanae 1300–1541: Volume 7, Chichester Diocese*, p. 2; B. Jones (ed.), *Fasti Ecclesiae Anglicanae 1300–1541: Volume 11, The Welsh Dioceses (Bangor, Llandaff, St Asaph, St David's)* (London: Athlone Press, 1965), p. 55.
65 *Fasti Ecclesiae Anglicanae 1300–1541: Volume 3, Salisbury Diocese*, p. 12.
66 Emden, *A Biographical Register of the University of Oxford*, i, p. 524; Hermann Keussen (ed.), *Die Matrikel der Universität Köln: Erster Band, 1389–1475* (Bonn: H. Behrendt, 1928), p. 105.
67 Emden, *A Biographical Register of the University of Oxford*, i, p. 524; *Fasti Ecclesiae Anglicanae 1300–1541: Volume 3, Salisbury Diocese*, p. 34. He is possibly the Griffin Crookadam who was present in the Roman court in May 1407 (*CCR 1405–9*, p. 195).
68 His name appears in a list of Welshmen who made payments to be exempted from the order that all Welsh-born who lived in England, with some exceptions, should return home: see *CPR 1413–16*, p. 124. The list includes mainly clergy and men in various trades. The chronicler Adam Usk as well as the future bishops Philip Morgan and Henry Ware also appear on the list.
69 *The Register of Robert Hallum*, pp. 9, 66.

70. *The Register of Robert Hallum*, pp. 199–200.
71. Emden, *A Biographical Register of the University of Oxford*, i, pp. 549–50. Other Welshmen include Henry Ware, Philip ap Rhys and Edward Vaughan: Emden, *A Biographical Register of the University of Oxford*, iii, pp. 1476, 1985; Emden, *A Biographical Register of the University of Cambridge*, pp. 607–8.
72. Virginia Davis, 'Irish Clergy in Late Medieval England', *Irish Historical Studies*, 32.126 (2000), 145–60, and in particular 148–51.
73. Davis, 'Irish Clergy in Late Medieval England', 151–2.
74. The numbers of Irish, the second largest group of non-English clergy, were much smaller than the Welsh and there were never more than five clerics per decade from France (the most populous group from continental Europe). For the numbers of Irish clergy in London by decade, see Davis, 'Irish Clergy in Late Medieval England', 151. See also Davis, *Clergy in London*, p. 30.
75. These eleven clerics were identified as London and Salisbury dioceses were studied for the purposes of this chapter; if this study of ordination lists was extended to other dioceses we would have a fuller idea of the travel patterns of Welsh clergy.
76. *The Register of Robert Hallum*, p. 185. The other individuals were Walter ap David, Peter Russell, Philip Payne, John Birde, Thomas Coyne, David John, Philip David, Richard Waryn, Thomas Hore and Reginald Phillip.
77. *The Episcopal Registers of the Diocese of St David's*, ii, pp. 632, 736, 744, 750, 752, 754, 768, 804, 812, 814.
78. *Fasti Ecclesiae Anglicanae 1300–1541: Volume 11, The Welsh Dioceses*, pp. 6, 17, 44. This does not necessarily mean that they were permanently resident back in Wales.
79. Griffiths, 'The Significance of St Davids and its Bishops during the Fifteenth Century', pp. 700–2.
80. It is likely that these men would have brought manuscripts and books with them as well. For cultural exchange through the travel of Welshmen, see Kathryn Hurlock's chapter in this volume, below.
81. E. F. Jacob (ed.), with the assistance of H. C. Johnson, *The Register of Henry Chichele, Archbishop of Canterbury 1414–1443*, 4 vols (Oxford: Clarendon Press, 1938–47), iii, pp. 530–2.
82. Emden, *A Biographical Register of the University of Oxford*, i, pp. 202–3, iii, p. 2126; Wyn Thomas, 'John Blodwell: St Asaph, Rome, Constance and Balsham', *National Library of Wales Journal*, 34.2 (2007), 186–95.
83. *The Register of Thomas Langton*, pp. 10, 14.

4

'A vice common in Wales': abduction, prejudice and the search for justice in the regional and central courts of early Tudor society

Deborah Youngs

In the 1530s, Rowland Lee, bishop of Coventry and Lichfield and the president of the Council in the Marches of Wales, claimed that rape was 'a vice common in Wales', and one that needed urgent reformation.[1] Lee is hardly to be trusted for a fair assessment of matters in Wales. He is well known, to borrow William Gerard's famous phrase, for being 'not affable to anye of the Walshrie'.[2] Yet the specific abduction case he used to support this assertion does appear at first reading to confirm all the worst prejudices officers and bureaucrats at Westminster had against the 'wild west' fringes of Henry VIII's kingdom. Occurring just as the first 'act of union' legislation came into force, it seemed to showcase the laxities of legal process, corrupt local gentry, the packing of juries in Wales and its Marches, and demonstrate why its peoples should be governed entirely by England's courts, laws and officials. In reviewing the case in full, this essay focuses on a series of incidents occurring in the small village of Llanwern (in the lordship of Caerleon), which were brought to the assizes at Gloucester and thence to the Westminster Court of Star Chamber. By listening to the various participants and exploring their motivations, it will demonstrate that the suit was far more complex than Lee's overblown rhetoric suggested it to be. It will also offer an important reminder of how Wales and the Marches as an idea and as the 'other' operated in the political and legal machinations of early Tudor governors at Westminster.

By the late 1520s, and increasingly in the early 1530s, pressure was building to reform the existing judicial and administrative structure of Wales and to bolster the king's prerogative power into the Marches. The fear felt in central government that conditions within the Marcher lordships were allowing lawlessness and disorder to go unchecked had prompted a number of actions, including the reinvigoration of the Council in the Marches of Wales in the summer of 1525. The latter's reconstitution had been partly justified by the observation that inhabitants of Wales and the Marches had found it difficult to take cases to Westminster, with the evident assumption that they would wish to do so.[3] During 1534–5 statutory legislation focused on the dire need for legal reform in Wales and the Marches. The direction and tone of the political rhetoric used to justify the changes is striking. Jurors in Wales and the Marches were believed to show a 'lack of diligent and sure custody' in the trials of murderers, felons and their accessories and had acquitted them 'openly and notoriously known contrary to equity and justice'.[4] Similarly the

> people of Wales and the Marches of the same, not dreading the good and wholesome laws and statutes of this realm, have of long time continued and persevered in perpetration and commission of divers and manifold thefts, murthers, rebellions, wilful burnings of houses and other scelerous deeds and abominable malefacts.[5]

This Westminster view was influenced by, and in accordance with, various voices from within the Marches that made their opinions known to Thomas Cromwell. The negative appraisal can be read in the oft-quoted letters of Thomas Philips ('All Wales is in great decay') and Sir Edward Croft of Croft Castle (the Welsh will 'wax so wild'), who denounced the Council in the Marches of Wales as woefully inadequate.[6] At the forefront of the drive for reform, however, was the man who became president of the Council in 1534, Bishop Rowland Lee, who made Wales and its Marches his primary concern for the rest of his life. To Lee felony was a common part of Welsh life and he aimed to instil order through show trials and public executions. His energetic pursuit of good government was infused with a deep scepticism about the cultural and social values of Welsh society.[7]

Modern historians have broadly agreed that reform was needed, or at least have accepted that those officials exercising power in the Marcher lordships were prone to 'neglect and misconduct'.[8] Yet the full extent of lawlessness is difficult to assess. We lack the kind of statistical data that in a later age might show comparison of crime rates across time and place, and we cannot assume that the level of fear expressed necessarily reflected the actual incidence of lawlessness. What can be done, however, is to examine more closely the events upon which this vision of Wales as disordered and mismanaged was based and why Welsh individuals may have felt the need to seek justice in English courts. One of the cases often used to justify Lee's campaign against packed juries is the acquittal of Roger Morgan and his accomplices over the abduction of the widow Jane Howell from Llanwern church in the mid-1530s. For Gwynfor Jones, writing in his *Wales and the Tudor State*, the acquittal had occurred 'because the law was inadequately enforced and officers unable to secure impartial justice'.[9] It is a fascinating incident, which has attracted some scholarly attention, but its details deserve to be better known because it was not the clear-cut case Lee assumed it to be.[10]

The first version of events, and the one Lee believed, is most clearly iterated in a Star Chamber bill made by William Johns, Sir James ap Howell clerk, Sanders Gent, William Wever and Thomas Bettes.[11] They deposed that one Friday during mass Roger Morgan accompanied by James ap Morgan, Philip Morgan, and six others, all heavily armed, burst into the church of Llanwern.[12] As soon as they did so Jane ferch Howell, who was sat in the nave, ran into the chancel towards the high altar and hid behind Anthony Welshe, gentleman. Nonetheless, she was caught by Roger Morgan who took her by force and dragged her out of the church shouting to others that 'they shuld not stere but upon their perill'. His men prevented others from leaving the church or pursuing the abductor. Three witnesses located outside the church are named in the petition – Thomas Fletcher, William ap Ieuan and Agnes Llywellyn – who, after seeing Jane's abduction, raised the hue and cry.

This dramatic series of events involved several, notable local individuals: William Johns was presumably the person who became mayor of Caerleon in 1542[13] and James ap Howell was the rector of Llanwern in 1535 and may well have been one of Jane's relatives; since the 'Statute of Rapes' in 1382, the prosecution of a ravisher did not need to be by the victim because the nearest relative was given the right to sue for felony.[14] This bill, however, had not been the first attempt to convict Roger Morgan of Jane's abduction because it echoes an earlier suit, which had been brought to the assize court in Gloucester. On that occasion the plaintiff was Anthony Welshe – portrayed in the bill as the protector of Jane – and a member of the Welshe or Walshe family who held land in Llanwern and Dinham (south Wales), and in Woolstrop and Netheridge (Quedgeley, Gloucestershire). He was the son of William Welshe of Llanwern and had married a daughter of Sir Christopher Beynam of Clearwell, Newland (Gloucestershire). He would later become high sheriff of Monmouthshire in 1546–7.[15] As plaintiff and as a landholder in Quedgeley, it was probably Welshe's decision to bring the case to the Gloucester assizes rather than a court within the lordship of Caerleon where the offence had allegedly taken place.

When the case went to the assizes it was presided over by four members of the Council in the Marches of Wales, including Bishop Rowland Lee and Thomas Holte, alongside two commissioned assize judges, Edward Montagu and John Port (who was also a councillor in his own right).[16] Copies of the witness statements given to the King's Commissioners between July–October 1537 and January–27 February 1538 on behalf of Anthony Welshe appear to confirm that the abduction had taken place.[17] All testimonies recount a similar story of the events of that day. Some were hearing mass at Llanwern, others had 'chanced to be there', and several were outside but had heard the commotion. Witnesses differed only on the dress and weapons of the men, and how many names of the supposed abductors they knew.

It is a terrifying rendition, and deliberately so. Anyone acquainted with abduction narratives, or Star Chamber bills, will recognise the familiar imagery and language. Accounts of abduction were shaped by legal, statutory requirements, which plaintiffs and their counsel needed to meet in order to indicate an offence had taken place.

The most recent legislation had been issued in 1487 – the 'Acte against taking awaye of women against theire willes' – which reaffirmed that abduction was a felony and stipulated that not only those who took 'any woman against her will' were committing a crime, but so too their 'procurors, abettors and receivers'.[18] In order to elicit sympathy for the plaintiffs, both the bill and witness statements consistently present Jane as a passive victim with no active voice.[19] She is introduced in the bill as on her knees in the aisles of the nave, and one witness recounted that he had seen a woman surrounded by men 'amonges theym like as she had fallen'. That Jane ran for safety when Morgan and his accomplices entered the church usefully signalled that she was unable to fight back and her only option was to flee and seek the support of others. She is described as holding on to Thomas Bettes for safety and hiding behind Welshe for protection. Bettes himself embellished their role remarking that Morgan's men had 'manassed the said Anthony Welshe to murder hym if he should stere'. Sometimes Jane is described as crying or as crying out in order to emphasise her unwillingness to go; others are explicit in stating that she went 'ayenst her wylle'. While William Johns was not sure whether Jane had cried out 'albeit he saithe that he thought by the countyneaunce of the said Jane that she went against her will'. For its iteration as a Star Chamber bill, it was also necessary to stress the armed nature of the men and how they had prevented anyone from pursuing Jane and her abductors. Finally, it was essential to show that the hue and cry had been raised. Witnesses outside the church usefully recounted that they had heard the outcry. John Hogge stated that when the company left the church he heard 'a grete crye of women without the churche that dyd followe after the said company'. Morgan Gwiliam had been ploughing in the field when he heard a cry. He ran towards the church and a place called Milton's Mile where he saw a group of seven or eight pass by with a woman. Agnes of Llanwern, widow, said she had run out of her own house to see Jane being led away and that she had made a 'grete outcrye'.

In both the bill and witness statements, therefore, key legal points were listed to indicate that abduction had taken place. It is also possible to detect a few 'paralegal' details, observations that were not vital legal requirements, but which helped make the case more credible and persuasive. One potential example is the record of the victim's name as Jane 'verch' Howell, a formulation which most commonly signifies a maiden name (verch/ferch = daughter of): it connected her to her natal family and suggested youth and singleness. However, we know from Lee and the witnesses that Jane was a widow and her husband was called Thomas ap Howell so her Howell (or Powell) surname may well have come through marriage.[20] Was the absence of her widow status in the Star Chamber bill an attempt to emphasise maidenhood and therefore the abduction as a potentially greater violation?[21] One might also include here the comments made on the use of the Welsh language. William ap Ieuan stated that he had heard Jane cry in Welsh and Thomas Bettes recalled that Roger Morgan had said 'in Welshe tong yonder she is, go fatche her'. It was also noted in a few places that the hue and cry had been given in Welsh or 'as it was done in that country'. Fletcher, for instance, indicated that he was dwelling near the church when he heard a woman 'cry in Welsh hobobe', which is presumably the scribe's phonetic rendering of the Welsh wbwb.[22] The strength of the case did not depend on the language in which the protagonists spoke, but these references may have been included to provide authenticity in the hope of convincing a Gloucestershire jury that the actions had actually happened over the border in Wales.

Given the local importance of the men who had brought the case, the supporting witness statements, and the carefully constructed case of the abduction, one might assume that it stood a good chance of succeeding. Yet instead of the conviction Anthony Welshe had hoped for – and perhaps expected in Gloucestershire – the jury found Roger Morgan not guilty. Records of the Gloucestershire sessions do not survive, but we know the outcome because a furious Bishop Lee wrote a series of letters to Thomas Cromwell. On 28 February 1538 Lee decried how Roger Morgan on a 'case of rape', forcibly carried away 'a wedowe against her will out of a churche', and that despite the 'pregnant' evidence given at the inquest, he and his company were acquitted.[23] There has been considerable academic discussion on the interpretation of the Latin *raptus* in legal records and its potential to mean sexual assault, abduction or theft (from *rapere* = to seize). While lawmakers may have deliberately conflated rape and abduction in drawing up legislation, it appears that medieval jurors and judges were often more precise in their distinguishing of the two crimes.[24] Lee's statement shows that he is fully aware that he is dealing with an abduction case, but his use of the vernacular 'rape' shows the continual use of the term to describe abduction into the sixteenth century. This, he believed, was a vice common in Wales and he had wanted the trial to send a strong message to any other would-be abductors. He sent copies of the evidence to Cromwell, and begged that the matter be considered or else 'farewell all goode rule'.[25]

In writing to Cromwell, it is clear that Lee was not particularly concerned with the crime of abduction or its victim. What exercised Lee was the perceived failure of the local legal process and his view that the verdict could only have been reached if the jury had been packed by supporters of Roger Morgan who had chosen to commit perjury. Lee's energetic actions in the Marches had convinced him that pressure was being placed on juries by friends, families and local, influential gentry. Lee saw this as a typical problem across the borders of Wales and contrasted it with the capital: 'For assuredly in these parts juries cannot be found as with you about London.'[26] He presented the jury as lowly men who lacked experience as jurors and who had only been selected because they were servants of certain gentry families who had wanted an acquittal. He complained that when the case had come before the assize judges and the council, the sheriff was unable to find the 'honest' gentlemen who had been originally appointed to the jury. The gentlemen 'by and by absented themselves in so much we caused the sheriff to seke them in the town, but none appearance would be hadd'. They had to take 'suche as remayned'.[27] In response to their actions, Lee had bound the jury over to appear at the assizes, and in the meantime before the council in the Star Chamber upon ten days' warning. Such actions were not out of line with sixteenth-century judges who were putting increasing pressure on juries: they could order their appearance at Star Chamber and even have them imprisoned if they seemed to be acquitting defendants against overwhelmingly incriminating evidence.[28] For Lee, justice could only be guaranteed if the case was taken out of the Marches and overseen by Westminster.

Lee had instructed Port and Montagu to fine all the gentry present at the assize for disobedience, but he had his sights on one family in particular, that of Sir William Morgan of Pencoed (d.1542), the uncle of Roger Morgan.[29] Sir William's eldest sons Thomas and Giles had been at the Gloucester assizes for the whole week and were present at the acquittal having, wrote Lee, 'no other matter there to do'.[30] The family undoubtedly enjoyed a position of power in south-east Wales, and had extended its influence throughout the English Marches. Sir William held several official roles and was a key figure in local government; among his positions was the stewardship of the lordships of Usk, Caerleon and Trelleck, and the chief steward of Newport and Machen; he had also been included in the commissions of the peace for Gloucestershire, Herefordshire, Worcestershire and Shropshire, and was named in the first commission of the peace for the newly formed county of Monmouth.[31] From 1525 he was vice-chamberlain of the household of Princess Mary and the only Welshman appointed to the Council in the Marches of Wales where his main role was to ensure its authority in the area where he held his offices. As a member of the council Sir William features in several Star Chamber and Chancery bills in the early sixteenth century, and these abound with accusations by his Welsh neighbours of corrupt and impartial justice in the localities.[32] Both his sons Thomas and Giles were in royal service and connected with Cromwell, although W. R. B. Robinson noted that they attracted 'unfavourable notice' and Cromwell had concerns over Giles's behaviour.[33] Whatever their connections, Lee had the sons imprisoned in Wigmore Castle where, he wrote to Cromwell, 'I shall stay to send them up till your further pleasure be known'.

Lee had similarly little trust in a number of Gloucestershire gentry, and was particularly unhappy with Sir John Brydges of Coberley, Gloucestershire (d.1557), who was Sir William Morgan's brother-in-law and had been with his Morgan nephews all week.[34] He held various offices in the county, including that of JP for both Gloucestershire and Wiltshire from 1529 until his death. While he was not among the jury, he claimed that if he had been a judge or jury foreman he would have come to the same verdict.[35] Brydges thought that the prosecution relied on the testimony of two female witnesses (only Agnes is named) whom he dismissed as speaking from 'malice' while the other side put forward 'a goode number of honest men, which deposed contrary to the accusers which men he thought on his conscience rather spake for the justice of the matter than upon any respect'. While Brydges made no explicit comment on the reliability of female witnesses, the gendered distinction may well reflect perceived prejudices on a woman's ability to tell the truth or be more easily coerced.[36] It was not a point that influenced Lee, however, who could not understand Brydges's position and assumed he must therefore be a 'favouror' of the cause.[37]

In many ways Lee's account of the acquittal is depressingly familiar and his frustrations shared broadly with England's ruling elite. The involvement of gentry families in the abduction of women, particularly heiresses, is well attested and at least two anti-ravishment statutes, those in 1382 and 1487, appear to have been prompted by the abduction of specific landed heiresses. Eric Ives's reading of the second is markedly downbeat on the ineffectiveness of statutes in preventing the abduction of women; indeed he went so far as to comment that the legislation 'might as well not have existed' bringing forth as it did 'perjured juries, legal ingenuity and a blanket of frustration'.[38] Historical analyses of rape and abduction more generally have pointed to the inability of juries to deal effectively with rape/abduction suits and their propensity to acquit offenders.[39] Such an analysis could be extended to Wales. While Lee's claim that rape was common is impossible to assess numerically, cases are in evidence during the 1520s and 1530s, a number of which were pursued in Star Chamber. A long-running dispute between the Morgan and Herbert family, which erupted into assault and affray in Newport in 1533, resulted in the abduction of two young maidens.[40] Jurors could be and were intimidated. In 1529 Kathryn Robert petitioned Star Chamber against Owen Gruffudd whom, she claimed, had abducted her from her father's house in Neath and forced her into marriage. Within her bill is an account of her first attempt to bring Owen to book in a trial at the local town court in Neath. When the judgment should have been given, Owen's brothers and '500 persons or above' heavily armed individuals came from neighbouring lordships and surrounded the court, at which point the jury refused to proceed.[41] Justice meant pursuing her abductor to London and urging redress from the king's council.

Lee evidently believed that a full examination of the jury, with the power of Star Chamber behind it, would lead to their swift punishment. As president of the council in the Marches of Wales, Lee could have investigated the jurors himself, but by calling on the authority of the King's Council, the responsibility fell to the king's attorney John Baker to give judgment. Baker, who was Attorney General 1536–40, had himself voiced concerns about juries in the Marches and their propensity for perjury.[42] The list of interrogatories compiled to investigate the jury had been designed to tease out their experience, the influence placed upon them and the justification for their decision.[43] They were asked who had selected them; whether they were servants of Gloucestershire gentlemen; if they had come to the sessions with the intent to sit on the trial of Roger Morgan; whether anyone had tried to influence their decisions directly or indirectly; the level of their experience as jurors; what evidence they had heard that caused them to acquit Roger; and, very pointedly, whether any had thought 'in their conscience' that Jane Howell had been abducted.

The answers the jurors provided, however, relay an entirely different tale to that told by the plaintiffs and this alternative version suggests the jury had strong grounds for questioning the substance of the petition.[44] The jurors, themselves, were no ingénues. When Thomas Holte, king's attorney and prone to see corruption in the Marches, rebuked the jury for their decision,[45] he received a short reply from the foreman Thomas Marston, an experienced official.[46] None of the jurors, it is true, was of gentry stock (one described himself as a 'clothur') and a couple were in the service of local landowners; nonetheless they came from that broad range of the middling sorts of society, including those who held the position of bailiff, tax collector or coroner, that was expected by this time.[47] Their responses to the questions raised by Star Chamber illustrate Geoffrey Elton's point that juries were 'thinking men' who were not always bowing to pressure or bribery; there are notable examples of diligence in the means by which they tried to determine the nature of offences.[48]

By the sixteenth century, jurors would learn most about the case from their time in court and the evidence presented there.[49] They were less likely to come from the hundred in which the offence took place, and this is alluded to by one of the Morgan jurors who commented that he lived 50 miles from the place of the rape and that none of the jury lived within 30 or 40 miles of the incident.[50] This can also be seen as a pointed comment on why an incident occurring in Llanwern should be brought before a Gloucestershire jury. The men themselves were keen to stress that they had been appointed correctly, they had previous experience of the sessions and they knew when to be distrustful of procedural irregularities. They highlighted the suspicious witness testimonies, which had been read out from a book by a clerk of the court: witnesses 'did not tell their tale by mouth but yt was redd unto them and thereupon demaunded whether yt were true and soo affirmed yt'. The choice of witnesses was also dubious: all were reckoned servants and tenants of Welshe, and men of little reputation. One jury member said he had acquitted Morgan because there were no substantial honest men of the parish who gave evidence against him. There was a sense that the impetus behind the case had been 'rather done of malice then of trouth'. Another was sceptical about the number of eyewitnesses who had apparently been in or around the church on a Friday. As he put it 'he thinketh that any person shuld comme to the churche xxti Fridayes in the yere, he shuld not fynde all them that gave evidence in the church upon a Fridaye at one tyme, being noo holy daye'.[51]

The alternative narrative, as mediated through the jurors' testimonies, can be pieced together as follows. When Jane Howell's husband, Thomas ap Howell,[52] died she called upon the aid of Anthony Welshe because she considered him her friend, and she stayed within his house. A marriage was proposed between Jane and Roger Morgan, but the financial settlement could not be agreed. As such, Welshe decided at first that she should marry one of his servants and when Jane refused, he took matters into his own hands. He pushed his servant into Jane's room with the words 'nowe playe the man, get her if thou can', and locked the door.[53] Jane cried out in fright, which drew the attention of Welshe's wife who went to investigate what was happening. Jane informed his wife that her husband's actions were shameful, and stated that she thought that she had come to friends, but they turned out to be her foes. Welshe's wife persuaded her husband to unlock the door, but it became clear to Jane that Welshe had sold her to a local man for a certain sum of money and Welshe had already received a deposit. It was at this point that she took matters into her own hands and sent word to her friend Alice Approsser to come to her. When Alice arrived, Jane begged her to travel to Caerleon and to Roger Morgan where she was to give him a ring as a token of her intent. Alice was to say to Roger that if he loved Jane as much as she loved him, then he was to fetch her away on Friday next for she was sold to another man.[54]

In this version of events, therefore, the abduction had been a consensual act between Jane and Roger, instigated by the former. Far from wickedly stealing her away, Roger had actually come to rescue Jane; it was Anthony Welshe, her protector in the first version, who was the villain of the piece. Evidence shown and spoken at the Gloucester trial appears to verify this interpretation. One of the jury, John Seymour, stated that Alice Approsser declared openly that she bore a ring that Jane had given her for Roger. It also fits with the witness statement of Thomas Latche who had been chopping wood about a quarter of a mile from Llanwern church when he saw Alice Approsser run by with her shoes in her hands from the direction of Llanwern town and entering a wood nearby. Immediately he saw others running out of the wood, over the meadow towards the church of Llanwern, and shortly afterwards he heard a cry at the church.[55]

That it might have happened this way would not be surprising. The use of consensual abduction – or elopement – was something known to, and feared by, medieval landed society. As Caroline Dunn has pointed out, 'anxieties about elopement and seduction loom large in the ravishment legislation of later medieval England'.[56] Bills in Star Chamber, as in other courts, reveal the claims and counter-claims over marriage alliances and false abduction cases.[57] There are also examples to be found of the abducted or ravished woman appearing at a trial herself and challenging the plaintiff's case: in fifteenth-century Norfolk Jane Boys contradicted her father by stating that she had consented to go with her accused abductor.[58] Consensual abduction was used actively by women as a means to avoid marriages, to leave a marriage or ensure one took place. As the case of Jane Howell shows, women's choices about their own marriages could be significantly restricted, especially if they held an attractive inheritance or dower. When she became a widow, Jane may have believed that she would gain more choice in future partners; her bitter disappointment perhaps coming through in a juror's account that Welshe had 'cast her awaye for money'. The restrictions on marriage are also heard in John Port's recorded intervention at Gloucester when he asked whether Jane was Welshe's ward. If she had been so, selling the marriage would have been lawful.[59] How a widow could also be a ward is not explained, but it may suggest that Jane was young and potentially under age.

Yet what is essential here is not to determine which version is right, but to underline the existence of two competing and conflicting accounts. It was not simply that bills and writs were shaped to fit legal requirements, but that they were creatively written to achieve particular ends. There is now a growing body of work on the fictional and performative nature of legal texts, which is sensitive to the possibility that accounts may contain what the litigant wanted or hoped had happened as much as what actually did.[60] This performative element can be extended to the trial itself where narratives were constructed to appeal to the prejudices of judges and juries. Jane may not have appeared as a plaintiff in her own alleged abduction case, but she was determined to play a strong role in Roger Morgan's defence. Not only did she turn up to the Gloucester trial, but Jane appears to have carefully stage-managed her intervention. One of the jurors, John Seymour, recalled how after the evidence had been given to support Welshe's claims, Jane Howell, realising that nothing had been produced on her behalf, demanded of Bishop Lee what had happened to the bills she had apparently presented to him at Hereford. And 'he layeng his hand apon his brest sayed they were goone'. Jane immediately requested, on bended knee, that she be allowed to tell her story, which was granted (the reported phrase was 'saye on woman'). The jury therefore heard what Jane had to say, a visible contrast to the witnesses for Welshe whose words were read.

It will not have gone unnoticed that the tale Jane recounted has several elements of the romance story, and provides more evidence for those who advocate the intertwining of law and chivalric culture. Kathryn Gravdal's reading of medieval French literature led her to demonstrate that 'linguistic paradigms first identified in fictional texts reappear in legal documents', while McSheffrey and Pope portrayed romances as providing 'culturally available models shaping how an event is understood'.[61] By the early Tudor period in England transmission did not necessarily travel in one direction and various linguistic models were available to our protagonists when it came to (re)telling their version of events. The 'Welshe' storyline itself echoes those popular romance and legal narratives which portray a hapless victim and a dishonourable abductor. But it is more palpable in Jane's version, which has at its heart a hero rescuing her from captivity. She has reframed the story so it is one of liberation rather than defilement. There is perhaps an element of the woman longing to be rescued from an arranged marriage and her desire to be whisked away.[62] In Jane Howell's case, this fantasy may have played out in a number of ways. Sat, locked in her room in the Welshe residence, Jane's mind might have worked through various scenarios and inspired her to convince others to assist in a rescue plan that had her dramatic escape at its centre. Equally, however, she may have found herself dragged unceremoniously out of the church by brutish thugs and chose to recast those events in a way that made sense to her afterwards. Did she really run towards Welshe and Bettes for help or for dramatic effect, or were the two men pinning her down so she could not escape? She, at least, could claim a champion who had risked a trial in order to carry her away,[63] and had done so in front of others (Roger secretly taking Jane away would have served the purpose of neither side in their desire to cast him as hero or villain).[64]

In either reading, Jane's account places her at the centre of the narrative in contrast to the legal petition where she is merely the passive victim. If most Star Chamber bills on abduction can be described as 'male stories', the account of this Gloucester trial might provide an example of a female one.[65] We are accustomed to seeing women play on their helplessness and vulnerability in court cases[66] – and Jane was careful to get on one knee and petition in front of Lee at Gloucester – but here she makes her personal situation the focus of that powerlessness. Choosing to describe her own dramatic solution may also have been the best legal strategy: that the abduction was the product of a young woman's desires could be seen to fit the jury's view of how a woman would act. That she was aided and abetted by women to achieve her aims may have similarly fitted a stereotype of female whimsy. There was Alice Approsser, the female messenger and go-between so redolent of romance stories. Not only does she appear to have delivered the ring, but also led the men to the church. There was also Welshe's wife who managed to convince her husband to release Jane. They can be celebrated as active women, a supportive sisterhood, who were willing to help Jane in her hour of need. But they may also have been part of an effective legal tactic that helped increase the authenticity of Jane's account. It was not Welshe, for example, who simply changed his mind about releasing Jane, but his wife who had persuaded him to do so.

Ultimately, however Jane's story came about, and whatever the balance between accuracy, embellishment, exaggeration and fiction, what is important is that the jury found it convincing. The jurors were all clear in their consciences that it was right to free Roger, not as Rowland Lee instinctively believed because this is what Welshmen do and how jurors in the Welsh Marches react, but because they were suspicious of the case and sided with Jane's understanding of fairness, acceptable behaviour and the law.

What can a detailed exploration of this cross-border abduction case tell us about relations between Wales and its largest neighbour in the early Tudor period? First, while Wales may well have needed legal reform, the evidence used to support the prevailing view is problematic, and more complex than previous commentators have supposed. There is no reason to assume that rape was more common in Wales or that the country was necessarily worse than other parts of the kingdom in terms of judicial process; certainly Star Chamber bills can provide evidence of unwelcome acquittals, local influence and prejudicial juries from around England. Nevertheless, for Cromwell and his faithful servant Lee, Wales was a problem that became one of (inter)national security in the years following Henry VIII's divorce. Lee needed the Morgan/Howell case for his own purposes, and he was adept at deploying rhetoric to this end: he is known to exaggerate the problems of the Welsh border in order to underline why the Council in the Marches of Wales needed to exist and why he was essential for the success of good government.[67] The Welsh people, therefore, needed to be brought fully into England's legal system, and juries from the Marches were subjected to the authority of Star Chamber.

Nevertheless, while Morgan's guilt is more questionable than Lee believed, it cannot be ignored that the case itself uncovered claims of witness manipulation, and that the suit was initially heard in Gloucester, a fair distance away from the royal lordship of Caerleon. One could explain it on the grounds that Welshe held lands in this area and point to the strong familial and business interconnections between south Wales and the English counties on the western March. Past kin and current marriages linked the families of Morgan, Howell, Welshe, Bridges and Beynam, among others, blurring distinctions of a 'Welsh' or 'English' identity in these areas; travel through this border region for trade and labour was frequent.[68] Yet, for Welshe, the choice of court must have offered greater potential for victory as the Gloucestershire jurors would have little knowledge of the Llanwern area. He perhaps had not counted on Jane Howell herself travelling to Hereford and then Gloucester in her own pursuit for justice.

Through his actions Welshe was adopting a common tactic, and by the early sixteenth century Welsh people, as elsewhere, were accustomed to choosing among the various jurisdictions the court(s) that suited their claims the best. During this article several examples have been mentioned of Welsh men and women taking their suits to Star Chamber and evidence indicates that these were becoming more frequent in the reign of Henry VIII.[69] Among these cases can be found examples of plaintiffs themselves blaming corruption, inadequate legal knowledge and process in the localities as part of their strategy for getting their suits heard. Katherine ferch David of Llandaff who petitioned Star Chamber when the murderers of her husband were acquitted, complained that the jury at Cardiff was packed, and condemned the bailiffs of Cardiff as ignorant and not learned in the law. The 'scarcytie of lerned men in thos parties in Wales' was a reason offered in another suit for it being taken to Star Chamber.[70] The argument that the Westminster courts could offer more impartial justice is also evident in a number of cases. It was clearly a trope not confined to Welsh suits, but it was a plea felt to ring true. When in the late 1520s, the president of the Council in the Marches of Wales received several complaints following the decision to direct all undecided cases in Star Chamber from parties in the Marches back to the council, the focus was on the 'indifferent justice' offered by the King's Council.[71]

Within these real and imagined legal contexts, therefore, it is understandable how local life events could be read in ways that confirmed the worst prejudices of those set on seeing the worst of Wales. We do not know Jane Howell's real story, although in any reading she is both a victim of the machinations of local gentlemen and a determined survivor. Yet this multivalent case of marital choice and misfortune could be conveniently shaped to fit the reforming agenda of Wales's legal union with England.

Notes

[1] TNA, SP 1/129, fo. 124.
[2] D. Lleufer Thomas, 'Further Notes on the Court of the Marches with Original Documents', *Y Cymmrodor*, 13 (1899), 159.
[3] Penry Williams, *The Council in the Marches of Wales under Elizabeth* (Cardiff: University of Wales Press, 1958), p. 13; C. A. J. Skeel, *The Council in the Marches of Wales* (London: Hugh Rees, 1904), particularly pp. 49–57.
[4] 26 Henry VIII, c.4; Ivor Bowen (ed.), *The Statutes of Wales* (London: T. Fisher Unwin, 1908), p. 51.
[5] 26 Henry VIII, c. 6; Bowen, *The Statutes of Wales*, p. 54.
[6] *Letters and Papers, Foreign and Domestic, Henry VIII*, v, ed. James Gairdner (London: HMSO, 1880), henceforth *LP*, p. 991; Glanmor Williams, *Renewal and Reformation: Wales, c.1415–1642* (Oxford: Oxford University Press, 1993), p. 258. See too the comments by Thomas Croft who supplied Thomas Cromwell with a steady stream of information on government in the Marches, generally with one eye closely on the dispersal of the recently dissolved monastic estates: *LP*, vi, ed. James Gairdner (London: HMSO, 1882), pp. 210, 946; S. T. Bindoff, *The House of Commons, 1509–1558*, 3 vols (London: Secker and Warburg, 1982), i, pp. 725–6.
[7] M. A. Jones, 'Cultural Boundaries within the Tudor State: Bishop Rowland Lee and the Welsh Settlement of 1536', *WHR*, 20.2 (2000), 234; Michael Jones, 'Lee, Rowland (*c.*1487–1543)', *Oxford Dictionary of National Biography* (2004), online at *www.oxforddnb.com/view/article/16307* (accessed 20 August 2016).
[8] E.g. T. B. Pugh (ed.), *Glamorgan County History, vol. III* (Cardiff: University of Wales Press, 1971), p. 563.
[9] J. Gwynfor Jones, *Wales and the Tudor State: Government, Religious Change and the Social Order, 1534–1603* (Cardiff: University of Wales Press, 1989), pp. 1–2.

[10] It is discussed in M. A. Jones, '"An earthly beast, a mole and an enemy to all godly learning": the life and career of Rowland Lee, Bishop of Coventry and Lichfield and Lord President of the Council in the Marches of Wales, c.1487–1543' (unpublished MPhil thesis, Cardiff University, 1997). The case is also briefly outlined in Geoffrey Elton, *Policy and Police: the Enforcement of the Reformation in the Age of Thomas Cromwell* (Cambridge: Cambridge University Press, 1985), pp. 312–13.

[11] TNA, STAC 2/20/223.

[12] For Llanwern church, which was completely rebuilt in fifteenth-century perpendicular, see Madeleine Gray, 'The pre-reformation church', in R. A. Griffiths (ed.), *The Gwent County History, vol. 2: The Age of the Marcher Lords* (Cardiff: University of Wales Press, 2008), p. 337.

[13] TNA, STAC 2/8/8; STAC 2/34/8.

[14] Joseph Bradney, *A History of Monmouthshire from the coming of the Normans into Wales down to the present time*, 5 vols (London: Mitchell Hughes and Clarke: 1904–23), iv, p. 256; J. B. Post, 'Sir Thomas West and the Statute of Rapes, 1382', *Bulletin of the Institute of Historical Research*, 53 (1980), 24–30.

[15] The history of the Welshe family is not easy to piece together although Anthony's father, William, was embroiled in a number of suits in the 1520s: TNA, REQ 2/5/59; REQ 2/10/69; his inquisition post-mortem is TNA, C 142/60/23. Anthony's wife is sometimes listed in genealogies as Catrin, but she is clearly named 'Margaret' in mid-sixteenth-century Llanwern deeds: Gwent Archives D43/3739, 3740 and 3987. For some sense of the family, see C. R. Elrington and N. M. Herbert (eds), *The Victoria History of the County of Gloucestershire* (Oxford: Oxford University Press, 1972), x, pp. 218–19.

[16] J. H. Baker, 'Montagu, Sir Edward (1480s–1557)', *Oxford Dictionary of National Biography* (2004), online at *www.oxforddnb.com/view/article/19006* (accessed 21 August 2016); J. H. Baker, 'Port, Sir John (c.1472–1540)', *Oxford Dictionary of National Biography* (2004), online at *www.oxforddnb.com/view/article/22552* (accessed 21 August 2016).

[17] The witness testimonies were taken at the following times and places; the given age of each witness is in parenthesis. Bishopsgate, 5 July 1537: William Jones of the parish of Llanwern (48); Sir James ap Howell, parson of Llanwern (34); John Hogge of Biston (34); Thomas Fletcher of Christchurch (30); William ap Ieuan of Christchurch (40); Morgan Gwilliam of Caerleon (25). Shrewsbury, 9 October 1537: Sander Gent of Wiston (31); William Terner (30). Bridgnorth, 23 January 1538: Agnes of Llanwern, widow (47). Gloucester, 27 February

1538: Thomas Bettes of Llanwern (24), Thomas Latche of Biston (26): TNA, SP 1/129, fos. 124–32.

[18] E. W. Ives, '"Agaynst taking awaye of women": the inception and operation of the abduction act of 1487', in E. W. Ives, R. J. Knecht and J. J. Scarisbrick (eds), *Wealth and Power in Tudor England: essays presented to S. T. Bindoff* (London: Athlone Press, 1978), pp. 25–6.

[19] This was not unusual because rape and abduction victims infrequently appear as plaintiffs in their own cases at Star Chamber. For a discussion of the conventions of narrative rape and abduction accounts in legal records, see Garthine Walker, 'Rereading Rape and Sexual Violence in Early Modern England', *Gender and History*, 10.1 (1998), 1–25, particularly 5–11; and Garthine Walker, '"A strange kind of stealing": abduction in early modern Wales', in Simone Clarke and Michael Roberts (eds), *Women and Gender in Early Modern Wales* (Cardiff: University of Wales Press, 2000), p. 64.

[20] In the juries' testimonies Jane is often called Jane ap Howell. There are contemporary examples of ap Howell (or Appowell) being adopted as a family name, and the prefix 'ap' (usually son of) being used as part of a woman's name. For example: Susan ap Howell, daughter of John ap Howell (TNA, C1/1346/23-24) and Margaret ap Gwillim, widow, who wrote her will in 1550 (TNA, PROB 11/38/16).

[21] For a reading of the use of 'filia' in relation to the case of Jane Boys, which connected her to her parents even though Boys was a widow, see Shannon McSheffrey and Julia Pope, 'Ravishment, Legal Narratives and Chivalric Culture in Fifteenth-Century England', *Journal of British Studies*, 48.4 (2009), 827.

[22] In the Star Chamber petition it is rendered *oob oobe* (STAC 2/20/223). Similar to hubbub, this would appear to be an early recording of wbwb, which is found elsewhere in the sixteenth century, but is more frequently seen in nineteenth-century texts on the hue and cry. For the Welsh hue and cry, see Helen Fulton, 'Fairs, feast-days and carnival in Medieval Wales: some poetic evidence', in Helen Fulton (ed.), *Urban Culture in Medieval Wales* (Cardiff: UWP, 2012), pp. 238–44. For derivations and dated examples of wbwb: see the *Geiriadur Prifysgol Cymru*: http://welsh-dictionary.ac.uk/gpc/gpc.html.

[23] TNA, SP 1/129, fo. 124.

[24] For a recent, detailed account of the legal definitions of raptus/rape, see Caroline Dunn, *Stolen Women in Medieval England. Rape, Abduction and Adultery, 1100–1500* (Cambridge: Cambridge University Press, 2013), chapter 1.

[25] TNA, SP 1/129, fo. 124.

[26] TNA, SP1/97, fo. 94; *LP*, ix, ed. James Gairdner (London: HMSO, 1886), p. 510.

[27] TNA, SP 1/130, fo. 63r.

[28] Thomas Andrew Green, *Verdict According to Conscience: Perspectives on the English Criminal Trial Jury, 1200–1800* (Chicago: University of Chicago Press, 1985), p. 106.

[29] Roger was son of John Morgan of Caerleon esq and his second wife Janet (daughter of David ap Morgan Rhys): Bradney, *Monmouthshire*, iii, pp. 263–4. Bartrum suggests that the three sons John had with her – the Roger, James and Philip mentioned in the Star Chamber bill – were all illegitimate: Peter C. Bartrum, *Welsh Genealogies, AD 1400–1500*, 18 vols (Aberystwyth: National Library of Wales, 1983), iii, p. 395.

[30] TNA, SP 1/130, fo. 63v.

[31] A full account of Sir William and his family can be found in W. R. B. Robinson, 'Sir William Morgan of Pencoed (d.1542) and the Morgans of Tredegar and Machen in Henry VIII's Reign', *National Library of Wales Journal*, 27.4 (1992), 405–29.

[32] These cases include: TNA C1/693/32 and C1/734/33; STAC 2/15/164-166, STAC 2/15/328, STAC 2/32/52 and STAC 2/32/54. On the other hand, Glanmor Williams saw Sir William as a hard-working official who, as a commissioner for the diocese of Llandaff during the dissolution of the monasteries, compiled the 'best returns we have for any part of Wales': Glanmor Williams, 'The Dissolution of the Monasteries in Glamorgan', *WHR*, 3 (1966), 25–6.

[33] Robinson, 'Sir William Morgan', 417. For the political careers of Thomas and Giles, see Bindoff, *House of Commons*, ii, pp. 627, 630; both were MPs in 1547.

[34] William Morgan was married to Florence, the daughter of Sir Giles Brydges of Coberley (d.1511) and sister to Sir John. For an account of the latter's lengthy service, which saw him raised to the peerage as Lord Chandos of Sudeley in 1554, see M. M. Norris, 'Brydges, John, first Baron Chandos (1492–1557) *Oxford Dictionary of National Biography* (2004), online at *www.oxforddnb.com/view/article/3807* (accessed 21 August 2016).

[35] TNA, SP1/131, fo. 137.

[36] For discussion on women as witnesses, see, e.g. Elisabeth van Houts, 'Gender and Authority in Oral Witnesses in Europe (800–1300)', *Transactions of the Royal Historical Society*, 6th ser., 9 (1999), 201–20; Sandy Bardsley, *Women's Roles in the Middle Ages* (Westport, CT: Greenwood Press, 2007), pp. 134–6.

'A vice common in Wales'

[37] TNA, SP1/131, fo. 137.
[38] Ives, 'Agaynst taking awaye of women', p. 40.
[39] E.g. John Bellamy, *The Criminal Trial in Later Medieval England* (Toronto: University of Toronto Press, 1998), p. 173; Gwen Seabourne, *Imprisoning Medieval Women: the Non-Judicial Confinement and Abduction of Women in England, c. 1170–1509* (Farnham: Ashgate, 2011), p. 159.
[40] TNA, STAC 2/25/16; STAC 2/34/18.
[41] TNA, STAC 2/26/105. The case is discussed in Deborah Youngs, '"She hym fresshely folowed and pursued": women and Star Chamber in early Tudor Wales', in Bronach Kane and Fiona Williamson (eds), *Women, Agency and the Law, 1300–1700* (London: Pickering and Chatto, 2013), pp. 73–85.
[42] J. D. Alsop, 'Baker, Sir John (*c.*1489–1558)', *Oxford Dictionary of National Biography* (2004), online at www.oxforddnb.com/view/article/1124 (accessed 21 August 2016).
[43] TNA, STAC 2/26/394
[44] TNA, STAC 2/24/34.
[45] Thomas Holte (d.1546) was educated at the Middle Temple, served as JP in several counties and was attorney for the Council in the Marches of Wales by 1534 (and until 1541). He had also served on a commission of inquiry into extortions and misdemeanours in the Marches of Wales which had reported early in 1533. Bindoff, *House of Commons*, II, pp. 381–2; TNA, E 163/11/34.
[46] He may have been the bailiff of Hinton and keeper of Whiteclifff Park in 1495–6: *Descriptive Catalogue of the Charters and Muniments in the Possession of Lord Fitzhardinge at Berkeley Castle*, ed. I. H. Jeayes (Bristol: C. T. Jefferies and Sons, 1892), p. 280.
[47] J. B. Post, 'Jury lists and juries in the later fourteenth century', in J. S. Cockburn and Thomas A. Green (eds), *Twelve Good Men and True: the Criminal Trial Jury in England, 1200–1800* (Princeton: Princeton University Press, 2014), p. 68; Edward Powell, 'Jury trial at gaol delivery in the late middle ages: the Midland circuit, 1400–1429', in Cockburn and Green (eds), *Twelve Good Men*, pp. 90–2.
[48] Elton, *Policy and Police*, p. 312; Sara M. Butler, *Divorce in Medieval England: from One Persons to Two in Law* (New York: Routledge, 2013), p. 68.
[49] Powell, 'Jury trial', pp. 78–116.
[50] Given that the case went to the Gloucestershire assizes, it is not surprising that the jurors were from that area. In recounting who had called them to the jury, they listed constables and bailiffs from Berkeley, Thornbury, Henbury, Haresfield, Grumbalds Ash and Whitstone (where part of Quedgely is situated).

51   TNA, STAC 2/24/34, fos. 1v, 2v, 3v and 5r.
52   It is possible that this Jane Howell is one and the same with the widow who petitioned Star Chamber concerning the murder of her husband Thomas ap Howell, who had been slain in the lordship of Ogmore: TNA, STAC 2/21/114. Another potential candidate for Thomas is the individual from Magor who was heavily involved in the dispute between the Herbert and Morgan families, which erupted in Newport in 1533: *LP*, x, ed. James Gairdner (London: HMSO, 1887), p. 91. Unfortunately, without a firm identification of Jane Howell, her wealth, connections and attractiveness as a marriage partner remain undetermined.
53   One of the jury declared this suitor to be Thomas Bettes, one of the men who had given evidence against Roger Morgan: TNA, STAC 10/4/82, f.1.
54   The main account of this narrative comes in the statement of the juror John Seymour who interestingly related Jane's words in the first person as she gave them in court: TNA, STAC 2/24/34.
55   TNA, STAC 2/24/34.
56   Dunn, *Stolen Women*, p. 98; a fuller treatment of elopement can be found in chapter 4 of Dunn's monograph.
57   E.g. TNA, STAC 2/10/54–5 and 186–7.
58   McSheffrey and Pope, 'Ravishment', 823.
59   See also Walker, 'A strange kind', p. 55, where a high proportion of alleged abduction cases for the purposes of forced marriages were of wards.
60   Examples include: Tim Stretton, *Women Waging Law in Elizabethan England* (Cambridge: Cambridge University Press, 1998), chapter 8; Shannon McSheffrey, 'Detective Fiction in the Archives: Court Records and the Uses of the Law in Late Medieval England', *History Workshop Journal*, 65 (2008), 65–78; Jeremy Goldberg, *Communal Discord, Child Abduction and Rape in the Later Middle Ages* (Basingstoke: Palgrave, 2008), particularly pp. 37–8.
61   Kathryn Gravdal, *Ravishing Maidens: Writing Rape in Medieval French Literature and Law* (Philadelphia: University of Pennsylvania Press, 1991), p. 140; McSheffrey and Pope, 'Ravishment', 834.
62   McSheffrey and Pope, 'Ravishment', 833.
63   Unfortunately we do not know what happened afterwards. According to surviving genealogies, Roger married Jenet, daughter and heir to James Adams of the Garn (Tredunnock) from whom the Morgan family of the Garn descended: Bradney, *Monmouthshire*, iii, p. 263. Potentially Jenet could be Jane, but there appears to be no surviving

records of James Adams or his family to indicate either way.
[64] Gravdal, *Ravishing Maidens*, p. 67; McSheffrey and Pope, 'Ravishment', 835.
[65] Walker, 'A strange kind', p. 51.
[66] Stretton, *Women Waging Law*, pp. 180, 212.
[67] Jones, 'Cultural Boundaries', 253.
[68] E.g. Ralph A. Griffiths, 'After Glyn Dŵr: an Age of Reconciliation?', *Proceedings of the British Academy*, 117 (2002), 139–64.
[69] Some indication of this increase can be found in Ifan ab Owen Edwards, *A Catalogue of Star Chamber Proceedings relating to Wales* (Cardiff: University Press Board, 1929); H. A. Lloyd, 'Wales and Star Chamber', *WHR*, 5 (1971), 257–60; and comments in Tim Thornton, *Cheshire and the Tudor State, 1480–1560* (Woodbridge: Boydell, 2000), pp. 109–14.
[70] TNA, STAC 2/32/23; STAC 3/3/73.
[71] National Library of Wales, MS 6620D.

PART II:

WALES, EUROPE AND THE WORLD

5

Welsh pilgrims and crusaders in the Middle Ages

Kathryn Hurlock

Pilgrimage and crusading were two aspects of the same impulse: to undertake a religious journey in the hope of spiritual reward, one of which was peaceable, the other undertaken with the specific aim of engaging in military activity against enemies of the Church, primarily in the Holy Land.[1] They were two of the most popular religious movements in the Middle Ages, and the Welsh were very much part of these pan-European phenomena. Although pilgrimage vows could be, and were, fulfilled in a more local or domestic context, for many people, overseas pilgrimage tended to gain the greatest spiritual reward, and so many pilgrims were willing to brave the dangers of a lengthy overseas journey to places like Jerusalem, Rome and Santiago de Compostela. Crusading to the Holy Land, too, had a particular cachet as crusaders were able to fulfil their vows whilst visiting the holiest sites of Christendom. Jerusalem was the primary destination of crusaders who sought to win back – and then defend – the holy sites of the east for Christians. Much has been said on what motivated people to engage in both activities across Europe, and more specifically from Wales,[2] but less is known on the impact that pilgrimage and crusading, which took people beyond the bounds of Wales, had on Wales, within Wales, and on the Welsh, and what impact the Welsh may have had in the places they went. This chapter will address these impacts by considering the role of international religious travel in the exchange of knowledge, ideas, interests and activities from the eleventh to the early sixteenth century.

Pilgrimage

The premier pilgrimage destination for Christians was the Holy City of Jerusalem, sites of Jesus' crucifixion and ascension to heaven. It was hugely popular throughout the Middle Ages despite problems over access and the dangers of the journey to reach it. Jerusalem pilgrimage from Wales had a long if poorly documented history. Models for pilgrimage to Jerusalem featured in various Welsh saints' *Lives* such as that of St David, and of that of St Padarn, written in the twelfth century and more reflective of the interests of that time than of the sixth century when Padarn probably lived.[3] In a similar vein, in some accounts of her life, St Winifred, the Welsh saint whose healing well at Holywell in Flintshire was one of the major pilgrimage destinations of Wales, was said to have gone on pilgrimage to Rome.[4] In the twelfth century, following the conquest of Jerusalem by the First Crusaders in 1099, pilgrimage and crusading to the City of Jerusalem were sometimes indistinguishable, though at times the aims of travellers are clearly identified. In 1128, for example, Morgan ap Cadwgan went on crusade in remorse for having killed his brother.[5] Some pilgrims or crusaders sailed to the Holy Land in 1144, drowning in the Mediterranean, and a substantial number joined the Third Crusade (1189–92) of Richard I.[6] In the following century, important figures like Ednyfed Fychan (seneschal of Llywelyn ap Iorwerth) and Llywelyn ap Gruffydd either planned to go, or did go, to Jerusalem for military and spiritual reasons. After the loss of Acre in 1291 Welsh interest in the long-distance journey to Jerusalem tailed off, arguably because of the combination of the loss of Welsh independence in 1282 and the re-focusing of crusade fighting on less traditional areas. At the close of the Middle Ages, however, there was a flurry of renewed interest as several prominent Welshmen, largely drawn from the gentry class of south Wales, set out for the Holy City once more.

Roman pilgrimage was also popular in the earlier Middle Ages when early pilgrims travelled to see the home of their popes, and the relics of the early martyrs. Over time the stock of relics was added to so that Rome boasted a vast array of spiritual delights, many of which could be visited on a circuit of the city by the committed pilgrim. One such early traveller was Cyngen, king of Powys, who went to Rome to die in 856; others were Hywel Dda (d.950), king of Deheubarth, who went to Rome in 928/9, and Joseph, bishop of Morgannwg, who went in 1045.[7] The story that Cadwallader, last king of the Britons, had undertaken a Roman pilgrimage in 682 and died in Rome was popularised by Geoffrey of Monmouth in the early twelfth century and reinforced in the early modern period with its inclusion in David Powell's 1584 *Historie of Cambria*.[8] Cadell ap Gruffydd, ruler of Deheubarth, undertook this pilgrimage in *c*.1153 and, given his status, it is entirely likely that he was accompanied by other Welshmen.[9] In the twelfth century, Gerald of Wales claimed that 'Of all pilgrimages they [the Welsh] prefer going to Rome, and when they reach St Peter's they pray most devoutly.'[10]

Of the three major international pilgrimage destinations, Santiago de Compostela on the western tip of Spain was the least popular among the Welsh, and interest in going there does not appear to have taken off until the mid-fourteenth century. There was already trade between Wales and the ports of the Bay of Biscay which meant that there were existing transport routes which pilgrims to Spain could take advantage of.[11] In 1361, three men departed from Welshpool for Santiago.[12] In the same period the poet Gruffudd Gryg (*fl.* 1340–80) wrote about his experience on the journey.[13] The small flurry of interest in this destination could have been because of the problems with reaching alternatives – the Holy Land had been lost by the Christians in the previous century and the city of Rome, missing the pope who was residing in Avignon by this time, had been allowed to fall into decay and 'shriveled [*sic*] like a severed branch'.[14] After the restoration of the papacy in the 1370s and the institution of a succession of jubilee years, an idea that had begun in 1300 but then fallen into abeyance, Roman pilgrimage was revived and began to appear more frequently in the Welsh sources.[15]

Although interest in the crusades waned significantly after the loss of Acre in 1291, overseas pilgrimage from Wales remained popular throughout the Middle Ages, and in the decades before the

Reformation it showed no signs of diminishing. In 1490, for example, Thomas Kenny of Llandaff requested in his will that John Gough undertaken a pilgrimage to Rome, and in *c.*1516, Miles Salley, the bishop of Llandaff, bequeathed ten pounds in his will so that someone could undertake a pilgrimage on his behalf to Santiago de Compostela and the Virgin of Gaudalupe in Castile.[16] Salley also wanted his heart and bowels to be buried before the image of St Theodoric in Mathern Church.[17]

Crusade

One of the most obvious contributions of Welsh crusaders overseas was, unsurprisingly, a military one. At the time of the First Crusade, the lord of Thouars in Poitou led a contingent made up of fighters from the British Isles; given that it is unlikely that they were drawn from his tenantry, but were perhaps recruited from lands that the lord of Thouars had links with, such as those on the Welsh border in Monmouthshire, some of these men could have been professional mercenaries.[18] Their reputation as fighters was well known even before there was significant crusading activity from Wales: Manuel Comnenus, emperor of Constantinople (r. 1143–80), was allegedly told by Henry II: 'there is a race of people called the Welsh who are so brave and untamed that, though unarmed themselves, they do not hesitate to do battle'.[19] If Gerald of Wales was giving us a true account of Henry's view of the Welsh, then this may have been a strong factor in influencing the decision to recruit heavily from Wales in 1188, the year in which Baldwin of Forde, archbishop of Canterbury, undertook a six-week preaching tour of Wales and the Welsh March in order to recruit men for Henry and the projected Third Crusade.

The Welshmen recruited for this Third Crusade were the first to make a real military contribution in the east. How many set out from Wales is open to debate – Gerald of Wales tells us 3,000 men signed up for the crusade, but delays among the leadership led numbers to drop off – but whatever the actual figure there were enough of them to find their way into some of the records of the Third Crusade.[20] At the Siege of Acre (1189–91), a Welsh archer engaged in an archery test with a Turkish archer.[21] According to one account:

> A Turk came out to shoot upon us and did not want to turn his back and a Welshman under provocation went out to fire in return. The Welshman was called Marcaduc and was not the son of a lord nor a duke. The Turk was called Grair; he was bold, strong, and seemed powerful. They immediately shot upon one another, the Welshman aiming at the Turk, the Turk at the Welshman. The Turk began to ask the Welshman where he came from, which country. The Welshman replied 'I am from Wales. It is mad of you to come down [here].' The Turk said 'You know how to shoot well. Would you like to play a game? I will shoot and you will stand still, not turning in any direction, and if I miss, I will stand still for you, not turning in any direction.' He said this so insistently and beseeched him to that the Welshman agreed. He drew against the Welshmen and missed, for he misfired. The Welshmen said, 'Now I will shoot. Stand still for me.' [But] he said, 'No, let me draw again and I will let you draw twice.' 'Certainly', said the Welshman. But while he (the Turk) was searching for a bolt in his quiver the Welshman, who was near to him and who did not like these terms, fired, and shot him in the head. Then he said, 'You did not keep your agreement with me, nor shall I with you, in the name of Saint Denis.'[22]

There has been some discussion about the veracity of this account, but whether or not it actually happened it is pertinent that the writer chose – out of an army drawn from a wide swathe of Europe's crusaders – to identify this archer as a Welshman. The archery skills of the Welsh were famed in the twelfth century, and the audience of Ambroise's tale would probably have been familiar with examples of Welsh prowess at archery, such as those recounted by Gerald of Wales.[23]

Throughout the thirteenth century Welsh combatants made contributions to all of the major crusade campaigns though in small numbers, and their activities on crusade are not recorded. In the fourteenth century, participation (or at least the identification of participants) all but disappears, perhaps because they were occupied fighting in the English army in France after the start of the Hundred Years War in 1337. Sir John Garin from the diocese of St Asaph enthusiastically set off for the crusades in the early 1340s, 'burning with zealous devotion': what he actually achieved is not known, but such keenness to fight could have translated into something positive for the crusade cause.[24] He is an almost isolated case. In the following century, Sir Hugh Johnnys of Landimore fought, perhaps as a mercenary, in the army of John VIII, emperor of Constantinople (r. 1416–48). According to his now-lost memorial brass,

> Sir Hugh was made Knight at the Holy Sepulchre of Oure Lord Jhesu Crist in the city of Jerusalem the xiii day of August in the yere of oure Lord Gode Mccccxlj. And the said Sir Hugh had contynuyd in the werris their long tyme byfore by the space of five yeres, that is to sey ageynst the Turkis and Sarsyns in the partis of Troy, Grecie and Turky under John, that tyme Emprowre of Constantyneople.[25]

Although there was not necessarily a spiritual element to this conflict, Sir John did receive knighthood in Jerusalem to become a Knight of the Holy Sepulchre, an order linked with late medieval crusading activity.[26]

The reasons for the comparatively limited Welsh participation in the crusade are several. The crusades appear to have been associated with English dominance in Wales, exemplified no better than when Archbishop John Pecham proposed that Dafydd ap Gruffydd go on crusade at Edward I's expense as a way of removing him from the Anglo-Welsh wars that resulted in the final conquest of Wales. Dafydd, perfectly aware that this was Pecham's intention, told him that he would go on crusade 'after taking a vow for God, and not for men'.[27] The Welsh had already seemed reluctant to support what was perceived as an English venture, and Welsh chroniclers were suspicious of the way in which King John took the Cross during his dispute with his barons in order to gain privilege and protection.[28]

Impact and exchange

The impact of these crusaders was not confined to military matters, as their overseas travel was also a means of transmitting and exchanging information with those they encountered. One crusader who probably took part in the Fifth Crusade (c.1219–22), for example, spread the fame of St David whilst he was in the Holy Land. During the course of his journey, he was taken captive by the Saracens. He was freed from captivity after crying 'Dewi wared' (David deliver me), appealing to the premier saint of Wales for assistance. His German cellmate, who spoke no Welsh, used the same words to gain his liberty without comprehending them, and afterwards learning of their significance went on pilgrimage to St David's where he confirmed the accuracy of this story for Bishop Iorwerth (1215–29).[29] Thus an event on crusade brought a German to the western tip of Wales, where his story was written down and no doubt used as evidence of the efficacy of appealing to St David and, by association, the benefits of pilgrimage to St David's itself.

Exchange naturally works both ways, and both crusaders and pilgrims were active in bringing information about the places they visited back to Wales, stimulating interest in the sites of the Holy Land, Santiago and Rome, and telling people of the routes taken to their various destinations. Some of the information on the crusades, for example, that found its way into the native Welsh chronicles probably came, directly or indirectly, from returning crusaders who knew about events in the Holy Land and in the countries they passed through en route. The Fifth Crusade in particular, when a large contingent went from Cheshire at a time when relations between Cheshire and the court of Gwynedd were amicable, is well represented in the sources, perhaps because of first-hand knowledge that was then conveyed to the scribe of the source material for the *Brut y Tywysogyon* or *Brenhinedd y Saesson*.[30] Overall, the chronicles written in the parts of Wales that were conquered by the Anglo-Normans in the late eleventh and early twelfth centuries, such as the *Margam Annals*, although shorter, contained a broader range of information on aspects of crusading history, which was in part a reflection of their location in areas that provided a greater number of crusaders.[31]

The more widespread travel engendered by crusading and pilgrimage arguably helped to promote interest in the world beyond Wales, both for the practical reason of knowing more about places people intended to visit, and for the intellectual stimulation that such works could provide. Transmission of information in this way was not the only way in which information came to Wales, of course, but it contributed to the information coming via other international routes, such as those fostered by trade or monastic and ecclesiastical networks, and added to the rise of manuscript transmission and translation into Welsh after the conquest of 1282 which worked to make Wales 'a region with close links to Europe, both cultural and political'.[32] *Delw y Byd* ('The form of the world'), a translation of part of the twelfth-century *Imago Mundi* of Honorious of Autun, was undertaken in at least three separate Welsh versions from the mid-thirteenth century onwards, though it was a work known in Wales before that time.[33] One version was undertaken by a scribe who may have been based at Aberconwy abbey in north Wales.[34] Motifs relating to the crusading romance cycle appeared in some of the poetry of thirteenth-century Gwynedd, where Prydydd y Moch alluded to Roland's horn when describing how his own work praised Llywelyn ap Iorwerth.[35] The Charlemagne tales themselves were translated so that they were accessible to, and suitable for, a Welsh audience. The *Song of Roland* was rendered into Welsh as *Cân Rolant* in c.1220, the *History of Charlemagne* and *Gests of Charlemagne* were translated and the *Pseudo-Turpin* was completed between 1265 and 1283.[36] In all, variant stories of the Charlemagne tales – the *Rhamant Otuel* and *Pererindod Siarlymaen*, survive in about ten manuscripts from the fourteenth and fifteenth centuries.[37] These tales took as theme conflict between Saracens and Christians. Whist the direct impetus for translation came from a variety of individuals, across Europe the general interest for vernacular works of this kind was underpinned by interest in crusading.[38] Although not directly about the crusading movement, the audience for these works would have been exposed to arguments about holy war, conflict with Muslims, and Jerusalem and the Holy Land.

Crusading imagery was also manifest in artistic productions in Wales, such as in the tiles made for the Cistercian abbeys of Neath and Tintern. The artistic exchange and influences on Welsh literature and art tailed off in the last centuries of the Middle Ages, perhaps because of the diversification of crusading activity in the wake of the loss of the Holy Land (as the Welsh showed interest in this to the exclusion of all other crusades), and because of the conquest of Wales by Edward I in 1282. The few late references to the crusades in artistic works, for example, are confined to works like the memorial brass of Sir Hugh Johnys, which references his fighting in the eastern Mediterranean, and the sixteenth-century memorial paintings to the Stradling family of St Donat's in Glamorgan that record the journey of some members to the Holy Land where they allegedly became Knights of the Holy Sepulchre: William Stradling (d.c.1407) did so,[39] as did a descendant Sir Edward (who died in Jerusalem in 1453) and Sir Edward's son Henry, who travelled to the Holy Land via Rome and Venice and died on the return leg on the island of Cyprus.[40]

The exchange of information engendered by returning pilgrims was much more widespread, in terms of geography, chronology and source type. Primarily, information about overseas pilgrimage was spread through poetry that was composed and reformed for the more high status houses of Wales. Some of this information focused on the journey that needed to be made to reach Rome or Santiago, or the route this took, or the dangers that pilgrims faced. Information on the sea journey to Santiago de Compostela appears in several poems: Robin Ddu, for example, described the 'wooden-chest of pilgrims' that he sailed there in,[41] and Gruffydd Gryg (*fl.* 1340–80) of Anglesey sang about his experience, recounting how his boat was almost shipwrecked.[42] When Lewis Glyn Cothi composed a poem about a Santiago-bound pilgrim called Gruffudd, he did so as a prayer being offered by the pilgrim's wife, Anne, for his safe return:

> Annes [*sic*] desires
> To bring him [Gruffudd] from sea to land.
> Hywel's daughter, she called upon St Elian
> And upon the saints the blessed cross.[43]

Information on pilgrimage routes was recorded and disseminated throughout the Middle Ages by Welshmen who went to Rome. Two of the most famous writers from Wales, Gerald of Wales (*c.*1146–1223) and Adam of Usk (*c.*1352–1430), both went to Rome and furnished detailed accounts of the routes they took: in Gerald's case he went four times, the last being a true pilgrimage, and each time took a varying route depending on his personal circumstances and the political and military upheavals of continental Europe.[44]

Adam of Usk described the route he followed via the St Gotthard pass,[45] Lewys Glyn Cothi simply stated that he travelled 'From Mon to the town of Rome'.[46]

Other texts actually explain the attractions of the major pilgrimage sites. According to Judith Champ, 'there were certainly Welsh-language versions of the *Libri Indulgentiarum*', which recorded the indulgences that could be obtained at particular shrines of Rome.[47] Late medieval Welsh poets told their audiences about specific aspects of the Roman pilgrimage. Gwilym Tew (*fl. c.*1460–80), for example, explained the Stations of the Cross walked by his patron Sir John ap Morgan:

> [he] traversed, under a divine aspiration,
> The holy places of the land of Israel.
> The Station of Christ and His Ages
> At the top of the Hill, it was
> And not a footstep trod he
> Without a prayer to the Three in One.[48]

Another feature that was referred to time and again was the Veil or Vernacle of St Veronica, the cloth used to wipe the face of Christ which afterwards left with the impression of Him upon it. Its fame was reasonably well known in late medieval Wales to judge from the surviving manuscripts of the *Ystorya Titus Aspasianus* (the History of Titus Vespasian), an account of the sack of Jerusalem which included the legendary story of Veronica and her Veil.[49] Lewis Glyn Cothi (*fl.* 1447–86) referred to it in his poem on the pilgrimage of David ap John.[50] A broad range of sites in Rome (including the Veil) were described by Huw Cae Llwyd (*fl.* 1431–1504) in his poem, composed as a result of his own pilgrimage in 1475.

> The best grave which even man obtained:
> To see the Veronica of God the judge,
> To lift up the curtain, to see the heads
> Of Peter and Paul, godly both.
> It is good to see the rod
> Which turned to seed for Aaron of old;
> . . . One of the bones of St Lawrence

> Which has been clothed in the holy Lateran,
> And a covering which was the garment
> Of the God of heaven while he suffered,
> And the cloth which dried the saints,
> The legs of Jesus' friends
> . . . Let us go to the chapel to see it.[51]

Other works in a similar vein were composed by Robin Ddu of Anglesey (*fl. c.*1450) and Llywelyn ap Hywel ab Ieuan ap Gronwy (*fl.* 1480) in the fifteenth century.[52] Rome was also used as a comparative example in other poems, particularly in works on St David's as two pilgrimages there were equal to one to Rome from the twelfth century onwards.[53] In some cases, Rome and Jerusalem were invoked:

> It is good for me from my region
> To go twice to David
> As if I went, a fine affinity,
> Once to Rome.
> Going three times (it is a splendid deed)
> With my soul as far as St David's,
> It's as good as going
> To Christ's sepulchre once, the blessing of Christendom.[54]

The recorded impact of Welsh pilgrims overseas is limited. We know that they often travelled together, and sometimes with pilgrims from other countries, so they contributed to the general pilgrim society of the major routes through Europe. When Harry Stradling made it to Rome he met a Welshman called Tom Gethin, and they walked the Stations of the Cross together as Tom had been there a decade before and knew the route.[55] A Welshman in Rome, originally from the diocese of St David's, Andrew Alene, contributed to the provision of pilgrim accommodation in the city by co-founding a hospice with a German.[56] Another contribution they could have made was to the sacred atmosphere of the shrine, specifically through music. According to the Codex Calixtus of *c.*1140 at Santiago pilgrims performed in the cathedral church: 'Some sang to the accompaniment of the . . . lyre, some to the timbrel, others to the flute, others to the British and Welsh harp and crwth.'[57]

In addition to information, crusaders and pilgrims brought back tangible items – often of spiritual value – to Wales. Those who went to Rome, for example, could and did secure remission of sins for their family and friends, acting as their proxies. The poet Huw Cae Llwyd, who was travelling on behalf of his patron, obtained spiritual benefits for himself and his neighbours, observing that it was possible for one person to go from a particular area to the benefit of all.[58] Harry Stradling's final pilgrimage destination was Jerusalem, but he appears to have gone via Rome – at least in part – to obtain papal indulgence on behalf of his wife; presumably she was in need of its benefits because he sent the resulting document, complete with its lead seal, home to her in the care of one of his fellow pilgrims while he continued his own pilgrimage.[59]

More broadly speaking, the crusading movement had an impact on the material and religious culture of those who were unable to fulfil their vows, who wanted to support the Holy Land in other ways, who needed to raise funds, or who wanted to make a pious donation in preparation for their journey. Margam Abbey, for example, could conceivably have been founded by Robert of Gloucester in 1147 because he could not fulfil a vow.[60] Concern for preparing oneself for the journey also led to acts of piety: in 1236 Ralph de Teoni of Painscastle granted two granges to the Cistercian house at Cwmhir.[61] When Gerald of Wales was preparing to embark on the Third Crusade, having spent six weeks travelling around Wales and the Welsh March to recruit for it with the archbishop of Canterbury, he sold his theological works to the abbey of Strata Florida in order to raise funds;[62] when the crusade was delayed and he found himself unable to go, Gerald was released from his vow on the condition that he contributed to the rebuilding of the cathedral church of St David's, work he presumably paid for using the money he gained from selling his books.[63]

The travel and exposure to the Continent brought by international pilgrimage and crusade were but two of the ways in which information, ideas and people moved across Europe. None of the resulting contributions were necessarily unique – Welshmen fought overseas in the king of England's armies, for example, and information about the Continent came to Wales via trade and ecclesiastical networks – but these exchanges all helped to spread the reputation of the Welsh as fighters overseas, or the fame of their premier saint, David, and in turn brought back information from across Europe and the Holy Land. This international travel helped to foster interest in lands that were otherwise distant and, although much of society was illiterate, through the performance of poetry (as opposed to the authoring of chronicles), motifs from crusade-themed tales set in Jerusalem, descriptions of the sea passage to Santiago, and descriptions of the routes to, and treasures of, Rome could be conveyed to a wider audience.

Notes

[1] The pilgrimage origins of the crusading movement are well known, as is the difficulty of identifying many crusaders in their contemporary sources because of the widespread use of pilgrim terminology to explain both groups and their journeys to the Holy Land. For the blurring of the lines between the two, see Léan Ní Chléirigh, '*Nova peregrinatio:* the First Crusade as a pilgrimage in contemporary Latin narratives', in Marcus Bull and Damien Kempf (eds), *Writing the Early Crusades: Text, Transmission and Memory* (Woodbridge: Boydell, 2014), pp. 63–74.

[2] For the Welsh context, see Kathryn Hurlock, *Wales and the Crusades, c.1095–1291*, Studies in Welsh History 33 (Cardiff: University of Wales Press, 2011) for crusaders; for pilgrimage, see Katharine Olson, '"Ar ffordd Pedr a Phawl": Welsh Pilgrimage and Travel to Rome, *c.*1200–*c.*1530', *WHR*, 24.2 (2008), 1–40.

[3] Meic Stephens (ed.), *The New Companion to the Literature of Wales* (Oxford: Oxford University Press, 1990), p. 564.

[4] Stephens (ed.), *The New Companion*, p. 293.

[5] *Brut y Tywysogyon: Red Book of Hergest Version*, ed. and trans. Thomas Jones (Cardiff: University of Wales Press, 1955), p. 111.

[6] *Brut y Tywysogyon: Red Book of Hergest*, p. 119. See also Hurlock, *Wales and the Crusades*, pp. 97–106.

[7] *Brut y Tywysogyon: Red Book of Hergest*, pp. 9, 13, 25; *Annales Cambriae*, ed. John Williams ab Ithel (London: Longman, Green, Longman and Roberts, 1860), p. 8.

[8] Elissa Henken, *The Welsh Saints: A Study in Patterned Lives* (Cambridge: D. S. Brewer, 1991), p. 2; Geoffrey of Monmouth, *The History of the*

Kings of Britain, trans. Lewis Thorpe (Harmondsworth: Penguin, 1973), pp. 282–3. For the endurance of the belief, see Jason Nice, *Sacred History and National Identity: Comparisons between Early Modern Wales and Brittany* (London: Routledge, 2009), pp. 145–50; David Powell, *The Historie of Cambria, now called Wales* (London: Rafe Newberie and Henry Denham, 1584).

[9] *Brut y Tywysogyon: Red Book of Hergest*, p. 133.

[10] Gerald of Wales, *The Journey Through Wales/The Description of Wales*, trans. Lewis Thorpe (Harmondsworth: Penguin Books, 1978), p. 253; Giraldus Cambrensis, *Itinerarium Kambriae et Descriptio Kambriae*, ed. James F. Dimock, in *GCO*, vi, p. 203.

[11] E. G. Bowen, 'Seafaring along the Pembrokeshire Coast in the Days of the Sailing Ships', *The Pembrokeshire Historian*, 4 (1972), 65. See also K. Lloyd Gruffydd, 'Maritime Wales' Export Trade in the Later Middle Ages', *Maritime Wales*, 21 (2000), 23–44. The poet Rhys Nanmor (*fl.* 1480–1513) refers to the privateer he travelled on: NLW, GB 0210 GOBOWEN 4/2; G. Hartwell-Jones, *Celtic Britain and the Pilgrim Movement* (London: Honourable Society of the Cymmrodorion, 1912), pp. 258–61.

[12] Olson, '"Ar ffordd Pedr a Phawl"', 8–9; *Cal. IPM*, xv, p. 269, n. 659.

[13] Huw M. Edwards, *Dafydd ap Gwilym: Influences and Analogues* (Oxford: Clarendon Press, 1996), p. 191; Eurys Rowlands, 'The continuing tradition', in A. O. H. Jarman and Gwilym Rees Hughes (eds), *A Guide to Welsh Literature, Volume 2 1282–c.1550* (Cardiff: University of Wales Press, 1997), p. 307; Gruffudd describes nearly being wrecked on Henry's land, presumably referring to Henry IV, which would place his pilgrimage between 1399 and 1413.

[14] Arthur White, *Plague and Pleasure: The Renaissance World of Pius II* (Washington DC: The Catholic University of America Press, 2014), p. 95. See also Diana Webb, *Medieval European Pilgrimage, c.700–c1500* (Basingstoke: Palgrave, 2002), pp. 27, 87.

[15] Gary Dickson, 'The Crowd at the Feet of Pope Boniface VIII: Pilgrimage, Crusade and the First Roman Jubilee (1300)', *JMH*, 25 (1999), 279–80.

[16] Glanmor Williams, *The Welsh Church from Conquest to Reformation* (Cardiff: University of Wales Press, 1962), p. 502.

[17] Robert W. Dunning, 'Miles Salley, Bishop of Llandaff', *Journal of Welsh Ecclesiastical History*, 8 (1991), 4.

[18] Carol Sweetenham and Linda L. Patterson (trans.), *Canso d'Antioca: an Occitan Epic of the First Crusade* (Aldershot: Ashgate 2003), p. 227; Hurlock, *Wales and the Crusades*, pp. 94–5; see also Susan B. Edgington

and Carol Sweetenham (trans.), *The Chanson d'Antioche: An Old French Account of the First Crusade* (Aldershot: Ashgate, 2011), p. 101. It was not unusual for Welsh mercenaries to be used by Anglo-Normans after the conquest of England: see Adam Chapman's chapter in this volume, and Sean Davies, *War and Society in Medieval Wales, 633–1283: Welsh Military Institutions* (Cardiff: University of Wales Press, 2004), pp. 61–2; I. W. Rowlands, '"Warriors fit for a prince": Welsh troops in Angevin service, 1154–1216', in John France (ed.), *Mercenaries and Paid Men: the Mercenary Identity in the Middle Ages* (Leiden: Brill, 2008), pp. 207–30.

[19] Hurlock, *Wales and the Crusades*, p. 2; *GCO*, vi, p. 181; Gerald of Wales, *The Journey Through Wales*, p. 234.

[20] For a discussion of the possible crusaders from Wales in this period, see Hurlock, *Wales and the Crusades*, pp. 99–101.

[21] Kathryn Hurlock, *Britain, Ireland and the Crusades, c.1000–1300* (Basingstoke: Palgrave, 2013), p. 80. See also Hurlock, *Wales and the Crusades*, p. 101 where the siege is erroneously placed at Tyre.

[22] Marianne Ailes and Malcolm Barber note that the reference to St Denis, unexpected for a Welshman who would more logically have chosen St David, 'is probably for the sake of the rhyme' in the original verse: Marianne Ailes (trans.), *The History of the Holy War: Ambroise's Estoire de la Guerre Sainte II: Translation*, with notes by Marianne Ailes and Malcolm Barber (Woodbridge: Boydell, 2003), p. 84; the Welsh are described as 'Gualeis' (*Gallois*, Welshman) in the French text. See Ambroise, *L'Estoire de la Guerre Sainte*, trans. Gaston Paris (Paris: Imprimerie Nationale, 1897), pp. 100–1, lines 3731–70.

[23] Davies, *War and Society*, p. 153.

[24] Timothy Guard, *Chivalry, Kingship and Crusade: the English Experience in the Fourteenth Century* (Woodbridge: Boydell, 2013), p. 35; Christopher Tyerman, *England and the Crusades, 1095–1588* (Chicago: Yale University Press, 1988), p. 281.

[25] A transcript of Sir Hugh Johnny's memorial brass, which hung in St Mary's church, Swansea until the Second World War, can be found in W. R. B. Robinson, 'Sir Hugh Johnys: a fifteenth century Welsh Knight', *Morgannwg*, 14 (1970), 6; his overseas activities are confirmed in the *CPR 1446–52*, p. 562; it is possible that Hugh Johnys went on pilgrimage again in 1445–6, as he and his wife were given a licence for a portable altar, and to hear mass in places that were placed under interdict: J. A. Twemlow (ed.), *Calendar of Papal Registers Relating to Great Britain and Ireland, volume 9, 1431–1447* (London: HMSO, 1912), p. 519.

[26] Francis Jones, 'Knights of the Holy Sepulchre', *Journal of the Historical Society of the Church in Wales*, 26 (1979), 23.

[27] Charles Trice Martin (ed.), *Registrum Epistolarum Fratris Johannis Pecham, Archiepiscopi Cantuariensis*, 3 vols (London: Longman, 1884), ii, p. 471.

[28] Kathryn Hurlock, 'Power, Preaching and the Crusades in Pura Walia c.1180–1280', *Thirteenth Century England*, 11 (2009), 94–108.

[29] Hurlock, *Wales and the Crusades*, pp. 200–1; Carl Horstmann (ed.), *Nova Legenda Anglie, by John of Tynemouth and John Capgrave* (Oxford: Clarendon Press, 1901), p. 262.

[30] Kathryn Hurlock, *Crusades and Crusading in the Welsh Annalistic Chronicles*, Trivium Occasional Series, no. 5 (Lampeter: Trivium Publications, 2009).

[31] For the text of the *Annals*, see 'Annals of Margam 1066–1232', in H. R. Luard (ed.), *Annales Monastici*, 5 vols (London: Longmans, 1864–9; repr. 1965), i.

[32] Helen Fulton, 'Translating Europe in medieval Wales', in Aidan Conti, Orietta de Rold and Philip Shaw (eds), *Writing Europe 500–1450: Texts and Contexts* (Cambridge: D. S. Brewer, 2015), p. 174.

[33] Nesta Lloyd and Morfydd E. Owen (eds), *Drych yr Oesoedd Canol* (Cardiff: University of Wales Press, 1986), pp. 117–18.

[34] Ceridwen Lloyd-Morgan, 'Manuscripts and the monasteries', in Janet Burton and Karen Stöber (eds), *Monastic Wales: New Approaches* (Cardiff: University of Wales Press, 2011), p. 217; H. Lewis and P. Diverre (eds), *Delw y Byd (Imago Mundi)* (Cardiff: University of Wales Press, 1928).

[35] A. D. Carr, 'Inside the tent looking out: the medieval Welsh world view', in R. R. Davies and Geraint H. Jenkins (eds), *From Medieval to Modern Wales: Historical Essays in Honour of Kenneth O. Morgan and Ralph A. Griffiths* (Cardiff: University of Wales Press, 2004), p. 31; Hurlock, *Wales and the Crusades*, pp. 39–42; Henry Lewis (ed.), *Hen gerddi crefyddol* (Cardiff: University of Wales Press, 1974), p. 75, ll. 47–50; *Gwaith Meilyr Brydydd a'i Ddisgynyddion*, ed. J. E. Caerwyn Williams, Peredur I. Lynch and R. Geraint Gruffydd (Cardiff: University of Wales Press, 1994), p. 337.

[36] Hurlock, *Wales and the Crusades*, pp. 44–55; Robert Williams, 'Ystoria de Carolo Magno', *Y Cymmrodor*, 20 (1907); R. Williams and G. H. Jones (eds), *Selections from the Hengwrt MSS* (London: Thomas Richards, 1892), ii, pp. 1–118, 437–517.

[37] Fulton, 'Translating Europe in medieval Wales', p. 172.

[38] For example, see Jace Stuckey, 'Charlemagne as crusader? Memory, propaganda, and the many uses of Charlemagne's legendary expedition

to Spain', in Matthew Gabriele and Jace Stuckey (eds), *The Legend of Charlemagne in the Middle Ages: Power, Faith and Crusade* (New York: Palgrave, 2008), pp. 137–52.

[39] Ralph A. Griffiths, 'The Rise of the Stradlings of St Donats', in his *Conquerors and Conquered in Medieval Wales* (Stroud and New York: Sutton/St Martin's Press, 1994), p. 32.

[40] Griffiths, 'Rise of the Stradlings', pp. 34–5.

[41] Rowlands, 'The continuing tradition', p. 307.

[42] E. D. Jones, 'Cartre Gruffudd Gryg', *National Library of Wales Journal*, 10 (1957–8), 230.

[43] Barry Lewis (ed. and trans.), *Medieval Welsh Poems to Saints and Shrines* (Dublin: Dublin Institute for Advanced Studies, 2015), pp. 95–7, 214–23, 366–8.

[44] Gerald of Wales, *The Autobiography of Gerald of Wales*, ed. and trans. H. E. Butler (Woodbridge: Boydell, 2005), pp. 163, 261.

[45] Gerald of Wales, *Autobiography*, p. 155.

[46] *Gwaith Lewis Glyn Cothi*, ed. E. D. Jones (Cardiff: University of Wales Press, 1953), p. 206, ll. 11–16; translation in Joseph P. Clancy (trans.), *Medieval Welsh Poems* (Dublin: Four Courts Press, 2002), p. 297.

[47] Judith Champ, *The English Pilgrimage to Rome: A Dwelling for the Soul* (Leominster: Gracewing, 2000), p. 42.

[48] D. R. Thomas, 'Sir John Morgan of Tredegar, Knt', *Archaeologia Cambrensis* (1884), 44.

[49] Williams, *Welsh Church from Conquest to Reformation*, p. 101; J. E. Caerwyn Williams, 'Ystorya Titus Aspassianus', *BBCS*, 9 (1938); Daniel Simon Evans, *Medieval Religious Literature* (Cardiff: University of Wales Press, 1986), p. 73.

[50] *Gwaith Lewis Glyn Cothi*, pp. 223–4.

[51] *Gwaith Huw Cae Llwyd ac eraill*, ed. Leslie Harries (Cardiff: University of Wales Press, 1953), pp. 83–5; *Medieval Welsh Poems to Saints and Shrines*, p. 379.

[52] Hartwell-Jones, *Celtic Britain and the Pilgrim Movement*, p. 223; for the text of Huw Cae Llwyd's poem, see *Medieval Welsh Poems to Saints and Shrines*, pp. 107–10, 378–81; Jane Cartwright, *Feminine Sanctity and Spirituality in Medieval Wales* (Cardiff: University of Wales Press, 2008), p. 56.

[53] William of Malmesbury, *Gesta Regum*, ed. and trans. R. A. B. Mynors, R. M. Thomson and M. Winterbottom (Oxford: Clarendon Press, 1998), pp. 778–81; Teresa Rodrigues (ed.), *Butler's Lives of the Saints: March* (New Full Edition, Collesville, Minnesota: The Liturgical Press, 1999), p. 1.

[54] For the poem by Ieuan ap Rhydderch (c.1430–70), see *Medieval Welsh Poems to Saints and Shrines*, pp. 16, ll. 15–22, 387, ll. 15–22; J. Wyn Evans, 'St David and St Davids: some observations on the cult, site and buildings', in Jane Cartwright (ed.), *Celtic Hagiography and Saints' Cults* (Cardiff: University of Wales Press, 2003), p. 11.

[55] West Glamorgan Archive Service, RISW GGF 3. Letter of Harry Stradling to his wife, 1456.

[56] Margaret M. Harvey, *The English in Rome, 1362–1420: Portrait of an Expatriate Community* (Cambridge: Cambridge University Press, 1999), pp. 12, 57.

[57] W. S. Gwynn, *Welsh National Dance and Music* (London: Curwen, 1932), pp. 35–6; Hartwell-Jones, *Celtic Britain and the Pilgrim Movement*, p. 569 n., quoting the *Codex of Pope Calixtus II* (c.1140).

[58] Glanmor Williams, 'Poets and Pilgrims in Fifteenth and Sixteenth Century Wales', *Trans. Hon. Soc. Cymm.* (1991), 86; *Gwaith Huw Cae Llwyd*, p. 109.

[59] West Glamorgan Archive Service, RISW GGF 3.

[60] Hurlock, *Wales and the Crusades*, pp. 129–30.

[61] Beatrice A. Lees (ed.), *Records of the Templars in England in the Twelfth Century: the Inquest of 185 with illustrative charters and documents* (London: Oxford University Press for the British Academy, 1935), pp. 213–15; Emma Mason, Jennifer Bray and Desmond J. Murphy (eds), *Westminster Abbey Charters, 1066–c.1214* (London: London Record Society, 1988), pp. 185–96; Michael Lower, *The Barons' Crusade: a Call to Arms and its Consequences* (Philadelphia: University of Pennsylvania Press, 2005), p. 144.

[62] Janet Burton, *Monastic and Religious Orders in Britain, 1000–1300* (Cambridge: Cambridge University Press, 1994), p. 192.

[63] James Conway Davies (ed.), *Episcopal Acts and Cognate Documents Relating to Welsh Dioceses, 1066–1272*, 2 vols (Cardiff: University of Wales Press, 1946–8), i, p. 326, document 367. Peter de Leia re-planned St David's in 1180. By the time Gerald was excused, the work on the building was already underway.

6

Welsh-French diplomacy in the Middle Ages

Gideon Brough

This chapter will discuss examples of Welsh diplomatic contacts with France during the medieval period. Far from being isolated and unknown, native leaders in medieval Wales were well able to communicate with their continental peers. Curiously, French-Welsh military and diplomatic relations lasted well beyond the extinction of native rule in 1282, as the careers of Owain Lawgoch and Owain Glyndŵr plainly demonstrated. The style and aims of the numerous French and Welsh leaders who engaged in these diplomatic relations are revealed by reading their exchanges. Some had a gentle, cautious style, which evolved with practice, while others were bellicose and threatened invasion and war.

Since the early nineteenth century, the idea of the nation in Europe has been shaped by the assumption that a people can only properly realise their destiny through political independence. History writing has tended to mirror and support that assumption, with the result that the study of the past in smaller and now stateless nations such as Wales has long been marginalised by dominant narratives of Anglo-Britishness. Although the intellectual foundations of this approach have been widely discredited over the past generation, the stifling weight of cultural inertia means that even today the study of medieval Wales attracts significantly less interest than the same period in England or France. Welsh history, seen on its own terms and judged in its own context, is every bit as deserving of scholarly attention as that of any other nation's past.[1]

Despite the invisibility of the Welsh in larger studies, they were apparent throughout medieval Europe, whether performers in Europe's courts, scholars in European universities or as troops on European battlefields.[2] In addition, Welsh principalities were indisputably engaged with neighbouring states and peoples connected to their geographical, economic, religious and political orbit.[3] The propagation of myths and legends across Europe, the Arthurian stories most prominent among them, also placed the Welsh firmly in the minds of their continental contemporaries. Even their enemies wrote about them, if Gerald of Wales was correct when he depicted Henry II of England describing the Welsh in a letter to the Byzantine emperor, Manuel Comnenus.[4] In this period, even the simple act of writing down a certain language gave it a status above that of a spoken dialect, and this elevation can be seen to be repeated across Europe, from Anglo-Norman to Welsh.[5] In the literary sphere, the Welsh were certainly well established. Medieval Wales and its people were not therefore parochial oddities, but part of a continental community.

While it could be reasonably argued that medieval Wales and its leaders habitually played a role commensurate to their size, and therefore do not register frequently in the records of the larger powers, the evidence clearly demonstrates that the Welsh princes were considered a distinct, identifiable part of the international community of the time. At different times, Welsh leaders established diplomatic relations with a variety of spiritual and temporal powers; this chapter will illuminate examples of Welsh engagement with one of the largest European powers, France. Welsh-French connections not only spanned the periods before Edward I's successful invasion of Gwynedd in 1282–3, but also recurred for some considerable time after. This invites reflection on the finality of the commonly termed 'conquest' and a revised view reveals a more complex situation than is first perceived. Although it is a convenient term, historically and politically, the French did not accept Edward's 'conquest' as a final position and subsequent events show that the Welsh did not either.

Exchanges in the twelfth century

While prior contacts could have occurred, the evidence for the first known connection between Welsh and French leaders comes in the form of three letters sent by Owain Gwynedd to Louis VII's court.[6] These letters date between 1163 and 1168, and demonstrate a striking evolution in Owain's diplomatic methods. The desire for contact with Louis was likely triggered by Henry II's demand of homage at Woodstock in July 1163 which subsequently ignited a Welsh uprising. Owain's quest for an alliance with France was rooted in the cultural mores of his time. Although Owain had humiliatingly defeated Henry in battle at Coleshill in 1157, conflict with his larger neighbour was evidently risky; yet Owain did not ask Louis for troops at any stage. Henry's insistence on a form of homage at Woodstock provided the accepted cultural expedient to allow an appeal to Louis, Henry's overlord. In addition, medieval French kings had a long history of arbitrating noble disputes and had dealt sympathetically and equitably with nobles and ecclesiastics of all ranks, mother tongue and nation.[7]

Owain's first letter appears naive: unsophisticated in its construction, but sufficiently humble and polite, it directly addressed Louis VII and was not sent through common diplomatic channels. Although it contained elements of the *politesse* required in courtly dialogue, it nonetheless reads as less florid, blunt even, when compared to other similar diplomatic approaches of the period. According to Gerald of Wales, anyone in Wales could speak their mind even in the presence of their ruler, a situation inconceivable in French or English courts. Owain's straightforwardness and lack of elaboration possibly denoted a norm among the Welsh.[8] He admitted that the two leaders were strangers to one another, yet Owain offered himself and his possessions to Louis. While Owain led a small power, he was more than an irrelevant minor player. Although geographically isolated from the Capetian domains, his neighbour and nemesis was Louis's troublesome, over-mighty vassal, Henry II. Therefore, Owain, his forces and his allies offered potential military and diplomatic opportunities for Louis to exploit.[9]

It should be highlighted that Welsh diplomatic isolation resulted from the assertion of Canterbury's primacy during the reign of

Henry I. When Archbishop Anselm (r. 1093–1109) demanded that the bishops of Wales swore allegiance to Canterbury, this effectively relinquished Welsh control or influence of future elections and candidates to those posts. The consequence was that in times of need, the Welsh leaders only had low-ranking and therefore less well-connected clergymen to rely on as messengers and advocates for their causes. Therefore, there was no powerful Welsh voice in Rome, nor anyone of rank in Europe's royal courts. Those Welshmen who did rise to positions of prominence in the church were, by necessity, loyal to Canterbury. A good example of this comes from Owain Gwynedd's reign, where Meurig, bishop of Bangor, was isolated by the princes of Gwynedd for being their outspoken critic, as well as being a sworn adherent of Canterbury and the king of England.[10]

For reasons unknown, Louis declined to respond formally to the first Welsh petition. This was not viewed as a rebuff, however, because Owain wrote again and subsequently received an apparently friendly response. The second letter was a better crafted proposition: the language is noticeably more elaborate, the theme of religion, key in dealing with Louis's regime, runs strongly through it and it was directed through an intermediary, Hugh de Champfleury, the French chancellor. This letter also acknowledges that the chancellor had instructed Owain how to improve his petitions.[11] It is worth also situating Owain's letters within the broader spectrum of contemporary affairs, for within this period Pope Alexander III and Archbishop Becket both sought Louis's protection from their respective enemies, Frederick Barbarossa and Henry II. Also, conflicts arose in Italy and western France, while the Welsh advanced against King Henry's interests in Wales.[12] Within that landscape, it is believable that Welsh appeals to France might be given an increasingly fertile reception.

The style and substance of Owain's third and last known letter to Louis mark impressive improvements in the form of his diplomacy and came shortly after Henry had again been humbled in a campaign against Owain at Berwyn in 1165. Owain began with an appropriate greeting introducing the two interlocutors, praising and thanking Louis. He sprinkled themes of piety and trust into his message, demonstrating that he had learned more about Louis's character and priorities. The manner in which Owain explained the causes and identified the agent of his distress, and in so doing gave the reason for his contacting Louis, were far more mature and diplomatically conventional than his previous missives. His depiction of the Welsh victory over Henry's unprovoked invasion in 1165 was intelligently presented: he let it be known that Henry had been beaten but acknowledged the influence of prayer and saintly intercession. The sub-text to this delivered two important messages: he was able to defeat Henry in battle and was therefore a worthy ally, but he was also respectful and pious and so, perhaps, deserved Louis's friendship and support. Then Owain revealed the crux of the message: his need for French intercession, as he had learned that Henry was due to muster another army destined for Wales after Easter 1166. The third letter ends by clarifying any confusion over the previous letters and thanking Louis for his help in another matter. In doing so, Owain presented his messenger as a man of the cloth and a man of the blood, which were the requisites for courtly messengers and ambassadors during the period.[13] Owain's final lines thanking Louis for his intercession with Thomas Becket and the pope suggest that the French king's barely discernible hand was, to a certain degree, already at work on Owain's behalf. This third letter was a bold and ultimately successful attempt at inducing Louis to take up Owain's cause. In effect, it proves that an amity, perhaps an alliance of sorts, was already active.[14]

While the Berwyn campaign has not entirely escaped the attention of historians, and is mostly recognised as a victory of sorts, it has not yet received the wider recognition it deserves.[15] Contemporary chroniclers observed:

> Let anyone turn his mind's eye to view the number and the quality of the enemies which the Lord has raised against the king [Henry II] since he lifted his heel against God to crush the Church. He will surely be astonished and, if he is wise, filled with reverence for God's judgement: for he has chosen not emperors or kings or the princes of the nations to quell him, but chose first the remotest of men, the Welsh of Snowdon; and later he fired them to withstand in open fight the king whose footprints they had been used to worship.[16]

> And against him [Henry II] came Owain and Cadwaladr, sons of Gruffudd ap Cynan, and all the host of Gwynedd with them, and Rhys ap Gruffudd and with him the host of Deheubarth, and Owain Cyfeiliog and Iorwerth Goch ap Maredudd and the sons of Madoc ap Maredudd and the host of all Powys with them, and the two sons of Madog ab Idnerth and their host.[17]

Even before conflict was joined, therefore, Owain Gwynedd had scored a staggering diplomatic success in Wales, creating an unprecedented alliance of the native powers, with armies from Gwynedd, Deheubarth, Powys and Gwent marching to his banner. Owain was not militarily strong enough to coerce these other Welsh rulers to join him, nor did they owe him military service required within a feudal arrangement; therefore they did so voluntarily. It is also striking that these Welsh leaders were not naturally allies, and several of them had opposed each other at certain moments: Gwynedd and Powys were longstanding adversaries.[18] In addition, most of the Welsh hosts who opposed Henry mustered and moved from areas outside Gwynedd, therefore from areas normally considered Marcher or Crown lands. The ability to raise forces and relocate many miles away, crossing other territories also considered to be under non-native control suggests an ongoing overestimation of the breadth and strength of Anglo-Norman power in twelfth-century Wales.[19]

Whether to frustrate Henry's territorial ambitions, or to support the liberties of a fellow Christian prince, Owain was invited to send ambassadors to sit in the session between Louis and Henry at La Ferté-Bernard in 1168 as guests of the French. The Welsh sat among their peers from Brittany, Scotland, Poitou and Gascony, and all left with commands, 'obligations', from Louis.[20] Although the conference at La Ferté-Bernard could be described as a precursor to the more significant meeting at Montmirail, six months later, it is nevertheless highly noteworthy because it appears to have been a first in Welsh history, in that the Welsh were invited to stand among other powers in such a conference. Also, it establishes a point after which Henry's behaviour towards the Welsh, particularly Rhys ap Gruffydd, became more amenable. There was no opportunity to improve relations with Owain Gwynedd, for he died peacefully in his bed in November 1170 while Henry was still occupied with his continental affairs. Given that there does not seem to have been any prior Welsh-French relationship, this first was solely due to Owain's diplomacy. These letters also demonstrate dimensions to Owain's personality that are not otherwise revealed by other sources concerning his life, notably his intelligence. They also demonstrate Owain as a man of some ambition: he was willing to reject Henry's overlordship and to meet him in battle. By appealing to Henry's feudal overlord, Owain operated within the political norms of his time, thereby dismissing any anachronistic notion that the Welsh princes were in any way culturally isolated. The third letter, written in the expected metre and form of such correspondence, exemplified Owain's diplomatic evolution. The result was the 1168 conference, which has been cautiously but credibly advanced as proof that an alliance of sorts existed between Louis and Owain.[21]

Llywelyn ap Iorwerth and Philip Augustus

The next significant French-Welsh connection joined Philip Augustus and Llywelyn ap Iorwerth, sometime between 1212 and 1216.[22] Within the febrile environment that existed on the British mainland, particularly in England, from 1212 to 1216, alliances were made between English, Welsh, French and Scots factions as well as the muscular papacy of Innocent III.[23] The treaty between Philip Augustus and Llywelyn was made during that period of prolific diplomatic and military effort.

Only one treaty document exists, although it is possible that two French-Welsh alliances were forged during this period. Whether coincidence or deliberate, the undated treaty document is too ambiguous to be uniquely identifiable: no places are explicitly named and the events it mentions could be interpreted as belonging to either moment.[24]

The opening contact, a letter from Philip to Llywelyn inviting alliance, is lost; however, the French king's motives appear evident in the concise, skilfully crafted reply from Gwynedd. The language indicates that Llywelyn and his council were able to express themselves in a style and standard comparable to Gwynedd's larger contemporaries. It began with an appropriately polite, perhaps flattering, greeting from Llywelyn, humbly submitting his lower status before Philip. While this realistically reflected the pre-eminence of France over Gwynedd, it also appears to be an intelligent way of opening a discourse with such a power, and likely used phrases in keeping with contemporary practice. Also, these softly rhyming phrases, for example, 'non tam munifice quam magnifice' and 'vestris amicis amici erimus et inimici inimicis', demonstrated the author's education and are arguably as important to the style and presentation of the letter as they are in the actual message they conveyed.[25] Throughout the period, the manner in which leaders projected themselves was highly important to their status. Perceptions of status helped shape how interlocutors perceived one another and consequently affected the course of their relations.[26]

Attached to the bold, overt promises of perpetual alliance to the French kings, their heirs and their allies, was a request that they acted similarly toward Llywelyn and his confederates. This demonstrates that Llywelyn was au fait with contemporary diplomatic procedure and the appropriate language to employ. Notably, similar clauses also appeared in the Welsh princes' agreement with the English barons in 1215 and between the Scots and the same barons during the winter of 1215–16.[27] While perhaps formulaic, the commonality of language in use between all parties at the same moment is suggestive of a contemporary link. This inclusive clause might also denote that, while pleased with the union with the French, Llywelyn was unwilling to act as Philip's sole pawn on the British mainland. Unilaterally attacking England would have almost certainly been disastrous for Llywelyn. Although it might have temporarily curtailed English actions across the channel, for Gwynedd, it would probably have resulted in a catastrophic defeat, similar to that of 1211. However, operating as part of a strong, multi-factional alliance would make joint actions viable. Although Philip was in contact with a few of John's nobles before 1212, in reality, that environment only existed from 1215 and connects the alliance to the events surrounding Magna Carta.

Llywelyn's enthusiasm to fight is unmistakeable and the Welsh had clearly already retaken some territory, although there is no indication of where or when. Nevertheless, these victories would be worth highlighting to his new French ally. Significantly, Llywelyn promised to make war on lands lost 'by fraud and guile', but made no mention of operating outside Wales. This could apply to any lands no longer under native control, but effectively delineated the operational boundaries for this alliance. Realistically, Llywelyn's forces were limited to Wales and the Marches.

Llywelyn's response to Philip ended with a dramatic but beautiful flourish which portrayed the prince of Gwynedd as a steadfast, worthy friend. He promised that he had not discussed any truce or held any negotiations with the English since Philip had contacted him. He evoked strong imagery, promising a long, unyielding fight, that he and all of the native powers 'unitedly confederated, will manfully resist our enemies, [and] yours'. Referring to lost land and castles, he added: 'we will recover [them] from the yoke of the tyrants' and that he would not make peace with their mutual enemy unless he had discussed it with Philip. The Welsh kept their word on this point.

Although the treaty presents ambiguities to modern historians as to its precise chronology and context, doubtless it was entirely clear to the parties involved. If in 1212, the treaty came at a time when the pope encouraged numerous factions to make war on King John, while Philip made initial, more covert machinations with certain discontented barons. If 1215–16, it engaged them with the barons responsible for Magna Carta and the French invasion of England, but in the face of papal opposition. Let us explore both scenarios.

One of the significant weaknesses of Angevin rule in England was that many of the king's magnates were very powerful men. They and their extended families held lands in England, Wales, Ireland, Scotland and France. Few, if any, were strong enough to challenge King John individually, but if united and committed, as later events would prove, even a handful would be able to attempt to dethrone him. For those holding lands on both sides of the Channel, there was an overlap in loyalties, particularly as Philip had swept John out of France and received the oaths of former Angevin lands.[28] Philip recognised this and sought to exploit it, with his first cross-channel intrigues coming to the fore as early as 1209 and running a course to confrontation in 1212.[29] The question of the nobles' loyalties was further exacerbated by John's brutal, demanding method of rule. When dispute arose between John and the de Braose and the de Lacy families, the king pursued them in England, Wales, Ireland and Scotland, and mercilessly destroyed those who had offended him.[30] John alienated much of the remainder of England's nobility with increased taxation and extending his demands for feudal service.[31] John had also come into conflict with his son-in-law, Llywelyn, supporting internal opposition against the prince of Gwynedd and finally coming to battle against him. Although Llywelyn was able to initially fend off John's army, a larger, better equipped force returned in 1211. On the advice of his wife and his council, Llywelyn submitted and agreed to humiliating terms. Subsequently, John swiftly built castles across Wales from which he mounted punitive campaigns against Welsh communities.[32] It is highly significant that John was also in conflict with Pope Innocent III, who, as a result, had placed England under an interdict in 1208, fully coming into effect the following year.[33] With John in conflict with the papacy, the French, Welsh, Scots, Irish and many of his own nobles, a major crisis seemed inevitable.[34]

In 1212, as John prepared an army to again attack Llywelyn, intelligence reached him of a baronial conspiracy to kill or seize him and hand him over to the Welsh.[35] John retreated to Nottingham and surrounded himself with mercenaries to protect him from his own nobles. The same year, the Welsh under Llywelyn were incited to revolt by Innocent III, seeking to increase pressure on John during the interdict. Under such pressures, and probably as a means of avoiding attack, John surrendered the Crown of England to the papacy in May 1213, making England a papal vassal.[36] Consequently, the papacy moved against all of John's foes, threatening them with interdict and excommunication, while seeming to give John carte blanche to act against them.

The second opportunity for alliance came amid the upheaval of the Barons' Revolt and Magna Carta. The barons allied themselves to the French and invited Louis, Philip's heir, to be proclaimed king of England in opposition to John. By November 1215, London had fallen to the barons, French troops had arrived in England and, in May 1216, Prince Louis landed and was proclaimed king.[37] In 1216, with the fight for the throne of England in full flow, John 'sent envoys . . . to the princes of Wales, and begged of them to be reconciled to him in every way; but they would not have it'. Instead of parley, Llywelyn arrayed his troops for battle with King John, who declined and withdrew.[38] Contemporary English, Welsh and papal sources independently demonstrate knowledge of a French-Welsh alliance in 1215 or 1216. The union between the Welsh and the English barons in 1215 was also noted by the respected contemporary chronicler, Walter of Coventry. The Waverley Annals described the Welsh being punished by interdict for being in league with Louis and the barons. That entry fell between John's death and Henry III's coronation, respectively 19 and 28 October 1216. The 1217 entry in the *Brut y Tywysogyon* recognised that the Welsh had taken an oath to the French at that moment: 'for the Welsh had no desire to agree to the peace which the barons had made, because they were still bound to their oath or else had been scorned and ignored in that peace'. This entry was set in the context of the Treaty of Lambeth made between the barons and the new king of England, the minor Henry III, which concluded the conflict between the barons of English and French allegiance. Peace had been made with Louis who, for a sum of money, relinquished his claim to the English throne. Louis forgot to discuss the matter with his Welsh or Scots allies, however.[39] Another first-hand English source, *L'Histoire de Guillaume le Maréchal*, also linked the Welsh and Louis through oath-taking:

> I almost forgot to mention that,
> Once the talks had taken place
> And the truce was concluded
> And agreed by all parties,
> Lord Louis told and ordered those loyal to him,
> Namely his own French,
> The Scots [and the] Welsh
> And English, come what may to
> Observe the truce throughout the land.[40]

William Marshal, earl of Pembroke, a Marcher lord with lands in Wales and a key adversary of the French and the Welsh at that crucial time, was well placed to identify when and to whom the Welsh were allied.

Moreover, the papacy was certainly aware of the Welsh-French alliance, although Louis was viewed as their partner, rather than

Philip. As Louis had openly invaded the papal vassal, England, and Philip was likely powerful enough to avoid direct condemnation, only the heir and his supporters in Britain were punished for the conflict (though Louis could not have acted without his father's knowledge, agreement and active support). The papal legate excommunicated Louis and all of his supporters in May 1216. He renewed that sentence and placed the whole of Wales under an interdict on 11 November 1216. In early 1217, the new pope, Honorius III, issued orders to the barons, the Scots and the Welsh, specifically 'Lewelin' and his supporters, to disregard the oaths they had taken to Louis.[41] There was certainly a French-Welsh alliance in force in 1216; everyone knew of it, but none wrote of such an alliance in 1212.

On concluding the treaty of Lambeth, which agreed to return possessions and boundaries to the state they had been prior to the Barons' Revolt and the French invasion, the pope ended the excommunication of Louis and his adherents. Louis returned to France and peace largely returned to England.[42] However, the terms of Lambeth were clearly unfavourable to Llywelyn and the Welsh, who had regained land, castles and even advanced their territorial possessions. Moreover, they had not been consulted in any case. The Welsh fought on, possibly because they had been excluded from the peace but also, as the evidence stated, they were bound by an oath. Clearly, they were not unilaterally holding to an oath made to the barons or Louis who, by that point, had already made peace and stopped fighting. The only other possible agreement therefore was with Philip Augustus with whom they had agreed not to seek peace without mutual consultation.[43] Since it was widely known that the Welsh had freely negotiated and maintained truces with the English, under the guidance of the papal legates during 1213–14, this mention of remaining faithful to their word cannot refer to an oath that they would have already openly broken.[44] This strongly advocates in favour of the treaty document being from 1215–16, rather than 1212.

A number of alliances were formed around the time of the Magna Carta rebellion between the Welsh, the French, the Scots and the English barons. Several of the treaties made in that period contain textual similarities which is suggestive of a common origin. The treaty between Llywelyn and Philip spoke of the princes uniting and agreeing not to make peace without informing or involving the other party. When describing the alliance between the Welsh and the English barons in 1215, the *Brut y Tywysogyon* revealed:

> all the leading men of England and the princes of Wales made a pact together against the king that no one of them, without the consent of all the others, would make peace or agreement or truce with the king until . . . there should be restored to each one of them their laws and their power and their castles, which he had taken from them without law or truth or justice.[45]

Similarly, when describing the agreement Louis and the English barons made with Alexander II, king of Scotland, the Melrose Chronicle recorded that Louis and the barons swore 'upon holy gospels, that they would never enter into any agreement for peace or truce with the king of England, unless the king of the Scots were included'.[46] In his response to Philip, Llywelyn asserted that he had made 'neither truce, nor peace, nor any negotiation whatever with the English' and required that 'without us, neither truce nor peace will you make with the English'. Although possibly formulaic, the fact that the four factions bound by alliances made similar terms, invoking similar articles of mutual faith at the same time, likely implies collaboration in a venture culminating in Philip Augustus permitting his sole heir be risked – for Louis could not muster a fleet and an army without his father's collaboration – in an attempted invasion of England.[47]

One of the main points of contention concerns the mention of assemblies of the native princes, Llywelyn's council and the clergy, before whom Llywelyn swore on sacrosanct relics. Gwynedd's noble council met in 1211, to encourage Llywelyn to surrender to John, and in 1212, to encourage him to take up arms against John's Welsh castles.[48] However, there is no mention of the clergy, the French or the pope in the supporting evidence. Considering papal encouragement to the Welsh, the lack of ecclesiastical mentions are notable omissions were the treaty made in 1212. The *Brut*, however, unambiguously described how the Welsh and English rebels met in 1215 to discuss their reasons for revolt, one of which was to restore the rights and liberty of the Church; a meeting at which, no doubt, clergymen of significant rank were present. Moreover, in 1216, the same chronicle noted at least two congresses of the Welsh nobility which included the native princes and 'all the learned men of Gwynedd' as well as the 'bishops and abbots and other men of great authority'.[49]

The geo-political decisions made by Llywelyn pitched Gwynedd and its allies into the most important events of their time: the barons' struggle with King John, Magna Carta and the attempted coup by the French heir. Aligning Gwynedd with the ascendant force at that time was shrewd; by 1214 Philip had swept John from France and fractured forever the Angevin dominions of his father.[50] The dearth of primary evidence for alliance in 1212 when compared to the full-blooded alliances of 1215–16 does not necessarily disprove that there was none. There certainly was a French-Welsh alliance between 1215 and 1217, but the extant document is sufficiently imprecise to cause this uncertainty. However, being enticed into Philip's amity in either or both periods underlines the little appreciated power of Gwynedd under Llywelyn ap Iorwerth.

The fourteenth century: Owain Lawgoch

The extinction of independent native governance after 1283 did not deter the French from including Wales within their strategic interests.[51] Given the numerous French-backed efforts to propagate revolt there or to muster invasion forces apparently destined for Wales over the following century, it is reasonable to propose that the fall of Gwynedd and the outbreak of conflict following Edward III's claim to their throne more starkly outlined Wales's potential value to the French. Even in the years following Edward I's invasion of 1282–3, native revolts found vent in Wales. Rhys ap Maredudd raised the standard of revolt in the south in 1287, while Madog ap Llywelyn proclaimed himself prince of Wales due to his royal blood and led a rebellion in 1294–5. Both revolts indicated deep dissatisfaction among the Welsh which expressed itself on the battlefield, in lesser acts of violent resistance as well as in poetic laments.[52]

In the 1330s, and probably in response to Edward III's deteriorating relations with the French, Wales once more became of interest to England's continental adversaries. The French and their Castilian allies also attempted to draw the Welsh into broader, European conflicts on their side, or at least they threatened to open another theatre of war on the British mainland through Wales. While 1338–9 brought the threat of a French-Scots invasion, the same spectre, but this time including Castilian support, reappeared in subsequent decades, notably in 1346 and 1359.[53]

However, as the peace made at Brétigny faded towards the end of the 1360s, and the French gained the initiative in the conflict with England, the prospect of attempted invasions of Wales was once again raised with missions in 1369 and 1372.[54] These expeditions were placed under the captaincy of a Welshman, Owain ap Thomas ap Rhodri, a soldier of allegedly Welsh royal lineage, more commonly called Owain 'Lawgoch': he proclaimed himself the senior male descendant of Llywelyn ap Gruffudd.

Owain was a remarkable character: born and raised in England, it seems probable that he had never been to Wales and there is no overt evidence that he had any close relations or supporters there. However, he did lead Welsh mercenaries in France who could certainly connect within Wales. He fought as a *routier* with the Free Companies in the 1360s and by 1369, following a dispute with English officials that led to the seizure of his estates in England, he swore allegiance to the French. It was under their colours that his career blossomed, where he participated in or led expeditions around French territories, into Switzerland, Spain, the Channel Islands, as well as conducting missions at sea.[55]

Almost as soon as he had taken an oath to Charles V, the French put him and some of his troops on a fleet along with a fighting force under his command in December 1369. They let it be known that they were heading for Wales – and perhaps that was the point. Predictably for a medieval fleet in the Channel in December, it did not successfully make the crossing but limped back to port after battling with high winds and rough seas for two weeks. However, authorities in England hurriedly reinforced a number of castles in Wales and held an enquiry into the level of native support for Lawgoch.[56]

In French literature, Lawgoch is called 'Yvain de Gales' or 'Owain of Wales'. This shows the respect with which the French treated him, accepting him as a prince of Wales's royal bloodline: the sobriquet 'de Gales' is a parallel to the French royal family's use of the title 'de France' as a surname. In Philippe Contamine's list of Charles V's forty war captains, there were only two foreigners, and both were Welshmen, Owain Lawgoch and his lieutenant, Ieuan Wyn.[57] Owain was considered an equal among the highest echelons of France's military elite. Due to his martial prowess under French colours and his high social rank, Owain was accorded the strikingly high honour of being commissioned to lead French troops into battle. On one memorable occasion, he was lauded for a fight in which 500 Englishmen were killed.[58]

However, undeterred by the unremarkable failure of 1369, on 10 May 1372, Owain wrote a defiant letter, declaring his alliance with Charles V and proclaiming himself prince of Wales and loyal ally of France.[59] The belligerent style of the treaty is noteworthy. In the first instance, Owain used the devices of nationality and oppression by the English to justify his claim. He also made a case for his lineage being legitimate, rather than that of the king of England, whose forebears he accused of unjust, treasonous killings of the true rulers of Wales. The fact that he opened with a discussion of legitimacy and lineage hints at French influences in the document's composition. In establishing an issue over succession and legitimacy, there is an obvious parallel with the English claim to the French throne. Once Owain's heritage was proclaimed, the French could more easily offer open support to a usurped, true, noble claimant rather than to a dubious pretender. As a consequence, England was obliged to make military preparations to repel this announced attack and also to later move against Owain in France, all of which diverted men, energy and resources from campaigns against the French. This declaration, most likely jointly conceived, also allowed Charles to signal his intent to take the war to the English through a proxy. According to Owain, this demonstrated that the French were showing the 'compassion . . . justice, grace and mercy to all those that are oppressed and requiring comfort'. He also alluded to wrongs 'that the present king of England has done unto me', referring to the seizure of his lands in 1369.[60]

Other key clauses concern Owain's ornate flattery of Charles and his statement that, having discussed the matter with a number of leaders, he intended to invade Wales with French forces. Clearly, he had acquired French support for this venture and he swore fealty to France for himself, his heirs, his subjects and his country. One treaty clause in particular appears problematic: Owain acknowledged that he owed the French 300,000 gold francs and he would make good that debt once he had reclaimed Wales. It is worth speculating over potential reasons for including mention of this amount of money. For any Welsh audience, the knowledge that they would owe the French a large sum of money, that presumably they would have to pay, might prove counter-productive to Owain's cause. It should be borne in mind that despite a few examples accusing cross-channel correspondence and a poem of unsure date that invited him to Wales, Lawgoch had no power base or influence there, and there is no evidence of any noteworthy measure of support for him there at that time.[61] At a glance, this might appear a large sum, however, when the English became aware of this declaration they are likely to have first considered what size force this might have afforded Owain. Therefore, it is worth giving air to the idea that this declaration aimed to provoke a defensive reaction in Britain, and was intended for French and English audiences, rather than a Welsh one. Aside from this consideration, the bellicose nature of the declaration left no doubt that Owain intended nothing less than war.

Although both missions were aborted or, in the case of 1372, redeployed to support other French operations, these efforts mark the first battlefield example of a combined French-Welsh force seeking to act in their perceived mutual interests on the British mainland. In 1372, after attacking Guernsey, Lawgoch's fleet sailed west along the Channel, then turned south at Brest. It combined with Castilian warships off La Rochelle and delivered a signal defeat to a large English fleet. Owain's troops put ashore and won a significant victory at Soubise, where they captured Sir Thomas Percy and Jean de Grailly, a key Gascon commander. These efforts, combined with the renowned Bertrand du Guesclin who took Niort and much of the region around La Rochelle, delivered a series of gains and victories for the French during that summer's campaigning season. Lawgoch's French-sponsored missions of 1369 and 1372 could readily be identified as part of a wider initiative by a France resurgent after Brétigny, to draw allies into the conflict with England. French machinations with Owain Lawgoch offer a microcosm of a broader strategy which also involved Portugal, Castile and Scotland.[62]

Owain Lawgoch could be depicted as an agent of French polity; although that is perhaps unfair. The 1372 declaration poses the intriguing question whether the venture was a well-developed ruse. Although the outcome of either the 1369 or the 1372 does not determine their true intent, it is noteworthy that England reacted to cover Wales on both occasions. English actions then proved that Wales was still not safely absorbed into England's body politic, irrespective of the wording of the 1284 Statute of Rhuddlan which declared Wales assimilate.[63]

The apogee of Welsh-French relations? Owain Glyndŵr and the court of Charles VI

In contrast to earlier examples of Welsh-French alliances, where there is no evidence of any enduring connection or even recollection of previous contact, Owain Glyndŵr was able to call upon the fond French memory of Owain Lawgoch.[64] Although Glyndŵr is widely remembered as a warrior and nobleman of fine lineage, his diplomatic successes arguably outstripped all his other achievements. Before the outbreak of the revolt, nothing hinted that Owain had talents in these areas. However, prior to his first formal documented exchange with the French in May 1404, Owain had already made contact with several other powers and factions, intending to construct alliances with them.[65] In France itself, Glyndŵr won significant support from the Orleanist party; the ruling faction at the French court at that key moment. As a consequence, the French also involved those under their influence: the Castilians, the pope in Avignon and the Bretons. Louis, duke of Orleans, bore Henry IV a personal enmity which helped Welsh appeals, which Owain exploited in his letters. French involvement with Owain Glyndŵr certainly pre-dated the formal treaty of alliance of 1404: French and Breton troops joined Welsh rebels to assault Kidwelly in October 1403, as well as landing soldiers from French and Breton pirate vessels for another joint attack on Caernarfon and the surrounding area the following year.[66]

Although the correspondence which initially enticed the French to support the Welsh rebellion is lost, were it ever committed to parchment, a body of Glyndŵr's letters has survived. Analysis of these reveals a clearly defined style: the voice of Owain Glyndŵr. While cautiously balancing this assertion against the knowledge that Owain attracted a number of skilled clergymen to his side prior to 1404, his letters pre-dating that point contain similar stylistic markers to those which followed.[67]

In his letters, Owain emerges as appropriately gracious, engaging and bright. Owain's classic traits are the use of colourful, emotive, often aggressive phraseology and repetition to emphasise the message he wished to convey. In addition, he frequently invoked themes of piety. The early letters consistently bear the classic hallmarks of Glyndŵr's style: intelligently reasoned, evoking the divine, using emotive imagery, repetition and aggression to deliver a decisively clear message. Glyndŵr's letters to the French would be similar, where appropriate.

In 1404, Owain's embassy party was led by his chancellor, Gruffudd Yonge, doctor of canon law and his acting bishop of Bangor, and John Hanmer, Owain's brother-in-law. Important ambassadorial missions of the period comprised a leading noble, preferably one of the royal blood, and a cleric of equivalent rank, usually a bishop, the keeper of the king's privy seal or a chancellor, who were empowered to act in place of their leader. It is noteworthy that the Welsh, although apparently excluded from such high-ranking affairs since the fall of Gwynedd in 1282, clearly knew the appropriate methods and requirements for diplomatic parties of the time. It is perhaps more striking that they were able to assemble a team capable of treating with the French.[68] The size and eminence of the French party conducting negotiations with Yonge and Hanmer demonstrated the importance they attached to the Welsh rebellion. In June 1404, the first negotiations were held with Jacques de Bourbon, count of la Marche, and Jean Montagu, bishop of Chartres and half-brother to the king. On 14 July, the alliance was ratified by another Bourbon count, Louis of Vendôme, also the French chancellor, Arnaud de Corbie, and no fewer than three bishops, those of Arras, Noyon and Meaux. Although largely formulaic, the treaty contained eleven clauses to bind the Welsh and French leaders in a 'most powerful union against Henry of Lancaster, adversary and enemy of both parties, and his adherents and supporters'.[69] In keeping with the mores of the time, the ambassadors solemnly exchanged promises, swearing for their masters on the holy gospels of God, thereby bringing the alliance into existence. This treaty was the first time Owain formally described himself in writing as *Owynus, Dei gratia princeps Wallie*: Owain, by the grace of God, prince of Wales.

The French wasted no time in honouring their promises, immediately writing to the Castilians, requesting them to send ships and soldiers. They joined French troops and ships in Brittany in August where they waited for their appointed commander, Jacques de Bourbon. He wasted the opportunity, vainly pursuing a love interest in Paris, reluctantly presenting himself in Brest in November. The fleet launched but only half-heartedly harassed shipping in the Channel before returning. The moment was lost and Jacques was vilified by French chroniclers.[70] The French resolved to make amends for the shame brought on their name by Jacques de Bourbon and sent another, smaller fleet the following year. That army, led by some of the brightest stars of the French military, landed in west Wales in August 1405 and campaigned in Wales with the rebels. That was a staggering achievement: no previous Welsh or French leader had managed to bring such close military cooperation between the two powers, and that event enabled the French to confront the English adversary on the British mainland. This is a signal moment in Welsh and British history, as well as demonstrating that the conflict in Wales was another theatre in the Hundred Years War.

In 1406, the relationship continued with perhaps Owain's best-known document, the Pennal Declaration. Whereas the 1404 alliance secured Wales's temporal allegiance to the king of France, the Pennal Declaration agreed to transfer Wales's spiritual loyalties to the papal candidate preferred by the French. As such, it bound the Welsh to the French in the temporal and spiritual spheres. While reasonable to sustain that Gruffydd Yonge and others of Owain's ecclesiastical entourage formulated the longer, religious parts of the declaration, for they understood the mechanics of Church business, the document gives another example of Owain Glyndŵr's voice:

the angry one that used repetition and colourful, violent phraseology. Two documents comprise the Pennal Declaration: a short preamble and a longer, more detailed letter.

The preamble appears to have been dictated by Owain, since the author speaks in the first person, referring to 'my nation', for example. Also, he referred to English barbarism three times in this short note and again described them as 'Saxons'. In the Pennal Declaration, the same voice that wrote the letters to the king of Scotland and Henry Don spoke of the Welsh Church being 'violently compelled, by the barbarous fury of those reigning in this country, to obey the church of Canterbury, and de facto still remains in this subjection'. It appealed for French support to 'remove violence and oppression from the Church and my subjects'. He also displayed a subtle, even gentle side to his language: 'as you deemed us worthy to raise us out of darkness into light'. In this brief letter, Owain's intelligence seems perceptible.[71]

The majority of the Pennal Declaration concerned the schism and was most likely scripted by Welsh churchmen with French advice. However, the final part also requested the Avignon pope to recreate the Welsh Church. In the short end section, the same aggressive voice identified elsewhere again becomes apparent. Owain repeatedly likened English behaviour to that of 'barbarous Saxons', yet elsewhere he used *Anglie* or the appropriate cognate.[72] Therefore, Owain deliberately referred to them as Saxons, and this would have been resonant with his contemporaries. That term tied into other European thought and literature of their time. A similar term to describe the English as *Sesnes* also appears in contemporary French treatises. Italian writers of the period also described the German armies which descended on Italy as barbarians. The Scottish chronicler, Walter Bower, described the English as Saxons in specific reference to this conflict with the Welsh, despite calling them English elsewhere in his works.[73] The theme and revulsion of barbarism was used to recount the unwarranted destruction of something innocent, perhaps holy. Characterising the English as Saxons and, by inference, pagan barbarians, resonated with other European writings and legitimised making war on them. Consequently, Owain used clever linguistic ploys in the declaration, shrewdly weaving French terminology into his reply while relating the case to comparable issues faced by the

Welsh. Similarly, the French letter to Owain identified the Roman pope as 'the intruder' and, in a repetition of the preamble's appropriation of French terms, Owain's articles referred to 'the intruder Henry of Lancaster'.[74] He also called for a crusade against Henry with a blend of aggression and religious zeal:

> Again, that the lord Benedict shall brand as heretics and cause to be tortured in the usual manner, Henry of Lancaster, the intruder of the kingdom of England, and the usurper of the crown of the same kingdom, and his adherents, in that of their own free will they have burnt or have caused to be burnt so many cathedrals, convents and parish churches; that they have savagely hung, beheaded, and quartered archbishops, bishops, prelates, priests, religious men, as madmen or beggars, or caused the same to be done.[75]

Owain closed by requesting that the French presented the letter to the Avignon pope, Benedict XIII, and that they supported the Welsh cause. However, the short preamble and the end section contain the classic elements of an address by Owain Glyndŵr: a well-structured argument, repetition of key ideas, religious references, violent language and emotive appeal. In his dealings with the French, Owain appears shrewd, pious, educated, well advised, intelligent and a dedicated opponent of King Henry. In addition, he appeared well versed in the political themes and arguments circulating European courts; he was certainly no isolated, unconnected uplander. In that light, it is easy to understand why they considered him worthy and loyally retained his amity. The French in this period were steadfast allies, although beset by civil war and invasion by Henry V, which limited their effectiveness to act elsewhere. The French called for Welsh ecclesiastical independence, perhaps after Owain's death, at the period's grand international conference, the Council of Constance, in sessions falling in March 1417.[76]

Conclusions

It is worth briefly asking whether, in each case of diplomacy outlined above, the Welsh were hostages to the whims of French political desire. Owain Gwynedd could not be described as a French proxy: he successfully courted Louis's support after twice defeating Henry II on the battlefield. The evolution of Owain's diplomatic efforts mark an impressive first in Welsh history. Although Louis did not articulate French power within the British Isles, he did exercise his authority over the recalcitrant Henry and the plaintiffs at La Ferté-Bernard. Henry likely understood the message delivered there: if Louis could bring those powers to peace, he might also bring them to war. Although Owain Gwynedd died peacefully shortly afterwards, for a time, he moved in similar political circles as other recognised powers, the Bretons, Gascons, Poitevins and Scots, as well as with the French and English.

During his five-decade reign, Llywelyn ap Iorwerth campaigned successfully against the kings of England before and after his alliance with Philip Augustus. Clearly, he did not enter any alliance at the command of the French king. When Philip proposed at least one alliance with Llywelyn, the prince of Gwynedd accepted to benefit his interests, without jeopardising his position. Significantly, he formed one part of a multi-factional alliance forged to support and protect Prince Louis's attempt to claim the throne of England, around the time of the Magna Carta rebellion.

Although Owain Lawgoch was clearly in the pay of the French, it would be incorrect to represent him solely as their pawn. He elected to join and remain under their colours, and was lauded and rewarded by the French. Owain Glyndŵr's achievements were genuinely remarkable. It is noteworthy that in spite of a long Welsh absence from international diplomacy, the composition of Glyndŵr's embassies mirrored the form, if not the size and eminence, of that of the French by containing men of the blood and the cloth, as well as legal specialists. By no measure could Owain Glyndŵr be viewed as a French creation or proxy; however, the more deeply entwined the Welsh became with their French allies, the more they appeared to depend on them.

So, throughout these periods of alliance, it is clear that the Welsh were not simply French pawns but powers in their own right. In fact, neither party appeared beholden to the other in any of these cases. The continuous appeal of the Welsh to a major power, combined with their role in some of the notable events of their continental region, elevates them beyond the fringe to which some general studies relegate them. These treaties also show that the Welsh were able to communicate appropriately within the norms of their time, and to organise themselves along similar lines to their contemporaries.

Medieval alliances commonly lacked permanence or continuity: relations were played out in an interrupted fashion through the movements of changing dynastic, military, economic, governmental and religious pressures.[77] The fact that official Welsh-French connections pre-date the Franco-Scots 'Auld Alliance' has not yet attracted the attention it is perhaps due. Perhaps Welsh-French relations should be known as 'the Aulder Alliance'. The examples of union from the later Middle Ages demonstrate French recognition of Wales's continued existence as a distinct entity a century after 'conquest'. The repetition and renewal of Welsh-French connections show that these links have a broader significance than simply being adjunct details of the long-lived dispute between France and England. It seems evident that each side found benefit in maintaining links, however fitful, irrespective of who considered themselves master of Wales. French-Welsh relations of the age highlight examples of France's military-political drive over a three-century span, as well as the capabilities of the Welsh with whom they sought these alliances.

APPENDIX 6.1:

Translated sources for Welsh-French diplomacy

a) Owain Gwynedd's third letter to the court of Louis VII, between September 1165 and 24 April 1166
(Pryce, 'Owain Gwynedd and Louis VII', 7–8, 27–8)

To the very excellent Louis, by the grace of God king of the French, Owain, prince of Wales, his very faithful man and friend, [sends] very devoted service with [his] greeting. Although the report of all, most serene king, proclaims you to be conspicuous as one in whom all can and should have complete trust, the clemency known to me by experience, and the kindness towards subjects and those having complete trust in you, make me choose you as the sole adviser to whom in difficulties I may complain loudly of my necessity. For as often as I have informed you about myself and my cares by the writing of letters, you have received not only the letters but their bearers benevolently and treated them kindly. Through the latter you have counselled me, thanks be to God and you, as a pious king should counsel someone having complete trust in him. Now that, therefore, difficulties are all around me at present, I do not wish my kind adviser to be ignorant of the situation. Preceded by no evil deeds of mine, in the past summer the king of England has waged against me the war which, as is known to you, he has planned for many days with the harshness of his tyranny. But when in the conflict the five armies of our side came together, thanks be to God and you, more of his men fell than mine. Having seen this, he wrongfully and harmfully mutilated my hostages, although he had not presented them previously for the keeping of peace. But, because all things are disposed of not by the wishes of man but by the will of God, he moved the army towards England, not through our merits, perhaps, but through the prayers of the humble to the saints, and by the saints' intercession to God; however, he left me uncertain of the outcome to the end, because he arranged neither a peace nor a truce with us. Angered therefore because the result had not turned out as he had hoped, on his departure he ordered the foreigners and all whom he gathered together to defeat us to come with him against us again after next Easter. On that account I vigorously entreat your clemency that you will inform me through the bearer of this present letter whether you are resolved to wage war against him, so that in that war I may both serve you by harming him according to your advice and take vengeance for the war he waged against me. But if you do not propose this, inform me by this bearer what you advise, what help you wish to bestow on me. I have no way of evading his snares unless you grant me advice and help. I commend to you moreover my private and familiar cleric and kinsman, Guiardus, that you may provide him with necessities for the love of God and us. I sent him before into your presence with my letters, which you did not believe were mine, so we were told. But they were mine, I bring in God as my witness, and through them I commended him to you from the depths of my heart. I vigorously entreat your clemency concerning this as well, that just as you have begun to render peaceful towards me the prelates of the Church, namely the pope and the archbishop of Canterbury, so you will continue to do so. Farewell.

b) Llywelyn ap Iorwerth's reply to Philip Augustus, c.1215–16 (Welsh Records, pp. 3–4, 57–8)

To our most excellent lord Philip, by the grace of God, the illustrious King of the French, Llywelyn, Prince of North Wales, his friend, sends greeting and such devotion as the debt of fealty and respectful service, which I will repay the excellency of your nobility, on account of the singular and priceless gifts, which you, King of the French, even prince of that country of kings, outstripping me, your friend, not more munificently than magnificently, have sent me by your knight, your letters, impressed by your golden seal in witness of the alliance of the kingdom of the French and the principality of North Wales, which I, before an assembly of clergy, even on the sacrosanct relics swear to observe as they will be a perpetual memorial and an inviolable testimony, that I and my heirs, cleaving inseparably to you and your heirs, shall be your friends' friends, to your enemies' enemies. This itself therefore stipulating, I expect and ask from your kingly dignity to be royally observed in every manner towards me and towards my friends, and in order that it may be inviolably observed, having called together a council of my chieftains, and with the common consent of all the princes of Wales all of whom I have joined with you in the friendship of this treaty promise you, under witness of my seal, fidelity in perpetuity, and as I thus faithfully promise I will carry out my promise more faithfully. Moreover, since I received letters of your excellency, I have made neither truce, nor peace, nor any negotiation whatever with the English. But, by the grace of God, I and all the princes of Wales, unitedly confederated, will manfully resist our enemies, even yours, and by the help of God and with a strong hand, we will recover from the yoke of the tyrants themselves the great part of the land and the strongly fortified castles, which they by fraud and guile have occupied. And being recovered, we will powerfully hold [them] in the Lord God, whence stipulating, we, the princes of all Wales, desire that without us, neither truce nor peace will ye make with the English, [for] let it be decreed, that by no pact or reward, unless by the foreknown kindness of your wish, will we be joined to them in any peace or treaty.

Endorsement – The Covenant of Llywelyn, Prince of North Wales, with the Lord King of France.

c) Owain Lawgoch's declaration of alliance with King Charles V of France, 10 May 1372
(Owen, 'Owain Lawgoch', 61–2)

Evain de Gales, to all those whom these letters shall come, Greeting. The kings of England in past times having treacherously and covetously, tortuously and without cause and by deliberate treasons, slain or caused to be slain my ancestors, kings of Wales, and others of them have put out of their country, and that country have by force and power appropriated and have submitted its people to divers services, the which country is and should be mine by right of succession, by kindred, by heritage and by right of decent from my ancestors the kings of that country, and in order to obtain help and succour to recover that country which is my heritage, I have visited several Christian kings, princes and noble lords, and have clearly declared and shown unto them my rights therein and have requested and supplicated their aid, and have latterly come unto the most puissant and renowned sovereign Charles, by the grace of God king of France, dauphin of Vienne, and have shown unto him my right in the aforesaid country and have made unto him the aforenamed requests and supplications, and he having had compassion upon my state and understanding the great wrong that the kings of England have done unto my ancestors in former times, and that the present king of England has done unto me, and of his beneficent and accustomed clemency in which he is the singular mirror and example amongst Christians of justice, grace and mercy to all those that are oppressed and require comforting, has granted me his aid and the assistance of his men-at-arms and fleet in order to recover the said realm, which is my rightful heritage, as has been said; know all ye, therefore, that in return for the great love that my said lord the king of France has shown unto me, and is truly showing by his expenditure of three hundred thousand francs of gold, and more, as well in the pay of men-at-arms, archers and arbalesters as in [the provision of] ships and the pay and expenses of the sailors, in harness and other matters in various expenses, the which sum I am at the present time not able to furnish, I promise loyally and by my faith and oath upon the holy evangelists, touched corporeally by me, and for my heirs and successors for ever, and the aforesaid sum of three hundred thousand francs of gold I will return and wholly repay, or my heirs and successors or those who may claim through them (ou ceul qui auront cause d'eulx), or by their will or command, without any other terms; and I herewith have made and entered into, for me my heirs an successors and for all my country and subjects for ever, with my said lord the king of France for him and his successors and for all their country and subjects, a good and firm treaty, union and alliance, by which I will aid and assist them by my person, my subjects and my country, to the utmost power and loyalty against all persons alive or dead (contre toutes personnes qui povent vivre et mourir). In witness of which I have sealed these letters with mine own seal Given at Paris the 10th day of May, the year of grace one thousand three hundred and seventy-two.

d) The relevant section of the 1406 Pennal Declaration (Welsh Records, pp. 95–9)

'Following the advice of our council, we have called together the nobles of our race, the prelates of our Principality and others called for this purpose, and, at length, after diligent examination and discussion of the foregoing articles and their contents being thoroughly made by the prelates and the clergy, it is agreed and determined that we, trusting in the rights of the lord Benedict, the holy Roman and supreme pontiff of the universal church, especially because he sought the peace and unity of the church, and as we understood daily seeks it, considering the hard service of the adversary of the same Benedict, tearing the seamless coat of Christ, and on account of the sincere love we specially bear towards your excellency, we have determined that the said lord Benedict shall be recognized as the true Vicar of Christ in our lands, by us and our subjects, and we recognize him by these presents.

Whereas, most illustrious prince, the underwritten articles especially concern our state and the reformation and usefulness of the Church of Wales, we humbly pray your royal majesty that you will graciously consider it worthy to advance their object, even in the court of the said lord Benedict:

First, that all ecclesiastical censures against us, our subjects, or our land, by the aforesaid Benedict or Clement his predecessor, at present existing, the same by the said Benedict be removed.

Again, that whatsoever vows and of whatsoever nature given by us or whomsoever of our principality, to those who called themselves Urban or Boniface, lately deceased, or to their adherents, shall be absolved.

Again, that he shall confirm and ratify the orders, collations, titles of prelates, dispensations, notorial documents, and all things whatso ever, from the time of Gregory XI., from which, any danger to the souls, or prejudice to us, or our subjects, may occur, or may be engendered.

Again, that the Church of St. David's shall be restored to its original dignity, from which time of St. David, archbishop and confessor, was a metropolitan church, and after his death, twenty-four archbishops succeeded him in the same place, as their names are contained in the chronicles and ancient books of the church of Menevia, and we cause these to be stated as the chief evidence, namely, Eliud, Ceneu, Morfael, Mynyw, Haerwnen, Elwaed, Gwrnwen, Llewdwyd, Gwrwyst, Gwgawn, Clydâwg, Aman, Elias, Maelyswyd, Sadwrnwen, Cadell, Alaethwy, Novis, Sadwrnwen, Drochwel, Asser, Arthwael, David II., and Samson; and that as a metropolitan church it had and ought to have the undermentioned suffragan churches, namely, Exeter, Bath, Hereford, Worcester, Leicester, which is now translated to the churches of Coventry and Lichfield, St. Asaph, Bangor, and Llandaf. For being crushed by the fury of the barbarous Saxons, who usurped to themselves the land of Wales, they trampled upon the aforesaid church of St. David's, and made her a handmaiden to the church of Canterbury.

Again, that the same lord Benedict shall provide for the metropolitan church of St. David's, and the other cathedral churches of our principality, prelates, dignitaries, and beneficed clergy and curates who know our language.

Again, that the lord Benedict shall revoke and annul all incorporations, unions, annexations, appropriations of parochial churches of our principality made so far, by any authority whatsoever with English monasteries and colleges. That the true patrons of these churches shall have the power to present to the ordinaries of those places suitable persons to the same or appoint others.

Again, that the said lord Benedict shall concede to us and to our heirs, the princes of Wales, that our chapels, &c., shall be free, and shall rejoice in the privileges, exemptions, and immunities in which they rejoiced in the times of our forefathers the princes of Wales.

Again, that we shall have two universities or places of general study, namely one in North Wales and the other in South Wales, in cities, towns, or places to be hereafter decided and determined by our ambassadors and nuncios for that purpose.

Again, that the lord Benedict shall brand as heretics and cause to be tortured in the usual manner, Henry of Lancaster, the intruder of the kingdom of England, and the usurper of the crown of the same kingdom, and his adherents, in that of their own free will they have burnt or have caused to be burnt so many cathedrals, convents, and parish churches; that they have savagely hung, beheaded, and quartered archbishops, bishops, prelates, priests, religious men, as madmen or beggars, or caused the same to be done.

Again, that the same lord Benedict shall grant to us, our heirs, subjects, and adherents, of whatsoever nation they may be, who wage war against the aforesaid intruder and usurper, as long as they hold the orthodox faith, full remission of all our sins, and that the remission shall continue as long as the war between us, our heirs, and our subjects, and the aforesaid Henry, his heirs, and subjects shall endure.

In testimony whereof we make these our letters patent. Given at Pennal on the thirty-first day of March, A.D. 1406, and in the sixth year of our rule.

Endorsement. – The letter by which Owen, Prince of Wales, reduces himself, his lands, and his dominions to the obedience of our lord the Pope Benedict XIII.

Notes

1. P. Geary, *The Myth of Nations: The Medieval Origins of Europe* (Princeton: Princeton University Press, 2003), p. 15; N. Evans, 'The changing context of Welsh historiography 1890–2000', in H. Brocklehurst and R. Philips (eds), *History, Nationhood and the Question of Britain* (Basingstoke: Palgrave Macmillan, 2004), pp. 20–32; R. A. Marsden, 'Gerald of Wales and Competing Interpretations of the Welsh Middle Ages c.1870–1910', *WHR*, 25.3 (2011), 314–45.
2. G. F. Warner (ed.), *Gerald of Wales, De principis instructione* in *GCO*, viii, pp. 292–3; J. Stevenson (trans.), *Concerning the Instruction of Princes* (Felinfach: Llanerch, 1991 [1858]), p. 93; M. Aurell, 'Henry II and the Arthurian Legend', in C. Harper-Bill and N. Vincent (eds), *Henry II, New Interpretations* (Woodbridge: Boydell, 2007), pp. 362–94.
3. D. Wyatt, 'Gruffudd ap Cynan and the Hiberno-Norse World', *WHR*, 19.4 (2000), 595–617.
4. Gerald of Wales, *The Journey Through Wales / The Description of Wales*, trans. L. Thorpe (London: Penguin Books, 1978), pp. 234–5, and see above, Kathryn Hurlock's chapter in this volume.
5. G. Duby, *France in the Middle Ages, 987–1460*, trans. J. Vale (Oxford: Oxford University Press, 1991 [1987]), p. 197; *The Mabinogion*, trans. S. Davies (Oxford: Oxford University Press, 2007), pp. xvii–xxiv.
6. M. Pacaut, *Louis VII et son royaume* (Paris: SEVPEN, 1964), pp. 38, 110; H. Pryce, 'Owain Gwynedd and Louis VII: The Franco-Welsh Diplomacy of the First Prince of Wales', *WHR*, 19.1 (1998), 1–28; J. Baldwin, *The Government of Philip Augustus: Foundations of French Royal Power in the Middle Ages* (Berkeley: University of California Press, 1986), p. 408; *AWR*, pp. 324–9; T. Bisson, *The Crisis of the Twelfth Century. Power, Lordship and the Origins of European Government* (Princeton: Princeton University Press, 2009), pp. 402–3; R. Turvey, *Owain Gwynedd, Prince of the Welsh* (Talybont: Y Lolfa, 2012), pp. 63–95. See Appendix 6.1, a).
7. D. Cathcart-King, 'Henry II and the Fight at Coleshill', *WHR*, 2 (1964–5), 367–73; Bisson, *Crisis*, pp. 229–33.
8. Gerald of Wales, *The Journey Through Wales*, p. 245.
9. Pacaut, *Louis VII*, pp. 187–94; Pryce, 'Owain Gwynedd and Louis VII', 13–14.
10. J. E. Lloyd, *A History of Wales from the Earliest Times to the Edwardian Conquest*, 2 vols (London: Longman, 1911–12; repr. 1939 and 1948), ii, pp. 480–4, 521; W. J. Millor, H. E. Butler and C. N. L. Brooke (eds), *The Letters of John of Salisbury*, 2 vols (Oxford: Oxford University

Press, 1979–86 [1955]), i, pp. 135–6; *AOC*, pp. 189–90; *The Correspondence of Thomas Becket, Archbishop of Canterbury, 1162–1170*, ed. A. J. Duggan, 2 vols (Oxford: Clarendon Press, 2000), i, pp. 32–3, 234–41.

[11] Pryce, 'Owain Gwynedd and Louis VII', 4–6.

[12] P. Barbier, *The Age of Owain Gwynedd* (London: David Nutt, 1908), pp. 99–102; Lloyd, *History of Wales*, ii, pp. 518–21; M. Pacaut, *Frederick Barbarossa*, trans. A. Pomerans (London: Collins, 1970), pp. 114–23; Y. Sassier, *Louis VII* (Paris: Fayard, 1991), pp. 293–306; W. Warren, *Henry II* (London: Eyre Methuen, 1973), pp. 97–105, 164, 451; M. Aurell, *The Plantagenet Empire, 1154–1224*, trans. D. Crouch (Harlow: Pearson Longman, 2007), p. 220.

[13] K. Fowler (ed.), *The Hundred Years War* (London: Macmillan, 1971), pp. 186–7.

[14] Pryce, 'Owain Gwynedd and Louis VII', 1, 7–8, 27–8; S. Duffy, 'Henry II and England's insular neighbours', in *Henry II: New Interpretations*, p. 136.

[15] Barbier, *Owain Gwynedd*, pp. 97–101; Lloyd, *History of Wales*, ii, pp. 514–18; Warren, *Henry II*, pp. 163–4; P. Latimer, 'Henry II's Campaign against the Welsh in 1165', *WHR*, 14.4 (1989), 523–52; *AOC*, p. 53; K. Maund, *The Welsh Kings. Warriors, Warlords and Princes* (Stroud: Tempus, 2000), pp. 168–9; D. Hosler, *Henry II, A Medieval Soldier at War, 1147–1189* (Leiden: Brill, 2007), pp. 140–2; Turvey, *Owain Gwynedd*, pp. 64–83.

[16] Millor et al., *John of Salisbury*, ii, pp. 106–9.

[17] *Brut y Tywysogyon or The chronicle of the princes. Peniarth ms. 20 version*, trans. T. Jones (Cardiff: University of Wales Press, 1952), henceforth *ByT*, p. 63.

[18] Barbier, *Owain Gwynedd*, pp. 86–102; Lloyd, *History of Wales*, ii, pp. 518–21; R. Turvey, *Lord Rhys: Prince of Deheubarth* (Llandysul: Gomer, 1997), p. 49; Maund, *Welsh Kings*, pp. 168–9.

[19] *AOC*, p. 38.

[20] Millor et al., *John of Salisbury*, ii, pp. 602–9.

[21] Duffy, 'Henry II and England's insular neighbours', p. 136; Turvey, *Owain Gwynedd*, pp. 84–95, 121–34.

[22] T. Matthews (ed. and trans.), *Welsh Records in Paris* (Carmarthen: Spurrell, 1910), henceforth *Welsh Records*, pp. xv–xvii; R. Treharne, 'The Franco-Welsh Treaty of Alliance in 1212', *BBCS*, 18 (1958), 60–75; G. Brough, 'Medieval Diplomatic History: France and the Welsh, 1163–1417' (unpublished PhD thesis, Cardiff University, 2013), 97–156.

[23] K. Norgate, *John Lackland* (London: Macmillan, 1902), pp. 253–4, 258–60; *ByT*, p. 89; W. L. Warren, *King John* (New Haven: Yale University Press, 1997), pp. 247–8; R. Turner, *King John* (London: Longman, 1994), pp. 252, 256; J. Bradbury, *Philip Augustus: King of France 1180–1223* (London: Longman, 1998), pp. 320–1; R. Turvey, *Llywelyn the Great: Prince of Gwynedd* (Llandysul: Gomer, 2007), pp. 59–60.

[24] *Welsh Records*, pp. xv–xvii. Matthews initially identified 1212 as the 'very probable' date, then built a more compelling case that the evidence 'decides in favour of the later rather than the earlier date'. According to primary sources, the later date seems almost certainly accurate, although there might have been two alliances. See also Brough, 'Medieval Diplomatic History', 97–156, and Appendix 6.1, b).

[25] 'not more munificently than magnificently' and 'friends to your friends and enemies to your enemies'.

[26] *Welsh Records*, pp. 3–4; Treharne, 'Franco-Welsh Treaty', 62; *AWR*, pp. 392–3.

[27] *Welsh Records*, pp. 57–8; *ByT*, p. 89; Treharne, 'Franco-Welsh Treaty', 65, 68; J. Stephenson (ed.), *Mediaeval Chronicles of Scotland. The Chronicles of Melrose and Holyrood* (Lampeter: Llanerch, 1988 [1850]), p. 45; Turvey, *Llywelyn*, pp. 59–60.

[28] Norgate, *John Lackland*, pp. 93–103, 114–17, 196–206; M. Powicke, *The Loss of Normandy, 1189–1204* (Manchester: Manchester University Press, 1961), pp. 93–4, 251–70; Turner, *King John*, pp. 115–35; Warren, *King John*, pp. 84–99, 116–20, 217–24.

[29] Turner, *King John*, pp. 13–17, 139, 226, 256; A. Duncan, 'King John of England and the king of Scots', and I. Rowlands, 'King John and Wales', in S. D. Church (ed.), *King John: New Interpretations* (Woodbridge: Boydell, 1999), pp. 265–7, 258–9, 285–7; B. Holden, *Lords of the Central Marches English Aristocracy and Frontier Society, 1087–1265* (Oxford: Oxford University Press, 2008), pp. 1–11, 166–229; C. Veach, *Lordship in Four Realms: The Lacy Family, 1166–1241* (Manchester: Manchester University Press, 2014), pp. 130–59, 167–86.

[30] Norgate, *John Lackland*, pp. 149–53, 163, 171–2, 210–7; C. Samaran et al. (eds), *Recueil des actes de Philippe Auguste, Roi de France*, 4 vols (Paris : Imprimerie Nationale, 1966–79), iii, pp. 161–2; C. Cheney, *Innocent III and England* (Stuttgart: Hiersemann, 1976), pp. 360–7; Warren, *King John*, pp. 105–16, 181–91, 224–40, 243, 246–56; Turner, *King John*, pp. 99–114, 126–8, 138, 175–224; J. Bradbury, 'Philip Augustus and King John: Personality and History', in Church (ed.), *King John*, p. 354; Rowlands, 'King John and Wales', p. 286.

31   J. A. Giles, *Roger of Wendover's Flowers of History* (London: Bohn, 1849), pp. 257–8, 275–8; *ByT*, pp. 86; Norgate, *John Lackland*, pp. 210–22; Cheney, *Innocent III*, pp. 326–8; Warren, *King John*, pp. 181, 224–32; D. Crouch, 'Baronial paranoia in King John's reign', in J. S. Loengard (ed.), *Magna Carta and the England of King John* (Woodbridge: Boydell, 2010), pp. 45–62.

32   *ByT*, pp. 79–82, 85; A. Carr, *Medieval Wales* (Basingstoke: Macmillan, 1995), p. 55; D. Walker, *Medieval Wales* (Cambridge: Cambridge University Press, 1990), pp. 93–4; Turvey, *Llywelyn*, pp. 35–41, 52–9.

33   C. Cheney, 'King John and the Papal Interdict', *Bulletin of the John Rylands Library*, 31, (1948), 297–300; Cheney, *Innocent III*, pp. 59, 272, 303–11, 319–25; A. Fliche, 'The advocate of church reform', in J. M. Powell (ed.), *Innocent III, Vicar of Christ or Lord of the World?* (2nd edn, Washington: Catholic University Press, 1994), p. 56; J. Sayers, *Innocent III, Leader of Europe, 1198–1216* (London: Longman, 1997), pp. 62–5, 175; C. Harper-Bill, 'John and the Church of Rome', in Church (ed.), *King John*, p. 305. And see Bryn Jones's chapter in this volume, n. 86.

34   Norgate, *John Lackland*, pp. 159, 169, 171–4; Cheney, *Innocent III*, pp. 324, 360–7; Turner, *King John*, pp. 16–19, 135; Warren, *King John*, pp. 224–32; N. Barratt, 'The Revenues of John and Philip Augustus Revisited', in Church (ed.), *King John*, p. 91.

35   Giles, *Wendover*, p. 257; Matthew Paris, *Chronica Majora*, ed. Henry R. Luard, 7 vols (London: Longman, 1872–83), ii., p. 534; A. O. Anderson (ed.), *Scottish Annals From English Chroniclers, A.D. 500 to 1286* (London: David Nutt, 1908; repr. Edinburgh: Oliver and Boyd, 1922), p. 331; Norgate, *John Lackland*, p. 169; Warren, *King John*, pp. 65, 200; *AWR*, pp. 392–3; Crouch, 'Baronial paranoia', pp. 58–9.

36   Norgate, *John Lackland*, pp. 167–9, 179–82; *ByT*, p. 87; Cheney, *Innocent III*, pp. 332–43; Turner, *King John*, pp. 139, 166–74; Turvey, *Llywelyn*, pp. 56–7.

37   T. Rymer (ed.), *Fœdera, conventiones, literae, et cujuscunque generis acta publica, inter reges Angliae, et alios quosvis imperatores, reges, pontifices, principes, vel communitates, ab ineunte saecula duodecimo, viz. ab anno 1101, ad nostra usque tempora, habita aut tractata; ex autographis, infra tempora, habita aut tractata; ex autographis, infra secretiores Archivorum regiorum thesaurarias, per multa saecula reconditis, fideliter exscripta*, 20 vols (London: HMSO, 1704–35), henceforth *Fœdera*, i, p. 207; H. R. Luard (ed.), *Annales Monastici*, 5 vols (London: Longmans, 1864–9), ii: *Waverleia*, p. 283; iii: *Dunstaplia*, p. 45; Giles, *Wendover*, pp. 307–8, 357–9; W. Stubbs (ed.), *Memoriale Fratris Walteri de Coventria*, 2 vols (London:

Longman and Co, 1873), ii, pp. 218–28; J. Stevenson (trans.), *Radulphi de Coggeshall Chronicon Anglicanum* (London: Longman and Co., 1875), pp. 171–85; Norgate, *John Lackland*, pp. 256–7; Turner, *King John*, p. 252; Warren, *King John*, pp. 251–2.

[38] F. Michel (ed.), *Histoire des ducs de Normandie et des rois d'Angleterre* (Paris: Société de l'histoire de France, 1840), p. 179 : 'Li Galois vinrent par nuit traire en l'ost, si lor fisent moult grant paour. Longhement furent armé por atendre la bataille; mais il ne l'orent pas, car li rois se traist arriere je ne sai pas par quel consel, et à tant remest. ('The Welsh came at night and drew up in battle order, and they were a very strong force. They were armed, ready for battle for a long time; but they did not have it, because the king drew back, I do not know by what advice, and so many returned.'); *ByT*, p. 93. King John's itinerary shows that he travelled along the Welsh border during the end of July and the first half of August 1216, during which time his efforts to reach agreement with Llywelyn and his allies were likely to have taken place. In addition, his letters show that he engaged Gwenwynwyn ab Owain Cyfeiliog to intercede with the king's allies and later, presumably when these initiatives failed, he held talks with minor border and southern nobles such as Gwallter Bychan, who sent a small force of three hundred men to serve the king: T. D. Hardy, ed., *Rotuli Litterarum Clausarum* (London: Public Records, 1833) vol. 1, p. 291; T. D. Hardy, ed., *Rotuli Litterarum Patentium* (London: Public Records, 1835) vol. 1, par. 1, pp. 189, 191. (With thanks to Rich Price for the references.)

[39] Giles, *Wendover*, p. 403; Stubbs, *Walteri de Coventria*, ii, pp. 220, 239; *Annales Monastici*, ii, pp. 286–7; A. O. Anderson (ed.), *Early Sources of Scottish History, A.D. 500 to 1286* (Edinburgh: Oliver and Boyd, 1922), p. 425; *ByT*, p. 96; Stephenson, *Melrose*, pp. 45, 51; R. Vaughan (ed. and trans.), *Chronicles of Matthew Paris: monastic life in the thirteenth century* (Gloucester: Alan Sutton, 1984), pp. 58–9; N. Vincent (ed.), *The Letters and Charters of Cardinal Guala Bicchieri, Papal Legate in England, 1216–1218*, Canterbury and York Society vol. LXXXIII (Woodbridge: Boydell, 1996), pp. 44–5; Barratt, 'The revenues of John and Philip Augustus revisited', p. 90; Duncan, 'John King of England and the Kings of Scots', p. 267.

[40] A. J. Holden, S. Gregory and D. Crouch (ed. and trans.), *History of William Marshal*, 3 vols (London: Anglo-Norman Text Society, 2004), ii, pp. 388–9; my brackets.

[41] P. Pressutti (ed.), *Regesta Honorii Papae III*, 2 vols (Rome, 1888), i, pp. 44–5; W. H. Bliss (ed.), *Calendar of Papal Registers Relating to Great Britain and Ireland, Volume 1: 1198–1304* (London: HMSO, 1893),

p. 43; A. Potthast (ed.), *Regesta Pontificum Romanorum de 1198 ab 1304*, 2 vols (Graz: Akademische Druck- u. Verlagsanstalt, 1957), i, pp. 473–4, 477; Vincent, *Letters and Charters*, pp. 43–5, 57, 82, 91–2, 124–5. See also Bryn Jones's chapter in this volume on Welsh relations with Honorius III.

[42] *Annales Monastici*, i: Burton, p. 224; ii: Wintonia, p. 83, Waverleia, pp. 285–8; iii: Dunstaplia, pp. 50–1; iv: Oseneia, p. 61, Wigornia, p. 409; Stubbs, *Walteri de Coventria*, ii, p. 239; H. F. Delaborde (ed.), *Œuvres de Rigord et de Guillaume le Breton. Historiens de Philippe-Auguste*, 2 vols (Paris: Librarie Renouard, 1882), i, pp. 307, 315; Anderson, *Early Sources*, p. 433.

[43] *Fœdera*, i, pp. 221–2 (no Welsh signatories); *ByT*, p. 96; Turvey, *Llywelyn*, p. 72.

[44] T. Hardy (ed.), *Rotuli Litterarum Patentium* (London: Record Commission, 1835), i, pp. 100, 103, 120; Norgate, *John Lackland*, pp. 193–4; *The Letters of Pope Innocent III (1198–1216) concerning England and Wales: a Calendar with an Appendix of texts*, ed. C. Cheney and M. Cheney (Oxford: Clarendon Press, 1967), p. 154; Warren, *King John*, p. 218; Turvey, *Llywelyn*, p. 59.

[45] *ByT*, p. 89; Turvey, *Llywelyn*, pp. 59–60.

[46] Stephenson, *Melrose*, p. 45.

[47] *Welsh Records*, pp. 3–4, 57–8.

[48] *Annales Monastici*, i: Wintonia, p. 81; Paris, *Chronica Majora*, ii, p. 534; *ByT*, pp. 85–6; Turvey, *Llywelyn*, pp. 52–7.

[49] *ByT*, pp. 89, 92–3. Note: if inaccurate on the matter of noble councils including clergy representation in 1212, then Treharne's argument largely collapses on this point. He conceded that there was a good case for there having been no such council in that year, Treharne, 'Franco-Welsh Treaty', 66, 70.

[50] Norgate, *John Lackland*, pp. 93–103, 114–17, 196–206; Powicke, *Loss of Normandy*, pp. 93–4, 251–70; Turner, *King John*, pp. 115–35; Warren, *King John*, pp. 84–99, 116–20, 217–24.

[51] Lloyd, *History of Wales*, ii, pp. 761–4; *AOC*, pp. 348–54; Walker, *Medieval Wales*, pp. 129–33; Carr, *Medieval Wales*, pp. 77–80.

[52] G. W. S. Barrow, *Feudal Britain* (London: Edward Arnold, 1956), pp. 359–62; *AOC*, pp. 353, 382–6; Walker, *Medieval Wales*, pp. 136–8, 154–7; Carr, *Medieval Wales*, pp. 84–8; J. N. Macdougall, 'L'Ecosse à la fin du XIIIe siècle: un royaume menacé', in J. Laidlaw (ed.), *The Auld Alliance, France and Scotland over 700 years* (Edinburgh: Edinburgh University Press, 1999), p.18; J. P. Clancy, *Medieval Welsh Poems* (Dublin: Four Courts Press, 2003), pp. 168–74. Note: financial

figures derived from the National Archives Currency Converter: www.nationalarchives.gov.uk/currency/results.asp#mid (accessed 21 August 2015).

53 *AOC*, p. 437; A. D. Carr, *Owen of Wales: The End of the House of Gwynedd* (Cardiff: University of Wales Press, 1991), pp. 78–9; D. Moore, *The Welsh Wars of Independence* (Stroud: Tempus, 2005), pp. 165–6.

54 E. Owen, 'Owain Lawgoch – Yeuain de Galles: Some Facts and Suggestions', *Trans. Hon. Soc. Cymm.* (1899–1900), 6–106; *AOC*, p. 438; Carr, *Owen of Wales*, pp. 21–37; M. Brown, *The Black Douglases. War and Lordship in Late Medieval Scotland, 1300–1455* (East Linton: Tuckwell Press, 1998), pp. 211–12.

55 Owen, 'Owain Lawgoch', pp. 52–4, 69–70; C. Allmand, *The Hundred Years War, England and France at war c. 1300–c. 1450* (Cambridge: Cambridge University Press, 1988), pp. 20–6, 73–6; A. D. Carr, 'Welshmen and the Hundred Years' War', *WHR*, 4 (1968), 32–3; M. Siddons, 'Welshmen in the Service of France', *BBCS*, 36, (1989), 162, 169, appendix n. 5; P. Galliou and M. Jones, *The Bretons* (Oxford: Blackwell, 1991), pp. 217–29; Carr, *Owen of Wales*, pp. 1–19, 21–37; K. A. Fowler, *Medieval Mercenaries, The Great Companies* (Oxford: Blackwell, 2001), pp. 155–239; A. J. Villalon and D. Kagay (eds), *The Hundred Years' War: A Wider Focus* (Leiden: Brill, 2005), pp. 3–209, 259–301.

56 *Fœdera*, vi, pp. 642–3; *CCR, 1369–1374*, pp. 61–2, 158; R. Delachanel, *Chronique des règnes de Jean II et Charles V*, 4 vols (Paris: Renouard, 1909–20), ii, pp. 137–9; Owen, 'Owain Lawgoch', 9–11, 59–60; C. de la Roncière, *Histoire de la marine Francaise, II: La guerre de cent ans: révolution maritime* (Paris: Plon-Nourrit, 1914), pp. 6–7; *AOC*, pp. 437–8; Carr, *Owen of Wales*, pp. 23–5.

57 P. Contamine, *Guerre, etat et société à la fin du Moyen Age: Etudes sur les armées des rois de France, 1337–1494* (Paris: Mouton, 1972), pp. 152, 576–7, 592–3.

58 N. Grèvy-Pons et al. (eds), *Jean de Montreuil, Opera*, 4 vols (Paris and Turin: Cemi and Giappichelli, 1964–86), ii, p. 113 (lines 703–5).

59 A. Thierry, *Histoire de la Conquête de l'Angleterre par les Normands* (Paris: Panthéon, 1851), iv, pp. 299–300; Owen, 'Owain Lawgoch', 61–2. See Appendix 6.1, c).

60 Owen, 'Owain Lawgoch', 13–15, 51–8, 80–1; *AOC*, p. 438; Walker, *Medieval Wales*, pp. 165–6; Carr, *Owen of Wales*, pp. 14–19, 23, 27, 53–6.

61 Owen, 'Owain Lawgoch', 9, 59–60; Carr, *Owen of Wales*, pp. 24–5, 42, 44–6, 50–1, 60, 78, 81–3; E. R. Henken, *National Redeemer, Owain*

Glyndŵr in Welsh Tradition (Cardiff: University of Wales Press, 1996), pp. 48–50.

62 Delachanel, Chronique, iii, p. 200; F. Autrand, 'Aux origines de l'Europe moderne : l'alliance Franco-Ecosse au XIVe siècle', in Laidlaw (ed.), *Auld Alliance*, p. 37.

63 I. Bowen (ed.), *The Statutes of Wales* (London: T. Fisher Unwin, 1908), pp. 2–27.

64 L. Bellaguet (ed.), *Chronique du religieux de Saint-Denys, le regne de Charles VI, de 1380 à 1422*, 6 vols (Paris: Crapelet, 1840), henceforth *Saint-Denys*, iii, pp. 164–5.

65 W. H. Bliss and J. A. Twemlow (eds), *Calendar of Entries in the Papal Registers Relating to Great Britain and Ireland, Papal Letters, Volume 5, AD 1396–1404* (London: HMSO, 1904), pp. 30, 44, 623–4; *Welsh Records*, pp. 23–54, 103–6, 108–10; R. A. Griffiths, 'Some Secret Supporters of Owain Glyn Dŵr?', *BBCS*, 20 (1962–4), 77–100; R. A. Griffiths, 'Some Partisans of Owain Glyn Dŵr at Oxford', *BBCS*, 20 (1962–4), 282–92; C. Given-Wilson (ed.), *The Chronicle of Adam Usk, 1377–1421* (Oxford: Oxford University Press, 1997), henceforth *Adam Usk*, pp. 148–53; R. A. Griffiths, 'Owain Glyn Dŵr's Invasion of the Central March of Wales in 1402: the Evidence of Clerical Taxation', *Studia Celtica*, 46 (2012), 111–22; M. Livingston and J. K. Bollard (eds), *Owain Glyndŵr, A Casebook* (Liverpool: Liverpool University Press, 2013), henceforth *OGC*, pp. 64–7, 431–4, 497–550.

66 J. E. Lloyd, *Owen Glendower (Owain Glyndŵr)* (Felinfach: Llanerch Press, 1992 [1931]), henceforth *Glendower*, pp. 77–82; *The History of the Gwydir Family and Memoirs*, ed. J. Gwynfor Jones (Llandysul: Gomer, 1990), p. 118.; R. R. Davies, *The Revolt of Owain Glyn Dŵr* (Oxford: Oxford University Press, 1995), p. 275.

67 Davies, *Revolt*, pp. 116, 163, 213–14; Griffiths, 'Owain Glyn Dŵr's Invasion', pp. 111–22. See Appendix 6.1, d).

68 *Welsh Records*, pp. 23–39, 75–82; Fowler (ed.), *Hundred Years War*, pp. 186–7; G. Cuttino, *English Medieval Diplomacy* (Bloomington: Indiana University Press, 1985), pp. 8–10, 18, 94.

69 *Welsh Records*, pp. 25, 28, 75, 76, 78.

70 *Saint-Denys*, iii, pp. 164–8, 198–201, 222–7 (my translation); H. Nicolas (ed.), *Proceedings and Ordinances of the Privy Council of England*, 7 vols (London: Record Commission, 1834–7), i, pp. 264–6; *Welsh Records*, pp. 107, 115; F. C. Hingeston, *Royal and Historical Letters during the Reign of Henry IV*, 2 vols (London: Longman, 1860–4), i, pp. 329–30, 331–5, 338–40, 367–70, 376–80, 384–5, 392. Note: the Saint-Denys

Chronicler described a far smaller force of 800 men-at-arms and many crossbowmen in a fleet of sixty-two sailing ships (*OGC*, pp. 152–5), various chronicles give different approximations of the size of the French force, *Royal and Historical Letters Henry IV* and *Saint-Denys* give the largest and smallest figures respectively.

[71] *Welsh Records*, pp. 40–1, 83–4.
[72] *Welsh Records*, pp. 51, 54, 95–6, 98.
[73] Grèvy-Pons, *Jean de Montreuil, Opera*, ii, pp. 96, 113, 201–2; E. R. Chamberlin, *The Count of Virtue, Giangaleazzo Visconti, Duke of Milan* (London: Eyre and Spottiswoode, 1965), p. 71; Walter Bower and D. Watt (eds), *Scotichronicon*, 9 vols (Aberdeen: Aberdeen University Press, 1987–98), viii, pp. 106–9; *Adam Usk*, pp. 147, 151, 199–210; A. Marchant, *The Revolt of Owain Glyndŵr in Medieval English Chronicles* (Woodbridge: Boydell, 2014), pp. 164–71.
[74] *Welsh Records*, pp. 53, 54, 96–8.
[75] *Welsh Records*, pp. 54, 98.
[76] J. R. Gabriel, 'Wales and the Avignon Papacy', *Archaeologia Cambrensis*, 78 (1923), 70–86; L. R. Loomis, 'Nationality at the Council of Constance: An Anglo-French Dispute', *American Historical Review*, 44.3 (1939), 508–27; A. Gwynn, 'Ireland and the English Nation at the Council of Constance', *Proc. of the Royal Irish Academy*, 45 (1939), 183–233; A. Jarman, 'Wales and the Council of Constance', *BBCS*, 14 (1951), 220–2; C. M. D. Crowder, *Unity, Heresy and Reform, 1378–1460: the Conciliar Response to the Great Schism* (London: Edward Arnold, 1977), pp. 24–8.
[77] Brown, *Black Douglases*, pp. 211–12; Autrand, 'Aux origines', p. 33; D. J. Kagay, 'Disposable Alliances: Aragon and Castile during the War of the Two Pedros and Beyond,' *Albany State University Papers* (2010), online at: *www.medievalists.net/2011/08/11/disposable-alliances-aragon-and-castille-during-the-war-of-the-two-pedros-and-beyond/* (accessed 10 April 2012), pp. 1–69.

7

Documents relevant to Wales before the Edwardian conquest in the Vatican archives[1]

Bryn Jones

The purpose of this chapter is to draw attention to some of the documents concerning Wales before the final Edwardian conquest (1282–3) held in the Vatican Secret Archives (ASV). This is a somewhat arbitrary date though in line with the contours of standard Welsh historiography, which tends towards looking at the Welsh before and after the extinguishing of Welsh princes who acted independently of the English crown. Discussion of Welsh relations with the papacy remains under researched until at least the period of the recusant writers of the sixteenth century.[2] To understand why such work is necessary, one might consider that Thomas Matthews addressed the Cardiff Naturalists Society over a century ago on 'Welsh records in Foreign Libraries', arguing that research ought to be conducted in order to establish if any documents were relevant to Welsh interests.[3] Matthews was hinting at a weakness in the historiography of medieval Wales, namely that, as a result of the fundamental need to edit Welsh historical sources to modern scholarly standard, very little consideration has been given to Wales in a European context.[4] A little over a century later it is hoped that some of this work might be completed.

Papal record-keeping

It seems possible that the papacy began conserving records at least as early as the fourth century, with more certain evidence from the pontificate of Gregory I (590–604).[5] By the middle of the seventh century the archive had found its first permanent home near the Lateran palace, but the idea of a central archive of the Church was not promoted until Pius IV (1559–65).[6] The contents of this original core are described thus by Leslie MacFarlane: 'The Vatican Archives contain the diplomatic and administrative correspondence of the Holy See, and are mainly a vast collection of the working records emanating from, and received by, the various departments of the papal curia.'[7] That the earliest continuous records survive from the time of Innocent III (1198–1216) should not be a surprise, as he appears to have been the first pope to regularise papal record keeping.[8] These earliest records are part of the *Registra Vaticana*, a series of records which runs until the registers of Clement VIII (1592–1605).[9] They contain letters sent and occasionally received by the papacy. The registers of this collection are divided for each pontificate and then further divided by a book for each year of a pope's pontificate.[10] Only two collections of letters from prior to Innocent III's time survive in the current Vatican Archives.[11] We have a limited idea of the registers prior to the pontificate of Gregory VII, but we know that they were utilised for standard phrases, accumulating legal proof and for setting precedents.[12]

Not all letters were registered by the papal chancery. Cheney draws attention to the thirty-six papal letters in the *registrum* of the bishopric of Glasgow from the thirteenth century, only one of which is to be found in the papal registers.[13] That letters were not always registered might perhaps explain the insistence by Gerald of Wales on having letters regarding the status of St David's entered in the register of Innocent III.[14]

Wales in the archives

In total almost three hundred documents either concerning the Welsh in the period before the Edwardian conquest or sent to recipients within Welsh diocese survive within the Vatican Archives from the pontificate of Innocent III to that of Martin IV (1281–5).[15] There is very little of specifically Welsh interest in many of these documents. One hundred and twenty-four documents were addressed either to all suffragan bishops in the province of Canterbury or to all bishops, or all the faithful, or all men or to a specific religious order 'in the realm of England'.[16] It seems likely that many of these letters made their way to Welsh polities as throughout the corpus there is no constant distinguishing between Wales on the one hand and England on the other, unlike the more common distinguishing between England, Ireland and Scotland. The lack of distinguishing between Wales and England caused a small problem for Innocent III when he threatened to place England under an interdict during the reign of King John. The first letter threatening an interdict, which did not mention Wales explicitly, was issued in August 1207. At the request of Mauger (bishop of Worcester, 1199–1212), Innocent III clarified the situation by reissuing the letter in November 1207, this time mentioning Wales.[17] Three letters that do make the distinction clear are letters from Innocent IV (1243–54) addressed to the bishop of Worcester concerning the crusade.[18] Urban IV (1261–4) also made the distinction in some of his letters of introduction and instruction concerning the tax collector Master Leonard during his time in England.[19] Most of the letters that mark the difference are letters of authority and instruction associated with Clement IV (1264–8). Twenty-four letters sent to him during his time as the legate in England (when he was known as Guy le Gros) mention Wales,[20] twenty-one letters were sent by him to his own legate, Ottobuono,[21] and a further five are concerned with the papal tax collector Master Sinicius.[22] This difference from previous and subsequent practice is most easily explained by the fact that he had spent time in England immediately prior to his election as pope, becoming aware of the distinctions and tensions in the years preceding the Second Barons' War. Beyond mentioning Wales however, these letters do not discuss or provide any information about Wales at all. The most useful thing to be said of this group is that it is through them that appeals for assistance in wider Church (such as appeals for assistance in the Holy Land), declarations for the whole Church (such as announcing the excommunication of the Emperor Frederick by Gregory IX (1227–41)) or notifications of papal approval for activities within the wider British Church (such as the series of letters concerned with the translation of Thomas Becket's relics issued by Honorius III (1216–27)) reached the Welsh polities.[23] We are then reduced to discussing a selection of 105 documents from the Vatican Archives.

Papal roles

These documents portray the papacy as a font of authority. It was to be obeyed when instructions were issued, but it could also be used for assistance in resolving disputes or problems. In this, the Welsh experience does not seem different from other parts of Europe and it would be surprising if this was not the case given the increase of papal activity by and during the thirteenth century.[24] Some cases however do provide illuminating details about medieval Wales, especially in consideration of its economic state. Let us first turn to the common experiences.

Many institutions wished to associate themselves with papal authority by receiving confirmation of land grants from the papacy. They wished to secure their rights to the land and there could be no higher authority on earth than the head of the Church. Institutions looked to the papacy as the ultimate guarantor of their rights and therefore, their property. Innocent IV confirmed a grant of land to the abbot and convent of Tintern Abbey.[25] Land and churches in Wales were also confirmed to institutions outside Wales. Honorius III confirmed the grant of an indult (a privilege) to the abbot and monastery of Tewkesbury by 'W. and H., bishops of Llandaf', for St Mary's, Cardiff.[26] Letters of confirmation were also issued to institutions outside the British Isles. The most notable of these is the grant of St Leonard's church, Magor by Gilbert Marshal, earl of Pembroke, to the abbey of St Mary in Glory, Anagni.[27] This abbey was a pet project of Gregory IX who issued two letters concerning the grant, one confirming Gilbert's gift.[28] Although originally given during the pontificate of Gregory IX, Earl Gilbert's grant is preserved in a later copy in the register of Innocent IV and was also the subject of a letter by Elias of Radnor (bishop of Llandaff,

1230–40).[29] The grant was further confirmed and expanded by Innocent IV and Alexander IV (1254–61).[30] Gilbert himself, along with his brothers Walter and Anselm, benefitted from the confirmation of lands in Wales by Gregory IX.[31] In light of his crusading vows, Henry III was similarly granted protection and confirmation of his family, possession and lands, with lands in Wales mentioned in particular by Innocent IV.[32]

Similarly, permission was requested by clerics to hold additional benefices after a prohibition on holding two benefices was proclaimed by the Fourth Lateran Council of 1215.[33] Two letters were addressed to clerics from the diocese of Llandaff[34] and seven to clerics from St David's.[35] Permission was also granted for benefices to be held in Wales by men from the dioceses of Bath and Wells and Hereford.[36] One of the St David's recipients, Maurice, rector of Abernant, was granted permission to hold two additional churches at Dinas and Llanboidy at the request of Annibale Annibaldi, Cardinal Priest of the church of the Twelve Apostles, and close friend of Thomas Aquinas.[37]

The papacy also provided assistance for ecclesiastical institutions and individuals. The abbots of the Cistercian houses of Cwm Hir and Valle Crucis, owing to their remote location, both received permission from Gregory IX to hear the confessions and administer the sacraments to their households.[38] An individual to benefit from papal aid was Abraham, a monk of Aberconwy, who was born illegitimately. Natural children were not automatically barred from holding sacred office with the pope able to grant dispensation as he saw fit.[39] Abraham was addressed by Honorius III who, in view of the support given to Abraham by his fellow brothers, the king of England and Stephen Langton (archbishop of Canterbury, 1207–28), granted him permission to enter religious life in April 1225.[40]

A rather more high-profile case of illegitimacy also attracted papal attention. This time, a bishop to benefit from contact with the papacy was Richard Carew (bishop of St David's, 1256–80).[41] He had been elected by the chapter of St David's in August 1255 but refused royal assent by Henry III.[42] It is not entirely clear why the king objected to Richard (he does not, for instance, raise the bishop's illegitimacy) but in a draft letter, dated on 12 November 1255, Henry appeals to Alexander IV not to admit the postulation of

Richard, along with the postulation of a new archbishop of York, promising that messengers will explain his reasons at the Curia.[43] Alexander IV cannot have found their reasons convincing as he consecrated Richard Carew in Rome and sent a series of letters in support of the new bishop in February and March of 1256. Ecclesiastical officials were to ensure that Richard Carew received his due rights in his diocese.[44] The chapter of St David's as well as the clergy and people of the diocese were to receive and obey Richard as their bishop despite his illegitimacy.[45] He was commended to Henry III, and the king commanded to ensure that the new bishop received his temporalities, to which end Henry directed his agents in May 1256.[46] The bishop himself was encouraged to govern his diocese well, a directive taken to heart as the chapter of St David's submitted an ordinance of diocese accounts for approval by Pope Alexander.[47]

One is also tempted to see the end of a dispute in an indult received by Thomas Wallensis (bishop of St David's, 1247–55) from Innocent IV.[48] The bishop was granted permission to build suitable dwellings near churches in Glascwm and Ceri, both in modern-day Powys.[49] At the most northern extremity of the medieval diocese of St David's, Ceri was a contentious place having been the location of a confrontation between Gerald of Wales and the bishop of St Asaph during the former's time as archdeacon of Brecon.[50] What prompted Thomas Wallensis to appeal to the papacy is again unknown, but the letter hints at the practice of those subject to him being 'uncorrected', and the location of the churches might indicate his willingness to use papal support against possible territorial encroachment by the bishop of St Asaph.[51] We see again the approximated use of papal authority by a Welsh ecclesiastic to solve problems.

Having granted assistance, the papacy is sometimes seen issuing follow-up instructions. Bishops were required to obtain papal permission before resigning their office.[52] Cadwgan of Llanddyfai (bishop of Bangor, 1215–36) sought and was granted permission to resign his see for unknown reasons.[53] Once he had given permission, Gregory IX wrote to the chapter of Bangor commanding them to canonically elect a new bishop and to use the former bishop's effects, barring his books and clothes, to pay the debts of the church.[54]

Assistance was also sought from Welsh ecclesiastics, which in turn meant that they became aware of events much further afield. Some were direct appeals for aid. Urban IV, for instance, wrote to the bishops of St David's, St Asaph and Llandaff asking for assistance in paying the debts incurred by the papacy during the Sicilian affair, although it is unknown if any such assistance was given.[55] The same pope also asked for aid in preaching the crusade. Although addressed in the main to Walter de Cantilupe (bishop of Worcester, 1236–66), some of these letters were addressed to the bishop of St David's: Richard Carew at the time of issue. He was granted a number of powers to encourage participation and letters were also sent to other ecclesiastics encouraging them to assist the bishop in his labours.[56] Hurlock suggests that the bishop of St David's was chosen for the task as the pope required an agent with local knowledge to undertake the task and that this is an example of the papacy taking more direct control of Welsh affairs.[57] She is undoubtedly correct on both counts and it is important to note that the letters directed to the bishop of St David's are amongst the letters of Urban IV to name Wales as a separate entity, already noted. On some occasions the request for help was in matters closer to home. Anian I of St Asaph was asked to ensure that papal decisions were adhered to whilst he oversaw the fallout from the brief tenure of William, sub-prior of Coventry, as abbot of Shrewsbury.[58]

Welsh ecclesiastics are also seen to be assisting the papacy in conducting enquiries and in being subject to them. Honorius III directed the abbots of Cymer and Whitland to investigate allegations of corruption against the bishop of St Asaph (Reiner, 1186–1224).[59] Gregory IX instructed the later bishop of St Asaph (Hywel, 1233–40), along with the abbot of Dore (Herefordshire), to resolve the ongoing dispute between Margaret de Lacey and her endowed foundation of Aconbury Priory.[60] Two further letters deal with disputed diocesan boundaries. Gregory IX appointed a commission to resolve a boundary dispute between St Asaph and Worcester on one hand and the see of Coventry and Lichfield on the other.[61] A second inquiry was launched by the same pope a few weeks later, the officials being charged with deciding on the boundaries between the diocese of St Asaph, Llandaff, St David's and Hereford.[62]

Gwynedd and the papacy

The princes of Gwynedd are the only secular Welsh lords with whom surviving papal letters are concerned. This makes these letters particularly valuable to the historian of medieval Wales as they provide information for both the princes' diplomatic activities and the evolving nature of their attitudes towards the papacy in Gwynedd. Three letters from the register of Innocent III are concerned with inquiries into the proposed marriage of Llywelyn ap Iorwerth (d.1240) to a daughter of Rögnvaldr, king of the Isles (1187–1229).[63] She had previously been betrothed to Llywelyn's uncle Rhodri ab Owain Gwynedd (d.1195), and Llywelyn did not wish to contravene canon law by marrying her.[64] The letters form an interesting series as we can see development from one stage to the next. The first letter established the original inquiry in November 1199,[65] the second letter confirmed the findings of the inquiry in April 1203 and gave instructions as to how to proceed[66] and the final letter overturned the previous findings following the presentation of 'new' evidence in February 1205.[67] Pryce is right to highlight that Llywelyn had twice utilised canon law to secure his own position.[68] The first time was the possibility of securing an ally in his fight to establish himself in Gwynedd: Rögnvaldr had, after all, sent military aid to Rhodri ab Owain Gwynedd in 1193. The second time (and the real reason for the discovery of 'evidence' establishing their consanguinity) was to gain himself an even more advantageous alliance.

Freed of his betrothal to Rögnvaldr's daughter, Llywelyn married Joan, an illegitimate daughter of King John, to seal an alliance that brought with it a greater stability to Gwynedd than an alliance with the kingdom of Man.[69] Taking further steps to strengthen his position, Llywelyn had Joan legitimised by Honorius III.[70] He had earlier gained recognition of Dafydd, Joan's son, as his sole heir from the same pope.[71] We also learn from a letter of Honorius to the bishops of St David's, Bangor and St Asaph that Llywelyn had obtained, by order of Henry III, a pledge of fealty from the leading men of Wales to Dafydd.[72] All of this formed part of Llywelyn's strategy for securing the succession of Dafydd as leader of Gwynedd.[73]

The significance of Llywelyn's seeking approval from the papacy in these matters cannot be overstated as it is a recognition of the increased importance of the papacy for Llywelyn and his advisers. His grandfather, Owain Gwynedd (d.1170), had repeatedly ignored Alexander III (1159–81) with regard to marrying within the degrees of consanguinity permitted by the Church. Based on correspondence with the French court, we can see that Owain regarded the papacy as important but also as an institution that could be ignored without much harm to his own position.[74] Indeed, Welsh attitudes to marriage continued to be a problem for the Church. In 1252, Innocent IV granted Thomas Wallensis of St David's the faculty to permit the continued marriage of two couples who had married within the degrees of consanguinity permitted by the Church and another couple who had married within the degrees of affinity.[75] We may say then that whilst the importance of papal teaching had become important to the Welsh elite it had not done so for common people. For Llywelyn, the papacy was an institution that could strengthen his hold on Gwynedd. Its support was essential to his attempt at securing the unity of Gwynedd for his son.

This is not to say that Llywelyn had everything his own way in his encounters with the papacy. Two letters were sent to remind Llywelyn to keep the peace with Henry III during his minority.[76] Llywelyn's lands were placed under interdict in October 1223.[77] After pressure from Gregory IX, Llywelyn twice came to terms with the Crown, leading to the Pact of Myddle in July 1234 and its renewal in July 1236.[78]

Two letters of Clement IV, addressed to the legate Ottobuono (who later became Adrian V (1276)), are concerned with Llywelyn ap Gruffudd (d.1282), the grandson of Llywelyn ap Iorwerth. They mandate the legate to induce and to aid Llywelyn to end his alliance with Simon de Montfort.[79] Both letters were issued in September 1265, a month after the Montfort defeat at the battle of Evesham, but they set the tone for Ottobuono's mission as regards the Welsh. He would lead peace negotiations between Llywelyn ap Gruffudd and the Crown, resulting in the Treaty of Montgomery in 1267.[80]

In this Ottobuono is by far the most prominent of the legates to have been concerned with Welsh affairs in the documents under consideration. Indeed, he is the only legate mentioned in these documents of whom we can say with certainty that he visited Wales. The earliest legate of whom there is any possibility that they visited

Wales is Theophylact, bishop of Todi, who may have done so in 786 as part of a delegation sent by Hadrian I (772–95) in response to the dispute between Offa of Mercia (d.796) and Jænberht, Archbishop of Canterbury (765–92).[81] The earliest legate who is certain to have travelled to Wales was John of Crema who, according to *Liber Landavensis*, visited Llandaff in connection with Bishop Urban's case to expand his diocese.[82]

Welsh ecclesiastics were of course expected to obey a legate, with Urban IV reminding Welsh ecclesiastics of their duties. Honorius III reminded all cathedral chapters in Wales and England to elect bishops who were faithful to the Church and king, and to pay attention to the advice of his legate Pandulf.[83] Judged by the evidence of papal letters alone, the legates only appear to have played a limited role in Welsh affairs. Pandulf was charged with reminding Llywelyn of his obligations to Henry III by Honorius, whilst the legate Otto was asked by Gregory IX to assist in the donation of land to Anagni by Gilbert Marshal.[84] Beyond letters of introduction and the letters just discussed, there is little evidence to suggest a great role in Welsh affairs for papal legates in the documents of the Vatican Archives.[85]

Returning to letters concerned with Llywelyn ap Gruffudd, several relate to the capture of Eleanor de Montfort and her brother Amaury de Montfort, a papal chaplain, by Edward I (1272–1307) in the winter of 1275.[86] Llywelyn had married Eleanor *per verba de presenti* and arranged for her to travel to him from France. Edward captured the siblings at sea, detaining Eleanor for almost three years and Amaury until 1282. In January 1277, John XXI (1276–7) addressed Edward I, asking for the release of Eleanor whilst the same pope also wrote to the prelates of the realm asking them to bring pressure to bear on the king for the release of Amaury.[87] Further letters concerning Amaury's release were sent by Nicholas III (1277–80) in February 1280 and by Martin IV in September 1281.[88]

Wales and papal revenues

Glimpses of the Welsh economy are also seen in the documents. Boniface of Savoy (Archbishop of Canterbury, 1241–70) was chided in a letter of April 1255 by Alexander IV for failing to visit the four

Welsh dioceses on account of war and the lack of sustenance available there, amongst other reasons.[89] Assuming that these were the reasons for not visiting the Welsh dioceses originally given by Boniface, they must have appeared to the pope like a list of poor excuses.[90] However, the reasons highlighted by Pope Alexander also deserve greater attention. War perhaps suggests the fighting between the sons of Gruffydd ap Llywelyn ap Iorwerth prior to the battle of Bryn Derwin in June 1255.[91] The lack of food available to sustain a visit by the archbishop perhaps indicates the high standards that a noble of Savoy might expect. It might also lead us to conclude that there were poor economic circumstances in the Welsh dioceses around the middle of the thirteenth century, a position supported both by the number of requests to hold additional benefices and by a letter addressed to the bishop of Llandaff by Gregory IX giving him the power to unite churches when their individual incomes were nor sufficient to support a rector.[92] It also chimes with Gerald of Wales's comments about the Welsh sees being poor half a century earlier.[93]

The citing of war by Boniface would have sounded familiar to Bishop Mauger of Worcester, who wrote to Innocent III complaining that he and his people were unable to appear before judges in Wales without risking their own safety, owing to the permanent state of conflict between the Welsh and English.[94] The pope advised Mauger to refer all such requests to appear before judges to the jurisdiction of the Apostolic See. Read alone, the letter might be taken as evidence for conditions along the Welsh border at the turn of the thirteenth century, perhaps an indication of the aftermath caused by the campaign led by Gwenwynwyn ab Owain Cyfeiliog of Powys (d.1216) between 1196 and 1198.[95] It might even be taken as suggesting that the bishop of Worcester was at times subject to Welsh law. Read and understood in its full context, the letter provides a greater interest. Mauger was known personally to Innocent III, having travelled to Rome to secure his election as bishop of Worcester. As the illegitimate son of a knight and a free woman, he was seemingly barred by canons of the Third Lateran Council from becoming a bishop. Whilst accepting that Mauger had been elected illegally, therefore quashing the election, Innocent III exercised his discretion in allowing the monks of Worcester to secure a dispensation for Mauger, before consecrating him personally.[96] Mauger also seems likely to have been a contemporary of Gerald of Wales at Paris, and one from whom Gerald presumed support at the beginning of his campaign to have his election as bishop of St David's ratified.[97] Even if Mauger had had sympathy for Gerald's cause, then by the beginning of 1202 he would have come under a great deal of pressure to change his position to be in line with that of the Crown and the Archbishop of Canterbury, at least to judge by the correspondence of Hubert Walter and letters patent of King John.[98] This was also a time when Mauger had been named as a papal commissioner inquiring into Gerald's twin causes of the status of St David's and his election.[99] Caught between the Scylla and Charybdis of disappointing an acquaintance and contradicting the wishes of two men to whom he had sworn obedience, Mauger sought to extricate himself from a difficult situation by appealing to the papacy for assistance. He exaggerated the dangers for Englishmen in Wales in order to achieve his aim.

The poor economic circumstances alleged by Archbishop Boniface might perhaps explain the difficulty of collecting papal levy in Wales. Several letters authorised this collection. Henry III was granted the right to collect tithes by Innocent IV, which was confirmed and extended by Alexander IV in March 1255.[100] Martin IV had instructed Geoffrey of Vezzano, a resident papal tax collector in England in the late thirteenth century, to collect Peter's Pence in Wales in a letter of March 1282,[101] and further instructed him to collect money for use in the Holy Land.[102] Export of this tenth was halted by Edward I in May 1282 and may have been used to finance his campaign against Llywelyn and Dafydd ap Gruffudd in 1282–3.[103] The earlier war of 1276–7 also appears to have made the collection of tax in Wales impossible.[104]

Conclusions

In the documents from the Vatican Secret Archives individuals and institutions are seen turning to the papacy for assistance and restitution. Thomas Wallensis used the papacy to strengthen his position as bishop and to maintain the rights of his see; Llywelyn ap Iorwerth appealed to the papacy several times in his attempts to secure his polity's future. Several clerics used the papacy to ensure greater financial stability for themselves. We also see the integration of the Welsh Church into the European mainstream through papal confirmation of the acquisition of land by foreign churches, through the issuing of orders to assist the papacy in some way and the imposition of ecclesiastical discipline in Welsh lands. The glimpses of Wales caught by chance are fascinating in the incidental detail that they provide, especially in the evidence they provide for the Welsh economy.

Much research into these documents remains to be done. The patterns of landholding described by the papal confirmations as well as the financial documents mentioned above may prove fruitful. Using these documents for comparative purposes with other regions of Europe might also prove instructive. It is hoped that this contribution might cast some light on the importance of documents in the Vatican Secret Archives for historians of medieval Wales, and help achieve a better understanding of Wales in the world.

Notes

[1] The research on which this chapter is based was sponsored by the Saunders Lewis Memorial Fund, with a view to publishing a handlist of relevant documents in the archives. The work benefitted greatly from the advice of the late Professor Emeritus R. G. Gruffydd and Mr Daniel Huws, the former keeper of manuscripts at the National Library of Wales. The generosity of the fund and through them Professor Gruffydd and Mr Huws is gratefully acknowledged. I would also like to thank Dr Alex Woolf, my doctoral supervisor, and Professor Patricia Skinner, the editor of this volume, for their comments on this chapter and to all who contributed to the discussion at Leeds. The handlist is in preparation for publication on the Memorial Fund's website. All errors are of course my own.

[2] For Welsh involvement with the papacy in the intervening period, the work of Glanmor Williams remains indispensable. Particular consideration has been given to Owain Glyndŵr's offer to switch the allegiance of the Welsh Church to the Avignon popes during his negotiations with the French crown (discussed also by Gideon

Brough in his chapter in the present volume). There has also been some consideration of the Welsh relations with the papal curia after this date in the work of Rhun Emlyn, who has addressed the presence of university graduates from Wales at the Curia. See G. Williams, *The Welsh Church from Conquest to Reformation* (rev edn, Cardiff: University of Wales Press, 1976); R. R. Davies, *The Revolt of Owain Glyn Dŵr* (Oxford: Oxford University Press, 1995), pp. 169–71 and Rh. Emlyn, 'Myfyrwyr canoloesol Cymreig a'u gyrfaoedd' (unpublished PhD thesis, Aberystwyth University, 2011). And see also his chapter in the present volume.

[3] T. Matthews, 'Welsh Records in Foreign Libraries', *Transactions of the Cardiff Naturalists' Society*, 43 (1910), 20–31.

[4] Consider for instance that edited texts of the *Acta* of Welsh rulers only appeared in print as recently as 2005: *AWR*; and that usable texts of the Welsh Latin chronicles in their entirety have only appeared more recently: *http://croniclau.bangor.ac.uk/* (accessed 16 December 2016), where editions of the chronicles may be found. This is also not to say that consideration has not been given at all to medieval Wales in a European context: see for instance H. Pryce, 'Welsh rulers and European change, c.1100–1282', in H. Pryce and J. Watts (eds), *Power and Identity in the Middle Ages: Essays in Memory of Rees Davies* (Oxford: Oxford University Press, 2007), pp. 37–51 and C. Wickham, 'Medieval Wales and European History', *WHR*, 25.2 (2010), 201–8.

[5] M. P. Sheehy (ed.), *Pontificia Hibernica*, 2 vols (Dublin: Gill, 1962–65), hereafter PH, i, p. xxx and L. E. Boyle, *A Survey of the Vatican Archives and of its Medieval Holdings* (Toronto: Pontifical Institute, 1972; rev. edn, 2001), hereafter *SVA*, p. 103.

[6] *SVA*, pp. 7 and 9–10.

[7] L. MacFarlane, 'The Vatican Archives', *Archives*, 4 (1959), 29–44, 84–101, at 29, n. 1.

[8] *SVA*, p. 7, and MacFarlane, 'Vatican Archives', 30.

[9] *SVA*, p. 10, and MacFarlane, 'Vatican Archives', 33. Five documents are taken from the *Collectoriae*, a series of papal tax accounts. For the *Collectoriae* see *SVA*, pp. 165–8 and MacFarlane, 'Vatican Archives', 41.

[10] PH, i, pp. xxx–xxxi.

[11] One is an eleventh-century copy of the register of John VIII (872–82) for the last six years of his pontificate, the other an incomplete copy of the registers for the reign of Gregory VII (1073–85). *SVA*, p. 103, MacFarlane, 'Vatican Archives', 30 and R. L. Poole, *Lectures on the History of the Papal Chancery* (Cambridge: Cambridge University Press,

1915), pp. 33–5 and pp. 85–6. The earliest extant original letter dates from 788. *PH*, i, p. xv and Poole, *Lectures*, p. 37. The register of John VIII was edited by E. Caspar and G. Laehr in *MGH, Epistolae VII: Karolini Aevi 5* (Berlin: Weidmann, 1928). The register of Gregory VII is found in *MGH, Epistolae Selectae II: Das Register Gregors VII*, ed. E. Caspar, 2 vols (Berlin: Weidmann, 1920–3) and translated in H. E. J. Cowdrey, *The Register of Pope Gregory VII 1073–1085* (Oxford: Oxford University Press, 2002). See also U. Blumenthal, 'Papal registers in the twelfth century', in P. Linehan (ed.), *Proceedings of the Seventh International Congress of Medieval Canon Law*, Monumenta iuris canonici., Series C, Subsidia, 8 (Vatican City: BAV, 1988), pp. 135–51.

[12] *PH*, i, p. xxx. See also Blumenthal, 'Papal registers', pp. 142–5.

[13] C. R. Cheney, *The Study of the Medieval Papal Chancery*, The Edwards Lectures 2 (Glasgow: Jackson, 1966), p. 15. Referring to the work of Franco Guerello, Sheehy drew attention to estimates of between 0 and 23 per cent of letters being registered, that is to say 'of every 100 documents found [at non Vatican Archives] between 77 and 100 of them were not registered'. See *PH*, i, p. xxxviii, n. 4.

[14] Gerald of Wales, *De Giraldo Archidiacono Menevensi*, in *GCO*, i, 398; Gerald of Wales, *De Invectionibus* (ed. W. S. Davies, *Y Cymmrodor*, 30 (1920)), in *GCO*, iv, 9 (p. 176), and *EAWD*, i, p. 226. Gerald received three letters establishing inquiries into the status of St David's, but the only text to survive in the register of Innocent III is that of the third proposed inquiry, with the only proof for the other commissions being the contents list of Gerald's *De Invectionibus*. See *De Invectionibus*, p. 77. The third commission seems unlikely to have convened following an agreement between Gerald and King John (1199–1216) and Hubert Walter (Archbishop of Canterbury, 1193–1205). See O. Hageneder, J. C. Moore, A. Sommerlechner, with C. Egger, and H. Weigl (eds), *Die Register Innocenz' III., 6. Pontifikatsjahr 1203/1204. Texte und Indices* (Vienna: ÖEAW, 1995), (hereafter *Reg. Inn. III.*,), 89; Gerald of Wales, *De Jure et Statu Menevensis Ecclesiae* (*GCO*, iii.282–4), hereafter *De Jure*; *EAWD*, i, D.374; C. R. Cheney and M. G. Cheney (eds), *The Letters of Pope Innocent III concerning England and Wales: a Calendar with an Appendix of Texts* (Oxford: Clarendon Press, 1967), 494, and Gerald of Wales, *The Autobiography of Gerald of Wales*, ed. and trans. H. E. Butler (Woodbridge: Boydell, 2005), pp. 306–7. See also *EAWD*, i, pp. 226–7.

[15] Five letters from the reign of Martin IV, which mention Wales, date from beyond the period set by this project, and are therefore not considered here.

[16] Phrases similar to *in regni Anglie* are commonly used in these letters.

[17] For the first letter, see R. Murauer, and A. Sommerlechner, with O. Hageneder, C. Egger, and H. Weigl (eds), *Reg. Inn. III. 10. Pontifikatsjahr 1207/1208. Texte und Indices* (Vienna: ÖEAW, 2007), 113; C. R. Cheney and W. H. Semple (ed. and trans.), *Selected Letters of Pope Innocent III concerning England* (1198–1216) (London: T. Nelson, 1953), 30; Cheney, *Calendar*, 763, and W. H. Bliss, *Calendar of Papal Registers Relating to Great Britain and Ireland, Volume 1: 1198–1304* (London: HMSO, 1893), hereafter *CPapReg*, p. 29. For the second letter, see *Reg. Inn. III.*, x.161, Cheney, Selected, 31, Cheney, *Calendar*, 770, *CPapReg*, p. 30, and *EAWD*, ii, L.272.

[18] Respectively, E. Berger (ed.), *Les registres d'Innocent IV*, 4 vols, Bibliothèque des Ecoles françaises d'Athènes et de Rome 2nd ser. i (Paris: Ernest Trobin, 1884–1921), hereafter *Reg. Inn. IV*, 2959, 2960 and 2962, *PH*, ii, 284–5 and *CPapReg*, pp. 234–5. On these letters, see K. Hurlock, *Wales and the Crusades, c.1095–1291*, Studies in Welsh History 33 (Cardiff: University of Wales Press, 2011), p. 202 and W. E. Lunt, *Financial Relations of the Papacy with England to 1327*, Studies in Anglo-Papal relations during the Middle Ages 1 (Cambridge: Cambridge University Press, 1939), pp. 435–6.

[19] There are five of these letters, J. Guiraud, L. Dorez and S. Clemenzet (eds), *Les registres d'Urbain IV*, 4 vols, Bibliothèque des Ecoles françaises d'Athènes et de Rome 2nd ser. xiii (Paris: Ernest Trobin, 1892–1958), hereafter *Reg. Urb. IV*, iii, 129–32, *CPapReg*, pp. 380, 383 and *EAWD*, i, D.652. *Reg. Urb. IV*, 129 and 131 are unedited and taken from, respectively, Vatican City, ASV Registra Vaticana (Reg. Vat.) 27, f. 31r–v and f. 32r.

[20] The edited letters are *Reg. Urb. IV*, 581, 586–8 and *CPapReg*, p. 396. The unedited letters are Vatican City, ASV Reg. Vat. 28, ff. 56r–58r, 59r–61v, *Reg. Urb. IV*, 582–3, 589–90, 593, 600, 602, 607–9, 611–12, 614–15, 617, 620, 624–5, 627, 629–30 and *CPapReg*, pp. 396–400.

[21] Only a few of these documents are edited, in E. Jordan (ed.), *Les registres de Clement IV*, Bibliothèque des Ecoles françaises d'Athènes et de Rome 2nd ser. xi (Paris: De Boccard, 1893–1945), hereafter *Reg. Clement IV*, 43, 115, 116, 324 and CPapReg, pp. 426, 429–30, 432–3. The unedited documents are respectively Vatican City, ASV Reg. Vat. 32, ff. 8v–9r, 10v–11v, 12v–13r, 23v–24r, 61r–62r and 63r, *Reg. Clement IV*, 40, 48, 50, 55, 56, 69–71, 73, 120–2, 228, 230, 234–5, and *CPR*, pp. 426–33. Another unedited letter of instruction to the legate is repeated in several manuscripts: Vatican City, ASV Reg. Vat. 31, 19v–20r, ASV Reg. Vat. 33, 21ra–21va, ASV Reg. Vat. 34,

Documents in the Vatican archives

27v–28v and ASV Reg. Vat. 35, 22v–23r, *Reg. Clement IV*, 986 and *CPapReg*, p. 419.

22 *Reg. Clement IV*, 764, 765, 767, 771, 782 and *CPapReg*, pp. 423–4. For Sinicius, see W. E. Lunt, *Papal Revenue in the Middle Ages*, 2 vols, Records of Civilization 19 (New York: Columbia University Press, 1934), i, p. 43.

23 For example, a letter for assistance in the Holy Land was issued by Gregory X and sent to the province of York but also to the province of Canterbury (amongst very many others). See J. Guiraud and E. Cadier (eds), *Les registres de Grégoire X (1272–1276) et de Jean XXI (1276–1277)*, 2 vols, Bibliothèque des Ecoles françaises d'Athènes et de Rome 2nd ser. xii (Paris: De Boccard, 1892–1960), hereafter *Reg. Greg. X et Jean XXI*, 569 and *CPapReg*, p. 449. The notice for the excommunication of Frederick is found in L. Auvray (ed.), *Les registres de Gregoire IX*, 4 vols, Bibliothèque des Ecoles françaises d'Athènes et de Rome 2nd ser. ix (Paris: De Boccard, 1890–1955), hereafter *Reg. Greg. IX*, 5102 and *CPapReg*, p. 188. The letters concerning the translation of Thomas Becket's relics are found in Vatican City, ASV Reg. Vat. 10, ff. 55v–56r, P. Pressutti (ed.), *Regesta Honorii Papae III*, 2 vols (Rome: Loescher, 1888–95; repr. Hildesheim: Olms, 1978), hereafter *Reg. Hon. III*, 1830, 1840–1 and *CPapReg*, p. 62. See also S. L. Reames, 'Reconstructing and Interpreting a Thirteenth-century Office for the Translation of Thomas Becket', *Speculum*, 80 (2005), 118–70.

24 On the papacy at this time, see W. Ullmann, *A Short History of the Papacy in the Middle Ages* (2nd edn, London: Routledge, 2003), pp. 201–79.

25 Vatican City, ASV Reg. Vat. 23, f. 1r, *Reg. Inn. IV*, 6820 and *CPapReg*, p. 288. For Tintern Abbey, see J. Burton and K. Stöber, *Abbeys and Priories of Medieval Wales* (Cardiff: University of Wales Press, 2015), pp. 204–9.

26 Honorius gave a general confirmation of lands and benefits to Tewkesbury mentioning the bishops of Llandaff in *Reg. Hon. III*, 3292, *CPapReg*, p. 81 and *EAWD*, ii, L.330. W. and H. and St Mary's are mentioned in *Reg. Hon. III*, 3323, *CPapReg*, p. 82 and *EAWD*, ii, L.331. The grant was confirmed by Gregory IX in 1230: Vatican City, ASV Reg. Vat. 15, f. 20v–21r, *Reg. Greg. IX*, 473, *CPapReg*, p. 123 and *EAWD*, ii, L.345. The H. is Henry of Abergavenny (bishop of Llandaff, 1193–1218) but the W. might conceivably be either William of Saltmarsh (bishop of Llandaff, 1186–91) or William of Goldcliff (1219–29). The latter was the subject of papal correspondence through

the papal legate Pandulf, who notified Henry III of his election. See *EAWD*, ii, L.322. For the bishops, see D. Crouch (ed.), *Llandaff Episcopal Acta 1140–1287* (Cardiff: University of Wales Press, 1988), pp. xiv–xv.

27 The church remains as the parish church of the modern Magor but was rededicated to St Mary at a later date. For Elias of Radnor, see Crouch, *Llandaff*, pp. xvi–xvii. For the history of this abbey, see G. Ercolani, D. Fiorani, G. Giammaria, with D. Durante, and I. Sanpietro, *La Badia della Gloria, Monumenti di Anagni* (Anagni: Istituto di storia e di arte del Lazio meridionale, 2001).

28 Vatican City, ASV Reg. Vat. 19, f. 131v, *Reg. Greg. IX*, 4932 and 4933 and *CPapReg*, p. 183.

29 Earl Gilbert's letter is edited in D. Crouch (ed.), *The Acts and Letters of the Marshal family: Marshals of England and Earls of Pembroke, 1145–1248*, Camden Fifth Series, 47 (Cambridge: Cambridge University Press for the Royal Historical Society, 2015), 200 (though Crouch here makes minor errors of reference, referring to Rome rather than the Vatican City, the Biblioteca Apostolica Vaticana rather than the ASV and the rather indistinct 'Register of Pope Innocent IV' rather than Reg. Vat. 21). For Elias of Radnor's letter, see Crouch, *Llandaff*, 67 and *EAWD*, ii, L.381.

30 Vatican City, ASV Reg. Vat. 21, f. 109v, f. 380r, ff. 474v–475r, ASV Reg. Vat. 22, ff. 218r–v, *Reg. Inn. IV*, 2873, 2586, 3373 and 6087, and *CPapReg*, pp. 234, 237 and 280; C. B. de la Ronciere, J. Loye, P. H. de Cenival and A. Coulon (eds), *Les registres d'Alexandre IV*, 3 vols, Bibliothèque des Ecoles françaises d'Athènes et de Rome 2nd ser. xv (Paris: A. Fontemoing, 1895–1959), hereafter *Reg. Alex. IV*, 443, 471, 2346, *CPapReg*, pp. 315, 316, 353 and *EAWD*, ii, L.477 and L.490. The lands would eventually be transferred to the permanent care of Tintern Abbey in 1442 as the income from the church lands was not any longer worth the expenditure of obtaining it to the monks of Anagni. See J. A. Twemlow, *Calendar of Papal Registers Relating to Great Britain and Ireland, Volume 9, 1431–1447* (London: HMSO, 1912), p. 266.

31 A. Theiner (ed.), *Vetera Monumenta Hibernorum et Scotorum* (Rome: Typis Vaticanis, 1864), p. lxxxi, *Reg. Greg. IX*, 2642, *CPapReg*, p. 147 and *PH*, ii, 226.

32 Vatican City, ASV Reg. Vat. 23, f. 19v, *Reg. Inn. IV*, 6985, *CPapReg*, p. 290 and *PH*, ii, 371. For Henry III and the crusade, see C. Tyerman, *England and the Crusades, 1095–1588* (Chicago: University of Chicago Press, 1988), pp. 111–23 and B. K. U. Weiler, *Henry III of England*

and the Staufen Empire, 1216–1272 (Woodbridge: Boydell, 2006), pp. 140–6.

[33] On the provision of benefices by the papacy during the twelfth and thirteenth centuries, see K. Pennington, *Pope and Bishops* (Philadelphia: University of Pennsylvania Press, 1984), pp. 115–53, especially pp. 135–48.

[34] Vatican City, ASV Reg. Vat. 27, f. 75r, *Reg. Urb. IV*, 274 and *EAWD*, i, L.507; Vatican City, ASV Reg. Vat. 27, f. 75r, *Reg. Urb. IV*, 275, *CPapReg*, p. 389 and *EAWD*, ii, L.517.

[35] Vatican City, ASV Reg. Vat. 19, ff. 29v–30r, *Reg. Greg. IX*, 4410, *CPapReg*, p. 175 and *EAWD*, i, D.515; Vatican City, ASV Reg. Vat. 21a, 218r (but cf. Reg. Vat 21a, 217v–218r), *Reg. Inn. IV*, 4465, *CPapReg*, p. 254 and *EAWD*, i, D.563; Vatican City, ASV Reg. Vat. 22, ff. 107v–108r, *Reg. Inn. IV*, 5424, *CPapReg*, p. 273 and *EAWD*, i, D. 583; Vatican City, ASV Reg. Vat. 22, ff. 228v–229r, *Reg. Inn. IV*, 6194 and *CPapReg*, p. 282; Vatican City, ASV Reg. Vat. 24, ff. 26v–27r, *Reg. Alex. IV*, 238 and *CPapReg*, p. 312; Vatican City, ASV Reg. Vat. 24, f. 155r, *Reg. Alex. IV*, 1237, *CPapReg*, p. 329 and *EAWD*, i, D.629.

[36] Vatican City, ASV Reg. Vat. 22, f. 180v, *Reg. Inn. IV*, 5836 and Bliss, *Calendar*, p. 278; Vatican City, ASV Reg. Vat. 27, f. 80r, *Reg. Urb. IV*, 292 and Bliss, *Calendar*, p. 390.

[37] Vatican City, ASV Reg. Vat. 29, f. 151v, *Reg. Urb. IV*, 1559, *CPapReg*, p. 412 and *EAWD*, i, D.666. Aquinas dedicated three books of *Catena Aurea* to the cardinal. Maurice is otherwise unknown. See J. Catto, 'Ideas and Experience in the Political Thought of Aquinas', *Past and Present*, 71 (1976), 3–21, at 16–17, and J. A. Weisheipl, *Friar Thomas D'Aquino: His Life, Thought and Works* (Oxford: Wiley-Blackwell, 1975), pp. 124, 129 and 136–7.

[38] Vatican City, ASV Reg. Vat. 16, f. 53r–v and f. 92v, *Reg. Greg. IX*, 963 and 1112 and *CPapReg*, p. 131. For Cwm Hir and Valle Crucis, see Burton and Stöber, *Abbeys and Priories*, pp. 80–3 and 213–17.

[39] Cheney discusses this very issue with regard to Bishop Mauger of Worcester for which see n. 97 below.

[40] Vatican City, ASV Reg. Vat. 13, f. 53r, *Reg. Hon. III*, 5437 and *CPapReg*, p. 102. Hays identifies him with Abraham, bishop of St Asaph, June 1225–32/3. See Rh. W. Hays, *The History of the Abbey of Aberconway* (Cardiff: University of Wales Press, 1963), pp. 37–8 and 'St Asaph: Bishops', in M. J. Pearson (ed.), *Fasti Ecclesiae Anglicanae 1066–1300: Volume 9, the Welsh Cathedrals (Bangor, Llandaff, St Asaph, St Davids)* (London: Institute of Historical Research, 2003), pp. 33–6,

British History Online, www.british-history.ac.uk/fasti-ecclesiae/1066-1300/vol9/pp33-36 (accessed 29 May 2016).

41 On Richard Carew, see J. W. Evans, 'The bishops of St Davids from Bernard to Bec', in R. F. Walker (ed.), *Medieval Pembrokeshire*, Pembrokeshire County History II (Haverfordwest: The Pembrokeshire Historical Society, 2002), pp. 270–311, at 297–302.

42 Evans, 'The bishops', p. 297.

43 London, The National Archives, E 135/5/43, *EAWD*, i, D.620 and Evans, 'The bishops', p. 297.

44 A. W. Haddan and W. Stubbs (eds), *Councils and Ecclesiastical Documents relating to Britain and Ireland*, 3 vols (Oxford: Clarendon Press, 1869–78), hereafter *CED*, i, pp. 481–2, *Reg. Alex. IV*, 1159, *CPapReg*, p. 327 and *EAWD*, i, D.623.

45 *Reg. Alex. IV*, 1158, *CPapReg*, p. 327 and *EAWD*, i, D.624; *CED*, i, pp. 482–3, *CPapReg*, p. 328 and *EAWD*, i, D.625–6.

46 *CED*, i, p. 483, *CPapReg*, p. 328 and *EAWD*, i, D.627; D.632–3 and Evans, 'The bishops', p. 298.

47 *CED*, i, pp. 483–4, *CPapReg*, p. 329, *EAWD*, i, D.628; Vatican City, ASV Reg. Vat. 25, 245r, *Reg. Alex. IV*, 3098 and *EAWD*, i, D.649. This document should be read with J. Barrow (ed.), *St Davids Episcopal Acta 1085–1280* (Cardiff: South Wales Records Society, 1998), p. 130, the document which established the treasurer at St David's.

48 For Thomas Wallensis, see Evans, 'The bishops', pp. 295–7, Barrow (ed.), *St Davids*, pp. 12–13 and *AoC*, pp. 193–4.

49 Vatican City, ASV Reg. Vat. 23, 97r–v, *Reg. Inn. IV*, 7554, *CPapReg*, p. 301 and *EAWD*, i, D.600.

50 Gerald of Wales, *De Rebus a se Gestis*, I.6 (*GCO*, i.32–9) and *Autobiography*, pp. 49–56.

51 The permission for Thomas Wallensis to build was granted only a few years after Gregory IX had ordered an inquiry into the boundaries between the two dioceses. See n. 62, below.

52 Pennington, *Pope and Bishops*, pp. 101–14.

53 On Cadwgan's life and his literary activities, see J. Goering and H. Pryce, 'The *De Modo Contifendi* of Cadwgan, Bishop of Bangor', *Mediaeval Studies*, 62 (2000), 1–27 at 1–15 and especially 6–8 where the possible reasons for the acceptance of his resignation are discussed. Cadwgan's resignation and the granting of that right by Gregory IX is recorded in all versions of *Brut y Tywysogyon*. See *Brut y Tywysogyon: Peniarth MS. 20*, ed. T. Jones (Cardiff: University of Wales Press, 1941), p. 196; *Brut y Tywysogyon: Peniarth MS. 20*, trans. T. Jones (Cardiff: University of Wales Press, 1952), hereafter *Brut (Pen. 20)*, 1236 (p. 104);

Brut y Tywysogyon: Red Book of Hergest Version, ed. and trans. T. Jones (Cardiff: University of Wales Press, 1955), hereafter *Brut (RBH)*, 1236 (pp. 234–5); and *Brenhinedd y Saesson*, ed. and trans. T. Jones (Cardiff: University of Wales Press, 1971), hereafter *BS*, 1236 (pp. 230–1).

54 *CED*, i, p. 464, *Reg. Greg. IX*, 2994 and *CPapReg*, p. 151.

55 *Reg. Urb. IV*, 128 and *CPapReg*, p. 383.

56 *Reg. Urb. IV*, 466, 468 and 470–2, D. Rees and J. G. Jones (eds), *Thomas Matthews's Welsh Records in Paris* (Cardiff: University of Wales Press, 2010), pp. 13–16, 7–12, 17, 18, 19–20 and 65–70, 59–66, 71, 72, and 73–4, *CPapReg*, pp. 394–5 and *EAWD*, i, D.665, D.662 and D.664. Page references are to Thomas Matthews's *Welsh Records in Paris* are to the texts and translation of the original volume. This was reissued in full in the recent reprint, but this volume also used roman numerals for pages in the new editors' introductions. See also Hurlock, *Crusades*, p. 36 and Lunt, *Financial Relations*, pp. 290–1.

57 Hurlock, *Crusades*, pp. 202–4. See also her chapter in this volume.

58 Vatican City, ASV Reg. Vat. 22, f. 62v, *Reg. Inn. IV*, 5190–1 and *CPapReg*, p. 269. Vatican City, ASV Reg. Vat. 22, f. 62v, *Reg. Inn. IV*, 5190 and *CPapReg*, p. 269. For the disputed election at Shrewsbury, see M. J. Angold, G. C. Baugh, Marjorie M. Chibnall, D. C. Cox, D. T. W. Price, Margaret Tomlinson and B. S. Trinder, 'Houses of Benedictine monks: abbey of Shrewsbury', in A. T. Gaydon and R. B. Pugh (eds), *A History of the County of Shropshire: Volume 2* (London: Institute of Historical Research, 1973), pp. 30–7, www.british-history.ac.uk/vch/salop/vol2/pp30-37 (accessed 7 January 2016). On the role of the executor in thirteenth-century England, see T. W. Smith, 'Papal Executors and the Veracity of Petitions from Thirteenth-century England', *Revue d'histoire ecclésiastique*, 110 (2015), 662–83.

59 Vatican City, ASV Reg. Vat. 11, f. 201r–v, *Reg. Hon. III*, 3835 and *CPapReg*, p. 85. See 'St Asaph: Bishops'. For Cymer and Whitland, see Burton and Stöber, *Abbeys and Priories*, pp. 84–6 and 218–21.

60 Vatican City, ASV Reg. Vat. 18 144v–145r, *Reg. Greg. IX*, 3103 and *CPapReg*, p. 152; *Reg. Greg. IX*, 3123 and *CPapReg*, p. 153. The case is analysed in detail by H. J. Nicholson, 'Margaret de Lacy and the Hospital of St John at Aconbury', *JEccH*, 50 (1999), 629–51. See also Hurlock, *Crusades*, pp. 162–3 and C. Veach, *Lordship in Four Realms: The Lacy Family, 1166–1241*, Manchester Medieval Studies (Manchester: Manchester University Press, 2014), pp. 221–3. For Bishop Hywel I see 'St Asaph: Bishops'.

61 Vatican City, ASV Reg. Vat. 18, f. 102r, *Reg. Greg. IX*, 2936 and *CPapReg*, p. 150.

[62] *CED*, i, pp. 464–5, *Reg. Greg. IX*, 3013, *CPapReg*, p. 151 and *EAWD*, i, D.510.
[63] The events are discussed in the context of Manx history in R. A. McDonald, *Manx Kingship in its Irish Sea Setting 1187–1229: King Rögnvaldr and the Crovan dynasty* (Dublin: Four Courts Press, 2007), pp. 101–4.
[64] Rögnvaldr campaigned on behalf of his son-in-law on Anglesey in 1193, for which see *Brut (RBH)* 1193 (pp. 172–3), *Brut y Tywysogyon: Peniarth MS. 20* (p. 134), *Brut (Pen. 20)* 1193 (p. 74), *BS* 1193 (pp. 188–9).
[65] O. Hageneder, W. Malczek and A. A. Strand (eds), *Reg. Inn. III., 2. Pontifikatsjahr 1199/1200. Texte* (Rome/Vienna: ÖEAW, 1979); K. Rudolf et al. (eds), *Reg. Inn. III., 2. Pontifikatsjahr 1199/1200. Indices* (Rome/Vienna: ÖEAW, 1983), 224, Cheney, *Calendar*, 168 and *CPapReg*, p. 8. Pryce draws attention to the use of the title *Princeps Norwalie* assigned to Llywelyn in the pope's letter. It seems likely that this echoes the use of the title in Llywelyn's petition to the pope and reflects an attempt at projecting dominance in Gwynedd at the time of the letter's writing: *AWR*, p. 25.
[66] *Reg. Inn. III*, vi, 47, Cheney, *Calendar*, 469 and *CPapReg*, p. 13.
[67] O. Hageneder, A. Sommerlechner, H. Weigl with C. Egger and R. Murauer (eds), *Reg. Inn. III., 7. Pontifikatsjahr 1204/1205. Texte und Indices* (Vienna: ÖEAW, 1997), 220, Cheney, *Calendar*, 600 and *CPapReg*, p. 19.
[68] H. Pryce, *Native Law and the Church in Medieval Wales* (Oxford: Oxford University Press, 1993), pp. 84–6.
[69] *AoC*, p. 10 and L. J. Wilkinson, 'Joan, Wife of Llywelyn the Great', in M. Prestwich, R. H. Britnell and R. Frame (eds), *Thirteenth Century England*, 10 (Woodbridge: Boydell, 2005), 81–93, at 82–3.
[70] Vatican City, ASV Reg. Vat. 13, f. 122v, *Reg. Hon. III*, 5906, *CPapReg*, p. 109 and *AWR*, 279. For the effect of this confirmation of legitimacy and the letters regarding the naming of Dafydd as heir in enhancing Joan's status see Wilkinson, 'Joan', p. 88.
[71] *AWR*, 253, *Reg. Hon. III*, 3996, and *CPapReg*, p. 87. Welsh law allowed for any natural children publicly acknowledged by their fathers to have an equal share of patrimony. Llywelyn had previously recognised Gruffudd, the son of Tangwystl, as his son. In securing this letter, Llywelyn appears to have been attempting to gain papal approval for his establishing the principle of a legitimate son taking precedence over a natural son in matters of inheritance. See J. B. Smith, 'Dynastic Succession in Medieval Wales', *BBCS*, 33 (1986), 199–232, at 218–19.

For the recognition of Dafydd, see Pryce, *Native Law*, pp. 86–7.

[72] Vatican City, ASV Reg. Vat. 13, f. 122v, *Reg. Hon. III*, 5907, *CPapReg*, p. 109 and *EAWD*, i, D.463.

[73] For Llywelyn's strategy, see G. A. Williams, 'The Succession to Gwynedd 1238–1247', *BBCS*, 20 (1962–4), 393–413 and *AoC*, pp. 249–50.

[74] H. Pryce, 'Owain Gwynedd and Louis VII: the Franco-Welsh Diplomacy of the First Prince of Wales', *WHR*, 19.1 (1998), 1–28 and *AoC*, p. 194. See also Gideon Brough's chapter in this volume, which translates one of Owain's letters.

[75] Vatican City, ASV Reg. Vat. 22, f. 198r, *Reg. Inn. IV*, 5880, *CPapReg*, pp. 278–9 and *EAWD*, i, D.591.

[76] Theiner, *Vetera*, p. iv; *Littere Wallie*, ed. J. G. Edwards (Cardiff: University of Wales Press, 1940), p. 304, *Reg. Hon. III*, 245 and *CPapReg*, p. 43; Vatican City, ASV Reg. Vat. 10, 83r, *Reg. Hon. III*, 1960 and *CPapReg*, p. 64. The text of the first letter from Honorius's register was addressed to the king of Scotland, with a similar letter recorded as being sent to Llywelyn among other recipients. Bliss is in error in stating that it was addressed to William I of Scotland (1165–1214), as the text is addressed to *Illustri regi scotie*, and was sent in January 1217.

[77] *CED*, i, pp. 459–61, *Reg. Hon. III*, 4517 and 4518, *CPapReg*, p. 93, J. E. Sayers, *Original Papal Documents in England and Wales from the Accession of Pope Innocent III to the Death of Pope Benedict XI (1198–1304)* (Oxford: Oxford University Press, 1999), p. 94. See also J. E. Sayers, *Papal Government and England during the Pontificate of Honorius III (1216–1227)*, Cambridge studies in medieval life and thought, Third Series 21 (Cambridge: Cambridge University Press, 1984), p. 170.

[78] Vatican City, ASV Reg. Vat. 17, ff. 152v–153r, *Reg. Greg. IX*, 1827 and *CPapReg*, p. 139; Vatican City, ASV Reg. Vat. 18, f. 152r, *Reg. Greg. IX*, 3134 and *CPapReg*, p. 153. For the Pact of Myddle, see *AWR*, 270–1. See also J. E. Lloyd, *A History of Wales from the Earliest Times to the Edwardian Conquest*, 2 vols (3rd edn, London: Longman, 1939), ii, pp. 678–81 and Hurlock, *Crusades*, p. 192.

[79] Vatican City, ASV Reg. Vat. 32, ff. 62r–v, *Reg. Clement IV*, 231–2, *CPapReg*, p. 431, Sayers, *Original*, 709–10 and *EAWD*, i, L.505.

[80] *AWR*, 363 and see J. B. Smith, *Llywelyn ap Gruffudd: Prince of Wales* (new edn, Cardiff: University of Wales Press, 2014), pp. 177–80.

[81] An extract from the report of the legates is translated in D. Whitelock (ed.), *English Historical Documents Volume I: c. 500–1042* (London: Eyre

and Spottiswoode, 1955), 191 (pp. 770–4). On the legation and the conflict between Offa and Jænberht, see F. M. Stenton, *Anglo-Saxon England* (3rd edn, Oxford: Oxford University Press, 1971), pp. 215–19, D. P. Kirby, *The Earliest English Kings* (London: Routledge, 1991), pp. 169–74 and C. Wickham, *The Inheritance of Rome: A History of Europe from 400 to 1000* (London: Allen Lane, 2009), p. 164.

82 The most comprehensive account of the case and analysis of *Liber Landavensis* as a source is J. R. Davies, *The Book of Llandaf and the Norman Church in Wales*, Studies in Celtic History 21 (Woodbridge: Boydell, 2003), which deals with John of Crema's involvement with Llandaff at pp. 39–40.

83 Vatican City, ASV Reg. Vat. 32, f. 9r, *Reg. Clement IV*, 41, Bliss, *Calendar*, p. 426; *PH*, i, 123, *Reg. Hon. III*, 2027 and *CPapReg*, p. 65.

84 See respectively nn. 77 and 26, above.

85 Some activities of legates are not reflected in the papal archives at all. For example, Guala Bicchieri placed the whole of Wales under an interdict in 1216 following Llywelyn's successful campaign of the winter of 1215. It was also Guala who lifted the interdict in 1218 having negotiated a settlement between Llywelyn and the young Henry III. See N. Vincent (ed.), *The Letters and Charters of Cardinal Guala Bicchieri, Papal Legate in England, 1216-1218*, Canterbury and York Society vol. LXXXIII (Woodbridge: Boydell, 1996), 124 and 125, *AoC*, pp. 242–3, Smith, *Llywelyn*, pp. 21–2, and Gideon Brough's discussion in his chapter in this volume.

86 The situation is explained thoroughly in Smith, *Llywelyn*, pp. 390–402.

87 *Reg. Greg. X et Jean XXI*, 78–9 and *CPapReg*, p. 452.

88 Vatican City, ASV Reg. Vat. 39, ff. 235v–236v, J. Gay and S. Vitte (eds), *Les registres de Nicolas III (1277–1280)*, Bibliothèque des Ecoles françaises d'Athènes et de Rome 2nd ser. xiv (Paris: A. Fontemoing, 1898–1938), pp. 629–31 and *CPapReg*, p. 461; F. Soehnée, G. de Puybaudet, R. Poupardin and F. Olivier-Martin (eds), *Les registres de Martin IV (1281–1285)*, Bibliothèque des Ecoles françaises d'Athènes et de Rome 2nd ser. xvi (Paris: Fontemoing, 1901–35), 18, *CPapReg*, p. 463 and Vatican City, ASV Reg. Vat. 41, ff. 10v–11r, Reg. Martin IV, i, 19–20 and *CPapReg*, p. 463.

89 *Reg. Alex. IV*, 407 and *CPapReg*, p. 315. For Boniface, see C. H. Knowles, 'Savoy, Boniface of (1206/7–70)', *Oxford Dictionary of National Biography*, Oxford University Press, 2004, *www.oxforddnb.com/view/article/2844?docPos=1* (accessed 30 April 2016).

90 The words *plura impedimenta alia* in particular would suggest this.

91 *AoC*, pp. 308–9 and Smith, *Llywelyn*, pp. 65–77.

92 Vatican City, ASV Reg. Vat. 20, f. 19r, *Reg. Greg IX*, 5238, *CPapReg*, p. 190 and *EAWD*, ii, L.402. On requests to hold additional benefices, see above p. 219.

93 See R. Bartlett, *Gerald of Wales: A Voice of the Middle Ages* (Stroud: Sutton, 2006), p. 47, n. 97 and the references found there.

94 O. Hageneder, with C. Egger, K. Rudolf and A. Sommerlechner (eds), *Reg. Inn. III., 5. Pontifikatsjahr 1202/1203. Texte* (Vienna: ÖEAW, 1993); A. Sommerlechner, with C. Egger and H. Weigl (eds), *Reg. Inn. III., 5. Pontifikatsjahr 1202/1203. Indices* (Vienna: ÖEAW, 1994), 22, *CPapReg*, p. 10 and Cheney, *Calendar*, 406.

95 *AoC*, p. 229 and Lloyd, *History*, pp. 582–7.

96 C. R. Cheney, *Pope Innocent III and England*, Päpste und Papsttum 9 (Stuttgart: Hiersemann, 1976), pp. 142–3 and M. Cheney, D. Smith, C. Brooke and P. M. Hoskin (eds), *English Episcopal Acta 34: Worcester 1186–1218* (Oxford: Oxford University Press, 2008), p. xxxv.

97 *English Episcopal Acta 34*, p. xxxiv.

98 *EAWD*, i, D.335 and D.346.

99 If this thesis is correct, then it may be likely that Mauger wrote to Innocent III following the first abortive hearing at Worcester on 26 January 1202 for which see *De Jure*, III (*GCO* iii.200–210), *Autobiography*, pp. 227–30, *EAWD*, i, pp. 220–2 and J. C. Davies, 'Giraldus Cambrensis 1146–1946', *Archaeologia Cambrensis*, 99 (1946–7), 85–108 and 256–80, at 266–7. It should be noted that Mauger was not present at this hearing.

100 *PH*, ii, 400, *Reg. Alex. IV*, 384 and *CPapReg*, p. 314.

101 G. Rudolph, with T. Frenz (eds), *Das Kammerregister Papst Martins IV* (Reg. Vat. 42) (Vatican City: BAV, 2007), 122 and *CPapReg*, p. 475.

102 Rudolph, *Kammerregister*, 127 and *CPapReg*, p. 476.

103 T. Rymer and R. Sanderson, *Foedera, Conventiones, Litterae etc.*, ed. A. Clarke and F. Holbrooke, 4 vols in 7 (London: G. Eyre and A. Strahan, 1816–69), I.ii, 608. Edward's actions drew condemnation from Martin IV who ordered the return of the money. According to a letter by Archbishop Pecham, Edward had paid the money back by the end of November 1283. See Lunt, *Financial Relations*, pp. 336–7, Hurlock, *Crusades*, p. 204 and the references found there.

104 W. E. Lunt, 'A Papal Tenth Levied in the British Isles from 1274–1280', *EHR*, 32 (1917), 49–89, document 13 and Lunt, *Papal Revenue*, p. 74.

8

Wales and the wider world: the soldiers' perspective

Adam Chapman

As Rees Davies has noted, Wales and the Welsh were considered strange, and alien, particularly in the thirteenth and early fourteenth centuries.[1] This was, of course, a function of their difference in culture, law, language and habits, themselves born from a history and geography that had existed alongside England, but had not been part of it. As Helen Fulton notes, Wales and Ireland had more in common with each other than either had in common with England. In relating their parallel traditions of bardic poetry, she notes that it was, 'shared by the native populations of the two countries and the product of a particular kind of society – kin-based, decentralized, hierarchical, linguistically distinctive – that existed long before the formation of an English state'.[2] Welsh perspectives on their neighbours ultimately hinged on the fact that the societies that co-existed in medieval Wales looked to very different models of authority than did inhabitants of the kingdom of England. The shires and March of Wales were part of the English realm, but its people were not, with a few contested exceptions, such as the citizens of Edward I's planted boroughs surrounding his castles in Gwynedd, considered English.[3] It is pertinent to note then, that for much of the later Middle Ages, for the majority of Europeans, Welshmen outside Wales were encountered primarily as soldiers.

It is certain that from the twelfth century at least, Welshmen had fought for the kings of England.[4] In the wars of conquest fought against the princes of Gwynedd, the princes of Deheubarth and Powys fought with the forces of Edward I for reasons of their own. For two generations after the conquest was completed, however, Welshmen were disproportionately represented in the armies of Edward I, his son and grandson. Thereafter the picture is more complex, but in summary, it can be said that Welsh soldiers were soldiers who happened to be Welsh, and their nationality did not mark them out.[5] Welshmen contributed to England's armies and also to the armies of England's enemies, either as followers of the self-declared prince of Wales, Owain ap Thomas ap Rhodri (Owain Lawgoch, d.1378) or later, as those adherents of Owain Glyndŵr who could not reconcile themselves to English rule.[6] The role of Wales and the Welsh in the course of what is generally known as the Hundred Years War has been well, if not exhaustively, studied with articles by D. L. Evans and Tony Carr providing dominant narratives.[7] These, together with Rees Davies's influential account of military lordship in the March of Wales have provided a framework on which the present author hung a more substantial account spanning the years from the conquest until the death of Henry V.[8]

Edward I – and his successors – exercised governance in Wales not in person, but by delegation: after 1295, Edward never returned to his conquests in Wales. Edward II was born in the midst of the construction of the great fortress of Caernarfon, as a symbolic statement of his father's imperium after his conquest. The end of his reign, and perhaps his death, believed by members of the Welsh elite to have been caused by the discovery of a plot to free him from Berkeley castle, were connected with Wales and perhaps give symbols of a different kind.[9] Edward III never visited at all. Richard II passed through on his way to and – infamously – from Ireland in the 1394 and 1399. Henry IV was, in essence, a Marcher lord whose reign – and the military apprenticeships of his sons – was defined by the opposition of the Welsh to his rule in Wales. In each case, the presence of the king of England in the Welsh parts of his realm were the product of necessity. Lordship was personal in Wales, but the person was only very rarely that of the king. As Rees Davies noted, this arm's length governance embedded ethnic rivalries and the impression of discrimination against the native populations.

The soldiers' perspective

More controversially, he went on to suggest that this fostered 'nationalism' and a 'two nation' mentality whereby the Irish (and Welsh) defined themselves against the English.[10] One of the difficulties of this approach is that it has come to define the historiography of the entire later Middle Ages in Wales, from the conquest of Gwynedd in 1282 to the end of the fifteenth century, with Owain Glyndŵr's rebellion (1400–c.1410) as the logical and near-inevitable conclusion of the exclusion of native Welshmen from the governance of shires and Marches of Wales. From the perspective of those Welshmen who made their careers – out of obligation and choice – serving the English crown as soldiers, the picture can be shown to be more complicated and conflicted. It is this complexity, as shown in the manner in which the Welsh were experienced beyond Wales and how they reflected upon this experience within their homelands, which will form the focus of this chapter.

Given the aims of this book, the chapter will look mainly at the wars of England's enemies – against France and Scotland – rather than Glyndŵr's rebellion or the Wars of the Roses. It will draw upon two important sets of sources, the records of English armies in the fourteenth and fifteenth centuries, and the large body of Welsh-language poetry surviving from the same period. Bringing these sources together is not without its problems since, fundamentally, the first is primarily concerned with money while the second deals with many other things besides, not least the image of poets' patrons. Involvement in war was, of course, an important part and the shires and March of Wales were a heavily militarised society. Rees Davies went so far as to suggest that the value of a Marcher lordship in the fourteenth century might readily be expressed not only in rents and profits, but in the number of men that could be recruited from it.[11] Like all young men, poets could be soldiers and muster rolls reveal that several were and the surviving work of others suggests that rather more might have been.

Welsh soldiers viewed by others

There are a number of well-known accounts of Welshmen fighting in English armies and two are especially vivid. The first was the eyewitness account of Welshmen around Ghent in the winter of 1297–8:

> Edward, king of England came to Flanders. He brought with him many soldiers from the land of Wales, and also some from England.[12] He came to Ghent . . . In the very depth of winter they were running about bare-legged. They wore a red robe. They could not have been warm. The money they received from the king was spent on milk and butter. They would eat and drink anywhere. I never saw them wearing armour. I studied them very closely, and walked among them to find out what defensive armour they carried when going into battle. Their weapons were bows, arrows and swords. They also had javelins. They wore linen clothing. They were great drinkers. Their camp was in the village of St Pierre. They endamaged the Flemings very much. Their pay was too small and so it came about that they took what did not belong to them.[13]

The second is found in Froissart's account of the battle of Crécy:

> Et lá entre ces Englés avoit et ribaus les gallois et cornillois, qui poursieuvoient gens d'armes et arciers, qui portient grandes coutilles, et venoient entre leurs gens d'armes et leurs arciers qui leur faisoient voie, et trouvoient ces gens d'armes en ce dangier, comtes, barons, chevaliers et escuires: si les occioient sans merci, commes grans sires qu' il fust.

> However, among the English there were pillagers and irregulars. Welsh and Cornishmen armed with long knives, who went out after the French (their own men-at-arms and archers making way for them) and, when they found any in difficulty, whether they were counts, barons, knights of esquires, they killed them without mercy.[14]

Both describe what outsiders thought of Welshmen and give a good indication of how Welshmen were experienced – knowingly – by English and continental observers: Welshmen were soldiers. Both accounts describe easily identifiable and obvious Welshmen and their coarse and unpredictable actions, the 'light-headedness' occasionally attributed to them in English sources.[15] Many examples appear in chronicles, including the unlikely account of a number of Welshmen being loaned as bodyguards to Albert, duke of Austria, one of whom, for sport, apparently leapt on to the duke's horse and attempted to slit the duke's throat.[16]

The chronicle of Lanercost for the year 1296 provides an example of the treachery of another Welshman, apparently named Lewyn or Lefwyn (Llywelyn being more likely) during the siege of Edinburgh castle and supposedly deriving from its Scottish constable:

> he (Edward I) chose a certain Welshman, his swiftest runner, whom he reckoned most trustworthy, committed to him many letters and, having provided him with money, ordered him to make his way to London with the utmost dispatch . . . Now, going straight to the tavern, he spent all in gluttony that he had received for travelling expenses. Early on the morning of the vigil, being Sunday, he made himself a laughing-stock to the English by ordering his comrade to carry his shield before him, declaring that he was not going to leave the place until he had made an assault on the castle. Presenting himself, therefore, with a balista [crossbow] before the gates, he cried upon the wall guard to let a rope down, so that having been admitted in that matter, he might reveal to them all the secrets of their enemy.[17]

This Welshman, it seems, was hung for this act, having been surrendered to the English. There may be some doubt that he ever existed since a similar story appears in the chronicle of Bury St Edmunds – this time concerning the siege of Ghent in the following winter of 1297–8. There, another Welshman was supposed to have swum the river, climbed a palisade, killed three defenders and returned to his fellows an act of boldness apparently rewarded with the sum of 100s. The bones of the story are reproduced some fifty years later in Thomas Gray's *Scalacronica* suggesting an origin in a now lost royal newsletter.[18] Further doubt may be shed on this anecdote because a very similar story was told about Welshmen, this time in the army of Henry II in 1167, swimming the river Epte at Chaumont and burning his stores there.[19] One might ask whether this love of water had become a narrative trope.

For the most part, however, Welshmen were ordinary: Welsh archers or men-at-arms just happened to be archers or men-at-arms who were Welsh.[20] They were valued by the kings of England: Welsh absence at the aftermath of the siege of Caerlaverock in 1300 (as a reward for their earlier good service) was noted as an unfortunate by the chronicler William Rishanger who suggested that the campaign suffered by their absence.[21] They were distinguished in pay accounts only by their shire or lordship of origin, much like levies from English counties, and were paid the same rates as their English contemporaries. Welsh infantry came with their own standard bearers, doctors, chaplains and criers (*proclamatores*), sometimes even interpreters, types of officers not seen among levies of the English counties, but the reasons for this must be primarily linguistic since many of these men would not have spoken English.[22] The Welshmen identified in the surviving plea roll of the same 1296 campaign seem to have been no more or less felonious than their English contemporaries and their stealing, brawling and murder (of one another, in the case of Einion Fychan who died at Jedburgh) appear wholly unremarkable in this context.[23] Welshmen, however, were disproportionately represented in the armies of Edward I and Edward II so it is unsurprising that their distinctive language and organisation with English armies should be remarked upon. What we cannot understand from these two accounts is what these Welsh soldiers thought about their involvement in war and how they thought about the world beyond Wales through that medium.

Despite this, external perspectives of Welshmen were stereotyped – the 'barefooted rascals' – of the English parliament's imagination in 1400 demonstrates a degree of contempt for the perceived poverty and roughness of the Welsh. This impression is at odds with that we get from the Welsh themselves.[24]

Military service in Welsh poetry

The military tactics of Edward I and Edward II and even in Edward III's early wars were dependent on enormous armies dominated by Welsh infantry. Tony Carr detailed some of the poetic references to service in France but the body of literature easily available for study has greatly increased.[25] The Beirdd yr Uchelwyr project at the University of Wales Centre for Advanced Welsh and Celtic

Studies has provided the historian with an abundance of material in a relatively accessible form to aid us in this quest.[26]

The destruction of the ambitions and the independence of Gwynedd destroyed the context for binary opposition of Welsh and English in poetry and it was only gradually that new forms of literary expression were established. It was, as Helen Fulton in particular has demonstrated, through contact with the wider world, on the part of both poets and patrons, that this came about.[27] This difference came about in form, with the couplet-based *cywydd*, best exemplified in the works of Dafydd ap Gwilym, master of that genre. Central to this, for many patrons, was praise of the Welsh squireachy (or *uchelwyr*: 'high men') as military leaders. Dafydd ap Gwilym, in an elegy for his most famous patron, Ifor Hael, called him 'Blade-hacker who scattered Englishmen in the splendid manner of anointed Llŷr'.[28] This despite the fact that Ifor (*fl. c.*1340–60) could only have served in English armies. The poem perpetuated mutual antagonism between English and Welsh dating from the period of Llywelyn ap Gruffudd's national ambitions after he declared himself 'prince of Wales' in 1258.[29] The celebration of leadership is striking, in part because by European standards even the wealthiest of the Welsh esquires were relatively impoverished and social advancement came with military success, generally in English armies, but also because Wales in the fourteenth and fifteenth centuries was a collection of heavily militarised societies. 'Celebrated' may not quite be the right word, of course, because the poets, as professional image makers, were concerned with making their patrons look good and might sometimes be guilty of hyperbole.

As the fourteenth-century grammar attributed to Einion Offeiriad (Einion the priest, *fl. c.*1320–40) suggests, such military attributes were just one among many of the qualities that could be praised in a lord or a baron. Einion's treatise, by drawing on the subjects and metres of popular verse, is an element in the reorientation which led to the development of praise poetry in the *cywydd* metre *c.*1350.[30]

> A lord is praised for his possession [i.e. dominion], and ability, and power, and valour, and might, and pride, and gentleness, and wisdom, and discretion and generosity, and meekness, and amiability towards his men and associates, and beauty of form, and beauty of body, and

nobility of thought, and of splendour of deeds and other gentle, honourable things.

A baron is praised for strength and prowess, and might, and loyalty towards his lord, and wisdom, and discretion, and generosity, and agreeableness, and beauty of body and of good breeding, and other commendable things.[31]

What mattered, then, was honour, favour and reward in other forms, praise by the poets being one. In this, as Helen Fulton has pointed out, Wales was adhering to a European norm.[32] It is significant that, with the exception of the period of the revolt of Owain Glyndŵr (1400–c.1410), military service for most Welshmen would have taken place outside Wales. That being the case, let us start with general perceptions. How was service in English armies perceived by the poets? It should be stated that from the Edwardian conquest onwards, members of English armies served for pay. This is almost never mentioned and, when it is, in disparaging or oblique terms.

After the conquest it was the descendants of Llywelyn ap Iorwerth's steward, Ednyfed Fychan (d.1246) that made the most of the situation, first by switching sides at an opportune moment and secondly, by securing most of the levers of power (this is never mentioned by the poets either). Sir Gruffudd Llwyd (d.1335) was the most important of the immediate post-conquest generation and praise to him takes profoundly archaic forms. He is most obviously prominent as a soldier in the records but this is not the focus of two surviving *awdlau* (odes) composed by Gwilym Ddu of Arfon. These poems date to the period of Gruffudd Llwyd's imprisonment in 1317 and a lament at this state of affairs is their principal theme. Sir Gruffudd's qualities as a warrior and as a leader are noted but Gwilym's references are thin on specific detail. The closest he comes to praising Sir Gruffudd's leadership in war is in describing Sir Gruffudd as '*Llew diymryson o Fôn Forudd*/The lion of strife from Anglesey to the English Channel'.[33] Gruffudd was dominant in his native Anglesey and had fought in Flanders in 1297 and in Scotland as leader of the men of north Wales, but this is hardly fulsome praise of his military leadership or of loyalty to English kings. As Morgan Thomas Davies notes, such reticence would be very unusual by the standards of the later fourteenth century. Sir Gruffudd's military service, leading armies far larger than those of any Welsh prince, is alluded to only gently and without detail. In fact, he spent almost every winter between 1294 and 1330 leading Welsh armies to Flanders, Scotland and around the March of Wales.

A man of a later generation, the poet Llywelyn Goch ap Meurig Hen (*fl. c.*1330–*c.*1390) was definitely a soldier. He was one of three men accused of attacking and wounding Gwyn ab Iorwerth Llwyd while waiting to embark for France on 3 June 1346. Gwyn died of his wounds at Penaran (Merion.) and Llywelyn was apprehended, having fled the scene and presumably deserted the army, but escaped the usual fate of murderers and lived into old age.[34] While Llywelyn may have expressed remorse for that act, his military experiences were not alluded to, but specific references to those of his patrons were. He described one of his patrons, probably Sir Rhys ap Gruffudd II who fought at Poitiers in 1356, as 'winner of a French castle'. In elegies to another descendant of Ednyfed Fychan, Tudur ap Goronwy of Penmynydd, Anglesey, Tudur's fame as a soldier was said to be known 'as far as Paris'.[35] One of Sir Hywel ap Gruffudd's elegies praised the knight for his exploits in 'Gwladoedd Ddolfin' (the Dauphin's lands), in France following the capture of Jean II.[36] This demonstrates that not only patrons, but also poets had a clear understanding not only of English and French politics and the realities of warfare. Even Dafydd ap Gwilym, by his own admission the least militaristic of men, though born of the class from which those whose status derived from their military utility frequently drew upon military imagery, not only in his court poetry but in his extensive body of love poetry which fits comfortably in the traditions of European troubadours.

> Ef a roes Duw, nawddfoes nawd,
> Gaer i'm cadw, gwiwrym ceudawd,
> Cystal, rhag ofn dial dyn,
> Â'r Galais rhag ei elyn.

> God, whose way is to protect,
> has granted a fortress to defend me – the heart's fine power,
> the equal (for fear of man's vengeance)
> of Calais against his enemy.[37]

It is the use of the strength of the walls of Calais, and by extension, the effort of the siege required to take the town that is of interest; it was a reference that would not only be familiar but totemic for his audience.

Poetry can, of course, offer some points of narrative to people's lives which have not otherwise been preserved, but it is worth pausing for a moment to consider how valid the poets' accounts of war might actually be. A great many of their lay patrons are known to have served in English armies in Scotland, France and even in Ireland, and this is reflected in praise composed to them. Military and judicial records prove that some poets also served in English armies though it is far from certain that a connection with a particular patron introduced the poet into military service. The exception is the fifteenth-century poet, Guto'r Glyn, of whom more below.

Other poets had military careers, though in some cases, more is known about these careers than survives of their verse. In 1372, the retinue of John Charlton III, lord of Powys included a man known as Crach Ffinnant (Scab of Ffinnant), who intended to go with Charlton as an archer.[38] This campaign was abandoned before the army had a chance to sail but he certainly served in Berwick under the command of the Flintshire knight, Sir Gregory Sais and with Owain Glyndŵr in 1384.[39] Of the two places in the medieval lordship of Powys called Ffinnant, it seems most probable that Y Crach, whose given name is unknown, came from the one near Cynllaith, one of Owain's own estates. Though he was named among twelve poets called upon by the poet Gruffudd Llwyd to pass judgement under the Welsh jurist Sir David Hanmer on Morgan ap Dafydd of Rhydodyn (Carmarthenshire), no indication is given of any wider fame.[40] His proven connection with Owain has brought him to the attention of scholars though none of his poems have survived. On 16 September 1400, he was present at the assembly that proclaimed Owain Glyndŵr prince of Wales and was named 'eorum propheta' by an Oswestry jury shortly afterwards. His involvement with the rebellion is also ambiguous: he was recorded as having come into the king's peace on 28 November 1400, but nothing more is known of him.[41] He was clearly a soldier and a poet though details of either career are limited, what little that is known suggests that his career as one had links with the other.[42]

The soldiers' perspective

Table 8.1: Hywel Swrdwal's military career

Date	Named as	Captain	Sub-captain	Role	Reference
1436	Hugh Sydual	Richard Plantagenet, duke of York		Rouen Garrison	BN ms Fr. 25773/1150
1443	Howel Sourdwall	Henry Griffith		Ordnance Company	BN ms Fr. 25777/1658
1443	Howel Sourdovill	Henry Griffith		Ordnance Company	BN ms Fr. 25777/1665
1445	Howell Sourdoual	Richard Plantagenet, duke of York	Georges Thibault	Rouen Garrison	BL Add. Ch. 8023
1447	Houel Sourdouel			Rouen Garrison (Gates)	BN ms Fr 25777/1772

The work of Hywel Swrdwal (*fl.* 1430–60) and Guto'r Glyn (*fl.* c.1430–c.1490) has survived in sufficient quantity to make some judgements on their lives and careers as people as well as poets. Guto is the most autobiographical about his military life and the careers of his patrons, though the most recent analysis of his career as a soldier suggest it to have been a relatively limited part of his life perhaps in 1436–7 and again, more certainly, in 1441–2. The first spell of service is suggested by his accounts of the Welsh captains, Sir Richard Gethin (d.*c*.1438) and Mathau (Mathew) Goch. Proven references to military service survive from a single muster roll of 1441 listed just above a Thomas Gitto who might plausibly have been his son.[43] The surviving poems attributed to Hywel Swrdwal are rather fewer, and without reference to his military life, but his documented military career is somewhat longer and, like the career of Guto, it seems probable that the connection with a patron, perhaps even the same Henry Griffith, advanced other elements of his career, leading to spending over a decade in Normandy. Table 8.1 outlines Hywel's possible career.

Guto'r Glyn was introduced to military service by one of his patrons, also a friend, Henry Griffith or Harri Ddu ap Gruffudd of Bacton, Herefordshire. He states this in a praise poem to Henry: 'He took me to the duke of York so that I might have 18 marks'. This sum represented a handsome bonus of £12, presumably for a year's service, being rather more than £9 2s. 6d. an archer would have received.[44] His take on war is revealed in a poetic account of a long, boozy evening at the house of another of his patrons, and fellow archer, Thomas ap Watkin of Llanddewi Rhydderch.[45] Poets, therefore, were not necessarily writing about war at one remove. Many were as much part of the culture of conflict as their patrons.

A comparison between two poems of Dafydd ap Gwilym and Iolo Goch show the differences in their attitudes to war. Dafydd, by his own admission, was no soldier and expressed regret over this. Insincere regret, but regret nonetheless. Nothing specific is known about Iolo Goch's military career nor even for certain whether he had one. While the most obvious example of his awareness of military affairs and several of his poems demonstrate his belonging to a highly militarised society.

This was not always the case, however: Iolo's poem of thanks for the gift of a knife is revealing of a more personal perspective and one that, ironically, accords better with the policies of the English realm. The knife itself is a baselard, a type of slim-bladed long dagger of a type originating in Basel, Switzerland.[46] As Iolo's poem makes clear, the purpose of such a weapon was solely military and, like a sword, possession of such an item, even given as a gift, implied high status both on the owner and on the giver:[47]

The soldiers' perspective

Ai gwell arf, gwiw yw'r llawrodd,
    Nag a roist im, enwog rodd?
        Cyllell hir cuall a llem,
        Callestrfin holltrin hylltrem,
    Bocs ei charn, pren cadarn prudd,
        Bygylwraig Ffrainc bogelrudd:

. . . Ychwaethach, hyach yw hyn,
    Lle brwydr, od â'r llu Brydyn,
        Eillio a hi a allwn
        Pen Ysgot coch – panis gwn? –
    Cnefio ei farf, arf erfai,
        Curo Ffrainc, dryllio cyff rhai,

. . . O daw dan llaw llu Ffichtiaid
    O'r mor hwnt, im nid mawr rhaid,
        I beri gewri a garn,
        Geisio na chledd nac isarm,
    Nac arf i'm llaw angiriol
        Eithr baslard ag ysbard bol.

Is there any better weapon, good is the handgift, / than the one you gave me, renowned gift? / A long knife, swift and sharp, / flint-tipped, good for cutting, grim-looking, / with boxwood hilt, hard sombre wood, / *French frightener* with a red pommel: / . . . Moreover, this is bolder, / place of battle, if the host goes to Scotland, / I could shave with it / the head of a red Scot – don't I know it? – / shear his beard, valiant weapon, / strike Frenchmen, chop the bodies of some, / . . . If the Pictish host comes furtively / from the sea yonder, there is no great need for me, / in order to cause shouts and commotion, / to seek either sword or battleaxe, / nor any weapon in my cruel hand / except a baselard with a blade on its belly.[48]

This, aside from thanking the patron for a generous gift, demonstrates that Iolo knew its use and was probably a soldier. Dafydd ap Gwilym's attitudes to weaponry are more ambivalent, most notably lending western literature one of its earliest firearm-based phallic metaphors.[49] More interesting, perhaps, are Dafydd ap Gwilym's reflections on the effects of war on the soldier:

253

Adam Chapman

Rhinwyllt fydd a rhy anwar.
Rhyfel ac oerfel a gâr.
O chlyw fod, catorfod tyn,
Brwydr yng ngwlad Ffrainc neu Brydyn,
Antur gwrdd, hwnt ar gerdded
Yn ŵr rhif yno y rhed.
O daw, perhôn a diainc,
Odd yno, medr ffrwyno Ffrainc,
Creithiog fydd, saethydd a'i sathr,
A chreulon, ddyn wych rylathr.
Mwy y câr ei drymbar draw
A mael dur a mul darian
A march o lu no merch lân.
Ni'th gêl pan ddêl poen ddolef,
Ni'th gais eithr i drais o'r dref.

He will be wild-natured and too savage.
He will love war and conflict.
That there is battle in France or Scotland,
a challenge for a mighty man,
he'll head straight off there to enlist in the ranks.
Should he escape and come back
He'll be scarred, an archer will leave his mark on him,
and bloody, you fine bright girl.
He'll have more affection for his heavy spear
And his sword (woe who puts faith in him)
and mail coat and dark shield
and war horse than for a pretty girl.
He won't protect you when cry of anguish comes,
He won't take you from your home except by force.[50]

Today we might say that what he describes was post-traumatic stress disorder. What it makes clear is that the effects of war might well be felt at home.

St George

We have seen how Sir Gruffudd Llwyd's involvement in the wars of Edward I and Edward II was viewed in distinctly lukewarm terms and how, as the fourteenth century went on, references to war, and praise for success in it were viewed more favourably without any sense that serving an English king as opposed to a Welsh prince was shameful. By the time that the poet Gruffudd Llwyd composed his *cywydd* to Owain Glyndŵr, probably in the 1380s, the poet felt able to describe the Flintshire knight, Sir Gregory Sais as 'Grigor Sais, a second St George'. The comparison to St George is interesting for two reasons. First because he was explicitly a martial saint, a soldier and patron of crusaders and soldiers. Secondly, because by the later Middle Ages he was the patron saint of England and inextricably linked with the English; even during Edward I's Welsh wars, his cross was a symbol used by Edward I to identify soldiers in his armies.[51] Since it was in the late thirteenth century that all Wales came under English rule the attitude to the Welsh of their new ruler's patron saint can be placed in the context of their place in England's armies.

The banner of St George, the red cross of a martyr on a white background, was adopted for the uniform of English soldiers possibly in the reign of Richard I, and later became the flag of England and the White Ensign of the Royal Navy. During Edward III's campaigns in France in 1345–9, pennants bearing the red cross on a white background were ordered for the king's ship and uniforms in the same style for the men-at-arms and in 1348, George was adopted by Edward III as principal patron of his new order of chivalry, the Knights of the Garter. It is believed that either in 1348 or in 1344 Edward proclaimed St George patron saint of England.

So Gruffudd Llwyd's comparison of a Welshman – even one who spent much of his career overseas – to the patron saint of England at the heart of a poem whose thrust is that Owain Glyndŵr deserved knighthood himself, bought into a set of international values: chivalry, and into belonging to the English realm. When Richard II invaded Scotland in 1385, the ordinances published for his campaign – the last raised by a feudal levy – were that every man was ordered to wear 'a signe of the arms of St George', both before and behind, whilst death was threatened against any of the enemy's soldiers 'who do bear the same crosse or token of Saint George, even if they be prisoners'. Similar ordinances were issued by Henry V and were a routine part of identifying fellow 'Englishmen' on the battlefield well into the sixteenth century. Guto'r Glyn's poem celebrating the wine of Thomas ap Watkin's table has the English battle cry (here taken up by beer): 'the soldiers of the hogsheads. / We, the righteous assembly, will shout / "St George!" all through the region of Gwent. / Your wine will shout "St Denis!"' Earlier in the same poem, however, he has the army – the alcohol of Thomas's table – appoint 'Tall St David as your herald.'[52] The Welsh soldier abroad, in other words, was English, but took his Welshness with him.

Modern commentators, particularly those attached to twentieth-century notions of nationalism have found this difficult and, as ever in the study of the Welsh past, aspirations for the Welsh present and future have coloured its perception and analysis. As Barry Lewis has remarked it is for this reason that the fifteenth century, between the failure of Glyndŵr – whose project was opposed by as many Welshmen as supported it – and the Acts of Union, is a Cinderella in Welsh historical writing.[53] The perception of St George lies at the heart of this as the evident fury of the critic Saunders Lewis demonstrates towards Guto'r Glyn's identification with that saint:

> yr oedd digon eto'n fyw Mhowys ac yng Ngwent a glywsai 'Sain Siôr' yn atseinio ar ddygwyl y sant, Ebrill 23, 1406, pan laddwyd dros fil o fyddin Glyndŵr a ma i'r tywysog yn eu plith. 'Dyw disgybyl Llywelyn ab y Moel yn cofio dim am hynny.'

> there were many still alive in Powys and in Gwent who had heard the cry of St George echoing on the saint's own day, April 23, 1406, when over a thousand men of Glyndŵr's army were killed, the prince's own son amongst them. The pupil of Llywelyn ab y Moel [Guto] doesn't recall any of this.[54]

Whether Guto, most probably born after 1406, would have identified himself with this is moot, but duality in the memorialisation of Glyndŵr's revolt by the poets is commonplace, a factor, no doubt of the requirement for Welshmen who survived that struggle to reach an accommodation with the English crown. For a great many, this accommodation was achieved by soldiering, perhaps as a condition of pardon, something which seems very probable for many of the archers from Carmarthenshire and Cardiganshire in 1415. While never made explicit, the fact that several proven rebels served, or had others serve in their place is suggestive. The names of these substitutes are listed alongside those who could not, for whatever reason, go in person.[55] For some, notably Gruffudd Dwnn, grandson of the incorrigible rebel Henry Dwnn of Cydweli, 1415 was the start of a new career and he and others became career soldiers in Normandy gaining letters of denizenship and de facto English status in 1421.[56] This duality was repeated frequently in poetry dedicated to the sons and grandsons of rebels and most remarkably, in Guto's praise of John Talbot, second earl of Shrewsbury, which referenced his family's careers in arms and in the service of the House of Lancaster:

> Cyfod, Meistr Talbod hy,
> Faner dy dad i fyny.
> Cywir fu dy daid cyoedd,
> Cadw Harri o Dderbi 'dd oedd.
> Cywir dy dad, gariad gŵr,
> I Ging Harri gwncwerwr.
> Cywir wyd, ni a'i credwn,
> Cywir i Harri hir yw hwn.

Raise your father's banner / valiant Master Talbot. / Your illustrious grandfather was loyal, / supporting Henry of Derby. / Your father, men's affection, was loyal /   to King Henry the conqueror. / You are loyal, we believe this, / loyal to tall Henry is this man.[57]

While it is notable that all three Lancastrian Henrys are named, the tone of the poem suggests that when Henry V is called 'the conqueror' it is not Wales and the defeat of Glyndŵr that is meant, but Normandy and thus France. Guto also notes Talbot's Welsh descent: 'You are the heir of Llywelyn ab Iorwerth Drwyndwn, as an oak is your might. / The prince of Gwynedd is on your seal / the Lord Rhys of golden sword is the second.' The two are combined, elsewhere in the poem, Talbot is the 'St David of the young barons' and 'mighty St George'.[58] What this demonstrates is the web of wider connections apparent in this poetry and in the lives of poets and patrons.

Not all English martial traditions were so neatly incorporated into Welsh culture as was St George. Elis Gruffudd, the 'soldier of Calais' compiled his chronicle in the 1540s.[59] In it, he referred to impressions of Arthurian tradition interpreted by Geoffrey of Monmouth. In Elis's day, it was the English, presumably his fellow soldiers in the Calais garrison, rather than the Welsh, who believed most fervently that Arthur was not dead but sleeping and would return.[60] Elis located this myth at Glastonbury in Somerset and included the tradition that people had actually seen Arthur there. In Lloyd-Morgan's view, given Elis's use elsewhere of oral tradition, this statement should be accepted without hesitation.

> Ac etto J mae yn vwy J son wyntt [sc. y Saeson] am danno ef nonnyni, hanis J maentt twy ym dywedud ac yn gadarn J kyuyd ef dracheuyn J vod yn vrenin . . .

> And yet they [the English] talk much more about his than we do, for they say and strongly believe that he will rise again to be king.[61]

Elis's exposure to the wider world came primarily as a soldier in the Calais garrison and it is his account of the early sixteenth century there that has brought him most scholarly attention, but not, as yet, a full edition of his chronicle.[62] It should be noted that in Welsh traditions of the fourteenth and fifteenth centuries, it was not Arthur, but Owain that was considered the returning saviour king. Owain Lawgoch was explicitly called *mab darogan* ('the son of prophecy') by the poets in his own lifetime and this undoubtedly drew support to his cause as much as his success in the service of the French.[63] Owain Glyndŵr and, later, Owain Tudur and his descendants consciously manipulated the same legend.[64] There is no explicit indication that it was the experience as soldiers that encouraged this, but Arthur was a martial archetype readily available for appropriation by those composing praise as well as more generally. Most striking of all in expressing this coming together of traditions in the fifteenth century are the recently restored wall paintings in the church of St Cadoc in Llancarfan, Glamorgan, depicting St George slaying a dragon. The English patron saint is depicted in the guise of a mounted knight on the walls of a church long dedicated to a native Welsh saint.[65]

As Gerald of Wales noted in 1188, 'Not only the leaders but the entire nation are trained in war. Sound the trumpet for battle and the peasant will rush from his plough to pick up his weapons as quickly as the courtier from his court.'[66] Gerald cannot be described as an outsider, though his perspective might have been coloured by his own sense of 'national' pride, albeit of a rather different nation to that of twenty-first-century aspirations. War provided the poets, through their patrons and their own experiences with new reference points and a new geography beyond Wales. Calais was added to the stock of poetic metaphor as sources of strength in the case of Dafydd ap Gwilym. Crécy could be a place of real achievement for Iolo Goch's praise to Sir Hywel ap Gruffudd. Their praise, however, seems to have looked at the English realm as a place apart with which the Welsh happened to be entangled. There was no pan-Celtic empathy: the Scots were to be defeated, the Irish slaughtered. France, however, as the home of chivalry, was the stage on which Welshmen participated in English victories as Englishmen.

Notes

[1] R. R. Davies, 'English Synopsis: the Manners and Morals of the Welsh', *WHR*, 12.2 (1984), 174–9.

[2] Helen Fulton, 'Poetry and nationalism in the reign of Edward I: Wales and Ireland', in P. Crooks, D. Green and M. Ormrod (eds), *The Plantagenet Empire, 1259–1453, Proceedings of the 2014 Harlaxton Symposium* (Donington: Shaun Tyas, 2016), pp. 169–70.

[3] David Stephenson, 'From Llywelyn ap Gruffudd to Edward I: expansionist rulers and Welsh society in thirteenth-century Gwynedd', in Diane M. Williams and John R. Kenyons (eds), *The Impact of the Edwardian Castles in Wales* (Oxford: Oxbow, 2010), pp. 9–15.

[4] Sean Davies, *War and Society in Medieval Wales, 633–1283: Welsh Military Institutions* (Cardiff: University of Wales Press, 2004).

5 Adam Chapman, *Welsh Soldiers in the Later Middle Ages, 1282–1422* (Woodbridge: Boydell, 2015), p. 76 and ch. 7.
6 M. P. Siddons, 'Welshmen in the Service of France', *BBCS*, 36 (1989), 161–84; A. D. Carr, *Owen of Wales: The End of the House of Gwynedd* (Cardiff: University of Wales Press, 1991). On Owain Lawgoch especially, see also Gideon Brough's discussion in this volume, above.
7 D. L. Evans, 'Some Notes on the Principality of Wales in the time of the Black Prince (1343–76)', *Trans. Hon. Soc. Cymm.* (1925–26), 25–110; A. D. Carr, 'Welshmen and the Hundred Years' War', *WHR*, 4 (1968), 21–46.
8 R. R. Davies, *Lordship and Society in the March of Wales, 1282–1400* (Oxford: Oxford University Press, 1978), pp. 80–4; Chapman, *Welsh Soldiers*.
9 J. Beverley Smith, 'Edward II and the Allegiance of Wales', *WHR*, 8 (1976), 139–71; T. F. Tout, 'The captivity and death of Edward of Caernarvon', in *The Collected Papers of Thomas Frederick Tout. With a Memoir and Bibliography* (Manchester: Manchester University Press, 1934), iii, pp. 145–90.
10 R. R. Davies, 'Lordship or Colony?', in J. Lydon (ed.), *The English in Medieval Ireland* (Dublin: Royal Irish Academy, 1984), p. 153.
11 Davies, *Lordship and Society*, p. 84.
12 Of 7,300 infantry in Edward's army in 1297, 5,297 were Welsh and only 2,000 English. See BL Add. MS 7965, fols 81–5; N. B. Lewis, 'The English forces in Flanders, August–November 1297', in R. N. Hunt, W. H. Pantin and R. W. Southern (eds), *Studies in Medieval History Presented to F.M. Powicke* (Oxford: Clarendon Press, 1948), pp. 310–18; M. Prestwich, 'Welsh infantry in Flanders in 1297', in R. A. Griffiths and P. R. Schofield (eds), *Wales and the Welsh in the Middle Ages: Essays presented to J. Beverley Smith* (Cardiff: University of Wales Press, 2011), pp. 56–69.
13 Lodewyk van Velthem, *Spiegel historiael of rym-Spiegel: zynde de Nederlandsche rym-chronym*, ed. I. le Long (Amsterdam: Hendrik van Eyl, 1727), pp. 215–16; a convenient translation of this passage is given in M. Strickland and R. Hardy, *From Hastings to the Mary Rose, The Great Warbow* (Stroud: Sutton, 2005), p. 166.
14 Jean Froissart, *Oeuvres*, ed. Kervyn de Lettenhove, 25 vols (Bruxelles: Victor Devaux, 1867–77), v, pp. 65–6. Translation from G. Brereton (trans.), *Jean Froissart, Chronicles* (London: Penguin, 1978), p. 93.
15 For example, R. W. Eyton, *Antiquities of Shropshire*, 12 vols (London: John Russell Smith, 1853–60), x, p. 367. For a fuller characterisation of the Welsh in English histories, R. R. Davies, 'Buchedd a Moes

y Cymry', *WHR*, 12.2 (1984), 155–74 with English synopsis: 'The Manners and Morals of the Welsh', 174–9.

[16] Carr, 'Welshmen and the Hundred Years' War', 23, citing Th. M. Chotzen, *Recherches sur la poésie de Dafydd ap Gwilym, barde gallois du XIVe siècle* (Amsterdam: H. J. Paris, 1928), p. 126, n.

[17] J. Maxwell (ed.), *The Chronicle of Lanercost 1272–1346* (Glasgow: James MacLehose and Sons, 1913), pp. 141–2.

[18] A. Gransden (ed.), *The Chronicle of Bury St Edmunds 1212–1301* (London: Nelson, 1964), pp. 143–5; A. King (ed.), *Scalacronica 1272–1363*, Surtees Society 209 (Woodbridge: Boydell, 2005), p. 17.

[19] Cited in Strickland and Hardy, *From Hastings*, p. 89.

[20] This applied to armaments, pay and treatment though not, significantly to organisation: Chapman, *Welsh Soldiers*, chapters 7 and 8.

[21] H. T. Riley (ed.), *Willelmi Rishanger, quondam monachi S. Albani, et quorundam anonymorum,chronica et annales, egnantibus Henrico Tertio et Edwardo Primo* (London: Rolls Series, 1865), p. 442.

[22] Chapman, *Welsh Soldiers*, pp. 201–11.

[23] C. J. Neville (ed.), 'A Plea Roll of Edward I's army in Scotland, 1296', in *A Miscellany of the Scottish History Society, Eleventh Volume* (Edinburgh: Pillans and Wilson for the Society, 1990), pp. 7–33; the death of Einion Fychan is noted at p. 83.

[24] In 1400, the rising of Owain Glyndŵr was dismissed as being no more than the frolic of 'bare-footed rascals' (de scurris nudipedibus): F. S. Haydon (ed.), *Eulogium (Historiarum sive temporis): Chronicon ab orbe condito usque ad Annum Domini M.CCC.LXVI. A monacho quodam Malmesburiensi exaratum*, 3 vols (London: Longman, Rolls Series, 1858–63), iii, p. 388. See also, R. R. Davies, 'Race Relations in Post-Conquest Wales: Confrontation and Compromise', The Cecil Williams Lecture for 1973, *Trans. Hon. Soc. Cymm.* (1974/5), 32–56.

[25] Carr, 'Welshmen and the Hundred Years' War'.

[26] *www.wales.ac.uk/cy/YGanolfanGeltaidd/ResearchProjects/ CompletedProjects/PoetsoftheNobility/CyflwyniadProsiect.aspx* (accessed 3 January 2017).

[27] In particular, H. Fulton, *Dafydd ap Gwilym in the European Context* (Cardiff: University of Wales Press, 1989); see also, A. T. E. Matonis, 'Traditions of Panegyric in Welsh Poetry: The Heroic and Chivalric', *Speculum*, 53 (1978), 667–87.

[28] Dafydd ap Gwilym, 'Marwnad Ifor a Nest', line 43: 'Llafnfriw, llwrw iawnwiw Llŷr ennaint – Einglgrwydr', ed. D. Johnston, at *www. dafyddapgwilym.net* (accessed 1 February 2017), text 17.

[29] Fulton, 'Poetry and nationalism', pp. 181–2.

30. Brynley F. Roberts, 'Einion Offeiriad (*d.* 1353?)', *Oxford Dictionary of National Biography* (2004), online at *www.oxforddnb.com/view/article/48544* (accessed 3 January 2017).
31. From *Llyfr Coch Hergest [The Red Book of Hergest]*, in G. J. Williams and E. J. Jones (eds), *Gramadegau'r Penceirddiaid [Grammars of the Celtic Bards]* (Cardiff: University of Wales Press, 1934), cited in Matonis, 'Traditions of Panegyric', 668.
32. Helen Fulton, *Dafydd ap Gwilym in the European Context* (Cardiff: University of Wales Press, 1989), pp. 143–4.
33. M. T. Davies, 'The Rhetoric of Gwilym Ddu's Awdlau to Sir Gruffudd Llwyd', *Studia Celtica*, 40 (2006), 167.
34. A. D. Carr, 'The Coroner in Fourteenth Century Merioneth', *Journal of the Merioneth Historical and Record Society*, 11.3 (1992), 250–1.
35. 'Marwnad i Gronwy ap Tudur o Benmynydd/Elegy to Gronwy ap Tudur of Penmynydd', in *Gwaith Llywelyn Goch ap Meurig Hen*, ed. D. R. Johnston (Aberystwyth: Canolfan Uwchefrydiau Cymreig a Cheltaidd Prifysgol Cymru, 1998), pp. 30–5.
36. N. A. Jones and E. H. Rheinallt (eds), 'Marwnad Hywel ap Gruffudd o Eifionydd' by Rhisierdyn, line 78, in *Gwaith Sefnyn, Rhisierdyn, Gruffudd Fychan ap Gruffudd ab Ednyfed a Llywarch Bentwrch* (Aberystwyth: Canolfan Uwchefrydiau Cymreig a Cheltaidd Prifysgol Cymru, 1995), p. 73; the notes, p. 104, provide further references to this phrase and the Dauphin in the works of other poets.
37. '*Caer Rhag Cenfigen*/A Fortress against Envy', *www.dafyddapgwilym.net*, poem 122, lines 17–20.
38. London, TNA, E 101/31/37 m. 1.
39. TNA, E 101/39/39 m. 3; E 101/39/40 m. 3.
40. *Gwaith Gruffudd Llwyd a'r Llygliwiaid Eraill*, ed. Rh. Ifans (Cardiff: University of Wales Press, 2000), p. 248.
41. *CPR 1399–1401*, 396.
42. TNA SC 6/774/11 and G. Aled Williams, 'Gwrthryfel Glyndŵr: Dau Nodyn', *Llên Cymru* 33 (2010), 180–7. Both J. E. Lloyd, *Owen Glendower* (Oxford: Oxford University Press, 1931), p. 31 and R. R. Davies, *Revolt of Owain Glyn Dŵr* (Oxford: Oxford University Press, 1995), p. 102 make note of the date of the declaration, but neither attaches any significance to it. Davies does discuss Owain's use of prophecy however (*Revolt of Owain Glyn Dŵr*, pp. 55, 159–61), and there has been a great deal of interest in the subject, some of the most recent work including J. A. Doig, 'The Prophecy of the "Six Kings to Follow John" and Owain Glyndŵr', *Studia Celtica*, 29 (1995), 257–67, and H. Fulton, 'Owain Glyndŵr and the Uses of Prophecy', *Studia Celtica*, 39 (2005), 105–21.

43 Barry Lewis, 'Late Medieval Welsh Praise Poetry and Nationality: The Military Career of Guto'r Glyn Revisited', *Studia Celtica*, 45 (2011), 113–18.
44 Guto'r Glyn, elegy for Henry Griffith of Newcourt, lines 23–4: 'Dug fi at y dug of Iorc/Dan amod cael deunawmorc', ed. Barry Lewis, at *www.gutorglyn.net* (accessed 5 January 2017), poem 36. For the career of Henry Griffith more generally and his relationship as a patron to Guto and other poets, see A. J. Chapman, '"He took me to the duke of York": Henry Griffith, a "Man of War"', in B. J. Lewis, A. P. Owen and D. F. Evans (eds), *'Gwalch Cywyddau Gwŷr': Essays on Guto'r Glyn and Fifteenth Century Wales* (Aberystwyth: Canolfan Uwchefrydiau Cymreig a Cheltaidd Prifysgol Cymru, 2013), pp. 103–34.
45 Guto'r Glyn, The battle of the bards with the wine of Thomas ap Watkin of Llanddewi Rhydderch, ed. Barry Lewis, at *www.gutorglyn.net* (accessed 5 February 2017), poem 4.
46 *https://medievallondon.ace.fordham.edu/exhibits/show/medieval-london-objects/baselard* (accessed 20 January 2017). For the use of weapons in Welsh poetry, see Jenny Day, 'Arfau yn yr Hengerdd a Cherddi Beirdd y Tywysogion' (unpublished PhD thesis, Aberystwyth University, 2010).
47 Such gift poems (and their counterpart 'request' poems) are common. Another with an overtly military theme is Guto'r Glyn, 'To thank Abbot Dafydd ab Ieuan of Valle Crucis' for a buckler (a type of small shield), ed. Ann Parry Owen, at *www.gutorglyn.net* (accessed 14 October 2016), poem 110.
48 'Diolch am Gyllell/Thanks for a Knife', in *Iolo Goch: Poems*, ed. and trans. D. Johnston (Llandysul: Gomer Press, 1993), pp. 42–6, lines 5–10, 21–6, 31–6.
49 'Y Gal/The Penis', at *www.dafyddapgwilym.net*, poem no. 85, lines 31–2.
50 'Merch yn Edliw ei Lyfrdra/A Girl Taunts Him for his Cowardice', at *www.dafyddapgwilym.net*, 72.27–42 (accessed 26 September 2017).
51 Henry Summerson, 'George (d. c.303?)', *Oxford Dictionary of National Biography* (2004), online at *www.oxforddnb.com/view/article/60304* (accessed 10 December 2016).
52 *www.gutorglyn.net* (accessed 8 February 2017), poem 4.
53 Lewis, 'Late Medieval Welsh Praise Poetry and Nationality', 112.
54 S. Lewis, 'Gyrfa filwrol Guto'r Glyn', in J. E. Caerwyn Williams (ed.) *Ysgrifau Beirniadol* IX (Denbigh: Gee Press, 1976), p. 88 cited by Lewis, 'Late Medieval Welsh Praise Poetry and Nationality', 112 and n. As Lewis notes, Guto was probably not a pupil of Llywelyn ab y Moel

but the two were certainly known to one another: see 'Marwnad i Lywelyn ab y Moel/Elegy for Llywelyn ab y Moel', at *www.gutorglyn.net*, poem 86, and accompanying notes (accessed 4 January 2017). For other recent perspectives on Guto and his attitude to Wales in his own time see two contrasting but complimentary essays by Helen Fulton and Rhidian Griffiths: H. Fulton, 'Guto'r Glyn and the Wars of the Roses' and Rh. Griffiths, 'Mwy o Gymro na Iorciad' [More Welsh man than Yorkist] in Lewis, Owen and Evans (eds), *'Gwalch Cywyddau Gwŷr', pp.* 53–68 and 69–82 respectively.

[55] A. J. Chapman, 'The King's Welshmen: Welsh involvement in the Expeditionary Army of 1415', *Journal of Medieval Military History*, 9 (2011), 41–64. Examples include Dafydd ap Rhys ap Llywelyn ap Cadwgan of Anhuniog (Cardiganshire) who provided Dafydd ab Ieuan Taillour in his place, and Dafydd ap Gruffudd ap y Person of Mabelfyw who sent Gruffudd ab Einion: TNA E 101/46/20, m. 2.

[56] R. A. Griffiths, *The Principality of Wales in the Later Middle Ages: The Structure and Personnel of Government*, volume I: *South Wales, 1277–1536* (Cardiff: University of Wales Press, 1972), pp. 201–2.

[57] Lewis, 'Late Medieval Welsh Praise Poetry and Nationality', 118–24; Guto'r Glyn, 'In praise of John Talbot, second earl of Shrewsbury', lines 15–22, ed. R. Iestyn Daniel and E. Salisbury, at *www.gutorglyn.net* (accessed 17 June 2016), poem 78.

[58] 'In Praise of John Talbot', lines, 37–9, 44, 64.

[59] Aberystwyth, NLW, 5276D; T. Jones, 'A Welsh Chronicler in Tudor England', *WHR*, 1 (1960–3), 1–17.

[60] C. Lloyd-Morgan, 'From Ynys Wydrin to Glasynbri: Glastonbury in the Welsh vernacular tradition', in L. Abrams and J. P. Carley (eds), *The Archaeology and History of Glastonbury Abbey, Essays in honour of the ninetieth birthday of C.A. Raleigh Radford* (Woodbridge: Boydell, 1991), pp. 311–12.

[61] Aberystwyth, NLW, 5276D, 342 r., cited by Lloyd-Morgan, 'From Ynys Wydrin to Glasynbri', p. 312.

[62] P. Morgan, 'Elis Gruffudd of Gronant: Tudor Chronicler Extraordinary', *Flintshire Historical Society Journal*, 25 (1975–6), 9–20; Brynley F. Roberts, 'Gruffudd, Elis (*b. c.*1490, *d.* in or after 1556)', *Oxford Dictionary of National Biography* (2004), online at *www.oxforddnb.com/view/article/56714* (accessed 25 January 2017).

[63] Carr, *Owen of Wales*, ch. 7, 'The Once and Future Prince'.

[64] R. Wallis Evans, 'Prophetic poetry', in A. O. H. Jarman and G. R. Jones (eds), *A Guide to Welsh Literature*, 2 vols (Cardiff: University of Wales Press, 1976–9), ii, pp. 278–97.

65 *www.flickr.com/photos/nickkaye/sets/72157636244430986/detail/?page=4* (accessed 21 June 2016).
66 Gerald of Wales, *The Journey through Wales/The Description of Wales*, trans. Lewis Thorpe (Harmondsworth: Penguin, 1978), p. 223.

9

The mixed jury in Wales: a preliminary inquiry into ethno-religious administration and conflict resolution in the medieval world, c.1100–1350 CE

Michael Hill

Around 1335, the English Marcher lords of Wales issued a petition to the English crown, complaining that their rights had been infringed because the Welsh had brought accusations and conducted inquisitions based on those accusations against them. They asserted that they were greatly wronged by these developments, arguing that neither Welshmen nor Englishmen should be forced to answer accusations made by the other community since, by implication, neither community could judge the other impartially.[1] Interestingly, the principle that ethnic impartiality in legal cases was impossible in the Anglo-Welsh border region was formally enshrined roughly twenty years earlier when Edward II issued a royal decree asserting that all cases involving both English and Welsh litigants in the royal territories of Wales must be resolved by a jury composed of half English and half Welsh and that all cases deriving from the Welshry or Englishry should be handled solely according to Welsh or English law, respectively.[2]

Yet the legal bifurcation articulated in the decree had been a feature of the Anglo-Welsh border region long before the early fourteenth century. For example, a witness provided testimony to a royal inquest conducted in 1281 and claimed that in any dispute between a Welsh and English lord in the March, half of the jurors were assembled from the 'confines of the March' (i.e. English) and half of them must be Welshmen.[3] Indeed, the development of the Englishries and Welshries and the principle of communal autonomy that reigned within those quasi-enclaves were cemented by the mid-thirteenth century and the use of mixed juries was extant in the Anglo-Welsh border region by the early thirteenth century at the latest.[4] The Marchers' plaint reveals the contemporary sensitivity about any attempt to erode that communal legal autonomy and the mistrust and fear that still existed in Wales over fifty years after Edward I's conquest in 1282–3. It was the mixed jury that was supposed to help alleviate that fear and mistrust from leading to greater violence and it was the perception of fairness enshrined in the mixed jury system that the Marchers argued was absent in the inquisitions mentioned.

Although the Anglo-Welsh mixed jury's particular features were distinct, the development of legal mechanisms for resolving cross-communal conflicts was common throughout medieval Eurasia, largely because the medieval era's relatively decentralised legal regimes typically allowed distinct religious and ethnic groups to adhere to their traditional laws and customs. Indeed, early medieval empires such as those of the Byzantines, the Sasanians and the Tang rulers of China had granted considerable legal autonomy to ethnic and religious communities.[5] Between the tenth and mid-fourteenth centuries, a series of settlement processes transformed Eurasia by creating new states and empires and refashioning the ethnic, religious and cultural paradigms of the Continent's border regions and contact zones. These settlement processes included the arrival of English, Flemish, German and French settlers in places such as Wales, Ireland, Scotland, Iberia, Sicily, the Levant, the Baltic regions, central and eastern Europe, in addition to the movement of Turko-Mongolic peoples into Anatolia, the Levant, Iran, the Caspian and Caucasus regions, Central Asia, the northern subcontinent, northern and western China and eastern Europe, and the movement of Chinese peoples into Sichuan and Guizhou. The legal paradigm of communal autonomy established in earlier periods persisted, which necessitated the development of methods for adjudicating cases that crossed ethnic and confessional lines so as to minimise conflict by maximising a perception of fairness.

This chapter will examine the mixed jury system in Wales within this wider context of communal contact and negotiation in medieval Eurasian history. Unlike other chapters in this volume, this chapter will analyse the influence of law on cultural change by comparing developments within the Anglo-Welsh border region to other regions across Eurasia in the period from roughly the early twelfth century to the mid-fourteenth. While the topic of cultural exchange has long dominated the historiography relating to communal contact in the medieval world, examining and comparing the legal frameworks of that contact in a global perspective has received far less attention. As I have argued elsewhere, examining systems of ethnic administration can illustrate how communities attempted to structure their interactions and how those structures influenced ethnic contact and cultural exchange and change. Although the Anglo-Welsh border region was a peripheral zone in the broader context of a Continent whose economic and political centre rested east of the Black Sea during the period under consideration, the system of dual-administration (of which the mixed jury was a part) that developed there provides an opportunity for global comparison both because the system itself had many parallels with other systems of ethnic and religious administration in Eurasia and because divergences in the context of contact in each border region provide interesting differences for analysis.[6]

For the purposes of this study, comparisons to the mixed jury system will attempt to address the following questions. First, to what extent did the system of intercommunal conflict resolution converge or diverge with the prevailing system(s) of ethnic or religious administration and how did those systems develop? Although modern scholars tend to draw more definitive demarcations between ethnic and religious identity, medieval Christians and Muslims in western Eurasia did not and deviations in the administration of ethnic vis-à-vis religious groups do not diverge sufficiently to warrant separate analysis.[7] Secondly, what was the relationship between personal status (i.e. one's ethnic or religious affiliation) and legal jurisdiction in deciding mixed cases? Thirdly, what was the relationship between law and communal power and how did that relationship affect communal conflict resolution? Finally, to what extent did methods of communal conflict resolution influence acculturation?

The comparisons used in this chapter will focus on the Islamic world and on the Khitan Liao (925–1115) and Mongol Yuan (1234–1368) dynasties of China for two principal reasons. First, the documentation from those regions is more complete and the contradictions in that documentary evidence less problematic than in most other Eurasian regions. Secondly, the Islamic world and China represented the largest geographical and demographic swath of Eurasia and the Islamic system of religious conflict resolution had tremendous influence on Christian systems that developed in Iberia, Sicily and the Crusader States. Hence, at any point during the medieval period and especially during the high-medieval period, the methods of ethno-religious conflict resolution developed in the Islamic world and China represented the Eurasian norm and provide the best opportunity to survey how the methods developed in the Anglo-Welsh border region compared and contrasted to those norms. There are, of course, limitations inherent in this approach and those limitations dictate that this study is a preliminary inquiry interested more in identifying patterns for further research and pinpointing potentially fruitful methods of investigation rather than attempting to draw definitive, comprehensive conclusions for global history.

The mixed jury – as were the other methods of conflict resolution in high-medieval Eurasia examined in this essay – was an integral component of the larger system of ethnic administration. Ethnic administration in Wales was a dualistic structure predicated on the development of Englishries and Welshries, within which each community maintained its own laws and customs and had its own ethnic courts.[8] Dual-administration granted each community considerable internal autonomy and aimed both to maintain communal separation (to the extent possible) and reduce the chances for communal conflict.

The mixed jury allowed dual administration to function because although Englishries and Welshries existed throughout the Anglo-Welsh border region (outside the major Welsh principalities of Powys, Deheubarth and Gwynedd where the overwhelming majority of the population was Welsh), it was impossible to prevent contact or legal conflicts emerging from that contact. Neither community accepted being judged by the other's laws and imposing one community's laws or customs on the other could have sparked violence and might have convinced the Welsh that justice was only possible through armed revolt.[9] The mixed jury, therefore, provided an outlet for resolving communal grievances in which each community could participate in the legal process in a manner that seemed fairest, in which one community's laws did not seem unjustly imposed on the other, and in which the broader structure of legal autonomy was preserved.

The mixed jury served a similar purpose to other systems of ethnic and religious conflict resolution where dual or multiple-administrative regimes existed. Yet differences in the historical context of each system's development led to some distinctions in principle, as well as juridical structure and methodology. In the Islamic world, for example, Jews, Christians and other religious minorities such as Zoroastrians and even Buddhists were granted *dhimmī* status, which provided them with protection (*dhimma*) within an Islamic state and considerable autonomy in exchange for enduring numerous restrictions that ensured their political, military and cultural subordination to the Muslim community.[10] While *dhimmī* communities retained their traditional laws and customs, all cases between distinct religious communities were referred to a Muslim judge (a *qāḍī*) who applied Islamic law. Furthermore, *dhimmīs* could bring their cases before Islamic courts if they so chose.[11] The Christian kings of Spain, the Norman kings of Sicily and the rulers of the Latin Christian Crusader States in the Levant retained many features of the Islamic system, including maintaining religious communities' legal autonomy and referring cases between distinct religious communities to Christian judges, but the restrictions on other religious communities were not nearly as extensive.[12]

In China under Khitan and Mongol rule, ethnic groups also utilised their own laws and customs. The Turko-Mongolic Khitans established the Liao dynasty (907–1125) that ruled over Mongolia, Manchuria, parts of northern Korea and a swath of northern China extending to modern Beijing. The Khitans managed their large and ethnically diverse empire by creating a dual-administrative system. A Northern Chancellery administered the Khitans and other Turko-Mongolic and Manchurian groups and a Southern Chancellery governed the sedentary Chinese population according to each groups' own laws and customs.[13] The Mongol Yuan dynasty (1234–1368) did not precisely follow the Khitan model. Instead, the Mongols established a discriminatory system whereby ethnic communities could utilise their own laws and customs, but were ranked into tiers of privilege. Mongols occupied the first tier, the *Semu ren* (mostly western and Central Asians, but also including other foreigners such as Europeans) occupied the second, and the *Han ren* (mostly northern Chinese, but also Jurchens and Khitans) and *Nan ren* (southern Chinese) filled the third and fourth tiers, respectively.[14] In addition, separate governmental bureaus adjudicated the legal affairs of ethnic groups. For example, the Grand Bureau of the Affairs of the Imperial Clan decided legal cases among Mongols, while the Bureau of Guardianship handled all cases involving the *Semu ren*. The Mongols effectively created a system of multiple-administration through which communities could acquire some degree of legal autonomy within a regime that sought to maintain Mongol political superiority and ensure Chinese subjugation.[15]

Inter-ethnic disputes in Khitan and Mongol China were also handled quite differently and highlight some unique methods for, and problems in, adjudicating such cases. In the Liao state, for example, it seems that a consistent law was not always used in inter-ethnic cases. In the tenth and early eleventh centuries it seems that Khitans were punished according to Khitan law in disputes with Chinese, while the Chinese were punished according to their own laws. However, for a short time in the mid-eleventh century both Chinese and Khitan testimony indicates that Chinese law was applied in all inter-ethnic disputes, a practice that adhered to former Tang policy and greatly angered the Khitan community.[16] Under the Mongol Yuan dynasty, commissions comprising representatives of each ethnic group tried inter-ethnic cases according to whichever dynastic law code was in force at the time. After 1229, these codes drew more and more heavily on Chinese laws. However, in many cases the law applied varied depending on the parties' particular legal circumstances.[17] Furthermore, Mongols typically received beneficial treatment and less severe punishments.[18]

The dual-administrative system in Wales and the use of mixed juries developed organically in a border region that was an amalgam of semi-autonomous, completely independent or dependent territories owing allegiance to the English crown, a Welsh prince or to some extent both. While the Arab conquerors and future caliphs instituted a nearly uniform model of communal administration fashioned along Byzantine and Sasanian precedents and while the Khitan and Mongol conquerors of China created a centralised governmental system based on Chinese models, the Anglo-Welsh border region's political fragmentation guaranteed that no single authority could impose dual-administration.[19] Roughly forty-nine semi-autonomous Marcher lordships existed in Wales and western England by the fourteenth century. The Marchers owed allegiance to the English crown, but each lord retained his own officers and military force and his own administration and courts that adjudicated and enforced his own laws. The Crown could and did intervene in Marcher affairs, increasingly so during the reign of Edward I, who not only conquered the Welsh principalities of Gwynedd, Powys and Deheubarth, annexed them to the English crown and created the principality of Wales, but also created new Marcher lordships of Denbigh, Dyffryn Clwyd, Bromfield and Yale, and Chirkland and made them directly subject to the royal principality. Furthermore, numerous lordships in southern Wales were also subject to the principality. Yet when Edward II issued his edict in 1315–16, it only applied to those territories under direct royal control, not to all lordships throughout the March.[20]

Remarkably, however, Englishries and Welshries were nearly ubiquitous across the Anglo-Welsh border region. Contemporary records indicate that Englishries and Welshries were located in the western regions of Shropshire, Maelor Saesneg, Bromfield and Yale, Denbigh, Dyffryn Clwyd, Hay, Brecon, Montgomery, Wigmore, Abergavenny, Glamorgan, Gower, Carmarthen, Cardigan, Narberth, Kidwelly, Caerleon and Striguil.[21] Written evidence for mixed juries is not as plentiful, largely because the jurors' names are not always given, because the need for a mixed jury is not always explicitly stated or only implicitly given, and because court records from the Marcher lordships in this period are not plentiful. For instance, in January 1328 the Crown ordered an inquisition into whether Hugh le Despenser had unjustly deprived the Welsh and English of the right to hunt in the woods of Rhos, Rhufoniog and Cymeirch. The letters patent state that the jurors should be summoned from certain regions. These regions happened to correspond to lands that were in the Englishry and the Welshry, but it is not explicitly stated and the letter does not state explicitly that the jurors had to be half Welsh and half English.[22] Nevertheless, we find explicit documentation for mixed juries resolving intercommunal matters in Dyffryn Clwyd, Builth, Hope, Montgomery, Oswestry, Kinnerly, Glamorgan, Denbigh and in Flintshire.[23] In addition, Edward II's statute of 1315–16 and the Marcher lords' petition to the Crown indicate that the principle of bifurcating intercommunal justice was pervasive.

As the Denbigh example given above illustrates, mixed juries performed diverse functions. Their most important was to adjudicate cross-communal disputes, with sometimes major implications for communal peace. In 1245, for example, Richard Seward, a member of the household of Richard de Clare (the earl of Gloucester and lord of Glamorgan), set off a diplomatic crisis in Glamorgan when he seized some of the followers of Hywel ap Maredudd, who was the lord of the commote of Meisgyn and eventually came to dominate upland Glamorgan. Steward's actions violated a truce and Hywel retaliated. The earl and Hywel agreed to resolve the dispute in the *comitatus* of Glamorgan through the 'decision of twelve upright and lawful men' (*per consideracionem xii proborum et legalium virorum*), half of whom were chosen by the earl and half by Hywel.[24] Most cases certainly involved far less politically significant matters. For instance, the court rolls of Dyffryn Clwyd record a case between a certain Cadwgan ap Bleddyn ap Hywel and Henry de Riggebi, whom Cadwgan accused of stealing his horse. The case went before six English and six Welsh jurors, who determined that Henry had taken the horse without asking, but not thievishly.[25]

Mixed juries were also formed to conduct local surveys, deduce the rights of lords and tenants, determine land boundaries, and ascertain tenurial customs and dues. For example, in 1326 a survey was conducted for the lands of the lord bishop of St David's in Pembrokeshire, Gower, Brecon and Ystrad Tywi. The name forms, while never a wholly concrete indicator of ethnicity, indicate that jurors from both the English and Welsh communities jointly participated in determining the bishop's landholdings, tenurial arrangements, dues and customs.[26] Another function of mixed juries was to determine whether lands lay within the Englishry or Welshry and,

The mixed jury in Wales

consequently, whether English or Welsh law applied in a particular locality. In 1281 the famous Hopton Commission, which Edward I established to hear pleas in Wales following his defeat of Llywelyn ap Gruffudd in 1277, heard a dispute between Roger Lestrange and William Audley over who held the right to the manor of Kinnerley in the Welshry of Oswestry. Officials summoned a mixed jury from the county of Shropshire and from the Welsh regions around Kinnerley to determine whether the land in dispute fell within the Englishry or the Welshry.[27]

A more famous example that came before the Hopton Commission arose at Oswestry in 1279. This case pitted John Giffard and his wife Maud de Clifford (Matilda in the assize roll – daughter of Walter de Clifford) against Rhys Bychan. At first, John and Maud only claimed Llandovery Castle and the commote of Perfedd against Rhys, arguing that Rhys's grandfather had improperly disseized Walter from the disputed lands during war.[28] The case became far more complicated and eventually involved the vill of Llandovery and the commote of Hirfryn, with both sides engaged in suits and countersuits. However, the central plea concerned whether the land was held in barony of the king as Giffard and his wife argued (meaning that English common law would apply), or whether (as Rhys claimed) Rhys's 'Welsh condition' (*condicionis Wallensice*) and the Treaty of Aberconwy's terms dictated that Welsh law settle the dispute.[29] In December 1279, the parties agreed to have the question regarding English or Welsh law decided by a jury, whose members hailed from both the Welsh regions (*per patriam Walensicam*) and the regions and counties neighbouring the March (*per patrias vicinas de marchia et comitatu propinquores*). The jury decided that because the land lay within Cantref Bychan, it was held in chief of the king and subject to common law.[30] The parties continued the dispute for two more years before Rhys Bychan joined with Llywelyn ap Gruffudd in rebellion, rendering further litigation moot.

Two important features of the Anglo-Welsh system of intercommunal adjudication and the relationship between power and law in high medieval Wales become evident. First, although the English crown was the dominant political player in Wales and although the English community was clearly politically ascendant following the fall of Gwynedd in 1283, the English had a relatively limited expectation of the extent to which it demanded the Welsh community to adopt English laws and customs. Many in England certainly would have shared the Archbishop of Canterbury John Pecham's position that Welsh law was diabolical.[31] Some of Edward I's statements about Irish law and 'the custom of the Scots and the Brets' in Scotland indicate that he embraced some of these ideas and the Statute of Rhuddlan introduced some changes to the operation of Welsh law in the new English principality, such as the right of women to inherit and laws outlawing illegitimate children from inheriting land, that would have pleased church reformers in England.[32] However, as Rees Davies asserted, Edward I had no intention of eliminating Welsh law and made numerous concessions to it. Further, contemporary evidence indicates that the Welsh sometimes blatantly ignored the Statute's proscriptions. For example, the Welsh custom of *galanas* (compensation payment for homicides) seems to have persisted, even though the Statute of Rhuddlan had stated that English criminal law would regulate such a felony.[33] We have little evidence that the Marchers attempted to change Welsh laws substantially in their territories.

Secondly, the laws and procedures that the English introduced into Wales were not outwardly discriminatory against the Welsh and were not designed to protect or privilege the English in intercommunal disputes. In fact, the English authorities were more concerned with not altering the status quo, which could trigger violence. Indeed, Llywelyn ap Gruffudd famously cited the defence of Welsh law as a rallying cry to resist Edward I's encroachments. Matthew Paris claimed that Welsh animosity about the imposition of English laws also helped Llywelyn rally the Welsh around him in the 1250s, leading to a far more successful war against the English crown and its Welsh allies and culminating in the Treaty of Montgomery in 1267.[34]

In the Islamic world and China, the relationships between personal status and jurisdiction, and between law and communal power in multi-ethnic and multi-religious societies were quite different. In Islamic Eurasia, the litigants' personal status solely determined the administration of law, but there was never any question that Islamic law always had theoretically limitless jurisdiction. If the dispute was purely intracommunal, *dhimmī* communities could expect autonomy, remembering always that they could litigate the case before a *qāḍī* according to *sharī'a*. *Dhimmī* communities obtained legal autonomy partly because the Arab conquerors of the seventh century had little capacity to impose their religious or legal norms on non-Muslim communities and instead negotiated surrender (*ṣulḥ*) agreements that implicitly and explicitly granted non-Muslims power over their own legal affairs, with certain restrictions.[35] Yet autonomy dissipated entirely when a case involving separate *dhimmī* groups appeared before a *qāḍī*. In such cases, Muslim authorities sought to make very clear that Islamic law was the sole source of legal authority.[36] The *qāḍī* pronounced judgment according to Islamic law, with little or no consideration of the respective communal religious laws that pertained to the *dhimmīs* involved. Islamic law also decided any case involving a Muslim and a *dhimmī*, with the further stipulation that *dhimmī* witnesses could not testify against Muslims, since their subordination to the *dhimma* strictures could arouse prejudice and hatred.[37]

Indeed, legal autonomy was stronger in practice than in theory. Many Muslim jurists argued that *dhimmī* courts only had arbitral power and that a *qāḍī* could intervene at any time.[38] The famous eleventh-century jurist al-Māwardī argued that the *dhimmī* courts' decisions were not binding on the Islamic community or its state.[39] Many Islamic jurists further claimed that Muslim courts and authorities had wide latitude to restrict *dhimmī* communities' jurisdiction or intervene in *dhimmī* cases involving marriage, monetary transactions, property rights, family, inheritance and criminal law.[40] Muslim authorities sometimes did show their power and ability to intervene in non-Muslim affairs. In the late twelfth century, for example, the Ayyūbid sultan Ṣalāḥ ad-Dīn (r.1174–93) heard a complaint from the Jewish community of Egypt that Muslim officials were forcing intracommunal disputes to be heard before Muslim courts. Mālikī and Shāfi'ī imams, however, counselled Ṣalāḥ ad-Dīn that *dhimmīs* should not be forced to bring such cases before the *qāḍīs*.[41]

Dhimmī communities enjoyed broad autonomy in practice because, as S. D. Goitein pointed out, medieval Islamic states were not very intrusive, even towards Muslims.[42] Although scholars from the Sunnī legal schools argued about the extent to which Muslim authorities could or should impose Islamic law on *dhimmīs*, Muslim authorities' interference was minimal. The debate about *dhimmī* autonomy in the Islamic world centred on the issues of Islamisation and communal dominance. The *dhimma* system emerged in an era when the early Arab conquerors generally discouraged non-Arab conversion to Islam and were loathe to allow non-Arab Muslims the same legal rights as Arab Muslims.[43] Hence, while the *dhimma* system always sought to ensure Muslim supremacy over non-Muslims, Islamisation was not a central objective. Over time, however, some jurists argued that the *dhimma* restrictions should encourage conversion and that all *dhimmīs* were ultimately subject to Islamic law.[44] Although intra-communal autonomy was seldom explicitly threatened, the assertion of Islamic superiority over the state and its religious communities ensured that autonomy could not prevent slow and inexorable Islamisation.

The superiority and application of Islamic law in all intercommunal cases highlights the fact that legal autonomy was not, unlike in Wales, based on a theoretical notion of equality. In the Anglo-Welsh border region, by contrast, both English and Welsh law was valid and enforceable and each had its own jurisdictional sphere. In the Islamic world, *dhimmī* laws were often barely tolerated, *dhimmī* laws had no jurisdiction if Islamic authorities chose to intervene, and *dhimmī* courts had purely arbitral power. In the Anglo-Welsh border region, the political authorities of one group did not explicitly use law to alter the cultural identification of another. In the Islamic world, Muslim jurists, intellectuals and political authorities increasingly came to believe that the *dhimma* compact should encourage conversion or at least some Islamisation. In this context, intercommunal cases became another vehicle to demonstrate to *dhimmīs* the hegemonic authority and moral superiority of the Islamic state and Islamic law. In the Anglo-Welsh border region, a person of one group could not circumvent the authority of their community's court easily, unless it pertained to specific cases reserved to the lord or the king. In the Islamic world, the verdict of any *dhimmī* court could be appealed to Islamic authorities, who most likely would not consider the *dhimmī* court's decision. These differences had implications for the nature of law's influence on cultural change and exchange in each region.

In Khitan and Mongol China, the relationship between personal status and jurisdiction was a little more complicated because different bureaucracies had jurisdiction over distinct communal cases, but as in the Islamic world, personal status was the driving principle of communal justice. Furthermore, intercommunal adjudication methods in both empires indicate that ensuring a privileged position for the politically dominant ethnic group was a concern, though much more so under Mongol than Khitan rule. Chinese contemporaries frequently complained that the Khitans received privileged judgments and greater leniency in inter-ethnic cases, but ethnic separation – not discrimination – was the stronger principle in the Khitan state.[45]

Under the Mongols' ethnically tiered structure of administration, however, only Mongols and the *Semu ren* were supposed to obtain high imperial offices such as the *darughachi* and Mongols received easier examinations for entry into the bureaucracy.[46] The principle of legal privilege extended into intercommunal disputes. While ethnic commissions composed of representatives from each group provided a veneer of equality to the proceedings and while imperial law seems to have decided most proceedings, the Mongols often retained privileges not afforded to other groups. For instance, in cases such as mixed marriages, Mongol law applied to both the husband and the wife if either were Mongols, while for other groups only the husband's law was enforceable.[47] In mixed cases, Mongols also received more lenient sentences than others who committed the same offences and received special legal exemptions denied to other groups.[48]

The lack of outright favouritism present in the system of ethnic administration in Wales and the lack of a single legal code to adjudicate intercommunal cases derived from the process of Anglo-European settlement and conquest. In the Islamic world (and in the Christian territories of Iberia, Sicily and the Crusader States) and in the Chinese conquest dynasties, the structure of ethnic and religious administration was solely designed to secure the position of the conquering community while simultaneously acknowledging the limited ability and desire of that community to impose its laws on defeated populations. In the Anglo-Welsh border region, the process of settlement was slow and uneven. Although the initial process of Anglo-European conquest and settlement had begun in the late eleventh century, the Marcher lords and the English crown had only tentative control in the upland regions of Wales – where most of the Welsh population lived – until the mid-thirteenth century, which provided the Welsh communities with extensive autonomy and sometimes outright independence. The development of Englishries and Welshries simply recognised previous circumstances of ethnic bifurcation and the mixed jury most likely emerged – in addition to parleys and love days – as a means of keeping peace between frequently warring communities.[49] After English control was consolidated, the Marcher lords and the English crown decided to retain the previous legal and administrative systems, including the principle of jurisdiction determining the law applied in a mixed case. While the English crown and the Marcher lords were interested in entrenching English normative procedures and laws to an extent, their greater concern was to prevent a potential Welsh rebellion and, therefore, they also avoided antagonising the Welsh population by imposing measures of ethnic favouritism.

The role of mixed juries and other methods of resolving intercommunal disputes in facilitating acculturation in contact zones is a subject that has been touched upon only indirectly, as such exchanges cannot be solely disassociated from wider forces driving cross-cultural interactions. Any discussion here, therefore, must recognise conjunctive factors. Indeed, the cases examined in this study indicate that methods of intercommunal dispute resolution could help augment acculturative processes, but there is little direct evidence that they played the sole or even primary role.

For example, in the Islamic world, the resolution of mixed religious cases was only one part of the wider legal structure and only one part of the wider policies of Muslim states to cement the normative values of Islamic law among non-Muslim communities by allowing non-Muslims to use *sharī'a* courts. Indeed, contemporary evidence indicates that Muslim authorities had many mechanisms to perforate the *dhimmī* communities' autonomy and thereby facilitate the establishment and acceptance of Islamic laws and norms among non-Muslims. The resolution of intercommunal cases by Islamic law was one of those mechanisms and it was not strictly necessary for the intercommunal case to involve members of entirely different faiths. Indeed, Muslim authorities also claimed jurisdiction over cases involving Christian and Jewish sects, such as those between Nestorian and Jacobite Christians, or between Karaite and Rabbanite

Jews.[50] As Richard Rose noted, fierce rivalries among *dhimmī* sects provided Muslim authorities numerous opportunities for juridical intervention.[51]

Many *dhimmī* communities responded to Muslim encroachment in their affairs by adopting two seemingly contradictory policies. On the one hand, communal leaders forbade their co-religionists from appealing to Muslim courts on pain of excommunication, though this tactic was used more often by Christian than Jewish authorities.[52] In addition, many Christian communities developed law codes that would clearly differentiate the laws of their communities. For example, the Nestorian patriarch Timothy I developed a series of canons in 805 in part to 'remove all excuses from Christians who turn to Muslim courts with the pretext that canon law is insufficient'. His successor then threatened to excommunicate any Nestorian who took their case to a *qāḍī*.[53] Between the eleventh and fourteenth centuries the Maronites, Jacobites and Nestorians each developed canons of civil law.[54] A Jacobite canon dated to the twelfth century and aimed at monks similarly threatened excommunication against anyone who dared to take his case outside the confines of the ecclesiastical authority.[55]

On the other hand, these *dhimmī* communities' laws became increasingly indistinguishable from Islamic laws in areas such as inheritance, taxation and commercial practices.[56] Indeed, since excommunicating co-religionists for appealing their cases to *sharī'a* courts violated Islamic law and could jeopardise communal autonomy, since the incentive for non-Muslims to attempt to gain a more favourable ruling through *sharī'a* courts was strong, and since sectarian strife persisted, the most effective way to limit Muslim intervention was to adopt Islamic laws. Limited Islamisation, furthermore, transpired within a framework of deep Arabisation fostered by the predominance of Arabic in administration, commercial exchanges and the legal system. Hence, just as *dhimmī* communities saw their autonomy and traditions eroded through state power, they also faced other cultural changes that further acculturated them to the Muslim Arabic community's norms.

Much like in the Islamic world, the mixed jury in Wales could help augment acculturative processes, in this case the embrace of English legal procedures among the Welsh population. The increasing popularity and use of jury procedure in Welsh districts in the thirteenth century is attested in petitions from the Welsh of Tempseter and Maelienydd demanding that their lords allow jury procedure in their respective Welshries.[57] Indeed, testimony from the Edwardian inquest indicates that jury procedure was the primary method of judgment in the Marcher districts and Crown territories at least by the late thirteenth century.[58] Since some form of mixed jury could be traced to the early thirteenth century, it is reasonable to deduce that the English and Welsh populations found the jury a preferable venue to resolving quarrels and that interactions in these settings helped facilitate its acceptance among the Welsh.

As in the Islamic world, the English community's growing political dominance certainly aided in the spread of jury procedure. Yet the Welsh use of English laws and legal norms was never as pervasive as the Islamisation of *dhimmī* legal systems. In the thirteenth and fourteenth centuries, Welsh communities tended to embrace English laws and procedures that conformed to their own cultural traditions and outlooks, while resisting others, such as the outlawing of *galanas*, which they saw as fundamentally alien. Hence, while the political relationship between the communities is important, it is not necessarily the central determining factor in the depth and breadth of cultural exchange and borrowing in every case.[59] Indeed, the power of the Muslim state was not only augmented by the economic and political factors that encouraged Arabisation, but also by the fact that Christian, Jewish and Islamic laws and methods of judgment were often fundamentally compatible, in large part due to the lasting influence of Roman rule. Likewise, the growing popularity of jury procedure and other methods of collective judgment among the Welsh population in the thirteenth and fourteenth centuries is also reflective of the fact that communal participation in judicial decisions was a long-established feature of Welsh law and English methods, therefore, would not have seemed entirely foreign.[60] In addition, other methods of collective judgment that were common in England, such as the use of suitors to render judgment in county courts, also became popular in places like Deheubarth.[61] The adoption of these methods of collective judgment was often initiated by Welsh princes or required their acquiescence and did not entail the complete abandonment of traditional methods of judgment in Wales.[62] Indeed, professional judges and communal elders knowledgeable in the law continued to carry on important, if diminished, roles.[63]

The dual importance of political dominance and cultural compatibility is evident in the relative lack of legal acculturation between Chinese and semi-nomadic communities in Khitan and Mongol China. Methods of communal dispute resolution in both realms exposed each community to the other's laws. As described above, it possibly led to the imposition of Chinese laws in cases between mixed ethnic groups in the Khitan realm for a short period. Yet there is little evidence that the exposure acquired in these cases led to the deep acculturation evident among the *dhimmī* communities in the Islamic world. Franke argues that the Khitans only borrowed Chinese laws selectively, mostly pertaining to administration, while retaining distinct criminal, marriage and property laws.[64] Similarly, while the Mongols adopted Chinese laws and practices into their legal codes, most of these laws pertained to administrative practices. Civil and criminal laws for Mongols remained entirely distinct from those applied to the Chinese.[65] The adoption of Chinese administrative practices and laws relating to imperial governance is best understood in the long-standing historical pattern of semi-nomadic conquest regimes adapting to the realities of governing complex sedentary societies, a task for which their traditional governance structures were ill-equipped to handle. Nevertheless, unlike the Jurchens under the Jin dynasty, the socio-economic differences between the Khitan and Mongol populations and their Chinese counterparts were never sufficiently reduced to permit for greater legal compatibility and borrowing.[66]

The mixed jury demonstrates the extent to which English procedures had pervaded Welsh legal practice and undoubtedly its role in helping expose the Welsh and English populations to each other's laws and customs. Its role in fostering acculturative change beyond the legal sphere is more open to speculation. While systems of intercommunal justice engendered contact and could, therefore, encourage cultural exchange, the evidence is not conclusive. For example, linguistic acculturation is undoubtedly an area in which one could expect to find substantial acculturation. George Owen of Henllys, however, asserted that linguistic barriers were a major problem for mixed juries in sixteenth-century Pembrokeshire.

Indeed, he claimed that neither the English nor the Welsh could understand each other. He mostly attributed this development to the fact that the region's Englishries and Welshries were ethnically homogenous.[67] Although his statement may be exaggerated for Pembrokeshire and certainly might not pertain to all of Wales, there is no documentation to prove otherwise.[68]

Evidence from the Islamic world and China is similarly inconclusive. Most scholars have attributed the Arabisation of *dhimmī* communities to Islamisation, the dominance of Arabic in state administration, commerce and (increasingly) scholarship.[69] Logically, the use of Arabic in legal settings and the need for *dhimmī* communities to understand *sharī'a* would also have contributed to Arabisation, but there is no definitive proof that it did. In China interpreters played a major role in administration and intercommunal cases and legal decisions and evidence were needed to be translated into multiple languages.[70] Such contact most certainly familiarised ethnic groups with different linguistic terminology. Yet the extent to which that contact facilitated the spread of language is difficult to determine precisely.

The analysis given above leads to the following findings. First, dual and multiple-administrative systems could only be effective in providing communal autonomy and reducing the chance for conflict if there existed mechanisms for adjudicating cross-communal disputes. Hence, while these mechanisms may have developed somewhat separately from the local system of ethnic or religious administration, they were still an integral and integrated part of that system. Secondly, since most ethnic and religious communities in high medieval Eurasia were able to retain their own laws and customs, mechanisms for resolving intercommunal disputes were present across the Continent and most of these mechanisms were centrally imposed.

The primary and most important difference in the Anglo-Welsh border region is that neither the system of ethnic administration nor the mixed jury were imposed by a central authority. In addition, since the Englishries and Welshries were the foundation of dual administration, ultimate legal jurisdiction was most often localised to the communal ethnic court. In this respect, the mixed jury could also serve as a geographical and social communal bridge. In the centralised models found in Khitan and Mongol China and Islamic

Eurasia, issues of personal status and legal jurisdiction were often more complex within structures that (with the Khitans excepted) were often designed to ensure the dominance of a single group. The Anglo-Welsh model of dual-administration and the mixed jury did not explicitly seek to promote English political dominance or cultural Anglicisation, unlike the *dhimmī* system that sought to ensure *dhimmī* subordination and promoted deep Arabisation and Islamisation. Finally, the mixed jury, unlike elsewhere in Eurasia performed numerous functions that went beyond adjudicating individual legal cases.

The systems of communal administration present throughout high medieval Eurasia allowed acculturation to occur within a framework that provided enough autonomy to prevent the large-scale assimilation (i.e. the loss of communal identity through cultural change) of one community into another because the retention of communal laws and customs promoted the persistence of ethnic and religious difference. By ensuring the efficacy of communal autonomy, methods of communal conflict resolution played an important role in maintaining this acculturative environment and structure. What role they played in fostering specific instances of cultural change is more difficult to pinpoint, though in the Islamic world they seemed to be very important. The major challenge in deducing this role derives from the fact that acculturation is dependent on conjunctive processes and it is those conjunctive processes that will need to be examined in more detail in future studies to determine the full impact of ethnic and religious administration on cultural change.

Notes

[1] William Rees (ed.), *Calendar of Ancient Petitions relating to Wales* (Cardiff: University of Wales Press, 1975), no. 7249, pp. 244–5.
[2] Ivor Bowen (ed.), *The Statutes of Wales* (London: T. Fisher Unwin, 1908), p. 28.
[3] *CWR*, p. 204. Compare the chapters by Cavell and Young in the present volume.
[4] Between 1227 and 1231, Henry III ordered a mixed jury to resolve a claim over a manor in Maelor Saesneg between an English and a Welsh litigant. See *CCR, 1227–1231*, p. 250.

5   For overviews of the Byzantine and Sasanian systems, see Milka Levy-Rubin, *Non-Muslims in the Early Islamic Empire: From Surrender to Coexistence* (Cambridge: Cambridge University Press, 2011), pp. 113–63. For the Tang, see Herbert Franke, 'Chinese Law in a Multinational Society: the Case of the Liao (907–1125)', *Asia Major*, 5 (1992), 113–16.

6   Michael Hill, 'Ethnic Administration and Dichotomization in a Eurasian Context: Wales, *c.*1100–1350CE', *WHR*, 27.2 (2014), 175–213.

7   For example, medieval English sources do not use the phrase *Judei Anglici* ('English Jews') with the adjectival nominative, instead preferring the regional genitive *Judei Angliae* ('Jews of England') since Christians in medieval England perceived the English as an exclusively Christian people. Likewise, Richard Hitchcock, *Mozarabs in Medieval and Early Modern Spain* (Aldershot: Ashgate, 2008), pp. ix–xi, notes that Arab Muslims in Iberia did not apply the term *musta'rab* ('Arabised') to the Christian Mozarabs because although these Christians had adopted the Arabic language and Arab customs, they were not Muslims and Arab Muslims saw the Arabs as exclusively Muslim.

8   Hill, 'Ethnic Administration', 175–6. Edward I's Statute of Rhuddlan, which created the royal principality of Wales, reserved cases of theft, homicide, rape, and arson to the Crown to be decided according to English law. See Bowen (ed.), *Statutes of Wales*, p. 26.

9   Hill, 'Ethnic Administration', 179, 206–7.

10 Theoretically, only the 'People of the Book' (*ahl al-kitāb*, namely Christians and Jews) were supposed to receive *dhimmī* status. However, the pragmatic necessities of ruling a vast multi-religious empire soon allowed Muslim jurists and officials to find exceptions for other groups, though the conditions granted to these groups were not always the same as for Christians and Jews. See Patricia Crone, *God's Rule – Government and Islam: Six Centuries of Medieval Islamic Political Thought* (New York: Columbia University Press, 2005), pp. 170–1; Anver M. Emon, *Religious Pluralism and Islamic Law: Dhimmīs and Others in the Empire of Law* (Oxford: Oxford University Press, 2012), pp. 68–9; and Johan Elverskog, *Buddhism and Islam on the Silk Road* (Philadelphia: University of Pennsylvania Press, 2010), pp. 48–50.

11 An early work from Antoine Fattal provides a sound overview of *dhimmī* communities' legal rights and the circumstances under which Islamic law applied to *dhimmīs*. See Fattal, 'How dhimmīs were judged in the Islamic world', in Robert G. Hoyland (ed.), *Muslims and Others in Early Islamic Society* (Burlington, VT: Ashgate, 2004), pp. 83–102. For a detailed analysis of Jewish and Christian appeals to Muslim authorities,

see Uriel Simonsohn, 'Communal Boundaries Reconsidered: Jews and Christians Appealing to Muslim Authorities in the Medieval Near East', *Jewish Studies Quarterly*, 14.4 (2007), 328–63.

[12] For the influence of the Islamic *dhimma* system in Iberia, see Thomas Glick, *Islamic and Christian Spain* (Leiden: Brill, 2005), pp. 187–95; L. P. Harvey, *Islamic Spain, 1250–1500* (Chicago: University of Chicago Press, 1990), pp. 110–11, 125–6; and Robert I. Burns, *Muslims, Christians, and Jews in the Crusader Kingdom of Valencia* (Cambridge: Cambridge University Press, 1984), pp. 58–9. For Sicily, see Alex Metcalfe, *The Muslims of Medieval Italy* (Edinburgh: Edinburgh University Press, 2009), p. 106; and Alex Metcalfe, *Muslims and Christians in Norman Sicily* (London: Routledge, 2011), pp. 34–6. For the Crusader States, see Jonathan Riley-Smith, 'Government and the indigenous in the Latin Kingdom of Jerusalem', in David Abulafia and Nora Berend (eds), *Medieval Frontiers* (Burlington, VT: Ashgate, 2002), pp. 126–30.

[13] See Hill, 'Ethnic Administration', 184–5.

[14] See Frederick Mote, 'Chinese Society under Mongol Rule, 1215–1368', in Herbert Franke and Denis Twitchett (eds), *The Cambridge History of China: Alien Regimes and Border States* (Cambridge: Cambridge University Press, 1994), pp. 629–32; and Frederick Mote, *Imperial China, 900–1800* (Cambridge, MA: Harvard University Press, 2003), pp. 489–90.

[15] See Paul Heng-chao Ch'en, *Chinese Legal Tradition Under the Mongols: The Code of 1291 as Reconstructed* (Princeton: Princeton University Press, 1979), pp. 79–80.

[16] Franke, 'Chinese Law', 113–17.

[17] See Ch'en, *Chinese Legal Tradition*, pp. 80–1; and H. Franke, 'The role of the state as a structural element in polyethnic societies', in S. R. Schram (ed.), *Foundations and Limits of State Power in China* (Hong Kong: The Chinese University Press, 1987), pp. 100–1.

[18] See below, p. XXX.

[19] See Levy-Rubin, *Non-Muslims*, pp. 114–62.

[20] Hill, 'Ethnic Administration', 195–6.

[21] Hill, 'Ethnic Administration', 196–200.

[22] *CPR (1324–1327)*, p. 354.

[23] Flintshire did not have discernible Englishries and Welshries. See R. A. Roberts (ed.), *The Court Rolls of the Lordship of Ruthin or Dyffryn Clwyd of the Reign of King Edward I* (London: C. J. Clark, 1893), pp. 2 and 38–9; *CPR (1292–1301)*, p. 162 and *CPR (1324–1327)*, p. 354; Rees (ed.), *Calendar of Ancient Petitions*, nos. 10188 and 10189, pp. 348–50; *CWR*, p. 204; *The Welsh Assize Roll, 1272–1284*, ed.

James Conway Davies (Cardiff: University of Wales Press, 1940), pp. 248–9, 308–9; Geoffrey T. Clark (ed.), *Cartae et Alia Munimenta Quae Ad Dominium De Glamorgan Pertinent*, 6 vols (Cardiff: University of Wales Press, 1885–1910), i, pp. 88–90; and J. G. Edwards (ed.), *Flint Pleas, 1283–1285* (Chester: G. R. Griffith, 1922), pp. 6–7, 25–6, and 39.

[24] Clark (ed.), *Cartae*, i, pp. 88–90.

[25] Roberts (ed.), *The Court Rolls of the Lordship of Ruthin*, p. 2.

[26] J. W. Willis-Bund (ed.), *An Extent of all the Lands and Rents of the Lord Bishop of St David's* (London: Honorable Society of Cymmrodorion, 1902), pp. 109 and 307.

[27] Davies (ed.), *Welsh Assize Roll*, pp. 248–9. *Nos assignaverimus vos ad inquirendum per sacramentum proborum et legalium hominum tam de comitatu Salopie quam de hominibus de Walscheria de partibus de Kynardeslege.*

[28] Davies (ed.), *Welsh Assize Roll*, pp. 261–2, 268–9.

[29] Davies (ed.), *Welsh Assize Roll*, p. 269.

[30] Davies (ed.), *Welsh Assize Roll*, pp. 290–1.

[31] For Pecham's statements about Welsh law, see Charles T. Martin (ed.), *Registrum Epistolarum Fratris Johannis Peckham, Archiepiscopi Cantuariensis*, 3 vols (London: Longman, 1884), i, pp. 77 and 136, and ii, pp. 475–6. For his arguments about 'civilizing' the Welsh, see A.W. Haddan and W. Stubbs (eds), *Councils and Ecclesiastical Documents relating to Great Britain and Ireland*, 3 vols (Oxford: Clarendon Press, 1869–78), i, pp. 570–1.

[32] For Edward I's views on Irish law, see *Irish Historical Documents, 1172–1922*, ed. Edmund Curtis and Robert B. McDowell (London: Methuen, 1943), no. 10, pp. 131–2. For Scotland, see E. L. G. Stones (ed.), *Anglo-Scottish Relations 1174–1328* (Oxford: Oxford University Press, 1965), p. 125. For the laws of inheritance in the principality of Wales, see Bowen (ed.), *Statutes of Wales*, pp. 25–6.

[33] *AoC*, p. 368.

[34] See Henry R. Luard (ed.), Matthew Paris, *Chronica Majora*, 7 vols (London, 1872–83), iv, p. 647; v, pp. 227, 288 and 592.

[35] For the early Islamic period and Arab relations with non-Muslim communities, see Crone, *God's Rule*, pp. 358–92; Levy-Rubin, *Non-Muslims*, esp. pp. 8–87 and Milka Levy-Rubin, 'Shurūṭ 'Umar and its Alternatives: the Legal Debate on the Status of the Dhimmīs', *Jerusalem Studies in Arabic and Islam*, 30 (2005), esp. 170–89; and Emon, *Religious Pluralism*, pp. 33–76.

[36] Islamic law was also applied to *dhimmīs* in any case involving serious crimes such as homicide or if *dhimmīs* referred their cases to Islamic courts.

[37] Emon, *Religious Pluralism*, pp. 136–41.

[38] Fattal, 'How dhimmīs were judged', pp. 90–2.
[39] Fattal, 'How dhimmīs were judged', pp. 94–5.
[40] See Néophyte Edelby, 'The legislative autonomy of Christians in the Islamic world', in Hoyland (ed.), *Muslims and Others*, pp. 58–82.
[41] Fattal, 'How dhimmīs were judged', pp. 95–6.
[42] S. D. Goitein, 'Minority Self-Rule and Government Control in Islam', in Hoyland (ed.), *Muslims and Others*, p. 103.
[43] For a summation of this argument, see Ira M. Lapidus, *A History of Islamic Societies* (Cambridge: Cambridge University Press, 2002), pp. 36–8, 40–4 and 50–4.
[44] For a thorough discussion of the jurists' discussions of these matters, see Emon, *Religious Pluralism*, pp. 79–87 and 99–102.
[45] Franke, 'Chinese law', 113.
[46] Elizabeth Endicott-West, *Mongolian Rule in China: Local Administration in the Yuan Dynasty* (Cambridge, MA: Harvard University Press, 1989), pp. 74–83; and Mote, *Imperial China*, pp. 490–1.
[47] Ch'en, *Chinese Legal Tradition*, pp. 80–1.
[48] Mote, *Imperial China*, pp. 489–90.
[49] Hill, 'Ethnic Administration', 195–7.
[50] Simonsohn, 'Communal boundaries', 340–1; and Richard B. Rose, 'Islam and the Development of Personal Status Laws among Christian Dhimmis: Motives, Sources, Consequences', *The Muslim World*, 72.3–4 (1982), 163.
[51] Rose, 'Islam', 166.
[52] Simonsohn, 'Communal boundaries', 356.
[53] Fattal, 'How dhimmīs were judged', p. 85.
[54] Fattal, 'How dhimmīs were judged', p. 85
[55] Simonsohn, 'Communal boundaries', 353.
[56] Rose, 'Islam', 172; and Goitein, 'Minority Self-Rule', p. 168.
[57] See Thomas Salt, *Concise Account of Ancient Documents relating to the Honor, Forest and Borough of Clun* (n.p., 1858), p. 6; and *CPR, 1292–1301*, p. 290.
[58] For the Edwardian inquest, see *CWR*, pp. 190–210.
[59] This argument is consistent with acculturation theories as developed by anthropologists, sociologists and psychologists. See, for example, the most influential explanation of acculturation theory in Bernard J. Siegel et al., 'Acculturation: an Explanatory Formulation', *American Anthropologist*, 56 (1954), 980–4; see also more recent studies such as Amado M. Padilla, 'The role of cultural awareness and ethnic loyalty in acculturation', in Amado M. Padilla (ed.), *Acculturation: Theory, Models and Some New Findings* (Boulder, CO: Westview Press, 1980),

pp. 48–67; John W. Berry, 'Acculturation', in Joan E. Grusec and Paul D. Hastings (eds), *Handbook of Socialization: Theory and Research* (New York: Rand McNally, 2007), pp. 543–60; Jean S. Phinney, 'Ethnic identity and acculturation', in Kevin M. Chun et al. (eds), *Acculturation: Advances in Theory, Measurement, and Applied Research* (Washington, DC: American Psychological Association, 2003), pp. 63–82.

60 See J. B. Smith, 'Judgement under the Law of Wales', *Studia Celtica*, 39 (2006), esp. 71–4, 83–4, and 90–3. Two of the clearest examples of collective judgment in Wales involving communal representatives come from early thirteenth-century Arwystli contained in the charters of Strata Marcella Abbey. In both these cases, communal elders (variously called 'good men' [*gwyrda*], 'elders' [*hynefyddion*], 'upright men' [*proborum virum*], 'wise men' [*sapientes*] and 'nobles' [*optimates*]) heard land disputes and played a variety of roles, such as advising judges, giving judgment themselves or hearing appeals: Graham C. G. Thomas (ed.), *The Charters of the Abbey of Ystrad Marchell* (Aberystwyth: National Library of Wales, 1997), nos. 63, 64, and 65, pp. 202–7.

61 Smith, 'Judgement', 74–88.

62 Smith, 'Judgement', 72–3 and 84–7.

63 See Huw Pryce, 'Lawbooks and Literacy in Medieval Wales', *Speculum*, 75.1 (2000), 46–7 and 61–4; and Smith, 'Judgement', 74–5.

64 Franke, 'Chinese law', 124–7.

65 See Mote, 'Chinese Society', p. 631 and Ch'en, *Chinese Legal Tradition*, pp. 14–40.

66 For Jurchen acculturation in China, see Tao Jing-shen, *The Jurchen in Twelfth-Century China: A Study of Sinicization* (Seattle: University of Washington Press, 1977); Herbert Franke and Hok-lam Chan (eds), *Studies on the Jurchens and the Chin Dynasty* (Aldershot: Ashgate, 1997); and Mote, *Imperial China*, pp. 265–88.

67 George Owen of Henllys, *The Description of Pembrokeshire*, ed. Dillwyn Miles (Llandysul: Gomer Press, 1994), pp. 50–1.

68 For the use and spread of English and French in Wales, see Llinos Beverley Smith, 'The Welsh and English language in late-Medieval Wales', in D. A. Trotter (ed.), *Multilingualism in Later Medieval Britain* (Cambridge: Cambridge University Press, 2000), pp. 7–21; and D. A. Trotter, 'L'anglo-français au Pays de Galles: une enquête préliminaire', *Revue de linguistique romane*, 58.231–2 (1994), 461–82.

69 See, for example, Kenneth Cragg, *The Arab Christian: A History in the Middle East* (Louisville, KY: Westminster/John Knox Press, 1991), pp. 61–6; Sidney H. Griffith, *The Church in the Shadow of the Mosque: Christians and Muslims in the World of Islam* (Princeton: Princeton University

Press, 2008), pp. 48–53; S. D. Goitein, *Jews and Arabs: A Concise History of their Social and Cultural Relations* (New York: Schocken, 1974), pp. 131–40; Lapidus, *History of Islamic Societies*, pp. 63–4; Richard Frye, *The Golden Age of Persia: The Arabs in the East* (London: Weidenfeld and Nicolson, 1996), pp. 68–72, 99–100, and 121–5; Maged S. A. Mikhail, *From Byzantine to Islamic Egypt: Religion, Identity and Politics After the Conquest* (London: I. B. Tauris, 2014), pp. 93–105; Metcalfe, *Muslims and Christians*, pp. 15–24; Glick, *Islamic and Christian Spain*, esp. pp. 196–8 and 203–16; and Pierre Guichard, *Al-Andalus (711–1492)* (Paris: Hachette 2000), pp. 143–5.

[70] See Franke, 'The Role of the State', pp. 110–11; Franke and Chan (eds), *Studies on the Jurchens*, pp. 398–9; and Ch'en, *Chinese Legal Tradition*, pp. 68–80.

Bibliography

Manuscript sources

Aberystwyth, National Library of Wales,
   5276D
   GB 0210 GOBOWEN 4/2
   MS 6620D
Ebbw Vale, Gwent Archives, D43/3739, 3740 and 3987
London, The National Archives,
   C1/693/32, C1/734/33, C1/1346/23-24, C47/4/1, C60/40,
   C142/60/23, C145/35, C146/9502;
   E 101/31/37, E 101/39/39, E 101/39/40, E 101/46/20,
   E 135/5/43, E 163/11/34;
   JUST1/1147;
   PROB 11/38/16;
   REQ 2/5/59, 2/10/69;
   SC 6/774/11;
   SP1/97, 1/129, 1/130, 1/131;
   STAC 2/8/8, 2/10/54-5, 2/10/186-7, 2/15/164-166, 2/15/328,
   2/20/223, 2/21/114, 2/24/34, 2/25/16, 2/26/105, 2/26/394,
   2/32/23, 2/32/52, 2/32/54, 2/34/8, 2/34/18, 3/3/73
Vatican City, Archivio Segreto Vaticano (ASV)
   Registra Vaticana (Reg. Vat.) 9–11, 13, 15–25a, 27–29, 31–35,
   41
West Glamorgan Archive Service
   RISW GGF 3

Bibliography

Printed sources

Ailes, Marianne (trans.), *The History of the Holy War: Ambroise's Estoire de la Guerre Sainte II: Translation*, with notes by Marianne Ailes and Malcolm Barber (Woodbridge: Boydell, 2003).

Anderson, A. O. (ed.), *Scottish Annals From English Chroniclers, A.D. 500 to 1286* (London: David Nutt, 1908; repr. Edinburgh: Oliver and Boyd, 1922).

Anderson, A. O. (ed.), *Early Sources of Scottish History, A.D. 500 to 1286* (Edinburgh: Oliver and Boyd, 1922).

Auvray, L. (ed.), *Les registres de Gregoire IX*, 4 vols, Bibliothèque des Ecoles françaises d'Athènes et de Rome 2nd ser. ix (Paris: De Boccard, 1890–1955).

Barrow, J. (ed.), *St Davids Episcopal Acta 1085–1280* (Cardiff: South Wales Records Society, 1998).

Bellaguet, L. (ed.), *Chronique du Religieux de Saint-Denys, le Regne de Charles VI, de 1380 à 1422*, 6 vols (Paris: Crapelet, 1840).

Berger, E. (ed.), *Les registres d'Innocent IV*, 4 vols, Bibliothèque des Ecoles françaises d'Athènes et de Rome 2nd ser. i (Paris: Ernest Trobin, 1884–1921).

Blake, N. F. (trans.), *Jómsvíkinga Saga / The Saga of the Jomsvikings* (Edinburgh: Thomas Nelson, 1962).

Bliss, W. H. (ed.), *Calendar of Papal Registers Relating to Great Britain and Ireland, Volume 1: 1198–1304* (London: HMSO, 1893).

Bliss, W. H., and J. A. Twemlow (eds), *Calendar of Entries in the Papal Registers relating to Great Britain and Ireland, AD 1404–1415* (London: HMSO, 1893–1960).

Bowen, Ivor (ed.), *The Statutes of Wales* (London: T. Fisher Unwin, 1908).

Bower, Walter, and D. Watt (eds), *Scotichronicon*, 9 vols (Aberdeen: Aberdeen University Press, 1987–98).

Brereton, G. (trans.), *Jean Froissart, Chronicles* (London: Penguin, 1978).

Brewer, J. S., J. F. Dimock and G. F. Warner (eds), Gerald of Wales (Giraldi Cambrensis), *Opera*, 8 vols, Rolls Series 21 (London, 1861–91).

Bromwich, R. (ed.), *Dafydd ap Gwilym: a selection of poems* (Llandysul: Gomer Press, 1982).

Bromwich, Rachel, and Ifor Williams (eds), *Armes Prydein: the Prophecy of Britain from the Book of Taliesin* (Dublin: Four Courts Press, 1982).

Butler, H. E. (ed. and trans.), Gerald of Wales, *The Autobiography of Gerald of Wales* (Woodbridge: Boydell, 2005).

Calendar of Inquisitions Miscellaneous (Chancery), preserved in the Public Record Office, 8 vols (London: HMSO, 1916–69).

Bibliography

Calendar of Various Chancery Rolls, Supplementary Close Rolls, Welsh Rolls, and Scutage Rolls contained in the Public Record Office, 1277–1326 (London: HMSO, 1912).

Caspar, E. (ed.), *MGH, Epistolae Selectae II: Das Register Gregors VII*, 2 vols (Berlin: Weidmann, 1920–3).

Caspar, E., and G. Laehr (eds), *MGH, Epistolae VII: Karolini Aevi 5* (Berlin, 1928).

Cheney, C. R., and M. G. Cheney (eds), *The Letters of Pope Innocent III (1198–1216) concerning England and Wales: a Calendar with an Appendix of Texts* (Oxford: Clarendon Press, 1967).

Cheney, C. R., and W. H. Semple (ed. and trans.), *Selected Letters of Pope Innocent III concerning England (1198–1216)* (London: T. Nelson, 1953).

Cheney, M., D. Smith, C. Brooke and P. M. Hoskin (eds), *English Episcopal Acta 34: Worcester 1186–1218* (Oxford: Oxford University Press, 2008).

Christie, Richard Copley (ed.), *Annales Cestrienses; or, Chronicle of the Abbey of S. Werberg, at Chester* (London: Record Society of Lancashire and Chesire, 1887).

Clancy, J. P. (trans.), *Medieval Welsh Lyrics* (London: Macmillan, 1965).

Clancy, J. P. (trans.), *Medieval Welsh Poems* (Dublin: Four Courts Press, 2003).

Clark, Geoffrey T. (ed.), *Cartae et Alia Munimenta Quae Ad Dominium De Glamorgan Pertinent*, 6 vols (Cardiff: University of Wales Press, 1885–1910).

Clarke, A., and F. Holbrooke (eds), T. Rymer and R. Sanderson, *Foedera, Conventiones, Litterae etc.*, 4 vols in 7 (London: G. Eyre and A. Strahan, 1816–69).

Cowdrey, H. E. J. (trans.), *The Register of Pope Gregory VII 1073–1085* (Oxford: Oxford University Press, 2002).

Crouch, D. (ed.), *Llandaff Episcopal Acta 1140–1287* (Cardiff: University of Wales Press, 1988).

Crouch, D. (ed.), *The Acts and Letters of the Marshal family: Marshals of England and Earls of Pembroke, 1145–1248*, Camden Fifth Series, 47 (Cambridge: Cambridge University Press for the Royal Historical Society, 2015).

Dafydd ap Gwilym, *www.dafyddapgwilym.net*.

Davies, James Conway (ed.), *The Welsh Assize Roll, 1272–1284* (Cardiff: University of Wales Press, 1940).

Davies, James Conway (ed.), *Episcopal Acts and Cognate Documents Relating to Welsh Dioceses, 1066–1272*, 2 vols (Cardiff: University of Wales Press, 1946–8).

Davies, J. S. (ed.), *An English Chronicle of the Reigns of Richard II, Henry IV, Henry V, and Henry VI written before the year 1471* (London: Printed for the Camden Society, 1856).

Davies, S. (trans.), *The Mabinogion* (Oxford: Oxford University Press, 2007).

Davies, W. S. (ed.), Gerald of Wales, *De Invectionibus*, Y Cymmrodor, 30 (1920).

de la Roncière, C. B., J. Loye, P. H. de Cenival and A. Coulon (eds), *Les registres d'Alexandre IV*, 3 vols, Bibliothèque des Ecoles françaises d'Athènes et de Rome 2nd ser. xv (Paris: A. Fontemoing, 1895–1959).

de Lettenhove, Kervyn (ed.), Jean Froissart, *Oeuvres*, 25 vols (Bruxelles: Victor Devaux, 1867–77).

Delaborde, H. F. (ed.), *Œuvres de Rigord et de Guillaume le Breton. Historiens de Philippe-Auguste*, 2 vols (Paris: Librarie Renouard, 1882).

Delachanel, R. (ed.), *Chronique des Règnes de Jean II et Charles V*, 4 vols (Paris: Renouard, 1909–20).

Deslisle, L., and E. Berger (eds), *Receuil des Actes de Henri II, roi d'Angleterre et duc de Normandie*, 4 vols (Paris: Imprimerie Nationale, 1909–27).

Douglas, D. C. (gen. ed.), H. Rothwell and A. R. Myers (eds), *English Historical Documents*, 12 vols (London: Eyre and Spottiswoode, 1968–77).

Duggan, A. J. (ed.), *The Correspondence of Thomas Becket, Archbishop of Canterbury, 1162–1170*, 2 vols (Oxford: Clarendon Press, 2000).

Edgington, Susan B., and Carol Sweetenham (trans.), *The Chanson d'Antioche: An Old French Account of the First Crusade* (Aldershot: Ashgate, 2011).

Edwards, Ifan ab Owen (ed.), *A Catalogue of Star Chamber Proceedings relating to Wales* (Cardiff: University Press Board, 1929).

Edwards, J. G. (ed.), *Flint Pleas, 1283–1285* (Chester: G. R. Griffith, 1922).

Edwards, J. G. (ed.), *Calendar of Ancient Correspondence Concerning Wales* (Cardiff: University of Wales Press, 1935).

Edwards, J. G. (ed.), *Littere Wallie* (Cardiff: University of Wales Press, 1940).

Emanuel, H. D., 'A Fragment of the Register of Stephen Patryngton, Bishop of St David's', *Journal of the Historical Society of the Church in Wales*, 2 (1950), 31–45.

Eubel, C. (ed.), *Hierarchia Catholica Medii Aevi* (Rome: Sumptibus et Typis Librariae Regensbergianae, 1898).

Fraine, Fr. (ed.), *Vita Antiqua Sancti Samsonis Dolensis Episcopi* (*Analecta Bollandiana*, 6, 1887), pp. 77–150.

Gairdner, James (ed.), *Letters and Papers, Foreign and Domestic, Henry VIII*, vols v, vi, ix and x (London: HMSO, 1880–7).

Gay, J., and Vitte, S. (eds), *Les registres de Nicolas III (1277–1280)*, Bibliothèque des Ecoles françaises d'Athènes et de Rome 2nd ser. xiv (Paris: A. Fontemoing, 1898–1938).

Giles, J. A. (ed.), *Roger of Wendover's Flowers of History* (London: Bohn, 1849).
Giles, J. A. (trans.), Nennius, *History of the Britons*, III.45 (Cambridge, ON: In parentheses Publications, 2000).
Given-Wilson, C. (ed.), *The Chronicle of Adam Usk, 1377–1421* (Oxford: Oxford University Press, 1997).
Given-Wilson, C., S. Phillips, M. Ormrod, G. Martin et al. (eds), *The Parliament Rolls of Medieval England, 1275–1504, vol 8, Henry IV, 1399–1413* (Woodbridge: Boydell, 2005).
Gransden, A. (ed.), *The Chronicle of Bury St Edmunds 1212–1301* (London: Nelson, 1964).
Grèvy-Pons, N., E. Ornato and G. Ouy (eds), *Jean de Montreuil, Opera*, 4 vols (Paris and Turin: Cemi and Giappichelli, 1964–86).
Guiraud, J., Dorez, L. and Clemenzet, S. (eds), *Les registres d'Urbain IV*, 4 vols, Bibliothèque des Ecoles françaises d'Athènes et de Rome 2nd ser. xiii (Paris, 1892–1958).
Guiraud, J., and Cadier, E. (eds), *Les registres de Grégoire X (1272–1276) et de Jean XXI (1276–1277)*, 2 vols, Bibliothèque des Ecoles françaises d'Athènes et de Rome 2nd ser. xii (Paris: De Boccard, 1892–1960).
Guto'r Glyn, *www.gutorglyn.net*.
Haddan, A. W., and Stubbs, W. (eds), *Councils and Ecclesiastical Documents relating to Great Britain and Ireland*, 3 vols (Oxford: Clarendon Press, 1869–78).
Hageneder, O., W. Malczek and A. A. Strand (eds), *Die Register Innocenz' III., 2. Pontifikatsjahr 1199/1200. Texte*, Publikationen der Abteilung für historische Studien des Österreichischen Kulturinstituts in Rom, 2. Abt., 1. Reihe, Bd. 2: Texte (Rome/Vienna: ÖEAW, 1979).
Hageneder, O., with C. Egger, K. Rudolf and A. Sommerlechner (eds), *Die Register Innocenz' III., 5. Pontifikatsjahr 1202/1203. Texte*, Publikationen des historischen Instituts beim Österreichischen Kulturinstituts in Rom, 2. Abt., 1. Reihe, Bd. 5: Texte (Vienna: ÖEAW, 1993).
Hageneder, O., J. C. Moore, A. Sommerlechner, with C. Egger and H. Weigl (eds), *Die Register Innocenz' III., 6. Pontifikatsjahr 1203/1204. Texte und Indices*, Publikationen des historischen Instituts beim Österreichischen Kulturinstituts in Rom, 2. Abt., 1. Reihe, Bd. 6: Texte und Indices (Vienna: ÖEAW, 1995).
Hageneder, O., A. Sommerlechner and H. Weigl, with C. Egger and R. Murauer (eds), *Die Register Innocenz' III., 7. Pontifikatsjahr 1204/1205. Texte und Indices*, Publikationen des historischen Instituts beim Österreichischen Kulturinstituts in Rom, 2. Abt., 1. Reihe, Bd. 7: Texte und Indices (Vienna: ÖEAW, 1997).

Bibliography

Hardy, T. D. (ed.), *Rotuli Litterarum Patentium* (London: Record Commission, 1835).

Harries, Leslie (ed.), *Gwaith Huw Cae Llwyd ac eraill* (Cardiff: University of Wales Press, 1953).

Haydon, F. S. (ed.), *Eulogium (Historiarum sive temporis): Chronicon ab orbe condito usque ad Annum Domini M.CCC.LXVI. A monacho quodam Malmesburiensi exaratum*, 3 vols (London: Longman, Rolls Series, 1858–63).

Hingeston, F. C. (ed.), *Royal and Historical Letters during the reign of Henry IV*, 2 vols (London: Longman, 1860–4).

Holden, A. J., S. Gregory and D. Crouch (ed. and trans.), *History of William Marshal*, 3 vols (London: Anglo-Norman Text Society, 2002–6).

Horn, Joyce M. (ed.), *Fasti Ecclesiae Anglicanae 1300–1541: Volume 3, Salisbury Diocese* (London: Athlone Press, 1962).

Horn, Joyce M. (ed.), *Fasti Ecclesiae Anglicanae 1300–1541: Volume 7, Chichester Diocese* (London: Athlone Press, 1964).

Horn, Joyce M. (ed.), *The Register of Robert Hallum, Bishop of Salisbury 1407–17* (York: Canterbury and York Society, 1982).

Horn, Joyce M. (ed.), *Fasti Ecclesiae Anglicanae 1300–1541: Volume 2, Hereford Diocese*, revised by David Lepine (London: Institute of Historical Research, 2009).

Horstmann, Carl (ed.), *Nova Legenda Anglie, by John of Tynemouth and John Capgrave* (Oxford: Clarendon Press, 1901).

Ifans, Rh. (ed.), *Gwaith Gruffudd Llwyd a'r Llygliwiaid Eraill* (Cardiff: University of Wales Press, 2000).

Isaacson, R. F. (ed.), *The Episcopal Registers of the Diocese of St David's 1397–1518*, 3 vols, with discussion by R. Arthur Roberts (London: Cymmrodorion, 1917–20).

Jacob, E. F. (ed.), with the assistance of H. C. Johnson, *The Register of Henry Chichele, Archbishop of Canterbury 1414–1443*, 4 vols (Oxford: Clarendon Press, 1938–47).

Jeayes, I. H. (ed.), *Descriptive Catalogue of the Charters and Muniments in the Possession of Lord Fitzhardinge at Berkeley Castle* (Bristol: C. T. Jefferies and Sons, 1892).

Johnston, D. (ed. and trans.), *Iolo Goch: Poems* (Llandysul: Gomer Press, 1993).

Johnston, D. R. (ed.), 'Marwnad i Gronwy ap Tudur o Benmynydd/Elegy to Gronwy ap Tudur of Penmynydd', in *Gwaith Llywelyn Goch ap Meurig Hen* (Aberystwyth: Canolfan Uwchefrydiau Cymreig a Cheltaidd Prifysgol Cymru, 1998), pp. 30–5.

Jones, B. (ed.), *Fasti Ecclesiae Anglicanae 1300–1541: Volume 11, The Welsh Dioceses (Bangor, Llandaff, St Asaph, St David's)* (London: Athlone Press, 1965).

Jones, E. D. (ed.), *Gwaith Lewis Glyn Cothi* (Cardiff: University of Wales Press, 1953).
Jones, N. A. and E. H. Rheinallt (eds), 'Marwnad Hywel ap Gruffudd o Eifionydd' by Rhisierdyn, in *Gwaith Sefnyn, Rhisierdyn, Gruffudd Fychan ap Gruffudd ab Ednyfed a Llywarch Benturch* (Aberystwyth: Canolfan Uwchefrydiau Cymreig a Cheltaidd Prifysgol Cymru, 1995).
Jones, T. (ed.), *Brut y Tywysogyon: Peniarth MS. 20* (Cardiff: University of Wales Press, 1941).
Jones, T. (trans.), *Brut y Tywysogyon: Peniarth MS. 20 Version* (Cardiff: University of Wales Press, 1952).
Jones, T. (ed. and trans.), *Brut y Tywysogyon: Red Book of Hergest Version* (Cardiff: University of Wales Press, 1955).
Jones, T. (ed. and trans.), *Brenhinedd y Saesson* (Cardiff: University of Wales Press, 1971).
Jordan, E. (ed.), *Les registres de Clement IV*, Bibliothèque des Ecoles françaises d'Athènes et de Rome 2nd ser. xi (Paris: De Boccard, 1893–1945).
Keussen, Hermann (ed.), *Die Matrikel der Universität Köln: Erster Band, 1389–1475* (Bonn: H. Behrendt, 1928).
King, A. (ed.), *Scalacronica 1272–1363*, Surtees Society 209 (Woodbridge: Boydell, 2005).
Kirby, J. L. (ed.), *Calendar of Signet Letters of Henry IV and Henry V (1399–1422)* (London: HMSO, 1978).
Lannette-Claverie, C. (ed.), *Collection Joursanvault, Sous-Série 6 J* (Orléans: Archives Départementales du Loiret, 1976).
le Long, I. (ed.), Lodewyk van Velthem, *Spiegel historiael of rym-Spiegel: zynde de Nederlandsche rym-chronym* (Amsterdam: Hendrik van Eyl, 1727).
Lees, Beatrice A. (ed.), *Records of the Templars in England in the Twelfth Century: the Inquest of 185 with illustrative charters and documents* (London: Oxford University Press for the British Academy, 1935).
Lewis, Barry (ed. and trans.), *Medieval Welsh Poems to Saints and Shrines* (Dublin: Dublin Institute for Advanced Studies, 2015).
Lewis, H., and P. Diverre (eds), *Delw y Byd (Imago Mundi)* (Cardiff: University of Wales Press, 1928).
Lewis, Henry (ed.), *Hen gerddi crefyddol* (Cardiff: University of Wales Press, 1974).
Livingston, M., and J. K. Bollard (eds), *Owain Glyndŵr, A Casebook* (Liverpool: Liverpool University Press, 2013).
Loomis, R., and D. Johnston (trans.), *Medieval Welsh Poems: an anthology* (Binghamton, NY: Medieval and Renaissance Texts and Studies, Pegasus, 1992).

Bibliography

Luard, H. R. (ed.), *Annales Monastici*, 5 vols (London: Longmans, 1864–9; repr. 1965).
— vol. 1 (1864): *Annales de Margan, Annales Monasterii de Theokesberia, Annales Monasterii de Burton*.
— vol. 2 (1865): *Annales Monasterii de Wintonia, Annales de Waverleia*.
— vol. 3 (1866): *Annales Prioratus de Dunstaplia, Annales de Bermundeseia*.
— vol. 4 (1869): *Annales Monasterii de Oseneia, Chronicon Vulgo Dictum Chronicon Thomæ Wykes, Annales Prioratus de Wigornia*.
Luard, Henry R. (ed.), Matthew Paris, *Chronica majora*, 7 vols (London: Longman, 1872–83).
Martin, Charles T. (ed.), *Registrum Epistolarum Fratris Johannis Pecham, Archiepiscopi Cantuariensis*, 3 vols (London: Longman, 1884).
Mason, Emma, Jennifer Bray and Desmond J. Murphy (eds), *Westminster Abbey Charters, 1066–c.1214* (London: London Record Society, 1988).
Matthews, T. (ed. and trans.), *Welsh Records in Paris* (Carmarthen: Spurrell, 1910).
Maund, K. L. (ed.), *Handlist of the Acts of Native Welsh Rulers, 1132–1283* (Cardiff: University of Wales Press, 1996).
Maxwell, J. (ed.), *The Chronicle of Lanercost 1272–1346* (Glasgow: James MacLehose and Sons, 1913).
Michel, F. (ed.), *Histoire des ducs de Normandie et des rois d'Angleterre* (Paris: Société de l'histoire de France, 1840).
Miles, Dillwyn (ed.), George Owen of Henllys, *The Description of Pembrokeshire* (Llandysul: Gomer Press, 1994).
Millor, W. J., H. E. Butler and C. N. L. Brooke (eds), *The Letters of John of Salisbury*, 2 vols (Oxford: Oxford University Press, 1979–86 [1955]).
Murauer, R., and A. Sommerlechner, with O. Hageneder, C. Egger and H. Weigl (eds), *Die Register Innocenz' III., 10. Pontifikatsjahr 1207/1208. Texte und Indices*, Publikationen des historischen Instituts beim Österreichischen Kulturinstituts in Rom, 2. Abt., 1. Reihe, Bd. 10: Texte und Indices (Vienna: ÖEAW, 2007).
Mynors, R. A. B., R. M. Thomson and M. Winterbottom (ed. and trans.), William of Malmesbury, *Gesta Regum* (Oxford: Clarendon Press, 1998).
Neville, C. J. (ed.), 'A Plea Roll of Edward I's army in Scotland, 1296', in *A Miscellany of the Scottish History Society, Eleventh Volume* (Edinburgh: Pillans and Wilson for the Society, 1990), pp. 7– 33.
Nicolas, N. H. (ed.), *Proceedings and Ordinances of the Privy Council of England*, 7 vols (London: Record Commission, 1834–7).
Paris, Gaston (trans.), Ambroise, *L'Estoire de la Guerre Sainte* (Paris: Imprimerie Nationale, 1897).

Bibliography

Pearson, M. J. (ed.), *Fasti Ecclesiae Anglicanae 1066–1300: Volume 9, the Welsh Cathedrals (Bangor, Llandaff, St Asaph, St Davids)* (London: Institute of Historical Research, 2003), www.british–history.ac.uk/fasti-ecclesiae/1066–1300/vol9/.

Potthast, A. (ed.), *Regesta Pontificum Romanorum de 1198 ab 1304*, 2 vols (Graz: Akademische Druck- u. Verlagsanstalt, 1957).

Pressutti, P. (ed.), *Regesta Honorii Papae III*, 2 vols (Rome, 1888–95; repr. Hildesheim: Olms, 1978).

Pryce, H., with C. Insley (eds), *The Acts of the Welsh Rulers 1120–1283* (Cardiff: University of Wales Press, 2005).

Rees, D., and J. G. Jones (eds), *Thomas Matthews's Welsh Records in Paris* (Cardiff: University of Wales Press, 2010).

Rees, William (ed.), *Calendar of Ancient Petitions relating to Wales* (Cardiff: University of Wales Press, 1975).

Riley, H. T. (ed.), *Willelmi Rishanger, quondam monachi S. Albani, et quorundam anonymorum, chronica et annales, egnantibus Henrico Tertio et Edwardo Primo* (London: Rolls Series, 1865).

Roberts, Charles (ed.), *Excerpta e Rotulis Finium in Turri Londinensi Asservatis. Henrico Tertio Rege A.D. 1216–1272*, 2 vols (London: Record Commission, 1835, 1836).

Roberts, R. A. (ed.), *The Court Rolls of the Lordship of Ruthin or Dyffryn Clwyd of the Reign of King Edward I* (London: C. J. Clark, 1893).

Rodrigues, Teresa (ed.), *Butler's Lives of the Saints: March* (New Full Edition, Collesville, Minnesota: The Liturgical Press, 1999).

Rudolf, K., et al. (eds), *Die Register Innocenz' III., 2. Pontifikatsjahr 1199/1200. Indices*, Publikationen des historischen Instituts beim Österreichischen Kulturinstituts in Rom, 2. Abt., 1. Reihe, Bd. 2: Indices (Rome/Vienna: ÖEAW, 1983).

Rudolph, G., with T. Frenz (eds), *Das Kammerregister Papst Martins IV (Reg. Vat. 42)* (Vatican City: BAV, 2007).

Rymer, T. (ed.), *Fœdera, conventiones, literae, et cujuscunque generis acta publica, inter reges Angliae, et alios quosvis imperatores, reges, pontifices, principes, vel communitates, ab ineunte saecula duodecimo, viz. ab anno 1101, ad nostra usque tempora, habita aut tractata; ex autographis, infra tempora, habita aut tractata; ex autographis, infra secretiores Archivorum regiorum thesaurarias, per multa saecula reconditis, fideliter exscripta*, 20 vols (London: HMSO, 1704–35).

Salt, Thomas, *Concise Account of Ancient Documents relating to the Honor, Forest and Borough of Clun* (n.p., 1858).

Samaran, C., J. Monicat, J. Boussard and M. Nortier (eds), *Recueil des Actes de Philippe Auguste, Roi de France*, 4 vols (Paris: Imprimerie Nationale, 1966–79).

Sayers, J. E. (ed.), *Original Papal Documents in England and Wales from the Accession of Pope Innocent III to the Death of Pope Benedict XI (1198–1304)* (Oxford: Oxford University Press, 1999).

Sheehy, M. P. (ed.), *Pontificia Hibernica*, 2 vols (Dublin: Gill, 1962–5).

Soehnée, F., G. de Puybaudet, R. Poupardin and F. Olivier–Martin (eds), *Les registres de Martin IV (1281–1285)*, Bibliothèque des Ecoles françaises d'Athènes et de Rome 2nd ser. xvi (Paris: Fontemoing, 1901–35).

Sommerlechner, A., with C. Egger and H. Weigl (eds), *Die Register Innocenz' III., 5. Pontifikatsjahr 1202/1203. Indices*, Publikationen des historischen Instituts beim Österreichischen Kulturinstituts in Rom, 2. Abt., 1. Reihe, Bd. 5: Indices (Vienna: ÖEAW, 1994).

Stamp, A. E. (ed.), *Calendar of the Close Rolls Preserved in the Public Record Office: Richard II*, 6 vols (London: HMSO, 1914–27), *Henry IV*, 5 vols (London: HMSO, 1927–38), *Henry V*, 2 vols (London: HMSO, 1929–32).

Stamp, A. E. (ed.), *Calendar of the Fine Rolls Preserved in the Public Record Office: Henry IV*, 2 vols (London: HMSO, 1931–3); *Henry V* (London: HMSO, 1934).

Stephenson, J. (ed.), *Mediaeval Chronicles of Scotland. The Chronicles of Melrose and Holyrood* (Lampeter: Llanerch, 1988 [1850]).

Stevenson, J. (trans.), *Concerning the Instruction of Princes* (Felinfach: Llanerch, 1991 [1858]).

Stevenson, J. (trans.), *Radulphi de Coggeshall Chronicon Anglicanum* (London: Longman and Co., 1875).

Stones, E. L. G. (ed.), *Anglo-Scottish Relations 1174–1328* (Oxford: Oxford University Press, 1965).

Strachey, J. (ed.), *Rotuli Parliamentorum ut et Petitiones, et placita in Parliamento tempore Edwardi R. III*, 6 vols (London, 1776–7).

Stubbs, W. (ed.), *Memoriale Fratris Walteri de Coventria*, 2 vols (London: Longman and Company, 1873).

Sweetenham, Carol, and Linda L. Patterson (trans.), *Canso d'Antioca: an Occitan Epic of the First Crusade* (Aldershot: Ashgate 2003).

Theiner, A. (ed.), *Vetera Monumenta Hibernorum et Scotorum* (Rome: Typis Vaticanis, 1864).

Thierry, A. (ed.), *Histoire de la Conquête de l'Angleterre par les Normands* (Paris: Panthéon, 1851).

Thomas, D. Lleufer, 'Further Notes on the Court of the Marches with Original Documents', *Y Cymmrodor*, 13 (1899).

Thomas, Graham C. G. (ed.), *The Charters of the Abbey of Ystrad Marchell* (Aberystwyth: National Library of Wales, 1997).

Thorpe, Lewis (trans.), Geoffrey of Monmouth, *The History of the Kings of Britain* (Harmondsworth: Penguin, 1973).
Thorpe, Lewis (trans.), Gerald of Wales, *The Journey Through Wales/The Description of Wales* (Harmondsworth: Penguin Books, 1978).
Twemlow, J. A., *Calendar of Papal Registers Relating to Great Britain and Ireland, volume 9, 1431–1447* (London: HMSO, 1912).
Vaughan, R. (ed. and trans.), *Chronicles of Matthew Paris: monastic life in the thirteenth century* (Gloucester: Alan Sutton, 1984).
Vincent, N. (ed.), *The Letters and Charters of Cardinal Guala Bicchieri, Papal Legate in England, 1216–1218*, Canterbury and York Society vol. LXXXIII (Woodbridge: Boydell, 1996).
Whitelock, D. (ed. and trans.), *English Historical Documents Volume I: c. 500–1042* (London: Eyre and Spottiswoode, 1955).
Williams, J. E. Caerwyn, Peredur I. Lynch and R. Geraint Gruffydd (eds), *Gwaith Meilyr Brydydd a'i Ddisgynyddion* (Cardiff: University of Wales Press, 1994).
Williams, R., and G. H. Jones (eds), *Selections from the Hengwrt MSS* (London: Thomas Richards, 1892).
Williams ab Ithel, John (ed.), *Annales Cambriae* (London: Longman, Green, Longman and Roberts, 1860).
Willis-Bund, J. W. (ed.), *An Extent of all the Lands and Rents of the Lord Bishop of St David's* (London: Honorable Society of Cymmrodorion, 1902).
Winterbottom, Michael (trans.), Gildas, *The Ruin of Britain and other Worlds* (Chichester: Phillimore, 1978).
Wright, D. P. (ed.), *The Register of Thomas Langton, Bishop of Salisbury 1485–93* (York: Canterbury and York Society, 1985).

Secondary works

Allaire, Gloria, and Regina F. Psaki (eds), *The Arthur of the Italians: the Arthurian Legend in Medieval Italian Literature and Culture* (Cardiff: University of Wales Press, 2014).
Allmand, C., *The Hundred Years War, England and France at War c. 1300–c. 1450* (Cambridge: Cambridge University Press, 1988).
Alsop, J. D., 'Baker, Sir John (c.1489–1558)', *Oxford Dictionary of National Biography* (2004), online at *www.oxforddnb.com/view/article/1124*.
Anderson, B., *Imagined Communities: Reflections on the Origin and Spread of Nationalism* (London: Verso, 2006).
Angold, M. J., G. C. Baugh, M. M. Chibnall, D. C. Cox, D. T. W. Price, M. Tomlinson and B. S. Trinder, 'Houses of Benedictine monks:

Bibliography

Abbey of Shrewsbury', in A. T. Gaydon and R. B. Pugh (eds), *A History of the County of Shropshire: Volume 2* (London: Institute of Historical Research, 1973), pp. 30–7, www.british-history.ac.uk/vch/salop/vol2/pp30-37.

Arnold, Christopher J., and Jeffrey L. Davies, *Roman and Early Medieval Wales* (Stroud: Sutton, 2000).

Aurell, M., *The Plantagenet Empire, 1154–1224*, trans. D. Crouch (Harlow: Pearson Longman, 2007).

Baker, J. H., 'Montagu, Sir Edward (1480s–1557)', *Oxford Dictionary of National Biography* (2004), online at www.oxforddnb.com/view/article/19006.

Baker, J. H., 'Port, Sir John (c.1472–1540)', *Oxford Dictionary of National Biography* (2004), online at www.oxforddnb.com/view/article/22552.

Baldwin, J., *The Government of Philip Augustus: Foundations of French Royal Power in the Middle Ages* (Berkeley: University of California Press, 2004 [1986]).

Barbier, P., *The Age of Owain Gwynedd* (London: David Nutt, 1908).

Bardsley, Sandy, *Women's Roles in the Middle Ages* (Westport, CT: Greenwood Press, 2007).

Barrell, A. D. M., *Medieval Scotland* (Cambridge: Cambridge University Press, 2000).

Barron, Caroline M., *London in the Later Middle Ages: Government and People 1200–1500* (Oxford: Oxford University Press, 2004).

Barrow, G. W. S., *Feudal Britain* (London: Edward Arnold, 1956).

Barrow, G. W. S., *Kingship and Unity; Scotland 1000–1306* (Edinburgh: Edinburgh University Press, 1989).

Barrow, G. W. S., *Scotland and its Neighbours in the Middle Ages* (London and Rio Grande: Hambledon Press, 1992).

Bartlett, Robert, *The Making of Europe: Conquest, Colonization and Cultural Change, 950–1350* (London: Penguin, 1993).

Bartlett, Robert, *Gerald of Wales: A Voice of the Middle Ages* (Oxford: Clarendon Press, 1982).

Bartrum, Peter C., *Welsh Genealogies, AD 1400–1500*, 18 vols (Aberystwyth: National Library of Wales, 1983).

Beard, Brian L., and Clark M. Johnson, 'Strontium Isotope Composition of Skeletal Material Can Determine the Birth Place and Geographic Mobility of Humans and Animals', *Journal of Forensic Science*, 45.5 (2000), 1049–61.

Bellamy, John, *The Criminal Trial in Later Medieval England* (Toronto: University of Toronto Press, 1998).

Bibliography

Ben-David, Merav, and Elizabeth A. Flaherty, 'Stable Isotopes in Mammalian Research: a Beginner's Guide', *Journal of Mammalogy*, 93.2 (2012), 312–28.

Bentley, R. Alexander, 'Strontium Isotopes from the Earth to the Archaeological Skeleton: a Review', *Journal of Archaeological Method and Theory*, 13.3 (2006), 135–87.

Berry, John W., 'Acculturation', in Joan E. Grusec and Paul D. Hastings (eds), *Handbook of Socialization: Theory and Research* (New York: Rand McNally, 2007), pp. 543–60.

Besly, Edward, 'The Rogiet Hoard and the Coinage of Allectus', *British Numismatic Journal*, 76 (2006), 45–146, online at *www.britnumsoc.org/publications/Digital%20BNJ/pdfs/2006_BNJ_76_1_4.pdf*.

Bethard, Jonathan, 'Isotopes', in E. A. DiGangi and M. K. Moore (eds), *Research Methods in Human Skeletal Biology* (Oxford: Academic Press, 2013), pp. 425–47.

Biancalana, Joseph, *The Fee Tail and the Common Recovery in Medieval England, 1176–1502* (Cambridge: Cambridge University Press, 2001).

Bindoff, S. T., *The House of Commons, 1509–1558*, 3 vols (London: Secker and Warburg, 1982).

Bisson, T. N., *The Crisis of the Twelfth Century. Power, Lordship and the Origins of European Government* (Princeton: Princeton University Press, 2009).

Blumenthal, U., 'Papal registers in the twelfth century', in P. Linehan (ed.), *Proceedings of the Seventh International Congress of Medieval Canon Law*, Monumenta iuris canonici, Series C, Subsidia, 8 (Vatican City: BAV, 1988), pp. 135–51.

Bowen, E. G., 'Seafaring along the Pembrokeshire Coast in the Days of the Sailing Ships', *The Pembrokeshire Historian*, 4 (1972).

Bowen, Lloyd, 'Information, Language and Political Culture in Early Modern Wales', *Past and Present*, 228 (2015), 125–58.

Boyle, L. E., *A Survey of the Vatican Archives and of its Medieval Holdings* (Toronto: Pontifical Institute, 1972; rev. edn, 2001).

Bradbury, J., *Philip Augustus: King of France 1180–1223* (London: Longman, 1998).

Bradney, Joseph, *A History of Monmouthshire from the coming of the Normans into Wales down to the present time*, 5 vols (London: Mitchell Hughes and Clarke: 1904–23).

Brettell, R., J. Montgomery and J. Evans, 'Brewing and Stewing: the Effect of Culturally Mediated Behavior on the Oxygen Isotope Composition of Ingested Fluids and the Implications for Human Provenance Studies', *Journal of Analytic Atomic Spectroscopy*, 27 (2012), 778–85.

Bibliography

Brettell, Rhea, Jane Evans, Sonja Marzinzik, Angela Lamb and Janet Montgomery, '"Impious Easterners": can Oxygen and Strontium Isotopes serve as Indicators of Provenance in Early Medieval European Cemetery Populations?', *European Journal of Archaeology*, 15.1 (2012), 117–45.

Brocklehurst, H., and R. Philips (eds), *History, Nationhood and the Question of Britain* (Basingstoke: Palgrave-Macmillan, 2004).

Brough, G., 'Owain's Revolt? Glyn Dŵr's Role in the Outbreak of the Rebellion', *Studies In History, Archaeology, Religion and Conservation*, 2.1 (2015), 1–30.

Brough, G., *The Rise and Fall of Owain Glyn Dŵr: England, France and the Welsh Rebellion in the Late Middle Ages* (London: I. B. Tauris, 2017).

Brown, M., *The Black Douglases. War and Lordship in Late Medieval Scotland, 1300–1455* (East Linton: Tuckwell Press, 1998).

Brown, M., *The Wars of Scotland, 1214–1371* (Edinburgh: Edinburgh University Press, 2004).

Budd, P., C. Chenery, J. Montgomery, J. Evans and D. Powlesland, 'Anglo- Saxon residential mobility at West Heslerton, North Yorkshire, UK from combined O- and Sr-isotope analysis', in J. G. Holland and S. D. Tanner (eds), *Plasma Source Mass Spectrometry: Applications and Emerging Technologies* (Cambridge: Royal Society of Chemistry, 2003), pp. 195–208.

Budd, P., J. Montgomery, B. Barreiro and R. G. Thomas, 'Differential Diagenesis of Strontium in Archaeological Human Dental Tissues', *Applied Geochemistry*, 15 (2000), 687–94.

Burns, Robert I., *Muslims, Christians, and Jews in the Crusader Kingdom of Valencia* (Cambridge: Cambridge University Press, 1984).

Burton, J. H., and T. Douglas Price, 'Seeking the local $87Sr/86Sr$ ratio to determine geographic origins of humans', in R. Armitage et al. (eds), *Archaeological Chemistry VIII, ACS Symposium Series* (Washington, DC: American Chemical Society, 2013), pp. 309–20.

Burton, Janet, *Monastic and Religious Orders in Britain, 1000–1300* (Cambridge: Cambridge University Press, 1994).

Burton, Janet, and Karen Stöber, *Abbeys and Priories of Medieval Wales* (Cardiff: University of Wales Press, 2015).

Butler, Sara M., *Divorce in Medieval England: from One Persons to Two in Law* (New York: Routledge, 2013).

Campbell, Ewan, *Continental and Mediterranean Imports to Atlantic Britain and Ireland, AD 400–800*, CBA Research Report 157 (York: Council for British Archaeology, 2007).

Carr, A. D., 'Welshmen and the Hundred Years' War', *WHR*, 4 (1968), 21–46.

Carr, A. D., 'An Aristocracy in Decline', *WHR*, 5 (1970), 103–29.
Carr, A. D., *Owen of Wales: The End of the House of Gwynedd* (Cardiff: University of Wales Press, 1991).
Carr, A. D., 'The Coroner in Fourteenth Century Merioneth', *Journal of the Merioneth Historical and Record Society*, 11.3 (1992).
Carr, A. D., *Medieval Wales* (Basingstoke: Macmillan, 1995).
Carr, A. D., 'Inside the tent looking out: the medieval Welsh world view', in R. R. Davies and Geraint H. Jenkins (eds), *From Medieval to Modern Wales: Historical Essays in Honour of Kenneth O. Morgan and Ralph A. Griffiths* (Cardiff: University of Wales Press, 2004).
Carr, A. D., 'A Welsh Knight in the Hundred Years' War', *Trans. Hon. Soc. Cymm.* (1977), 40–53.
Cartwright, Jane, *Feminine Sanctity and Spirituality in Medieval Wales* (Cardiff: University of Wales Press, 2008).
Carver, Martin, 'Wasperton in context', in M. Carver, C. Hills and J. Scheschkewitz (eds), *Wasperton: A Roman, British and Anglo-Saxon Community in Central England* (Woodbridge: Boydell, 2009), pp. 127–40.
Cathcart-King, D., 'Henry II and the Fight at Coleshill', *WHR*, 2 (1964–5), 367–73.
Catto, J., 'Ideas and Experience in the Political Thought of Aquinas', *Past and Present*, 71 (1976), 3–21.
Cavendish, Richard, 'Owen Glendower's French Treaty', *History Today*, 54.6 (June 2004), 54–5.
Chadwick, Nora K., *Studies in the Early British Church* (Cambridge: Cambridge University Press, 1958).
Chamberlin, E. R., *The Count of Virtue, Giangaleazzo Visconti, Duke of Milan* (London: Eyre and Spottiswoode, 1965).
Champ, Judith, *The English Pilgrimage to Rome: A Dwelling for the Soul* (Leominster: Gracewing, 2000).
Chapman, A. J., 'The King's Welshmen: Welsh Involvement in the Expeditionary Army of 1415', *Journal of Medieval Military History*, 9 (2011), 41–64.
Chapman, A. J., '"He took me to the duke of York": Henry Griffith, a "Man of War"', in B. J. Lewis, A. P. Owen and D. F. Evans (eds), *'Gwalch Cywyddau Gwŷr': Essays on Guto'r Glyn and Fifteenth Century Wales* (Aberystwyth: Canolfan Uwchefrydiau Cymreig a Cheltaidd Prifysgol Cymru, 2013), pp. 103–34.
Chapman, Adam, 'Wales, Welshmen and the Hundred Years War', in L. J. Andrew Villalon and Donald J. Kagay (eds), *The Hundred Years War: Further Considerations* (Leiden: Brill, 2013), pp. 217–31.

Chapman, Adam, *Welsh Soldiers in the Later Middle Ages, 1282–1422* (Woodbridge: Boydell, 2015).

Charles-Edwards, T. M., *Wales and the Britons 350–1064* (Oxford: Oxford University Press, 2013).

Charles-Edwards, Thomas, 'Wales and Mercia, 613–918', in Michelle P. Brown and Carol Ann Farr (eds), *Mercia: an Anglo-Saxon Kingdom in Europe* (London: Continuum, 2001), pp. 88–105.

Ch'en, Paul Heng-chao, *Chinese Legal Tradition Under the Mongols: The Code of 1291 as Reconstructed* (Princeton: Princeton University Press, 1979).

Chenery, C., H. Eckardt and G. Müldner, 'Cosmopolitan Catterick? Isotopic Evidence for Population Mobility on Rome's Northern Frontier', *Journal of Archaeological Science*, 38 (2011), 1525–36.

Chenery, Carolyn, Gundula Müldner, Jane Evans, Hella Eckardt and Mary Lewis, 'Strontium and Stable Isotope Evidence for Diet and Mobility in Roman Gloucester, UK', *Journal of Archaeological Science*, 37 (2010), 150–63.

Cheney, C. R., 'King John and the Papal Interdict', *Bulletin of the John Rylands Library*, 31, (1948), 295–317.

Cheney, C. R., *The Study of the Medieval Papal Chancery*, The Edwards Lectures 2 (Glasgow: Jackson, 1966).

Cheney, C. R., *Pope Innocent III and England* (Stuttgart: Hiersemann, 1976).

Cheney, C. R., *The Papacy and England, 12th–14th Centuries* (London: Variorum, 1982).

Chotzen, T. M., *Recherches sur la poésie de Dafydd ap Gwilym, barde gallois du XIVe siècle* (Amsterdam: H. J. Paris, 1928).

Chotzen, T. M., 'Yvain de Galles in Alsace-Lorraine and Switzerland', *BBCS*, 4 (1928), 231–40.

Church, S. D. (ed.), *King John: New Interpretations* (Woodbridge: Boydell, 1999).

Clarke, Giles, *Winchester Studies 3: Pre-Roman and Roman Winchester, Part II: The Roman Cemetery at Lankhills* (Oxford: BAR, 1979).

Contamine, P., *Guerre, etat et société à la fin du Moyen Age: Etudes sur les armées des rois de France, 1337–1494* (Paris: Mouton, 1972).

Cooper, N. J., 'Searching for the blank generation: consumer choice in Roman and post-Roman Britain', in J. Webster and N. J. Cooper (eds), *Roman Imperialism: Post-Colonial Perspectives* (Leicester: School of Archaeological Studies, 1996), pp. 85–98.

Copplestone-Crow, Bruce, 'The Dual Nature of the Irish Colonization of Dyfed in the Dark Ages', *Studia Celtica*, 16/17 (1981/2), 1–24.

Bibliography

Cragg, Kenneth, *The Arab Christian: A History in the Middle East* (Louisville, KY: Westminster/John Knox Press, 1991).

Crone, Patricia, *God's Rule – Government and Islam: Six Centuries of Medieval Islamic Political Thought* (New York: Columbia University Press, 2005).

Crowder, C. M. D., *Unity, Heresy and Reform, 1378–1460: the Conciliar Response to the Great Schism* (London: Edward Arnold, 1977).

Curta, Florin (ed.), *Borders, Barriers and Ethnogenesis: Frontiers in Late Antiquity and the Middle Ages* (Turnhout: Brepols, 2005)

Cuttino, G. P., *English Medieval Diplomacy* (Bloomington: Indiana University Press, 1985).

Dark, Ken, *Britain and the End of the Roman Empire* (Stroud: The History Press, 2010).

Darling, W. G., A. H. Bath and J. C. Talbot, 'The O & H Stable Isotopic Composition of Fresh Waters in the British Isles. 2. Surface Waters and Groundwater', *Hydrology and Earth System Sciences*, 7.2 (2003), 183–95.

Darling, W. G., and J. C. Talbot, 'The O & H Stable Isotopic Composition of Fresh Waters in the British Isles. 1. Rainfall', *Hydrology and Earth System Sciences*, 7.2 (2003), 163–81.

Daux, V., C. Lécuyer, M. Héran, R. Amoit, L. Simon, F. Martineau, N. Lynnerup, H. Reychler and G. Escarguel, 'Oxygen Isotope Fractionation between Human Phosphate and Water Revisited', *Journal of Human Evolution*, 55 (2008), 1138–47.

Davies, J. C., 'Giraldus Cambrensis 1146–1946', *Archaeologia Cambrensis*, 99 (1946–7), 85–108 and 256–80.

Davies, J. R., *The Book of Llandaf and the Norman Church in Wales*, Studies in Celtic History 21 (Woodbridge: Boydell, 2003).

Davies, M. T., 'The Rhetoric of Gwilym Ddu's Awdlau to Sir Gruffudd Llwyd', *Studia Celtica*, 40 (2006).

Davies, R. G., 'Henry Despenser, d. 1406', *Oxford Dictionary of National Biography* (2008; subsequently updated), online at *www.oxforddnb.com/view/article/7551*.

Davies, R. R., *Lordship and Society in the March of Wales, 1282–1400* (Oxford: Oxford University Press, 1978).

Davies, R. R., 'Buchedd a Moes y Cymry'/'English Synopsis: the Manners and Morals of the Welsh', *WHR*, 12.2 (1984), 155–74, 174–9.

Davies, R. R., 'Lordship or Colony?', in J. Lydon (ed.), *The English in Medieval Ireland* (Dublin: Royal Irish Academy, 1984).

Davies, R. R., 'Race Relations in Post-Conquest Wales: Confrontation and Compromise', The Cecil Williams Lecture for 1973, *Trans. Hon. Soc. Cymm.* (1974/5), 32–56.

Davies, R. R., *The Revolt of Owain Glyn Dŵr* (Oxford: Oxford University Press, 1995).

Davies, R. R., *The Age of Conquest: Wales 1063–1415* (Oxford, 2000) [originally *Conquest, Coexistence, and Change: Wales 1063–1415* (Oxford: Oxford University Press, 1987)].

Davies, R. R., 'Mortimer, Roger (V), first earl of March (1287–1330)', *Oxford Dictionary of National Biography* (2008; subsequently updated), online at *www.oxforddnb.com/view/article/19354?docPos=1*.

Davies, Sean, *War and Society in Medieval Wales, 633–1283: Welsh Military Institutions* (Cardiff: University of Wales Press, 2004).

Davies, Wendy, *Wales in the Early Middle Ages* (Leicester: Leicester University Press, 1982).

Davies, Wendy, *Welsh History in the Early Middle Ages* (Aldershot: Variorum, 2009).

Davis, R. H. C., *History of Medieval Europe* (Harlow: Longman, 2006).

Davis, Virginia, 'Episcopal ordination lists as a source for clerical mobility in England in the fourteenth century', in N. Rogers (ed.), *England in the Fourteenth Century* (Stamford: Paul Watkins, 1993), pp. 152–70.

Davis, Virginia, 'Irish Clergy in Late Medieval England', *Irish Historical Studies*, 32.126 (2000), 145–60.

Davis, Virginia, *Clergy in London in the Late Middle Ages: A Register of Clergy Ordained in the Diocese of London Based on Episcopal Ordination Lists 1361–1539* (London: Centre for Metropolitan History, 2002).

de la Roncière, C., *Histoire de la marine Francaise, II: La guerre de cent ans: révolution maritime* (Paris: Plon-Nourrit, 1914).

Dickson, Gary, 'The Crowd at the Feet of Pope Boniface VIII: Pilgrimage, Crusade and the First Roman Jubilee (1300)', *JMH*, 25 (1999).

Dodd, G., and D. Biggs, *Henry IV: the Establishment of the Regime, 1399–1406* (Woodbridge: York Medieval Press in association with Boydell Press, 2003).

Dodd, G., and D. Biggs, *The Reign of Henry IV, Rebellion and Survival, 1403–1413* (York: York University Press, 2008).

Doig, J. A., 'The Prophecy of the "Six Kings to Follow John" and Owain Glyndŵr', *Studia Celtica*, 29 (1995), 257–67.

Donaldson, G., *The Auld Alliance; The Franco-Scottish Connection* (Edinburgh: Saltire Society – Institut Français d'Ecosse, 1985).

Duby, G., *France in the Middle Ages, 987–1460*, trans. J. Vale (Oxford: Blackwell, 1991 [1987]).

Duncan, A., *Scotland: the Making of the Kingdom* (Edinburgh: Oliver and Boyd, 1975)

Dunn, Caroline, *Stolen Women in Medieval England. Rape, Abduction and Adultery, 1100–1500* (Cambridge: Cambridge University Press, 2013).

Dunning, Robert W., 'Miles Salley, Bishop of Llandaff', *Journal of Welsh Ecclesiastical History*, 8 (1991).

Dyer, Alan, 'Appendix: ranking lists of English medieval towns', in D. M. Palliser (ed.), *The Cambridge Urban History of Britain Volume I: 600–1540* (Cambridge: Cambridge University Press, 2000), pp. 747–70.

Echard, Siân (ed.), *The Arthur of Medieval Latin Literature* (Cardiff: University of Wales Press, 2011).

Eckardt, H., C. Chenery, P. Booth, J. A. Evans, A. Lamb and G. Müldner, 'Oxygen and Strontium Isotope Evidence for Mobility in Roman Winchester', *Journal of Archaeological Science*, 36 (2009), 2816–25.

Eckardt, H., G. Müldner and G. Speed, 'The Late Roman Field Army in Northern Britain? Mobility, Material Culture, and Multi-isotope Analysis at Scorton (N. Yorks.)', *Britannia*, 46 (2015), 1–33.

Eckardt, Hella (ed.), *Roman Diasporas: Archaeological Approaches to Mobility and Diversity in the Roman Empire*, Journal of Roman Archaeology Monograph, Supplementary Series 78 (Portsmouth, Rhode Island: Journal of Roman Archaeology, 2010).

Edelby, Néophyte, 'The legislative autonomy of Christians in the Islamic world', in Robert G. Hoyland (ed.), *Muslims and Others in Early Islamic Society* (Burlington, VT: Ashgate, 2004), pp. 58–82.

Edwards, Huw M., *Dafydd ap Gwilym: Influences and Analogues* (Oxford: Clarendon Press, 1996).

Edwards, J. F., and B. P. Hindle, 'The Transportation System of Medieval England and Wales', *Journal of Historical Geography*, 17.2 (1991), 123–34.

Edwards, Nancy, 'Early medieval sculpture in South-West Wales: the Irish Sea connection', in Rachael Moss (ed.), *Making and Meaning in Insular Art* (Dublin: Four Courts Press, 2007), pp. 184–97.

Edwards, Nancy, and Alan Lane (eds), *The Early Church in Wales and the West* (Oxford: Oxbow, 1992).

Elrington, C. R., and N. M. Herbert (eds), *The Victoria History of the County of Gloucestershire* (Oxford: Oxford University Press, 1972).

Elton, Geoffrey, *Policy and Police: the Enforcement of the Reformation in the Age of Thomas Cromwell* (Cambridge: Cambridge University Press, 1985).

Elverskog, Johan, *Buddhism and Islam on the Silk Road* (Philadelphia: University of Pennsylvania Press, 2010).

Emden, A. B., *A Biographical Register of the University of Oxford to A.D. 1500*, 3 vols (Oxford: Oxford University Press, 1957–9).

Emden, A. B., *A Biographical Register of the University of Cambridge to A.D. 1500* (Cambridge: Cambridge University Press, 1963).

Bibliography

Emlyn, Rhun, 'Serving Church and state: the careers of medieval Welsh students', in Linda Clark (ed.), *The Fifteenth Century XI: Concerns and Preoccupations* (Woodbridge: Boydell, 2012), pp. 25–40.

Emon, Anver M., *Religious Pluralism and Islamic Law: Dhimmīs and Others in the Empire of Law* (Oxford: Oxford University Press, 2012).

Endicott-West, Elizabeth, *Mongolian Rule in China: Local Administration in the Yuan Dynasty* (Cambridge, MA: Harvard University Press, 1989).

Ercolani, G., D. Fiorani and G. Giammaria with D. Durante and I. Sanpietro, *La Badia della Gloria*, Monumenti di Anagni (Anagni: Istituto di storia e di arte del Lazio meridionale, 2001).

Evans, D. L., 'Some Notes on the Principality of Wales in the time of the Black Prince (1343–76)', *Trans. Hon. Soc. Cymm.* (1925–26), 25–110.

Evans, Daniel Simon, *Medieval Religious Literature* (Cardiff: University of Wales Press, 1986).

Evans, J., N. Stoodley and C. Chenery, 'A Strontium and Oxygen Isotope Assessment of a Possible Fourth Century Immigrant Population in a Hampshire Cemetery, southern England', *Journal of Archaeological Science*, 33 (2006), 265–72.

Evans, J. A., C. A. Chenery and J. Montgomery, 'A Summary of Strontium and Oxygen Isotope Variation in Archaeological Human Tooth Enamel excavated from Britain', *Journal of Analytical Atomic Spectrometry*, 27 (2012), 754–64.

Evans, J. A., J. Montgomery, G. Wildman and N. Boulton, 'Spatial Variations in Biosphere 87Sr/86Sr in Britain', *Journal of the Geological Society*, 167 (2010), 1–4.

Evans, J. A., and S. Tatham, 'Defining "Local Signature" in Terms of Sr Isotope Composition using a Tenth- to Twelfth-century Anglo-Saxon Population living on a Jurassic Clay-carbonate Terrain, Rutland, UK', *Geological Society, London, Special Publications*, 232 (2004), 237–48.

Evans, J. W., 'The bishops of St Davids from Bernard to Bec', in R. F. Walker (ed.), *Medieval Pembrokeshire*, Pembrokeshire County History 2 (Haverfordwest: Pembrokeshire Historical Society, 2002), pp. 270–311.

Evans, J. Wyn, 'St David and St Davids: some observations on the cult, site and buildings', in Jane Cartwright (ed.), *Celtic Hagiography and Saints' Cults* (Cardiff: University of Wales Press, 2003).

Evans, J. Wyn, and Jonathan M. Wooding (eds), *St David of Wales: Cult, Church and Nation* (Woodbridge: Boydell, 2007).

Evans, R. Wallis, 'Prophetic poetry', in A. O. H. Jarman and G. R. Jones (eds), *A Guide to Welsh Literature*, 2 vols (Cardiff: University of Wales Press, 1976–9), ii, pp. 278–97.

Bibliography

Eyton, R. W., *The Antiquities of Shropshire*, 12 vols (London: John Russell Smith, 1854–60).
Fattal, Antoine, 'How dhimmīs were judged in the Islamic world', in Robert G. Hoyland (ed.), *Muslims and Others in Early Islamic Society* (Burlington, VT: Ashgate, 2004), pp. 83–102.
Fenwick, H., *The Auld Alliance* (Kineton: The Roundwood Press, 1971).
Foucault, M., 'The Subject and Power,' *Critical Inquiry*, 8.4 (1982), 777–95.
Fowler, K. (ed.), *The Hundred Years War* (London: Macmillan, 1971).
Fowler, K. A., *Medieval Mercenaries, The Great Companies* (Oxford: Blackwell, 2001).
Frame, R., 'The Bruces in Ireland, 1315–18', *Irish Historical Studies*, 19 (1974), 3–37.
Franke, Herbert, 'The role of the state as a structural element in polyethnic societies', in S. R. Schram (ed.), *Foundations and Limits of State Power in China* (Hong Kong: The Chinese University Press, 1987).
Franke, Herbert, 'Chinese Law in a Multinational Society: the Case of the Liao (907–1125)', *Asia Major*, 5 (1992), 113–16.
Franke, Herbert, and Hok-lam Chan (eds), *Studies on the Jurchens and the Chin Dynasty* (Aldershot: Ashgate, 1997).
Frye, Richard, *The Golden Age of Persia: The Arabs in the East* (London: Weidenfeld and Nicolson, 1996).
Fulton, Helen, *Dafydd ap Gwilym in the European Context* (Cardiff: University of Wales Press, 1989).
Fulton, Helen, 'Tenth-century Wales and *Armes Prydein*', *Trans. Hon. Soc. Cymm.*, n.s. 7 (2001), 5–18.
Fulton, Helen, 'Owain Glyndŵr and the Uses of Prophecy', *Studia Celtica*, 39 (2005), 105–21.
Fulton, Helen (ed.), *A Companion to Arthurian Literature* (Oxford: Blackwell, 2009).
Fulton, Helen, 'Fairs, feast-days and carnival in Medieval Wales: some poetic evidence', in Helen Fulton (ed.), *Urban Culture in Medieval Wales* (Cardiff: University of Wales Press, 2012), pp. 238–44.
Fulton, Helen, 'Guto'r Glyn and the Wars of the Roses', in B. J. Lewis, A. P. Owen and D. F. Evans (eds), *'Gwalch Cywyddau Gwŷr': Essays on Guto'r Glyn and Fifteenth Century Wales* (Aberystwyth: Canolfan Uwchefrydiau Cymreig a Cheltaidd Prifysgol Cymru, 2013), pp. 53–68.
Fulton, Helen, 'Translating Europe in medieval Wales', in Aidan Conti, Orietta de Rold and Philip Shaw (eds), *Writing Europe 500–1450: Texts and Contexts* (Cambridge: D. S. Brewer, 2015).
Fulton, Helen, 'Poetry and nationalism in the reign of Edward I: Wales and Ireland', in P. Crooks, D. Green and M. Ormrod (eds), *The*

Plantagenet Empire, 1259–1453, Proceedings of the 2014 Harlaxton Symposium (Donington: Shaun Tyas, 2016), pp. 169–70.
Gabriel, J. R., 'Wales and the Avignon Papacy', *Archaeologia Cambrensis*, 78 (1923), 70–86.
Galliou, P., and M. Jones, *The Bretons* (Oxford: Blackwell, 1991).
Garcia, Michael, 'Gildas and the "Grievous Divorce from the Barbarians"', *EME*, 21.3 (2013), 243–53.
Geary, P. J., *The Myth of Nations: The Medieval Origins of Europe* (Princeton: Princeton University Press, 2003).
German, Gary, 'L'"Armes Prydein Fawr" et "La Bataille de Brunanburgh": les relations géopolitiques entre Bretons, Anglo-Saxons et Scandinaves dans la Bretagne insulaire du Xe siècle', in Magali Coumert and Yvon Tranvouez (eds), *Landévennec, les Vikings et la Bretagne: en hommage à Jean-Christophe Cassard* (Brest: Editions du CRBC, 2015), pp. 171–209.
Gerrard, James, *The Ruin of Roman Britain: An Archaeological Perspective* (Cambridge: Cambridge University Press, 2013).
Glick, Thomas, *Islamic and Christian Spain* (Leiden: Brill, 2005).
Goering, J., and H. Pryce, 'The *De Modo Contifendi* of Cadwgan, Bishop of Bangor', *Mediaeval Studies*, 62 (2000), 1–27.
Goitein, S. D., *Jews and Arabs: A Concise History of their Social and Cultural Relations* (New York: Schocken, 1974).
Goitein, S. D., 'Minority self-rule and government control in Islam', in Robert G. Hoyland (ed.), *Muslims and Others in Early Islamic Society* (Burlington, VT: Ashgate, 2004).
Goldberg, Jeremy, *Communal Discord, Child Abduction and Rape in the Later Middle Ages* (Basingstoke: Palgrave, 2008).
Golding, Brian, 'Transborder Transactions: Patterns of Patronage in Anglo-Norman Wales', *The Haskins Society Journal*, 16 (2005), 27–46.
Gough, Henry, *Itinerary of King Edward I throughout his reign A.D. 1272–1307, exhibiting his movements from time to time so far as they are recorded*, 2 vols (Paisley: Alexander Gardner, 1900).
Gravdal, Kathryn, *Ravishing Maidens: Writing Rape in Medieval French Literature and Law* (Philadelphia: University of Pennsylvania Press, 1991).
Gray, Madeleine, 'The pre-reformation church', in R. A. Griffiths (ed.), *The Gwent County History, vol. 2: The Age of the Marcher Lords* (Cardiff: University of Wales Press, 2008).
Green, Thomas Andrew, *Verdict According to Conscience: Perspectives on the English Criminal Trial Jury, 1200–1800* (Chicago: University of Chicago Press, 1985).
Griffith, Sidney H., *The Church in the Shadow of the Mosque: Christians and Muslims in the World of Islam* (Princeton: Princeton University Press, 2008).

Bibliography

Griffiths, R. A., 'Some Partisans of Owain Glyn Dŵr at Oxford', *BBCS*, 20 (1962–4), 282–92.

Griffiths, R. A., 'Some Secret Supporters of Owain Glyn Dŵr?', *BBCS*, 20 (1962–4), 77–100.

Griffiths, R. A., *The Principality of Wales in the Later Middle Ages: The Structure and Personnel of Government*, volume I: *South Wales, 1277–1536* (Cardiff: University of Wales Press, 1972).

Griffiths, Ralph A., 'The Glyndwr Rebellion in North Wales through the Eyes of an Englishman', *BBCS*, 22 (1966–8), 151–68.

Griffiths, Ralph A., *King and Country: England and Wales in the Fifteenth Century* (London: Hambledon, 1991).

Griffiths, Ralph A., *Conquerors and Conquered in Medieval Wales* (Stroud and New York: Sutton/St Martin's Press, 1994).

Griffiths, Ralph A., 'After Glyn Dŵr: An Age of Reconciliation?', *Proceedings of the British Academy*, 117 (2002), 139–64.

Griffiths, Ralph A. (ed.), *The Fourteenth and Fifteenth Centuries* (Oxford: Oxford University Press, 2003).

Griffiths, Ralph A., 'Owain Glyn Dŵr's Invasion of the Central March of Wales in 1402: the Evidence of Clerical Taxation', *Studia Celtica*, 46 (2012), 111–22.

Griffiths, Ralph A., 'The Significance of St Davids and its Bishops during the Fifteenth Century', *WHR*, 27.4 (2015), 672–706.

Griffiths, Rh., 'Mwy o Gymro na Iorciad' [More Welshman than Yorkist] in B. J. Lewis, A. P. Owen and D. F. Evans (eds), *'Gwalch Cywyddau Gwŷr': Essays on Guto'r Glyn and Fifteenth Century Wales* (Aberystwyth: Canolfan Uwchefrydiau Cymreig a Cheltaidd Prifysgol Cymru, 2013), pp. 69–82.

Groom, Polly, Duncan Schlee, Gwilym Hughes, Pete Crane, Neil Ludlow and Ken Murphy, 'Two Early Medieval Cemeteries in Pembrokeshire: Brownslade Barrow and West Angle Bay', *Archaeologica Cambrensis*, 160 (2011), 133–203.

Gruffydd, K. Lloyd, 'Maritime Wales' Export Trade in the Later Middle Ages', *Maritime Wales*, 21 (2000), 23–44.

Guard, Timothy, *Chivalry, Kingship and Crusade: the English Experience in the Fourteenth Century* (Woodbridge: Boydell, 2013).

Guichard, Pierre, *Al-Andalus (711–1492)* (Paris: Hachette 2000).

Gwynn, A., 'Ireland and the English Nation at the Council of Constance', *Proc. of the Royal Irish Academy*, 45 (1939), 183–233.

Gwynn, W. S., *Welsh National Dance and Music* (London: Curwen, 1932).

Hagger, Mark, *The Fortunes of a Norman Family: the de Verduns in England, Ireland and Wales, 1066–1316* (Dublin: Four Courts Press, 2001).

Hakenbeck, Susanne, 'Potentials and Limitations of Isotope Analysis in Early Medieval Archaeology', *Post-Classical Archaeologies*, 3 (2013), 109–25.

Halloran, Kevin, 'Welsh Kings at the English Court, 928–956', *WHR*, 25.3 (2011), 297–313.

Halsall, Guy, 'Ethnicity and Early Medieval Cemeteries', *Arqueologia y Territorio Medieval*, 18 (2011), 18–21.

Harper-Bill, C., and N. Vincent (eds), *Henry II, New Interpretations* (Woodbridge: Boydell, 2007).

Hartwell-Jones, G., *Celtic Britain and the Pilgrim Movement* (London: Honourable Society of the Cymmrodorion, 1912).

Harvey, L. P., *Islamic Spain, 1250–1500* (Chicago: University of Chicago Press, 1990).

Harvey, Margaret M., *The English in Rome, 1362–1420: Portrait of an Expatriate Community* (Cambridge: Cambridge University Press, 1999).

Hays, Rh. W., *The History of the Abbey of Aberconway* (Cardiff: University of Wales Press, 1963).

Hays, Rh. W., 'Welsh Students at Oxford and Cambridge Universities in the Middle Ages', *WHR*, 4.4 (1969), 325–61.

Heath, Peter, *The English Parish Clergy on the Eve of the Reformation* (London: Routledge & Kegan Paul, 1969).

Hemer, K. A., 'Are we nearly there yet? Children and migration in early medieval Britain', in D. M. Hadley and K. A. Hemer (eds), *Medieval Childhood: Archaeological Approaches*, Childhood in the Past Monograph Series 3 (Oxford: Oxbow Books, 2014), pp. 131–44.

Hemer, K. A., J. A. Evans, C. A. Chenery and A. L. Lamb, 'Evidence of Early Medieval Trade and Migration between Wales and Mediterranean Sea Region', *Journal of Archaeological Science*, 40 (2013), 2352–9.

Hemer, K. A., J. A. Evans, C. A. Chenery and A. L. Lamb, 'No Man is an Island: Evidence of pre-Viking Age Migration to the Isle of Man', *Journal of Archaeological Science*, 52 (2014), 242–9.

Henken, E. R., *National Redeemer, Owain Glyndŵr in Welsh Tradition* (Cardiff: University of Wales Press, 1996).

Henken, Elissa, *The Welsh Saints: A Study in Patterned Lives* (Cambridge: D. S. Brewer, 1991).

Higham, Nicholas, *Rome, Britain and the Anglo-Saxons* (London: Seaby, 1992).

Hill, Michael, 'Ethnic Administration and Dichotomization in a Eurasian Context: Wales, c.1100–1350CE', *WHR*, 27.2 (2014), 175–213.

Hindle, B. P., 'The Road Network of Medieval England and Wales', *Journal of Historical Geography*, 2.3 (1976), 207–21.

Hines, John, 'Welsh and English: Mutual Origins in Post-Roman Britain?' *Studia Celtica*, 34 (2000), 81–104.

Hitchcock, Richard, *Mozarabs in Medieval and Early Modern Spain* (Aldershot: Ashgate, 2008).

Holbrook, Neil, and Alan Thomas, 'An Early-medieval Monastic Cemetery at Llandough, Glamorgan: Excavations in 1994', *Medieval Archaeology*, 49 (2005), 1–92.

Holden, B., *Lords of the Central Marches English Aristocracy and Frontier Society, 1087–1265* (Oxford: Oxford University Press, 2008).

Holmes, Claire, and Keith Lilley, 'Viking Swansea', at www.medievalswansea.ac.uk/en/context/viking-swansea/.

Hosler, D., *Henry II, A Medieval Soldier at War, 1147–1189* (Leiden: Brill, 2007).

Hughes, S. S., A. R. Millard, S. J. Lucy, C. A. Chenery, J. A. Evans, G. Nowell and D. G. Pearson, 'Anglo-Saxon Origins Investigated by Isotopic Analysis of Burials from Berinsfield, Oxfordshire, UK', *Journal of Archaeological Science*, 42 (2014), 81–92.

Hurlock, Kathryn, *Crusades and Crusading in the Welsh Annalistic Chronicles*, Trivium Occasional Series, no. 5 (Lampeter: Trivium Publications, 2009).

Hurlock, Kathryn, 'Power, Preaching and the Crusades in *Pura Walia* c.1180–1280', *Thirteenth Century England*, 11 (2009), 94–108.

Hurlock, Kathryn, *Wales and the Crusades, c.1095–1291*, Studies in Welsh History 33 (Cardiff: University of Wales Press, 2011).

Hurlock, Kathryn, *Britain, Ireland and the Crusades, c.1000–1300* (Basingstoke: Palgrave, 2013).

Hurlock, Kathryn, 'The Norman influence on crusading from England and Wales', in Kathryn Hurlock and Paul Oldfield (eds), *Crusading and Pilgrimage in the Norman World* (Woodbridge: Boydell, 2015), pp. 65–80.

Ives, E. W., '"Agaynst taking awaye of women": the inception and operation of the abduction act of 1487', in E. W. Ives, R. J. Knecht and J. J. Scarisbrick (eds), *Wealth and Power in Tudor England: essays presented to S. T. Bindoff* (London: Athlone Press, 1978).

Jankulak, Karen, Thomas O'Loughlin and Jonathan M. Wooding (eds), *Ireland and Wales in the Middle Ages* (Dublin: Four Courts, 2007).

Jankulak, Karen, 'The absent saint: St Samson in Wales', in J.-C. Cassard et al. (eds), *Mélanges offerts au professeur Bernard Merdrignac* (*Britannia Monastica* 17, Landevennec, 2013), pp. 197–212.

Jarman, A., 'Wales and the Council of Constance', *BBCS*, 14 (1951), 220–2.

Jarman, A. O. H., and G. R. Hughes (eds), *Guide to Welsh Literature* (Swansea: Davies, 1976).

Jenkins, Dafydd, and Morfydd Owen (eds), *The Welsh Law of Women: studies presented to Daniel Binchy on his eightieth birthday* (Cardiff: University of Wales Press, 1980).

Jing-shen, Tao, *The Jurchen in Twelfth-Century China: A Study of Sinicization* (Seattle: University of Washington Press, 1977).

Jones, E. D., 'Cartre Gruffudd Gryg', *National Library of Wales Journal*, 10 (1957–8).

Jones, Francis, 'Knights of the Holy Sepulchre', *Journal of the Historical Society of the Church in Wales*, 26 (1979).

Jones, J. Gwynfor (ed.), *Sir John Wynn: History of the Gwydir family, and Memoirs* (Llandysul: Gomer Press, 1990).

Jones, J. Gwynfor, *Wales and the Tudor State: Government, Religious Change and the Social Order, 1534–1603* (Cardiff: University of Wales Press, 1989).

Jones, M., *Ducal Brittany, 1364–1399: Relations with England and France during the Reign of Duke John IV* (London: Oxford University Press, 1970).

Jones, M. A., 'Cultural Boundaries within the Tudor State: Bishop Rowland Lee and the Welsh Settlement of 1536', *WHR*, 20.2 (2000), 227–53.

Jones, Michael, 'Lee, Rowland (c.1487–1543)', *Oxford Dictionary of National Biography* (2004), online at *www.oxforddnb.com/view/article/16307*.

Jones, T., 'A Welsh Chronicler in Tudor England', *WHR*, 1 (1960–3), 1–17.

Kagay, D. J., 'Disposable Alliances: Aragon and Castile during the War of the Two Pedros and Beyond', *Albany State University Papers* (2010), online at: *www.medievalists.net/2011/08/11/disposable-alliances-aragon-and-castille-during-the-war-of-the-two-pedros-and-beyond/*, pp. 1–69.

Kalinke, Marianne E. (ed.), *The Arthur of the North: The Arthurian Legend in the Northern and Rus' Realms* (Cardiff: University of Wales Press, 2011).

Kaye, J. M., *Medieval English Conveyances* (Cambridge: Cambridge University Press, 2009).

Kinoshita, Sharon, 'Colonial possessions: Wales and the Anglo-Norman imaginary in the *Lais* of Marie de France', in Albrecht Classen (ed.), *Discourses on Love, Marriage and Transgression in Medieval and Early Modern Literature* (Tempe, AZ: Arizona University Press, 2004), pp. 147–62.

Kirby, D. P., *The Earliest English Kings* (London: Routledge, 1991).

Knowles, C. H., 'Savoy, Boniface of (1206/7–70)', *Oxford Dictionary of National Biography* (2004), online at *www.oxforddnb.com/view/article/2844?docPos=1*.

Laidlaw, J. (ed.), *The Auld Alliance, France and Scotland over 700 years* (Edinburgh: Edinburgh University Press, 1999).

Lapidus, Ira M., *A History of Islamic Societies* (Cambridge: Cambridge University Press, 2002).
Latimer, P., 'Henry II's Campaign against the Welsh in 1165', *WHR*, 14.4 (1989), 523–52.
Leach, S., M. Lewis, C. Chenery, G. Müldner and H. Eckardt, 'Migration and Diversity in Roman Britain: a Multidisciplinary Approach to the Identification of Immigrants in Roman York, England', *American Journal of Physical Anthropology*, 140 (2009), 546–61.
Lepine, David, *A Brotherhood of Canons Serving God: English Secular Cathedrals in the Later Middle Ages* (Woodbridge: Boydell, 1995).
Lepine, David, '"Loose canons": the mobility of higher clergy in the later Middle Ages', in Peregrine Horden (ed.), *Freedom of Movement in the Middle Ages: Proceedings of the 2003 Harlaxton Composium* (Donington: Shaun Tyas, 2007), pp. 86–103.
Levinson, A. A., B. Luz and Y. Kolodny, 'Variations in Oxygen Isotopic Compositions of Human Teeth and Urinary Stones', *Applied Geochemistry*, 2 (1987), 367–71.
Levy-Rubin, Milka, 'Shurūṭ 'Umar and its Alternatives: the Legal Debate on the Status of the Dhimmīs', *Jerusalem Studies in Arabic and Islam*, 30 (2005).
Levy-Rubin, Milka, *Non-Muslims in the Early Islamic Empire: From Surrender to Coexistence* (Cambridge: Cambridge University Press, 2011).
Lewis, B. J., A. P. Owen and D. F. Evans (eds), *'Gwalch Cywyddau Gwŷr': Essays on Guto'r Glyn and Fifteenth Century Wales* (Aberystwyth: Canolfan Uwchefrydiau Cymreig a Cheltaidd Prifysgol Cymru, 2013).
Lewis, Barry, 'Late Medieval Welsh Praise Poetry and Nationality: The Military Career of Guto'r Glyn Revisited', *Studia Celtica*, 45 (2011), 113–18.
Lewis, N. B., 'The English forces in Flanders, August–November 1297', in R. N. Hunt, W. H. Pantin and R. W. Southern (eds), *Studies in Medieval History Presented to F.M. Powicke* (Oxford: Clarendon Press, 1948), pp. 310–18.
Lewis, S., 'Gyrfa filwrol Guto'r Glyn', in J. E. Caerwyn Williams (ed.), *Ysgrifau Beirniadol IX* (Denbigh: Gee Press, 1976).
Lloyd, H. A., 'Wales and Star Chamber', *WHR*, 5 (1971), 257–60.
Lloyd, J. E., *A History of Wales from the Earliest Times to the Edwardian Conquest*, 2 vols (London: Longman, 1911–12; repr. 1939 and 1948).
Lloyd, J. E., *Owen Glendower* (Oxford: Oxford University Press, 1931; repr. Felinfach: Llanerch Press, 1992).
Lloyd, Nesta, and Morfydd E. Owen (eds), *Drych yr Oesoedd Canol* (Cardiff: University of Wales Press, 1986).

Lloyd-Morgan, C., 'From Ynys Wydrin to Glasynbri: Glastonbury in the Welsh vernacular tradition', in L. Abrams and J. P. Carley (eds), *The Archaeology and History of Glastonbury Abbey, Essays in honour of the ninetieth birthday of C.A. Raleigh Radford* (Woodbridge: Boydell, 1991).

Lloyd-Morgan, Ceridwen, 'Manuscripts and the monasteries', in Janet Burton and Karen Stöber (eds), *Monastic Wales: New Approaches* (Cardiff: University of Wales Press, 2011).

Loengard, J. S. (ed.), *Magna Carta and the England of King John* (Woodbridge: Boydell, 2010).

Longinelli, A., and E. Selmo, 'Oxygen Isotopes in Mammal Bone Phosphate: a New Tool for Palaeohydrological and Palaeoclimatological Research', *Geochimica et Cosmochimica Acta*, 48 (1984), 385–90.

Loomis, L. R., 'Nationality at the Council of Constance: An Anglo-French Dispute', *American Historical Review*, 44.3 (1939), 508–27.

Lower, Michael, *The Barons' Crusade: a Call to Arms and its Consequences* (Philadelphia: University of Pennsylvania Press, 2005).

Lunt, W. E., 'A Papal Tenth Levied in the British Isles from 1274–1280', *EHR*, 32 (1917), 49–89.

Lunt, W. E., *Papal Revenue in the Middle Ages*, 2 vols, Records of Civilization 19 (New York: Columbia University Press, 1934).

Lunt, W. E., *Financial Relations of the Papacy with England to 1327*, Studies in Anglo-Papal relations during the Middle Ages 1 (Cambridge: Cambridge University Press, 1939).

McDonald, R. A., *Manx Kingship in its Irish Sea Setting 1187–1229: King Rögnvaldr and the Crovan dynasty* (Dublin: Four Courts Press, 2007).

Macdougall, N., *An Antidote to the English: The Auld Alliance, 1295–1560* (East Linton: Tuckwell Press, 2001).

MacFarlane, L., 'The Vatican Archives', *Archives*, 4 (1959), 29–44, 84–101.

McSheffrey, Shannon, 'Detective Fiction in the Archives: Court Records and the Uses of the Law in Late Medieval England', *History Workshop Journal*, 65 (2008), 65–78.

McSheffrey, Shannon, and Julia Pope, 'Ravishment, Legal Narratives and Chivalric Culture in Fifteenth-Century England', *Journal of British Studies*, 48.4 (2009).

Marchant, A., *The Revolt of Owain Glyndŵr in Medieval English Chronicles* (Woodbridge: Boydell, 2014).

Marsden, R. A., 'Gerald of Wales and Competing Interpretations of the Welsh Middle Ages *c*.1870–1910', *WHR*, 25.3 (2011), 314–45.

Matonis, A. T. E., 'Traditions of Panegyric in Welsh Poetry: The Heroic and Chivalric', *Speculum*, 53 (1978), 667–87.

Matthews, T., 'Welsh Records in Foreign Libraries', *Transactions of the Cardiff Naturalists' Society*, 43 (1910), 20–31.

Maund, K., *The Welsh Kings. Warriors, Warlords and Princes* (Stroud: Tempus, 2000).

Meisel, Janet, *Barons of the Welsh Frontier: the Corbet, Pantulf and FitzWarin Families, 1066–1272* (Lincoln, NB and London: University of Nebraska Press, 1980).

Metcalfe, Alex, *The Muslims of Medieval Italy* (Edinburgh: Edinburgh University Press, 2009).

Metcalfe, Alex, *Muslims and Christians in Norman Sicily* (London: Routledge, 2011).

Mikhail, Maged S. A., *From Byzantine to Islamic Egypt: Religion, Identity and Politics after the Conquest* (London: I. B. Tauris, 2014).

Montgomery, Janet, Jane Evans and Carolyn Chenery, 'Strontium and oxygen isotope analysis of burials from Wasperton, Warwickshire', in M. Carver (ed.), *Wasperton Anglo-Saxon Cemetery* [data set] (York: Archaeology Data Service, 2008). DOI: 10.5284/1000052.

Montgomery, Janet, 'Passports from the Past: Investigating Human Dispersals using Strontium Isotope Analysis of Tooth Enamel', *Annals of Human Biology*, 37.3 (2010), 325–46.

Moore, D., *The Welsh Wars of Independence* (Stroud: Tempus, 2005).

Moreland, John, 'Going Native, becoming German: Isotopes and Identities in Late Roman and Early Medieval England', *Postmedieval: A Journal of Medieval Cultural Studies*, 1.1/2 (2010), 142–9.

Morgan, P., 'Elis Gruffudd of Gronant: Tudor Chronicler Extraordinary', *Flintshire Historical Society Journal*, 25 (1975–6), 9–20.

Mortimer, I., 'The Death of Edward II in Berkeley Castle', *EHR*, 120 (2005), 1175–1214.

Mote, Frederick, 'Chinese Society under Mongol Rule, 1215–1368', in Herbert Franke and Denis Twitchett (eds), *The Cambridge History of China: Alien Regimes and Border States* (Cambridge: Cambridge University Press, 1994), pp. 629–32.

Mote, Frederick, *Imperial China, 900–1800* (Cambridge, MA: Harvard University Press, 2003).

Ní Chléirigh, Léan, '*Nova peregrinatio*: the First Crusade as a pilgrimage in contemporary Latin narratives', in Marcus Bull and Damien Kempf (eds), *Writing the Early Crusades: Text, Transmission and Memory* (Woodbridge: Boydell, 2014), pp. 63–74.

Nice, Jason, *Sacred History and National Identity: Comparisons between Early Modern Wales and Brittany* (London: Routledge, 2009).

Nicholson, H. J., 'Margaret de Lacy and the Hospital of St John at Aconbury', *JEccH*, 50 (1999), 629–51.

Nicolas, N. H., *History of the Royal Navy* (London: Bentley, 1847).
Norgate, K., *John Lackland* (London: Macmillan, 1902).
Norris, M. M., 'Brydges, John, first Baron Chandos (1492–1557)', *Oxford Dictionary of National Biography* (2004), online at *www.oxforddnb.com/view/article/3807*.
Olson, Katherine K., '"Ar Ffordd Pedr a Phawl": Welsh Pilgrimage and Travel to Rome *c*.1200–*c*.1530', *WHR*, 24.2 (2008), 1–40.
Over, Kristen Lee, *Kingship, Conquest and* Patria: *Literary and Cultural Identities in Medieval French and Welsh Arthurian Romance* (New York and Abingdon: Routledge, 2005)
Owen, E., 'Owain Lawgoch – Yeuain de Galles: Some Facts and Suggestions', *Trans. Hon. Soc. Cymm.* (1899–1900), 6–106.
Owen, E., 'Owain Lawgoch – A Rejoinder', *Trans. Hon. Soc. Cymm.* (1900–1), 98–113.
Pacaut, M., *Louis VII et son royaume* (Paris: SEVPEN, 1964).
Pacaut, M., *Frederick Barbarossa*, trans. A. Pomerans (London: Collins, 1970).
Padilla, Amado M. (ed.), *Acculturation: Theory, Models and Some New Findings* (Boulder, CO: Westview Press, 1980).
Pennington, K., *Pope and Bishops* (Philadelphia: University of Pennsylvania Press, 1984).
Petts, David, 'Cemeteries and boundaries in western Britain', in S. Lucy and A. Reynolds (eds), *Burial in Early Medieval England and Wales*, Society for Medieval Archaeology Monograph Series 17 (London: Society for Medieval Archaeology, 2002), pp. 23–46.
Petts, David, 'Burial in western Britain, AD 400–800: late antique or early medieval?', in R. Collins and J. Gerrard (eds), *Debating Late Antiquity in Britain*, BAR British Series 365 (Oxford: Archaeopress, 2004), pp. 77–88.
Phinney, Jean S., 'Ethnic identity and acculturation', in Kevin M. Chun et al. (eds), *Acculturation: Advances in Theory, Measurement, and Applied Research* (Washington, DC: American Psychological Association, 2003), pp. 63–82.
Pohl, Walter, 'Introduction: strategies of distinction', in W. Pohl and H. Reimitz (eds), *Strategies of Distinction: The Construction of Ethnic Communities, 300–800* (Leiden: Brill, 1998), pp. 1–15.
Polk, Dora, *A Book Called Hiraeth* (Port Talbot: Alun Books, 1982).
Poole, R. L., *Lectures on the History of the Papal Chancery* (Cambridge: Cambridge University Press, 1915).
Post, J. B., 'Sir Thomas West and the Statute of Rapes, 1382', *Bulletin of the Institute of Historical Research*, 53 (1980), 24–30.

Bibliography

Post, J. B., 'Jury lists and juries in the later fourteenth century', in J. S. Cockburn and Thomas A. Green (eds), *Twelve Good Men and True: the Criminal Trial Jury in England, 1200–1800* (Princeton: Princeton University Press, 2014).

Powell, David, *The Historie of Cambria, now called Wales* (London: Rafe Newberie and Henry Denham, 1584).

Powell, Edward, 'Jury trial at gaol delivery in the late middle ages: the Midland circuit, 1400–1429', in J. S. Cockburn and Thomas A. Green (eds), *Twelve Good Men and True: the Criminal Trial Jury in England, 1200–1800* (Princeton: Princeton University Press, 2014).

Powell, J. M. (ed.), *Innocent III, Vicar of Christ or Lord of the World?* (2nd edn, Washington DC: Catholic University Press, 1994).

Power, Daniel, 'The Briouze Family in the Thirteenth and Early Fourteenth Centuries: Inheritance Strategies, Lordship and Identity', *JMH*, 41.3 (2015), 341–61.

Powicke, M., *The Loss of Normandy, 1189–1204* (Manchester: Manchester University Press, 1961).

Prestwich, M., 'Welsh infantry in Flanders in 1297', in R. A. Griffiths and P. R. Schofield (eds), *Wales and the Welsh in the Middle Ages: Essays presented to J. Beverley Smith* (Cardiff: University of Wales Press, 2011), pp. 56–69.

Pryce, H., *Native Law and the Church in Medieval Wales* (Oxford: Oxford University Press, 1993).

Pryce, H., 'Owain Gwynedd and Louis VII: The Franco-Welsh Diplomacy of the First Prince of Wales', *WHR*, 19.1 (1998), 1–28.

Pryce, H., 'Lawbooks and Literacy in Medieval Wales', *Speculum*, 75.1 (2000), 29–67.

Pryce, H., 'Welsh rulers and European change, c.1100–1282', in H. Pryce and J. Watts (eds), *Power and Identity in the Middle Ages: Essays in Memory of Rees Davies* (Oxford: Oxford University Press, 2007), pp. 37–51.

Pryce, H., and J. Watts (eds), *Power and Identity in the Middle Ages. Essays in Memory of Rees Davies (Oxford: Oxford university Press, 2007)*.

Pugh, T. B. (ed.), *Glamorgan County History, vol. III* (Cardiff: University of Wales Press, 1971).

Reames, S. L., 'Reconstructing and Interpreting a Thirteenth-Century Office for the Translation of Thomas Becket', *Speculum*, 80 (2005), 118–70.

Redknap, Mark, 'Glitter in the dragon's lair: Irish and Anglo-Saxon metalwork from pre-Viking Wales', in James A. Graham-Campbell and Michael Ryan (eds), *Anglo-Saxon/Irish Relations before the Vikings, Proceedings of the British Academy*, 157 (Oxford: Oxford University Press, 2009), pp. 281–310.

Rees, E. A., *Welsh Outlaws and Bandits, Political Rebellion and Lawlessness in Wales, 1400–1603* (Birmingham: Caterwen Press, 2001).

Rees, E. A., *A Life of Guto'r Glyn* (Tal-y-bont: Y Lolfa, 2008).

Richards, Gwenyth, *Welsh Noblewomen in the Thirteenth Century: An Historical Study of Medieval Welsh Law and Gender Roles* (Lewiston, NY, Queenstown, ON and Lampeter: Edwin Mellen Press, 2009).

Riley-Smith, Jonathan, 'Government and the indigenous in the Latin Kingdom of Jerusalem', in David Abulafia and Nora Berend (eds), *Medieval Frontiers* (Burlington, VT: Ashgate, 2002), pp. 126–30.

Roberts, Brynley F., 'Einion Offeiriad (d. 1353?)', *Oxford Dictionary of National Biography* (2004), online at www.oxforddnb.com/view/article/48544.

Roberts, Brynley F., 'Gruffudd, Elis (b. c.1490, d. in or after 1556)', *Oxford Dictionary of National Biography* (2004), online at www.oxforddnb.com/view/article/56714.

Robinson, W. R. B., 'Sir Hugh Johnys: a fifteenth century Welsh Knight', *Morgannwg*, 14 (1970).

Robinson, W. R. B., 'Sir William Morgan of Pencoed (d.1542) and the Morgans of Tredegar and Machen in Henry VIII's Reign', *National Library of Wales Journal*, 27.4 (1992), 405–29.

Rose, Richard B., 'Islam and the Development of Personal Status Laws among Christian Dhimmis: Motives, Sources, Consequences', *The Muslim World*, 72.3–4 (1982).

Rousseau, Marie-Hélène, *Saving the Souls of Medieval London: Perpetual Chantries at St Paul's Cathedral, c.1200–1548* (Farnham: Ashgate, 2011).

Rowlands, Eurys, 'The Continuing Tradition', in A. O. H. Jarman and Gwilym Rees Hughes (eds), *A Guide to Welsh Literature, Volume 2 1282–c.1550* (Cardiff: University of Wales Press, 1997).

Rowlands, I. W., '"Warriors fit for a prince": Welsh troops in Angevin service, 1154–1216', in John France (ed.), *Mercenaries and Paid Men: the Mercenary Identity in the Middle Ages* (Leiden: Brill, 2008), pp. 207–30.

Sassier, Y., *Louis VII* (Paris: Fayard, 1991).

Saul, N. (ed.), 'The Despensers and the Downfall of Edward II', *EHR*, 99 (1984), 1–33

Sayers, J., *Innocent III, Leader of Europe, 1198–1216* (London: Longman, 1994).

Sayers, J. E., *Papal Government and England during the Pontificate of Honorius III (1216–1227)*, Cambridge studies in medieval life and thought, Third Series 21 (Cambridge: Cambridge University Press, 1984).

Schiffels, Stephan, Wolfgang Haak, Pirita Paajanen, Bastien Llamas, Elizabeth Popescu, Louise Loe, Rachel Clarke, Alice Lyons, Richard

Mortimer, Duncan Sayer, Chris Tyler-Smith, Alan Cooper and Richard Durbin, 'Iron Age and Anglo-Saxon Genomes from East England reveal British Migration History', *Nature Communications* (2015), 1–9. DOI: 10.1038/ncomms10408.

Schlee, Duncan, *The Pembrokeshire Cemeteries Project: Excavations at Porthclew Chapel, Freshwater East, Pembrokeshire 2009, Second Interim Report*, Dyfed Archaeological Trust Report, 2010/20 (Llandeilo: Dyfed Archaeological Trust, 2010).

Seabourne, Gwen, *Imprisoning Medieval Women: the Non-Judicial Confinement and Abduction of Women in England, c. 1170–1509* (Farnham: Ashgate, 2011).

Seebohm, Frederic, *The Tribal System in Wales: being part of an inquiry into the structure and methods of tribal society* (2nd edn, London and New York: Longmans Green, 1905).

Shennan, J. H., *The Bourbons: The History of a Dynasty* (London: Continuum, 2007).

Siddons, M., 'Welshmen in the Service of France', *BBCS*, 36 (1989), 161–84.

Siegel, Bernard J. et al., 'Acculturation: an Explanatory Formulation', *American Anthropologist*, 56 (1954).

Simonsohn, Uriel, 'Communal Boundaries Reconsidered: Jews and Christians Appealing to Muslim Authorities in the Medieval Near East', *Jewish Studies Quarterly*, 14.4 (2007), 328–63.

Skeel, C. A. J., *The Council in the Marches of Wales* (London: Hugh Rees, 1904).

Skinner, Patricia, *Living with Disfigurement in Early Medieval Europe* (New York: Palgrave, 2017).

Skinner, Patricia, 'The mountainous problems of Wales and southern Italy', in Ross Balzaretti, Julia Barrow and Patricia Skinner (eds), *Italy and Early Medieval Europe: Papers for Chris Wickham* (Oxford: Oxford University Press, in press).

Smith, David M., *Guide to Bishops' Registers of England and Wales: A Survey from the Middle Ages to the Abolition of Episcopacy in 1646* (London: Royal Historical Society, 1981).

Smith, David M., *Supplement to the 'Guide to Bishops' Registers of England and Wales: A Survey from the Middle Ages to the Abolition of Episcopacy in 1646'* (York: Canterbury and York Society, 2004).

Smith, J. B., 'Dower in Thirteenth-Century Wales: a Grant of the Commote of Anhuniog, 1273', *BBCS*, 30 (1983), 348–55.

Smith, J. B., 'Dynastic Succession in Medieval Wales', *BBCS*, 33 (1986), 199–232.

Smith, J. B., 'Judgement under the Law of Wales', *Studia Celtica*, 39 (2006).
Smith, J. B., 'Gruffudd Llwyd, Sir (d. 1335)', *Oxford Dictionary of National Biography* (2008; subsequently updated), online at *www.oxforddnb.com/view/article/16864?docPos=1*.
Smith, J. B., *Llywelyn ap Gruffudd: Prince of Wales* (new edn, Cardiff: University of Wales Press, 2014).
Smith, J. Beverley, 'Edward II and the Allegiance of Wales', *WHR*, 8 (1976), 139–71.
Smith, Ll., 'Glyn Dŵr, Owain (c.1359–c.1416)', *Oxford Dictionary of National Biography* (2008; subsequently updated), online at *www.oxforddnb.com/view/article/10816?docPos=1*.
Smith, Ll. B. 'The Welsh and English language in late-medieval Wales', in D. A. Trotter (ed.), *Multilingualism in Later Medieval Britain* (Cambridge: Cambridge University Press, 2000), pp. 7–21.
Smith, T. W., 'Papal Executors and the Veracity of Petitions from Thirteenth-Century England', *Revue d'histoire ecclésiastique*, 110 (2015), 662–83.
Stacey, R. C., 'Hywel in the World', *Haskins Society Journal*, 20 (2009), 175–203. Stenton, F. M., *Anglo-Saxon England* (3rd edn, Oxford: Oxford University Press, 1971).
Stenton, F. M., 'The Road System of Medieval England,' *The Economic History Review*, 7.1 (November 1936), 1–21.
Stephens, Meic (ed.), *The New Companion to the Literature of Wales* (Oxford: Oxford University Press, 1990).
Stephenson, D., '*Potens et Prudens*: Gruffudd ap Madog, lord of Bromfield 1236–69', *WHR*, 22 (2005), 409–31.
Stephenson, David, 'From Llywelyn ap Gruffudd to Edward I: expansionist rulers and Welsh society in thirteenth-century Gwynedd', in Diane M. Williams and John R. Kenyons (eds), *The Impact of the Edwardian Castles in Wales* (Oxford: Oxbow, 2010), pp. 9–15.
Stephenson, David, *Medieval Powys. Kingdom, Principality and Lordship, 1132–1293* (Woodbridge: Boydell, 2016).
Stokes, Kaele L., 'The Educated Barbarian? Asser's *Life of King Alfred* and Welsh Learning', *Quaestio Insularis*, 3 (2002), 45–58.
Stretton, Tim, *Women Waging Law in Elizabethan England* (Cambridge: Cambridge University Press, 1998).
Strickland, M., and R. Hardy, *From Hastings to the* Mary Rose, *The Great Warbow* (Stroud: Sutton, 2005).
Stuckey, Jace, 'Charlemagne as crusader? Memory, propaganda, and the many uses of Charlemagne's legendary expedition to Spain', in Matthew Gabriele and Jace Stuckey (eds), *The Legend of Charlemagne in the Middle Ages: Power, Faith and Crusade* (New York: Palgrave, 2008), pp. 137–52.

Bibliography

Summerson, Henry, 'George (*d. c.*303?)', *Oxford Dictionary of National Biography*, Oxford University Press (2004), online at *www.oxforddnb.com/view/article/60304*.

Swanson, R. N., *Universities, Academics and The Great Schism* (Cambridge: Cambridge University Press, 1979).

Swanson, R. N., *Church and Society in Late Medieval England* (Oxford: Blackwell, 1989).

Thomas, D. R., 'Sir John Morgan of Tredegar, Knt', *Archaeologia Cambrensis* (1884).

Thomas, Wyn, 'John Blodwell: St Asaph, Rome, Constance and Balsham', *National Library of Wales Journal*, 34.2 (2007), 186–95.

Thornton, Tim, *Cheshire and the Tudor State, 1480–1560* (Woodbridge: Boydell, 2000).

Tout, T. F., 'The captivity and death of Edward of Caernarvon', in *The Collected Papers of Thomas Frederick Tout. With a Memoir and Bibliography* (Manchester: Manchester University Press, 1934), iii, pp. 145–90.

Tout, T. F., 'Llywelyn Bren (*d.* 1318)', rev. R. Griffiths, *Oxford Dictionary of National Biography* (2008; subsequently updated), online at *www.oxforddnb.com/view/article/16876?docPos=1*.

Treharne, R., 'The Franco-Welsh Treaty of Alliance in 1212', *BBCS*, 18 (1958), 60–75.

Trotter, D. A., 'L'anglo-français au Pays de Galles: une enquête préliminaire', *Revue de linguistique romane*, 58.231–2 (1994), 461–82.

Turner, R., *King John* (London: Longman, 1994).

Turvey, R., 'The Marcher Shire of Pembroke and the Glyndŵr Rebellion', *WHR*, 15.2 (1990), 151–68.

Turvey, R., *Lord Rhys: Prince of Deheubarth* (Llandysul: Gomer, 1997).

Turvey, R., *Llywelyn the Great: Prince of Gwynedd* (Llandysul: Gwasg Gomer, 2007).

Turvey, R., *Owain Gwynedd, Prince of the Welsh* (Talybont: Y Lolfa, 2012).

Tyerman, Christopher, *England and the Crusades, 1095–1588* (Chicago: Chicago University Press, 1988).

Tyler, D. J., 'Offa's Dyke: a Historiographical Appraisal', *JMH*, 37 (2011), 145–61.

Ullmann, W., *A Short History of the Papacy in the Middle Ages* (2nd edn, London: Routledge, 2003).

Usher, Gwilym, 'Welsh Students at Oxford in the Middle Ages', *BBCS*, 16 (1954–5), 193–8.

van Houts, Elisabeth, 'Gender and Authority in Oral Witnesses in Europe (800–1300)', *Transactions of the Royal Historical Society*, 6th ser., 9 (1999), 201–20.

Veach, C., *Lordship in Four Realms: The Lacy Family, 1166–1241* (Manchester: Manchester University Press, 2014).

Veninger, Jacqueline, 'Landscapes of conflict: patterns of Welsh resistance to the Anglo-Norman conquest of North Wales, 1070–1250 – an overview of a new study', in Peter Ettel (ed.), *Château et frontière: actes du colloque international d'Aabenraa (Danemark, 24–31 août 2012)* (=*Chateau Gaillard*, 26, Caen: Université de Caen, 2014), pp. 353–6.

Villalon, A. J., and Kagay, D. (eds), *The Hundred Years' War: A Wider Focus* (Leiden: Brill, 2005).

Villalon, A. J., and Kagay, D. (eds), *The Hundred Years War (Part II): Different Vistas* (Leiden: Brill, 2008).

Voerkelis, Susanne, Gesine D. Lorenz, Susanne Rummel, Christophe R. Quétel, Gerhard Heiss, Malcolm Baxter, Christophe Brach-Papa, Peter Deters-Itzelsberger, Stefan Hoelzl, Jurian Hoogewerff, Emmanuel Ponzevera, Marleen Van Bocxstaele and Henriette Ueckermann, 'Strontium Isotopic Signatures of Natural Mineral Waters, the Reference to a Simple Geological Map and its Potential for Authentication of Food', *Food Chemistry*, 118 (2010), 933–40.

Walker, D., *Medieval Wales* (Cambridge: Cambridge University Press, 1990).

Walker, Garthine, 'Rereading Rape and Sexual Violence in Early Modern England', *Gender and History*, 10.1 (1998), 1–25.

Walker, Garthine, '"A strange kind of stealing": abduction in early modern Wales', in Simone Clarke and Michael Roberts (eds), *Women and Gender in Early Modern Wales* (Cardiff: University of Wales Press, 2000).

Warren, W. L., *Henry II* (London: Eyre Methuen, 1973).

Warren, W. L., *King John* (New Haven: Yale University Press, 1997).

Watkin, Thomas Glyn, *The Legal History of Wales* (2nd edn, Cardiff: University of Wales Press, 2012).

Weale, Michael E., Deborah A. Weiss, Rolf F. Jager, Neil Bradman and Mark G. Thomas, 'Y Chromosome Evidence for Anglo-Saxon Mass Migration', *Molecular Biology and Evolution*, 19.7 (2002), 1008–21.

Webb, Diana, *Medieval European Pilgrimage, c.700–c1500* (Basingstoke: Palgrave, 2002).

Weiler, B. K. U., *Henry III of England and the Staufen Empire, 1216–1272* (Woodbridge: Boydell, 2006).

Weisheipl, J. A., *Friar Thomas D'Aquino: His Life, Thought and Works* (Oxford: Wiley-Blackwell, 1975).

White, Arthur, *Plague and Pleasure: The Renaissance World of Pius II* (Washington DC: The Catholic University of America Press, 2014).

Wickham, C., *The Inheritance of Rome: A History of Europe from 400 to 1000* (London: Allen Lane, 2009).
Wickham, C., 'Medieval Wales and European History', *WHR*, 25.2 (2010), 201–8.
Wickham, Chris, *Framing the Early Middle Ages: Europe and the Mediterranean 400–800* (Oxford: Oxford University Press, 2005).
Wilkinson, L. J., 'Joan, Wife of Llywelyn the Great', in M. Prestwich, R. H. Britnell and R. Frame (eds), *Thirteenth Century England* 10 (Woodbridge: Boydell, 2005), pp. 81–93.
Williams, G. A., 'The Succession to Gwynedd 1238–1247', *BBCS*, 20 (1962–4), 393–413.
Williams, G. Aled, 'Gwrthryfel Glyndŵr: Dau Nodyn', *Llên Cymru*, 33 (2010), 180–7.
Williams, G. J., and E. J. Jones (eds), *Gramadegau'r Penceirddiaid [Grammars of the Celtic Bards]* (Cardiff: University of Wales Press, 1934).
Williams, Glanmor, *The Welsh Church from Conquest to Reformation* (Cardiff: University of Wales Press, 1962).
Williams, Glanmor, 'The Dissolution of the Monasteries in Glamorgan', *WHR*, 3 (1966).
Williams, Glanmor, *Welsh Reformation Essays* (Cardiff: University of Wales Press, 1967).
Williams, Glanmor, *The Welsh Church from Conquest to Reformation* (rev. edn, Cardiff: University of Wales Press, 1976).
Williams, Glanmor, *Religion, Language and Nationality in Wales: Historical Essays* (Cardiff: University of Wales Press, 1979).
Williams, Glanmor, 'Poets and Pilgrims in Fifteenth and Sixteenth Century Wales', *Trans. Hon. Soc. Cymm.* (1991).
Williams, Glanmor, *Renewal and Reformation: Wales c. 1415–1642* (Oxford: Oxford University Press, 1993).
Williams, Gwyn, *Madoc: the Making of a Myth* (London: Eyre Methuen, 1979).
Williams, J. E. Caerwyn, 'Ystorya Titus Aspassianus', *BBCS*, 9 (1938).
Williams, Penry, *The Council in the Marches of Wales under Elizabeth* (Cardiff: University of Wales Press, 1958).
Williams, Robert, 'Ystoria de Carolo Magno', *Y Cymmrodor*, 20 (1907).
Wright, Lori E., and Henry P. Schwarcz, 'Stable Carbon and Oxygen Isotopes in Human Tooth Enamel: Identifying Breastfeeding and Weaning in Prehistory', *American Journal of Physical Anthropology*, 106 (1998), 1–18.
Wyatt, D., '*Gruffudd ap Cynan and the Hiberno-Norse World*', *WHR*, 19.4 (2000), 595–617.

Wyatt, David R., *Slaves and Warriors in Medieval Britain and Ireland, 800–1200* (Leiden: Brill, 2009).

Youngs, Deborah, '"For the Preferement of their Marriage and Bringing Upp in their Youth": The Education and Training of Young Welshwomen, *c.*1450—*c.*1550', *WHR*, 25.4 (2011), 463–85.

Youngs, Deborah, '"She hym fresshely folowed and pursued": women and Star Chamber in early Tudor Wales', in Bronach Kane and Fiona Williamson (eds), *Women, Agency and the Law, 1300–1700* (London: Pickering and Chatto, 2013), pp. 73–85.

Unpublished secondary sources

Brough, Gideon, 'Medieval Diplomatic History: France and the Welsh, 1163–1417' (PhD thesis, Cardiff University, 2013).

Day, Jenny, 'Arfau yn yr Hengerdd a Cherddi Beirdd y Tywysogion' (PhD thesis, Aberystwyth University, 2010).

Delin, Alexandre, 'Les étudiants Gallois à l'université d'Oxford, 1282–1485' (PhD thesis, Université Paris 1 Panthéon-Sorbonne, 2013).

Emlyn, Rh., 'Myfyrwyr canoloesol Cymreig a'u gyrfaoedd' (PhD thesis, Aberystwyth University, 2012).

Jones, M. A., '"An earthly beast, a mole and an enemy to all godly learning": the Life and Career of Rowland Lee, Bishop of Coventry and Lichfield and Lord President of the Council in the Marches of Wales, c.1487–1543' (MPhil thesis, Cardiff University, 1997).

Kay, Janet, 'Old, New, Borrowed, and Buried: Burial Practices in Fifth-Century Britain' (PhD thesis, Boston College, 2017).

Montgomery, Janet, 'Lead and Strontium Isotope Compositions of Human Dental Tissues as an Indicator of Ancient Exposure and Population Dynamics: The Application of Isotope Source-Tracing Methods to Identify Migrants Among I Archaeological Burials and a Consideration of Ante-Mortem Uptake, Tissue Stability and Post-Mortem Diagenesis' (PhD thesis, University of Bradford, 2002).

Index

abduction 131–53
Aberconwy
  abbey 99, 105–7, 164, 219
  Treaty of 53, 64, 72, 275
Abergavenny 231, 273
Abergwili 79
Aconbury, priory 221, 235
Adam of Usk 129, 165–6, 213
Adrian V, pope 223
Aethelstan, king of England 7
Alexander II, king of Scotland 187
Alexander III, pope 178, 223
Alexander IV, pope 219–20, 224–6
Alfred, king of Wessex 7, 12
Americas 2
amobr 61, 63, 72
Anagni 218, 224, 232
Anglesey 6, 18, 99, 165, 167, 236, 248–9
Anglo-Saxons 5–7, 11–13, 18–19, 24, 32, 36–8, 40, 42–3, 45
archaeology 17–47
archbishops *see* Canterbury
archers 14, 160–1, 202, 244–5, 250, 252, 254, 257
Armes Prydein 7, 13
Arthur 1, 9–10, 176, 206, 258
Asser 7, 12, 204

Australia 2, 10
Avignon 159, 192, 195–6, 214, 227

Bangor 77, 81–2, 85–8, 94, 98–100, 103–4, 120, 122–3, 125–6, 128, 178, 193, 204, 220, 222, 234
  Cadwgan, bishop 220, 234
  Meurig, bishop, 178
Bath and Wells, diocese 79, 89, 204, 219
Benedict XIII, pope 196, 203–5
benefices 77, 79, 90–1, 94–6, 125, 204, 219, 225, 233
Berkshire 91
Berwyn, battle 178–9
bishops *see* Bangor; Llandaff; St Asaph; St David's
Bjorn 'the Welshman' 3, 11
Black Death 80, 82
Brecon 8, 79, 81, 109, 220, 273–4
Brenhinedd y Saesson 163, 235
Bristol 79, 86, 101–3, 126
Britons 5–6, 11, 159
Brittany 6, 18, 34, 37, 170, 180, 194
Bromfield 52, 54, 60, 66, 68, 273
Brut y Tywysogion 163, 185, 187
burials 18, 20, 24–5, 27–34, 37

Index

Bury St Edmunds 245
Byzantium 3, 4, 160, 162, 176, 268, 273, 286

Cadell ap Gruffydd 159
Caerleon 5, 101, 131, 134, 138, 142, 146, 273
Caernarfon 193, 242
Calais 249–50, 258–9
Cambridge 75, 79, 85–6, 107
Cân Rolant (*Song of Roland*) 164
Canterbury 6, 75, 168, 177–8, 195, 200, 204, 217, 219, 224, 226, 229, 231, 276
   Baldwin of Forde, archbishop 8, 160
   Becket, Thomas, archbishop 178–9, 218, 231
   Boniface of Savoy, archbishop 224–6, 238
   Hubert Walter, archbishop 226, 229
   Jaenberht, archbishop 224, 238
   John Pecham, archbishop 162, 239, 276
   Stephen Langton, archbishop 219
Cardiff 146, 215, 218
Cardiganshire *see* Ceredigion
Carlisle 79, 82
Carmarthen/shire 5, 79, 81, 108, 110, 112, 114, 117–18, 250, 257, 273
Castile 160, 192
Ceredigion (Cardiganshire) 57, 67, 108, 119, 257, 264, 273
Channel Islands 189, 191
Charlemagne 164, 172
Charles V, king 189–91, 201
Charles VI, king 192–6
Charles the Bald, king 6
Cheshire 52, 71, 163

Chester 50, 55, 107
Chichester 91, 129
children 11, 20, 24–5, 30, 32, 34, 36, 46, 50, 66, 152, 219, 236, 276
China 268, 270–3, 276, 278, 283–4
Chirk 66, 103, 105, 273
chivalry 143, 255, 259
chronicles 68, 69, 129, 162–3, 169, 179, 185, 187–8, 194–5, 204, 213, 228, 245–6, 258
Cilmeri 65
Cistercians 52, 164, 168, 219
Clement IV, pope 217, 223
Clement VIII, pope 216
clothing 134, 140, 220, 244
coinage 5, 6, 11
Cologne 92
Constance, Council of 92, 196, 214
Constantinople *see* Byzantium
Cornish, Cornwall 18, 25, 36, 244
Coventry and Lichfield, diocese 79, 85, 131, 204, 221
Croft, Sir Edward 132
Cromwell, Thomas 132, 136–8, 145, 147
crusade/rs 4, 8, 76, 157, 160–5, 168–74, 196, 217, 221, 255, 270, 279
Cwm Hir, abbey 219
Cymer, abbey 108, 221
Cyngen, king of Powys 159
Cyprus 165

D'Audley, Emma 49–73
Dafydd ap Gruffydd 162, 226
Dafydd ap Gwilym, poet 170, 247, 249, 252–3, 259, 261
Dafydd ap Llywelyn 51, 222
David Blodwell 75, 95, 124
de Braose family 9, 183

332

Index

de Lacey family 221
Deheubarth 159, 180, 242, 270, 273, 282
Delw y Byd (*The Form of the World*) 164
Denbigh 273–4
Derbyshire 50, 61, 257
dhimmī 271, 276–8, 281–5
dispensations 77, 203, 219, 226
Donetsk *see* Hughesovska
Dore, abbey 221
dower 50, 52–62, 70, 142
Durham 79, 82
Dyfed 18, 39
Dyffryn Clwyd 273–4

Edinburgh 245
Ednyfed Fychan 158, 248–9
Edward I, king 9, 49, 55, 57–8, 60, 67, 70, 75, 162, 164, 176, 188, 216, 224, 239, 241–2, 244–6, 255, 268, 273, 275–6
Edward II, king 242, 246, 255, 267, 273–4
Edward III, king 188–9, 242, 246, 255
Einion Offeiriad 247, 262
Elis Gruffudd 258, 264
Ely 79, 95

Flanders, Flemish 244, 248–9, 268
Flintshire 158, 250, 255, 274, 287
food 19–20, 225
France, Francia 5, 7, 8, 24, 130, 161, 175–214, 224, 237, 243, 246, 249–50, 254–5, 257, 259
Frederick I, emperor 178
Frederick II, emperor 217
friendship 84, 137, 141–2, 168, 179, 183, 199–201, 219, 252
Froissart 244

Gaul *see* France, Francia
gender 2, 32–3, 139
Geoffrey of Monmouth 159, 169, 258
George Owen of Henllys 283
Gerald of Wales 8–9, 13, 159–61, 165, 168, 176–7, 216, 220, 225–6, 229, 259
Germans, Germany 3, 24, 26, 32, 37, 163, 167, 195, 268
Ghent 244–5
Gilbert Marshal 218–19, 224, 232
Gildas 5
Glamorgan 24–5, 43, 165, 259, 273–4
Glasgow 216
Glastonbury 258, 264
Gloucester 27–8, 34, 36, 50–1, 70, 114, 131, 134, 136, 138, 141–4, 146, 148, 151, 168, 274
Gower 273–4
grave goods *see* burial
Gregory I, pope 216
Gregory VII, pope 216, 228
Gregory IX, pope 218–21, 223–5
Gregory X, pope 231
Gregory XI, pope 203
Gregory Sais, Sir 250, 255
Gruffudd ab Einion 54, 63
Gruffudd ap Llywelyn 3
Gruffudd ap Madog 49–53, 55–6, 59, 66, 68
Gruffudd Llwyd, poet 250, 255
Gruffudd Llwyd, Sir 248–9, 255
Gruffudd Dwnn 257
Gruffydd Gryg, poet 159
Guala Bicchieri, papal legate 210, 238
Guto'r Glyn, poet 75, 124, 250–2, 256–7, 263

Index

Gwent 180, 256
Gwilym Ddu of Arfon, poet 248
Gwilym Tew, poet 166
Gwynedd 3, 6–7, 51–2, 163–4, 176, 178, 180, 182, 184, 187–8, 197, 222–4, 241–3, 247, 257, 270, 273, 275

Harri Ddu ap Gruffudd 252
Haverfordwest 79, 81, 111–16
Hay 273
Henry I, king 50–1, 178
Henry II, king 160, 176–81, 197, 245
Henry III, king 50, 52, 185, 219–20, 222–4, 226, 232, 238, 285
Henry IV, king 170, 192, 196, 204–5, 242
Henry V, king 196, 242, 256–7
Henry VII, king 84–5, 88
Henry VIII, king 131, 145–6
Henry Griffith *see* Harri Ddu
Herbert family 139, 152
Hereford/shire 52, 60, 75, 79, 82, 87–8, 90, 127–9, 138, 143, 146, 204, 219, 221, 252
hiraeth 2, 10
Holy Land 4, 6, 157–9, 162–9, 217, 226, 231
Honorius III, pope 186, 210, 218–19, 221–2, 224, 231, 237
honour 144, 190, 248
Hugh Johnys/Johnnys 162, 165, 171
Hugh le Despenser 273
Hughesovska (Donetsk) 2
Hundred Years' War 194, 242
Huw Cae Llwyd, poet 166, 168, 173
Hywel ap Gruffudd, poet 249
Hywel ap Maredudd 274

Hywel Dda, king 7–8, 56, 63–4, 67, 159
Hywel Swrdwal, poet 251

Iberia 4, 5, 159, 189, 192, 268, 270–1, 279, 286
Ifor Hael 247
imprisonment 137–8, 151, 248, 256
Innocent III, pope 181, 184, 216–17, 222, 225, 229, 239
Innocent IV, pope 217–20, 223, 226
inscriptions 18
intermarriage 4, 49–50, 63, 222, 279
Iolo Goch, poet 252, 259
Ireland, Irish 5–7, 9, 18, 34, 36, 93, 130, 183–4, 217, 241–3, 250, 259, 268, 276
isotope analysis 17–47

Jerusalem *see* Holy Land
Jewish, Jews 271, 277, 280–2, 286
John, king 162, 182–8, 217, 222, 226, 229
John VIII, pope 228
John XXI, pope 224
John of Crema, papal legate 224, 238
Jómsvikinga Saga 3–4, 10–11
juries 131, 133, 137, 139–40, 143, 145, 267, 272–4, 280, 283

Kent 24, 27, 91
see also Rochester
Kidwelly 192, 273

language 9, 23, 134, 136, 166, 176, 178, 181–2, 195–6, 204, 241, 243, 246, 284
see also translation

Index

Lateran Council, Fourth 219
Lateran Council, Third 225
law 4, 7–8, 49–73, 75, 78, 92, 97, 131–3, 136, 143, 145–6, 187, 193, 222, 225, 236, 241, 267–91
Lee, Rowland, bishop 131–4, 136–40, 143–6
legitimacy 50, 150, 190, 219–20, 222, 225, 236, 276
  see also children
letters 1, 52, 60, 71, 77–8, 132, 136, 176, 177–82, 190, 192–3, 195, 199–202, 205, 216–39, 245, 257, 273–4
Lewis Glyn Cothi, poet 165–6
Lincoln 79, 89–90, 121
Llancarfan 259
Llandaff 77, 81–2, 86–8, 101–3, 120–2, 146, 150, 160, 204, 218–19, 221, 224–5
  Elias of Radnor, bishop 218
  Henry of Abergavenny, bishop 231
  Miles Salley, bishop 160
  William of Goldcliff, bishop 231
  William of Saltmarsh, bishop 231
Llandovery 275
Llanwern 131, 133–5, 141–2, 146, 148
Llawhaden 79
Llywelyn ap Gruffudd, prince 52, 55–6, 58, 60, 62, 158, 189, 223–4, 247, 275–6
Llywelyn ap Hywel ab Ieuan ap Gronwy, poet 167
Llywelyn ap Iorwerth, prince 158, 164, 181–8, 197, 200–1, 222–3, 225, 257
Llywelyn Goch ap Meurig Hen, poet 249

London 79–90, 92–118, 137, 139, 245
Louis VII, king 177–81, 199–200

Madog ab Owain Gwynedd, prince 2
Madog ap Gruffudd 51
Madog ap Llywelyn 188
Maelor 51–62, 273
March, Marcher families 50, 59, 66, 131–2, 134, 137–8, 140, 145–6, 160, 168, 180, 183, 185, 241–3, 249, 267–8, 273–6, 279–80, 282
Margam, abbey 121, 168
Marshal family *see* Gilbert, William
Martin IV, pope 217, 224, 226, 229
Mary, princess 138
Matilda, empress 50
Matthew Paris 51, 276
Mauger, bishop of Worcester 217, 225–6
Mediterranean 18, 23–4, 26, 31–6, 158, 165
Mercia 6, 224
mining 2
monasteries 164, 204
  see also Cwm Hir; Cymer; Margam; Neath; Strata Florida; Tintern; Valle Crucis; Whitland
Monmouthshire 134, 160
Montgomery 70, 273–4
  treaty of 223, 276
Mortimer family 60, 66
murder 132, 135, 146, 152, 246, 249
music 167
Muslims 164, 269, 271, 277–8, 280–1
muster rolls 243, 251

335

Index

Narberth 110, 273
nationhood, nationalism 2, 4, 175, 190, 195, 242–3, 246–7, 256, 259
Neath 139
  abbey 101, 103, 164
Nennius 5
Newport 138–9
Nicholas III, pope 224
Normandy, Normans 7–9, 75, 77, 163, 171, 176, 180, 251, 257, 271

Offa's Dyke 6
ordination 77–130
Oswestry 53–4, 59–60, 62–5, 250, 274–5
Otto, papal legate 224
Ottobuono, papal legate 217, 223
  see also Adrian V, pope
Owain ap Maredudd 57, 67
Owain Glyndŵr 9, 66, 175, 192–6, 205, 227, 242–3, 248, 250, 255
Owain Gwynedd 2, 177–81, 197, 199–200, 223
Owain Lawgoch 175, 188–92, 197, 201–2, 242, 258
Owain Tudur 258
Owen, Goronwy, poet 2
Oxford/shire 27, 75, 79, 86–9, 92, 100, 102, 105, 108–9, 112, 116–17

Pandulf, papal legate 224
papal legates *see* Guala Bicchieri; John of Crema; Otto; Ottobuono; Pandulf; Theophylact
Paris 194, 202, 226, 249
Patagonia 2

patronage 91, 95–6, 166, 168, 204, 243, 247, 249–53, 255, 258–9
payments 9, 60–1, 92, 129, 191, 197, 202, 220–1, 244, 246, 248, 276
Pembroke/shire 24–7, 79, 185, 218, 274, 283–4
Pennal Declaration 194–5, 203–5
Philip Augustus, king 181–8, 197, 200–1
Philips, Thomas 132
pilgrimage 4, 6, 76, 158–60, 163, 165–8
Pisa, council of 92
Pius IV, pope 216
poetry 2, 8, 164–5, 169, 241, 243, 246–54, 256–9
Port Talbot 5
Porthclew 26–8, 31, 36, 38
pottery 18
Powys 49–73, 159, 180, 220, 225, 242, 250, 256, 270, 273
Prophecy of Britain see Armes Prydein
Prydydd y Moch, poet 164

rape 131, 134, 136–7, 139, 145, 286
relics 159, 187, 200, 218
Rhodri ab Owain Gwynedd 222
Rhodri Mawr 3, 7
Rhys ap Maredudd 188
Richard I, king 158, 255
Richard II, king 242, 255
Robert of Gloucester 168
Robin Ddu, poet 165, 167
Rochester 82
Rögnvaldr, king 222, 236
Romans 3–5, 17, 23–4, 26, 36
Rome 5, 73, 159, 165–6, 178, 220, 225
  see also pilgrimage

336

Index

St Asaph 54, 77, 81–2, 84–8, 94, 103–8, 121–2, 126, 161, 204, 220–2
  Abraham, bishop 233
  Anian I, bishop 221
  Hywel, bishop 221, 235
  Reiner, bishop 221
St David's 6, 7, 77, 79–82, 85–7, 89, 92, 94, 100, 108–18, 119–21, 163, 167–8, 203–4, 216, 219–26, 274
  Iorwerth, bishop 163
  Richard Carew, bishop 219–21
  Thomas Wallensis, bishop 220, 223, 226
Salisbury 79, 86–92, 119–23,
Santiago de Compostela 157, 159–60, 163, 165, 167, 169
Scandinavia 3, 6, 32
Scotland 18, 25, 37, 180–7, 189, 192, 195, 197–8, 217, 237, 243, 245, 248–50, 253–5, 259, 268, 276
Shrewsbury 148, 221, 235, 257
Shropshire 50, 52, 73, 138, 273, 275
Sicily 268, 270–1, 279
slavery 2, 7
soldiers 4, 8, 75–6, 189, 192, 194, 241–65,
Staffordshire 50
Star Chamber 131, 133–40, 142, 144–6
Statute of Rhuddlan 192, 276
Stradling family 165, 167–8
Strata Florida, abbey 113, 168
Striguil 273
students 75, 85, 87–9, 93
surnames 4, 96, 136, 190
Swansea 6, 79, 109, 171
Switzerland 189, 252

Talbot family 257
teeth 19–20
Tewkesbury 218
Theophylact, papal legate 224
Thomas ap Watkin, archer 252, 256
Thomas Wolsey 84, 94
Tintern, abbey 101, 164, 218, 232
trade 2, 6, 18–19, 36, 146, 159, 164, 170
translation 164, 284
  see also language
treaties *see* Aberconwy; Montgomery
Trelleck 138
Tudur ap Goronwy of Penmynydd 249

universities *see* Cambridge; Oxford; Paris
Urban IV, pope 217, 221, 224
Usk 138
  see also Adam of Usk

Valle Crucis, abbey 52, 69, 103, 106–7, 122, 219, 263
Vatican 4, 8, 215–39
Venice 165

water 19–20, 26, 29, 245
weapons 134, 244, 252–3, 259, 263
Welshpool 159
Wessex 7
Westminster 60–1, 131–2, 137, 146
Whitland, abbey 104, 221
widowhood 49, 52–3, 55–9, 61, 63, 67, 133, 136, 142–3
Wigmore 138, 273

Index

William Marshal 185
wills 77, 95, 149, 160
Wiltshire 91, 138
Winchester 26, 28, 79, 82, 84, 88
witnesses 7, 56–7, 60, 95, 133–6, 138–9, 141–3, 146, 148, 150, 244, 267, 277

Worcester/shire 44, 54, 55, 62, 72, 79, 82, 85, 102, 138, 204, 217, 221, 225

York/shire 27, 36, 75, 128, 220, 251–2